AMERICA

AND

HER RESOURCES;

OR

A VIEW

OF

THE AGRICULTURAL, COMMERCIAL,

MANUFACTURING, FINANCIAL, POLITICAL, LITERARY,

MORAL AND RELIGIOUS CAPACITY

AND CHARACTER

OF THE

AMERICAN PEOPLE.

BY JOHN BRISTED,

COUNSELLOR AT LAW,

AUTHOR OF THE RESOURCES OF THE BRITISH EMPIRE.

Εν δε φαει και ολεσσον!

LONDON:
PRINTED FOR HENRY COLBURN,
PUBLIC LIBRARY, CONDUIT STREET, HANOVER SQUARE.

1818.

Research Reprints Inc. · New York

First Published 1818
Reprinted 1970

B. CLARKE, Printer, Well-street, London.

LIBRARY OF CONGRESS CATALOG CARD NUMBER:
76-124780

PRINTED IN THE UNITED STATES OF AMERICA

DEDICATION.

TO THE

HON. JAMES KENT,

CHANCELLOR OF THE STATE OF NEW-YORK.

SIR,

WILL you permit me to place under your protection the following pages, in which it is attempted to present a brief outline of the Resources and Character of a Country, whose public weal you have so powerfully upheld by your judicial talents and learning; whose private interests have been promoted, and whose private relations have been uniformly gladdened, by your social and domestic virtues?

I have the honour to be,
Sir,
Your much obliged
And most obedient Servant,

JOHN BRISTED.

New-York, 1818.

ADVERTISEMENT.

———

TOWARDS the close of the year 1809, when the result of the battle of *Wagram* had convinced the American public that the continent of Europe was finally subdued, and that England alone remained " an easy prey to the all-conquering arms of the Great Napoleon, I ventured to oppose the headlong current of popular opinion; and in the "*Hints on the National Bankruptcy of Britain, and on her resources to maintain the present contest with France,*" (afterward republished under the title of "*Resources of the British Empire,*") undertook to demonstrate that the final destruction of the overgrown power of France was to be expected; *First,* from the *nature* of the French political and military institutions; *Secondly,* from the resistance of the *people* of continental Europe; and, *Thirdly,* from the resources of the British Empire.

This work was no sooner published than many profound politicians pronounced the author to be " a visionary fanatic, a mere closet recluse, unacquainted with men and things, deficient in judgment, and wanting common sense;" and persisted, with increased vehemence, as they inhaled fresh inspirations from the " *sævi spiracula Ditis,*" to prophesy that France "would soon stretch her sceptre over the whole of Europe, plant her tri-coloured flag on the Tower of London,

and establish a Gallic viceroy in the palace of St.
James." *That* controversy, I presume, is now closed,
by the events of the years 1812, 1813, 1814, and 1815;
and by the present residence of the Imperial and Royal
Exile, whom those sagacious statesmen so long worshipped as the god of their idolatry.

In the advertisement to the " *Hints on the National
Bankruptcy of Britain*," it was said, "the consideration
of the domestic policy, the foreign relations, the manners and habits, the laws, religion, morals, literature,
and science of *this* very interesting and unparalleled
country, whose institutions are almost entirely unknown
to the people of Europe, and not sufficiently understood,
at least in their remoter consequences, by the general
body of our own citizens, I shall take up, as soon as I
have leisure and opportunity to arrange the great mass
of materials, facts, documents, and state-papers, respecting these United States, with which I am furnished
by the careful and diligent collection of more than *three*
years, aided by the abundant and liberal communications of some American gentlemen, who have distinguished themselves as stetesmen of the highest order,
by the zeal, fidelity, industry, and talent, with which
they have discharged the most arduous political duties,
both in their own country and in the courts of the most
powerful European kingdoms."

More than *eight* years have now elapsed, since it was
then proposed to publish a " *View of the resources of
the United States*." Those eight years have added very
considerably to the bulk and interest of the collection
then formed; and the following pages, selected and di-
gesting from the voluminous masses of materials relating
to our federative Republic, are offered to the reader as

an effort to redeem the pledge given so long since as October, 1809.

It is *not* intended in the present work to give a *statistical* view of the United States. This has been done already with so much ability and accuracy by the Honourable Mr. Pitkin, a member of Congress, from Connecticut, that the political economist has only to resort to his book for ample instruction on the commerce, agriculture, manufactures, public debt, revenues, and expenditures of the United States. To Mr. Pitkin's " *Statistical View*" the following pages are much indebted ; and I beg leave to embrace this opportunity of presenting to that gentleman my grateful acknowledgments for his very kind and liberal offer to furnish me with his own collection of documents respecting the United States ; a collection unrivalled in extent and value, and containing, in more than a hundred printed volumes, besides innumerable manuscripts, all the necessary information respecting North America, from her earliest settlement; and, more especially, respecting these United States, from their first establishment to the present hour.

The object proposed in the following work, is merely to give a brief outline of the physical, intellectual, and moral character, capacity, and resources of the United States, with an entire determination to steer clear of all undue bias for or against either of the great contending political parties, which divide, agitate, and govern this ever-widening republic. As I have never received nor sought any favour or benefit from any one of the numerous parties which have had their day of triumph and defeat, in the quick succession and rapid alternations which so peculiarly characterize all the movements of men and things under our popular institutions, I may perhaps be permitted to say, in relation to those parties, whether dominant or defeated,

" *Tros, Tyriusque* mihi nullo discrimine agetur."

After a few introductory remarks on the importance of a right acquaintance with the resources and character of the United States, and the grievous misrepresentation of them by European writers, the *first* chapter exhibits the territorial aspect, population, agriculture, and navigable capacities of the United States; the *second*, their commerce, home and foreign ; the *third*, their manufactures ; the *fourth*, their finances; the *fifth*, their government, policy, and laws ; the *sixth*, their literature, arts, and science; the *seventh*, their religion, morals, habits, manners, and character. The work is concluded by an eye-glance at the present condition of Europe, particularly of Spain, France, England, and Russia, and the probable consequences of the present European coalition to these United States.

JOHN BRISTED.

New-York, April, 1818.

CONTENTS.

CHAPTER III.

MANUFACTURES OF THE UNITED STATES,

CHAPTER IV.

FINANCES OF THE UNITED STATES.

CHAPTER V.

GOVERNMENT, POLICY, AND LAWS OF THE UNITED STATES.

CHAPTER VI.

ON THE LITERATURE OF THE UNITED STATES.

CHAPTER VII.

ON THE HABITS, MANNERS, AND CHARACTER OF THE UNITED STATES.

CONCLUSION.

PRESENT STATE OF EUROPE.

AMERICA,

AND

HER RESOURCES.

INTRODUCTORY REMARKS.

Importance of the United States.—Misrepresentations of Travellers, &c.

THE resources and character, the present power, and future prospects, of the *United States*, are very imperfectly appreciated or understood by the nations of Europe. Nay, one of the great British critics has recently informed us, that the Americans themselves have not yet told their own story well; nor sufficiently directed their mind towards fathoming the capabilities of their own country.

To ascertain and exhibit the resources of this extended and rapidly-rising empire, is worthy the attention of every one who feels a deep interest in the well-being of the republic. Indeed, no object can be presented more worthy of the contemplation of all the nations of the globe, than the growing capacities of a commonwealth which has borne itself triumphantly through two severe and bloody conflicts, against the most fearful odds; and run a career of peace, unexampled in enterprise and prosperity throughout the history of the world.

Humanly speaking, no circumstances *can* prevent these United States from becoming, eventually, and at no distant period, a great and powerful nation, in-

B

fluencing and controlling the other sovereignties of the world ;—seeing that they are secure from the dread of powerful neighbours ; that they are not composed of detached and distant territories ; but that one connect-ed, fertile, wide-spreading country is the goodly heri-tage of their dominion ; that they are blessed with a vast variety of soils and productions, and are watered with innumerable streams for the delight and accom-modation of their inhabitants ; that a succession of na-vigable rivers forms an ocean-chain around their bor-ders, to bind them together ; while the most capacious waters, running at convenient distances, present them with so many highways for the mutual transportation and exchange of all their various commercial commo-dities, both rude and manufactured ; and also for the easy communication of all friendly aids, political and military.

In addition to the *Atlantic* States, exhibiting up-wards of *two thousand* miles of sea-coast, with innu-merable bays, creeks, rivers, ports, and harbours, and covering a surface of nearly *one million* of square miles, displaying every variety of soil and produce,—a *new* empire has suddenly sprung up within the bosom of the union, like an exhalation from the earth. I mean that immense region called the *Western Country*; bound-ed on the north by the great lakes Erie, Huron, and Superior, and the chain of waters between the Grand Portage and the Lake of the Woods ; on the west by the Rocky Mountains ; on the south by the Gulf of Mexico ; on the east by the Alleghany Hills ; com-prising full *fifteen hundred thousand* square miles, and more than *fifty thousand* miles of internal ship and boat navigation. It contains *two thousand* miles of lake ; *one thousand* miles of gulf ; and *one hundred thousand* miles of river *coast*. The whole country is one continued intersection of rivers, communicating with each other.

These vast territorial domains are held by a popula-tion, free as the air they breathe—a population, pow-erful in physical activity and strength ; patient of toil.

and prodigal of life; brave, enterprising, intelligent, and persevering; presenting, both in body and in mind, the noblest materials for the formation of national greatness, prosperity, and influence.

There are many and obvious reasons why the nations of Europe are unacquainted with the resources and character of the United States; which present institutions political and social, altogether unique, and unparalleled in the annals of humankind. It is sufficient merely to mention one very broad source of European ignorance, with respect to this country; namely, the opposite, but equally erroneous views which the various travellers from Europe have given of the American Republic. By far the greater portion of these writers have fallen into the vitious extreme of unbounded praise, or of indiscriminate censure.

Many persons, frustrated in their pernicious hopes at home, and sometimes smarting from the recent scourge; men who have been arraigned at the bar of justice in their own land, as traitors and felons, and have exchanged the well-merited gallows for an ignominious exile, have generally depicted *this* country as the seat of uncontaminated purity, and uninterrupted happiness. If we may believe the assertions of these political philosophers, the soil every where teems with spontaneous plenty; the air is balmy and fragrant; the soft delights of perpetual spring dwell upon the land; the form of government, as it is written down upon paper, and appears in a printed book, is the model of all human perfection; the *rulers* are, of necessity, all virtue, wisdom, and strength; and the *people*, who elect, and from the midst of whom are elected these rulers, are, invariably, all incorruptible in their political integrity, pure in their personal conduct, simple and refined in their social manners. Vice knows no habitation here; and Paradise is again restored on earth, as it existed, in all the bloom of innocence and love, before the fall of our primeval parents.

Another set of writers, either rankling under the disappointment of their too sanguine expectations of suc-

cess in this country; or, from a very slight and superficial view of what they did not understand, and under
the guidance of that self-sufficient malignity, which is
the inseparable concomitant of dulness and ignorance,
and measuring every thing they saw here by the habits
and manners of the people in their own country, and
resolutely condemning whatsoever differed from the
standard to which they themselves had been accustomed; without ever once reflecting upon the very different states of society which must necessarily take
place in an old, long-established, and fully peopled
country, and in one which labours under all the peculiar
circumstances of national infancy—a thin and a scattered
population over an immense extent of territory. The
unfinished condition of its social habits, the fluctuation
of its political institutions, the uncertainty of its popular movements, have taken upon themselves to represent these United States as cursed with a barren
and inhospitable soil; an ungenial and dreary clime;
a government full of weakness, fraud, and violence; a
people made up and compounded of the sweepings and
refuse of Europe—" the taint of anarchy, and the blast
of crime,"—fickle and turbulent in their politics, rude
and coarse in their behaviour, and steeped in all the
vulgar brutality of vice and faction.

  Gilbert Imlay, and *M. St. John de Crevecœur*, author of " The American Farmer," and of pretended
" Travels in Upper Pennsylvania and the State of New
York," have exceedingly exaggerated the excellencies
of the United States, by representing them as the abode
of *more* than all the perfection of innocence, happiness,
plenty, learning, and wisdom, than *can* be allotted to
human beings to enjoy. A far greater number of writers, however, have outraged decency, by loading the
American people with abuse and calumny. Among
the vilest and silliest of these, are *Parkinson*, an
English farmer; *Ashe*, a *soi-disant* military officer;
and one *Jansen*, a non-descript.

  These writers, as appears from their own confession,
never herded with any other companions than the

lower classes of society in the union, such as stage-drivers, masters of sloops, keepers of ale-houses, low mechanics, retail tradesmen, and labouring peasants. It is not, indeed, pretended by any of the advocates of American character and claims, that among these classes of the community can be discovered any very great refinement of breeding, or any very extensive information, or any very profound reflection.

Another set of travellers in this country have come hither with letters of introduction to some very respectable gentlemen in the United States ; and, in consequence, have been received into their families, and the families of their friends and acquaintance : and, in every instance, have been treated with hospitality and kindness. These men have gone away to Europe, and published anecdotes of private families, have given to the world accounts of mere domestic incidents, such as could only have been imparted in the moments of unsuspecting confidence ; and the relation of which can serve no other purpose than to sadden the heart of those who have been betrayed, and stamp, in characters of lasting infamy, the baseness of the being who could thus drag into painful notice individuals wishing to pass their lives in the privacy of cultivated retirement, occasionally diversified by the more select intercourse of the social circle.

On the height of this bad eminence stand the *Marquis de Chastilleux,* and the *Duke de la Rouchefaucault Laincourt,* who have repaid the kindness of American hospitality, by descanting on the vulgarity of American manners, and by detailing to the world occurrences and conversations which they could never have known, had they not, unfortunately, been mistaken for gentlemen by those whose civilities and confidence they thus abused. But, surely, private individuals, who do not obtrude themselves upon the public, but rather shun the eye of vulgar observation, are *not* fit subjects for a traveller's merriment, or satire. In a world, bursting with vice and folly, there are always knaves and cox-combs, in sufficient number, to exhaust all the powers of ridicule and invective; and these are the *only* legitimate objects, against which the laugh of the wit, and the declamation of the moralist, ought to be directed.

The well-known poet, Mr. Thomas Moore, when quite a young man, published a book, made up of prose and verse, in which he, very unmercifully, abused and misrepresented the people of this country. Some little time since, however, he addressed a letter to Mr. John E. Hall, the editor of the Port-Folio, in Philadelphia, in which he expresses his deep repentance for having slandered America, and swings into the opposite extreme of unmeasured praise, representing it, *now*, as the *only* land where freedom, and happiness, and so forth, are to be found.

It would, indeed, be superfluous to descant upon the credulity of *Mr. Weld*, who, in enumerating the perilous wild beasts of this country, gravely asserts, and, as he says, upon the authority of General Washington, that the *moschetto* of the United States is so terrible in its attacks as to bite through the *thickest boot*. Now, the moschetto, which is a species of *gnat*, is no more troublesome or offensive *here* than the gnats are in the fens of Lincolnshire, or the lowlands of Essex, in England. Besides, General Washington merely told Mr. Weld, that the moschetto will bite through the thickest *stocking*, above the boot-top, when there is any space between the boot and the knee-band. But Mr. Weld has substituted the word *boot* for *stocking*; and thus, very reasonably, alarmed all cautious people with a tale of terror, respecting the dreadful ravages of the *moschetto tribe* of North America upon the human body.

Still more insufferable would it be to dwell upon the meagre, miserable trash, that is occasionally foisted into the *Monthly Magazine*, of London, under the signature of a little obstetrical Quixote, at Alexandria, in the district of Columbia; and, by a singular misnomer, called " *Information* as to the United States."

But the character of *M. Brissot de Warville*, the leader of the Gironde revolutionary faction in France, is too notorious to permit *his* observations on the United

States to be passed over in silence.   In a printed book of his, on the commerce of this country, he very profusely praises the Americans, and calls himself a Quaker. Brissot had led a very wandering life, and had written an incredible number of books on politics, none of which were over-wise.   He had been a subaltern in the police, under the old French monarchy, and had been sent to London on some service, in the line of his vocation, by the lieutenant of police in Paris. The revolution in France, of course, raised him to the level of his merit, and he became the *doer* of a newspaper, an office of high importance in all revolutionary societies. He was, however, a better disorganizer than philosopher : for, in a *manuscript* volume of his, now, or lately in the city of Philadelphia, in the hands of some elderly Friends, or Quakers, to whom he sent it for the express purpose of being published in this country (a step which his more prudent correspondents declined), he solemnly maintains that the *character* of the American people can always be known, infallibly, by the course of the *rivers* throughout the union.

For instance, says this profound observer of men and things, when he illustrates this notable proposition, " in the Northern and Eastern States, the rivers are violent and irregular in their progress, and so is the character of the inabitants of these States."—Alas ! for the people of New England, who have always, hitherto, been deemed the most sober, orderly, steady, and persevering in their habits and manners of all the Americans ! " In the Middle States," continues Brissot, " the rivers are strong and majestic, and so are the people. In the Southern departments, as Virginia, the two Carolinas, and Georgia, the rivers are muddy, slow, ebbing, and flowing capriciously; and, accordingly, the people on these states are dull, stagnant, and fickle."

This consolatory mode of determining the national character of a people was never equalled, but once, in the annals of philosophism. An obscure madman, called *William Gilbert*, in the year 1797, published, in London, a poem, entitled " 'I ' ·· Hurricane, a theoso-

phical and western eclogue ; to which is subjoined, a
solitary effusion in a summer's evening." In the notes
appended to this solitary effusion, Mr. Gilbert assures
us (I quote his own words), " First, that all countries
have a *specific mind*, or determinable principle. This
character may be traced, with as much satisfaction, in
the vegetable as in the animal productions. Thus,
strength, with its attributes, namely, asperity, &c. is
the character, or mind of *England* Her leading productions are the oak, peppermint, sloes, crabs, and sour
cherries. All elegance, all polish *is* superinduced ; and
primarily, from *France*, of which *they* [Query, *who ?*]
are natives. *Secondly*, that a country is subdued when
its *mind*, or *life*, (its prince, according to Daniel,) or its
genius, according to the modern easterns, or its *principle*, according to Europeans, is either suppressed or
destroyed, or *chymically* combined with that of a foreign country, in a form that leaves the foreign property
predominant, and not till then. And this cannot ensue
but upon suicide, upon a previous abandonment, on the
part of a nation, of its *own* principle. For when the
Creator made every thing very good, he also made it
tenable on the one hand, and on the other complete ;
consequently, without the necessity, without the desire
of encroaching ; and also without the capability, except under the penalty of surrendering, with its own
complete roundness, its own tenability."

" Thus," continues Mr. Gilbert, " I arrive at a *primary* law of nature, that every one must fall into the
pit that he digs for others, either before or after, or
without success. *Thirdly*, that in the European subjugation of *America*, the American mind or life, only
suffered under a powerful *affusion* of the European ;
and that, as the *solution* proceeds, it acquires a stronger
and stronger tincture of the subject, till, at length, that
which was first subdued, assumes an absolute, unexpug-
nable predominancy, and a final ; inasmuch as the contest is between the *two last* parts of the world, and
there is no prospective umpire to refer to ; but it must
be decided by the possession of first principles, or the

highest mind in the hierarchy of minds; and the *European* possession of mind, having previously arrived at perfection, from her long intercourse with *Africa* and *Asia*; and not being able to rescue her from the present grasp and predominancy of *American* mind, the question is now settled for ever, and *Europe* yields to the influence, mind, and power of *America*, linked in essential principle with *Africa* and *Asia* for ever. Besides, Europe had full success in her encroachments; she succeeded in throwing America into the pit; and, *of course*, it must be her own turn to go in now; she depopulated America, and, now, America must depopulate her."—Q. E. D.

It would be unjust not to recommend the work of *M. Beaujour*, late Consul from France, residing at Philadelphia: his view of the commerce, policy, finances, agriculture, manners, and habits of the United States, is written with great spirit and intelligence; and cannot fail to repay an attentive perusal with a rich harvest of instruction and amusement.

To which may be added M. de Marbois's preliminary discourse to his account of Arnold's conspiracy, where the United States, their institutions, and people, are spoken of in terms of high eulogy, and ardent admiration. For a splendid and interesting account, and an excellent translation of this work, the reader is referred to the second volume of Mr. Walsh's American Register. Mr. Volney's " View of the Soil and Climate of the United States of America;" and Mr. Schultz's " Travels on an inland voyage through the States of New-York, Pennsylvania, Virginia, Ohio, &c." may also be consulted with pleasure and profit.

Much useful information, conveyed in a plain, unostentatious style, may likewise be derived from Mr. Mellish's " Travels through the United States, in the years 1806, 1807, 1809, 1810, and 1811;" a work which is particularly valuable for its account of the Western States, and for the candour with which it treats, generally, of the country, its people, institutions, habits, and manners. The reader will also find " Travels in the Interior of the United States," by John Bradbury, F. L. S., an entertaining and instructive book. Mr. Morris Birkbeck's " Notes of a Journey in America, from the coast of Virginia to the territory of Illinois," with the exception of some Jacobin slang against England and her institutions, will be found a valuable and interesting little work.

Let it not be imagined, that I seek, by thus censuring many of the writers who have treated of this country, to recommend to the notice of the reader the opinions contained in the present work. It is merely desired to state the simple fact, that the people of this country have been grossly misrepresented; and some publications have been referred to, as proving the correctness of this statement. The chief intention of the following pages is to show, that the truth, as is generally the case in all human opinions and transactions, lies between the two extremes, which have been chosen by the calumniators and panegyrists of the United States; that this country is neither the garden of Eden nor the valley of Tophet; that the Americans themselves are neither angels nor fiends, but human beings, clothed with flesh and blood, possessing the appetites and passions, the powers and frailties of mortality; and greatly influenced in their feelings, sentiments, and conduct, by the peculiar circumstances in which they are placed. It is wished, " nothing extenuating, nor setting down aught in malice," to give a faithful portrait, a living likeness of the habits and condition of an enterprising, intelligent, spirited, aspiring people, that *must* be, ere long, and that *ought*, before this period, to have been better known, and more justly appreciated by the potentates and nations of Europe.

CHAPTER I.

On the Aspect, Agriculture, Population, &c. of the
United States.

It is *not* intended, in the following pages, to give a
minute detail of the agriculture, commerce, finances,
politics, religion, education, literature, habits, and manners of the United States ; but merely to present a brief
outline of their resources and character, such as they
appear, from an inspection and examination during several years. The reader who wishes for more ample
information upon the statistics of this country, is referred to the second edition of *Mr. Pitkin's* very valuable work, entitled " A statistical View of the Commerce of the United States of America ; its connexion
with Agriculture and Manufactures," &c. giving an account of the public debt, revenues, and expenditure of
the United States, &c. to *Mr. Tench Coxe's* " View of
the United States of America," exhibiting the progress
and present state of civil and religious liberty, population, agriculture, exports, imports, fisheries, navigation,
ship-building, manufactures, and general improvements;
to *Mr. Blodget's* " Economica, a Statistical Manual for
the United States of America ;" to *Mr. Jefferson's*
" Notes on Virginia," in answer to certain questions
proposed by M. Barbe de Marbois; to the *Western
Gazetteer*, or Emigrant's Directory," containing a geographical description of the Western States and Territories, including the *States* of Kentucky, Indiana, Louisiana, Ohio, Tennessee, and Mississippi, and the *Territories* of Illinois, Missouri, Alabama, Michigan, and
Northwestern; out of which may be carved at least

twelve new states, *each* as large as the United Kingdom of Great-Britain and Ireland. And, finally, the reader may consult *Dr. Morse's* " American Universal Geography," which contains much valuable information, respecting the United States generally, and each separate state in particular.

The United States possess prodigious *physical* capabilities of wealth and greatness, in a *home* territory, spread out to an enormous extent, and fertile in most of those productions which minister to the necessities and gratifications of man ; in navigable rivers, capacious and convenient ports, and the Atlantic main, which connects them with the other portions of the world. All these advantages, brought into exercise by the spirit and perseverance of an intelligent and enterprising people, afford the means and facilities of acquiring ample power, and permanent strength. Indeed, the whole aspect of *Nature* here, in America, has a direct tendency to enlarge and elevate the mind of the sensible and refined spectator. Little are the feelings of that being to be envied, whose heart does not swell with sublime emotions, when he sees with what a bold and magnificent profusion the living God has scattered the great works of his creation in this quarter of the globe ; on how vast and awful a scale of grandeur *He* has piled up the mountains, spread out the vallies, planted the forests, and poured forth the floods.

Some political writers and moral philosophers have asserted, that assemblages of the grander objects of nature tend directly to elevate the minds of those who live in their vicinity, and to give them a magnanimity of thought and action, which we look for in vain from the inhabitants of less favoured regions. And the elevation of mind, which is supposed to characterize the Scottish Highlander and the peasant of Switzerland, is referred to the effect produced by the sublime scenery which the rugged mountains, the winding streams, the sunken glens, and the roaring torrents of their respective countries continually offer to their perception and contemplation. This position, however, ought to be restricted in its application, and considered as relating only to those who are endowed with quick perceptions and acute feelings ; for all experience proves, that upon ordinary minds, upon the great and grosser mass of human animals, no such exalting effect is produced, by the contemplation of nature in any of her visible forms, either of magnificence or beauty.

The great majority of mankind, either employed in providing for the necessities of the passing day, or in- tent upon the pursuit of wealth, or engaged in adminis- tering to the gratification of the grosser senses, have neither the inclination nor the ability to derive pleasure from surveying the calm or the agitated ocean; or from observing the various beauties of nature that adorn the fair face of the earth.   All that the sea can present of value or delight to them is contained in her depths, or wafted on her bosom, in the shape of marketable com- modities; and all of satisfaction or comfort that they can derive from the earth is either pent up within her bow- els, in the form of the more precious minerals or metals, or appear upon her surface, in all the variety of those animal and vegetable productions that can be converted into nutriment or profit.   Much stress, therefore, is *not* to be laid upon the grand disposition of natural scenery in the United States, as regulating or affecting the moral and political character of the American people.

President Montesquieu, and other political philoso- phers (besides M. Brissot de Warville and Mr. Gil- bert), do, indeed, attribute much of national character to *physical* circumstances, as scenery, soil, climate, &c. But the physical circumstances of Greece and Rome are the *same* now as in the days of Pericles and Plato, of Cæsar and Cicero.   Yet how different now are the *Men* of Athens and Rome, *quantum matatus ab illo Hectore !* Such is the quickening power of *liberty*, not only to render man, individually, great and power- ful, but also, to render his country, for its allotted hour, lord of the ascendant over other nations ; while *des- potism* debases the individual citizens into slaves, and makes their country the vassal of vassals.   Witness

Greece, once the pride and terror of the world, now a bondwoman to the ignorant and barbarous Turk ; witness Rome, once mistress of the earth, now the miserable asylum of a cumbrous superstition, decaying even to the last faint gleam of extinction.

Prior to the reign of the Imperial Charles the Fifth, *Spain* was the *freest* nation in Europe : the power of her kings was guardedly limited; all orders were admitted to an equal representation in the diet; she maintained an entire independence on the Roman Church ; she engaged and excelled in every walk of literature, science, and erudition; she influenced and controlled every other European sovereignty. Now, she is the forlorn and abject slave of papal superstition, the victim of the inquisition, dark, ignorant, helpless, a prey to the most despicable civil and religious bondage. Yet the plains of Castile and Arragon show as wide a champaign, and the range of the Pyrenees, the chain of the Sierra Morena, and the Mountains of the Asturias, lift their heads as proudly to the skies, now in the darkest hour of Spanish thraldom and degradation, as in her brightest day of civil and religious liberty, chivalric heroism, and mental illumination. The character of nations, therefore, is formed, *not* by physical, but by *moral* causes and influences, as government, religion, laws, and education, which will, hereafter, be shown at length.

The United States are situated between 25° 50′ and 49° 17′ north latitude, and between 10° east and 48° 20′ west longitude from Washington. The most northern part is bounded by a line, running due west from the northwest corner of the Lake of the Woods, and the southern extremity is the outlet of the Rio del Norte. The eastern extremity is the Great Menan Island, on the coast of Maine, and the western extremity is Cape Flattery, north of Columbia River, on the Pacific Ocean. Their greatest extent from north to south is 1,700 miles, and from east to west 2,700. Their surface covers more than 2,500,000 square miles, or 1,600,000,000 acres ; and their population is ten millions, or about four persons to every square mile. The following table shows the popu lation and surface of some of the most important part s of the world ; namely, in round numbers, which is sufficient for our present purpose, to point out the propoi tion of territory and people between the United Stat es and other sovereignties.

States in 1817.	Po pulation.	Square Miles.
All Russia	52, ,000,000	3,650,000
Italy	20, ,000,000	100,000
France	29 ,000,000	250,000
Austria	26 ,000,000	280,000
Turkey	57 ,000,000	940,000
British Isles	20 ,000,000	100,000
Spain	14 ,000,000	150,000
Prussia	11 ,,000,000	96,000
Sweden and Norway . . .	1,500,000	270,000
Denmark	800,000	60,000
United Netherlands	6,,000,000	47,000
Switzerland	2,20 0,000	16,000
Portugal	2,30 0,000	28,000
China	200,000, ,000	1,200,000
United States N. America	10,000, 000	2,500,000
Total	435,800,0 00	9,687,000

So that the United States have the large st *home* territory of all the nations in the world, exc ept Russia ; and their population is gaining fast upon th at of all the European powers.   China is laid out of t he question, because she is barbarous, helpless, and eff ete; she can never contend for the sovereignty or controlling influence of the world; *that* question m ust be decided hereafter, between America and the f irst-rate potentates of Europe.   Britain possesses a *hu ndred and fifty millions* of subjects in her colonial empire, and covers a dominion equal to nearly *one-fifth* of the whole surface of the globe; but her main strength must always depend upon the resources, intelligence, spirit, and character of her native population in the British Isles. If these fail, her colonial empire will be soon dissipated into thin air. The following table shows the gross population and surface of the four quarters of the world.

Quarters of the World.	Population.	Square Miles.
All Asia	600,000,000	11,000,000
Africa	150,000,000	9,000,000
Europe	200,000,000	2,700,000
America	40,000,000	18,000,000
Total	990,000,000	40,700,000

The following tables show how fast the people increase in an extensive country, under the auspices of free and popular institutions. In the year 1749, the whole white population of the North American colonies, now the United States, amounted only to 1,046,000 souls, in the following proportions, as to the respective colonies, now states:

New-Hampshire - - - -	30,000
Massachusetts - - - - -	220,000
Rhode-Island - - - - -	35,000
Connecticut - - - - - -	100,000
New-York - - - - - -	100,000
New-Jersey - - - - -	60,000
Pennsylvania and Delaware -	250,000
Maryland - - - - - -	85,000
Virginia - - - - - - -	85,000
North-Carolina - - - - -	45,000
Georgia - - - - - - -	6,000

States.	Square Miles.	POPULATION.		
		1790.	1800.	1817.
Vermont	10,000	85,539	154,465	296,450
New Hampshire	9,800	141,885	183,858	302,733
Maine ⎫	31,750	96,540	151,719	318,647
Massachusetts ⎬	8,500	378,787	422,845	564,392
Rhode-Island	1,700	68,825	69,122	98,721
Connecticut	4,500	237,946	251,092	349,568
New-York	54,000	340,120	586,050	1,486,739
New-Jersey	6,500	184,139	211,149	345,822
Pennsylvania........	48,700	434,373	602,545	986,494
Delaware...........	1,800	59,094	64,273	108,334
Maryland	14,000	319,728	349,692	502,710
Virginia ⎫	75,000	747,610	886,149	1,347,496
Kentucky ⎬	52,000	73,677	220,959	683,753
North Carolina......	49,000	393,751	478,105	701,224
South Carolina	32,700	240,073	345,591	564,785
Georgia............	64,000	82,548	162,685	408,567
Western Territories ..	———	35,691	45,365	———
District of Columbia..	100	———	14,093	37,892
Tennessee	63,000	———	105,602	489,624
Ohio	45,000	———	———	394,752
Louisiana	49,000	———	———	108,923
Indiana	38,000	———	5,641	86,734
Mississippi	55,000	———	———	104,550
Illinois Territory	66,000	———	———	39,000
Michigan do.........	47,500	———	———	9,743
Missouri do.	1,987,000	———	———	68,794
Total..	2,814,550	3,929,336	5,303.666	10,405,547

What the national capacities of the State of New-York are, may be inferred, not only from her territorial extent, which is ten thousand square miles larger than all England and Wales taken together, but also from the fact, that she has already, in 1817, outstripped every other State in the Union, in the number of her population; although, at the close of the revolutionary war in 1783, she did *not* contain half the number of souls which the States of Massachusetts, Pennsylvania, Maryland, and Virginia, respectively possessed. The following facts will show how rapid has been the growth of some particular places in the United States. In the

c

year 1783, the population of the city of New-York was only 26,000; in the year 1790, 33,000; in 1800, 60,439; in 1810, 93,914; in 1817, 122,000; thus multiplying four times in thirty-four years. Its harbour, formed by the union of the Hudson with the strait of the Sound, called East river, makes a roadstead capable of containing all the navies of the world. Its commerce far surpasses that of any other city in the Union, and in the course of a few years will be second only to that of London. It imports most of the goods consumed between the Raritan and the Connecticut, a coast of one hundred and thirty miles, and between the Atlantic ocean and the lakes, a range of four hundred miles. In the year 1816, the *foreign* imports into the city exceeded fifty-six millions of dollars.

Fifty years since, no such place as Baltimore existed; and now it is a city, abounding in commerce, wealth, and splendour, and contains a population of nearly sixty thousand souls.

In the year 1770, there was not a single white inhabitant in all Kentucky; in 1790, there were 73,677 souls; in 1800, 220,960; and now, in 1817, nearly 700,000. In 1783, the city of New-Orleans was inhabited by a few miserable Spaniards, who carried on a small smuggling trade. Now, in 1817, it numbers nearly 40,000 inhabitants: and its *exports*, during the last year, exceeded those of all the New-England States taken together: the *steam-boats* have been found able to stem the current of the Mississippi; and henceforth, the struggle to engross the foreign trade of the whole western country will be between New-Orleans, New-York, Montreal, and Philadelphia. The difficulty of ascending the Mississippi, had until the experiment of the steam-boats, prevented New-Orleans from supplying the western States with foreign merchandise, which was purchased cheaper in New-York or Philadelphia, and carried by land to Pittsburgh, at the confluence of the Monongahela and Alleghany rivers, and thence down the Ohio, to the various settlements on its banks, than it could be transported up the Mississippi and the Ohio. The chief part of this immense and rapidly augmenting commerce will fall, of course, to that place which can supply foreign goods at the lowest rate; the difference of price depending chiefly on the expense of internal transportation. At present, Montreal seems to have the advantage over her rivals. The single portage, at the falls of Niagara excepted, there is a free navigation for vessels from Montreal to Lake Erie, and the vast extent of waters beyond; unless, indeed, the canal, to be opened between Lake Erie and the Hudson, may succeed in diverting the trade of the western country from Montreal to New-York.

The population of New-Orleans is rapidly increasing by emigrations from all the other States in the Union, and from almost every country in Europe. The *exports* of Louisiana already exceed those of all the New-England States. Nearly four hundred sea vessels arrive and depart annually. And about one thousand vessels, of all denominations, departed during the year 1816, from the Bayou St. John, a port of delivery in the Mississippi district, and were employed in carrying the produce of the Floridas, belonging to the United States. Six hundred flat-bottomed boats, and three hundred barges brought down, last year, to New-Orleans, produce from the Western States and Territories. Ten millions of pounds of sugar are made on the Mississippi alone. And twenty thousand bales of cotton are exported annually.

If the population of the United States shall increase for the next twenty-five years in the same ratio that it has increased during the last twenty-five years, what European country, *single handed,* will be able to compete with them, on the land or on the ocean? or what European power will be able to preserve its American colonies, whether in the West-Indies or on the continent, from their grasp? And why the population should not increase as rapidly, in time to come, as in the past periods, it is difficult to prove; for the extent

c 2

of fertile territory, yet uncleared, is immense; and any one, in any vocation, manual or mechanical, may, by honest industry and ordinary prudence, acquire an independent provision for himself and family; so high are the wages of labour, averaging, at least, double the rate in England, and quadruple that in France; so comparatively scanty the population; so great the demand for all kinds of work; so vast the quantity, and so low the price of land; so light the taxes; so little burdensome the public expenditure and debt.

The recent convulsions and distresses of Europe have, during the last two or three years, thrown a more than usual quantity of foreign emigrants into the United States.

For the rapid increase of population, however, this country is much less indebted to foreign emigration than is generally believed. The number of emigrants from other countries, into the Union, has not averaged more than *five thousand* annually, during the twenty-five years preceding the peace of Europe in 1815; and full half that number have, during the same period, migrated from the United States, partly into Upper Canada, and partly as seafaring adventurers, all over the world. The proof that this country owes the rapid increase of its population chiefly to its own exertions in that universal domestic manufactory, the production of children, lies in the fact, that the average births are to the deaths, throughout the whole United States, as 100 to 48; in the healthiest parts, as New-England and the Middle States, as 100 to 44;—in the least healthy, namely, the two Carolinas and Georgia, as 100 to 52.—The annual deaths average, throughout the United States, one in forty; in the healthiest districts, one in fifty-six; in the most unhealthy, one in thirty-five. There die, annually, in all Europe, in great cities, one in twenty-three; in moderately-sized towns, one in twenty-eight; in the country, one in thirty-five; and in the most healthy parts, one in fifty-five.

The aggregate salubrity of the United States surpasses that of Europe; the males are, generally, active, robust, muscular, and powerful, capable of great exertion and endurance; the females display a fine symmetry of person, lively and interesting countenances, frank and engaging manners. Neither the men nor the women exhibit such ruddy complexions as the British, Dutch, Swedes, Danes, Russians, Norwegians, and the northern Europeans generally. The Americans average a longer life than the people in Europe; where only *three*, out of every thousand births, reach the ages of eighty to ninety years; whereas, in the United States, the proportion is *five* to every thousand.

The population of the whole United States has, hitherto, doubled itself in rather less than *twenty-five* years. The New-England States, of course, do *not* retain their proportion of this increase, because large bodies of their people migrate annually to the western country; which, in consequence, has increased much faster than do the States on the seaboard. Kentucky, for example, has increased eighty per cent. in ten years; Tennessee, ninety-five; Ohio, one hundred and eighty; Louisiana, one hundred and fifty; Indiana, eight hundred; Mississippi Territory, one hundred and sixty; Illinois Territory, seven hundred; Missouri Territory, six hundred; and Michigan Territory, six hundred;—while, of all the Atlantic States, the greatest increase is only forty-four per cent. the population growth of New-York; and the least is twenty per cent. that of Virginia. So that, in the course of a few years, the States will range, if the future be like the past, as to their aggregate population in the following order; New-York, Pennsylvania, Virginia, Kentucky, Ohio, North-Carolina, Massachusetts, South-Carolina, Tennessee, Maryland, Georgia, New-Jersey, Connecticut, Vermont, Louisiana, New-Hampshire, Indiana, Missouri, Mississippi, Illinois, Delaware, and Rhode-Island.

Although the Western Country draws off large migrations from the Atlantic States, particularly from New-England, yet the annually-increasing surplus of population in those States has become so great, that they will not very sensibly feel the drain ; because the *whole* of the annual increase will never migrate in any given year, until the older States shall be overstocked. Massachusetts proper, Connecticut, and Rhode-Island, appear to be approximating to that point ; for their population averages a very slow increase ; and they furnish, yearly, great numbers of recruits to the Western Country. As long as the Federal Union lasts, every succeeding year will diminish the relative importance of New-England in the American commonwealth, by rendering her population and resources less and less proportionate to those of the Western States, whose preponderance in the national councils is already begun to be felt. Supposing, however, that the national councils shall be directed for the benefit of the *whole* United States, and not, exclusively, or too abundantly, for the local interests of some particular districts, then no injury can accrue to the older States, on account of their annual migrations to the west : because, by augmenting the population and resources of the Union at large, they do, in fact, augment their own strength, as an integral part of that Union. If otherwise, indeed, —— but it is not pleasant to indulge in ill-omened anticipations – sufficient for the day is the evil thereof.

The migrations to the west, at present, are supposed to average *one-third* of the annual increase of the older States; to this, add the importation of foreigners from Europe, and the growth of their own native stock of population, in an extensive country, a fertile soil, and a favourable climate, and it requires no great skill in political arithmetic to calculate how soon the Western States will outweigh all the rest of the Union in the general government, by the mere force of a more numerous people. An overstock of inhabitants must always be measured by the habits and manners prevalent in any given country. In the earlier stages of barbarous life, for instance, such as our aboriginal Indians pursue, *one* hunter for every square mile is considered by them a full stock ; and when there is more than this proportion, they say, " it is time for our young men to

go to war, or we shall *starve*." Hence arises their mer-
ciless mode of fighting, and extermination after conquest,
so common to all savage hostilities. In the next, or
pastoral state of human society, an increase, at the rate
of *three* or *four* to each square mile, takes place; as is
seen in Arabia, and other parts of Africa, and in Asia.
In the more advanced stages of social life, in countries
where agriculture and commerce prevail, the rate of
population varies from *three* to *three hundred* for each
square mile of territory, according to the different degrees of advancement in the arts of civilization, and
commercial, horticultural, agricultural, mechanical, and
scientific pursuits. In the most populous parts of China,
there are upwards of three hundred persons to each
square mile; in England, Ireland, the Netherlands,
and Italy, the average is two hundred; in France, one
hundred and fifty; in Scotland, seventy; in Massachusetts, Rhode-Island, and Connecticut, fifty-two;
New-York, twenty; Virginia, fifteen; the whole United
States, four.

It is a fact worthy of observation, that in the State
of Virginia there appear to be three distinct races of
people; those on the seaboard, up to the head of the
tidewater, are a sickly, indolent, feeble tribe; from
the head of the tidewater to the base of the Blue-ridge
the soil is inhabited by as fine, robust, athletic, powerful a body of men as may be found in the world; on
the ridge of the Blue-mountains the population is less
in stature, but extremely active, hardy, strong, and
enterprising.

The rapid increase of a healthy and vigorous population implies a flourishing state of agriculture; and,
accordingly, the United States, during the last twenty
years, except 1808 (the embargo year), and 1814, in
addition to maintaining their own fast-growing population, have, on an average, exported *one-fourth* of their
agricultural produce. For the tables, showing these
exports, from the year 1791 to 1816, both inclusive,
the reader is referred to Mr. Pitkin's Statistical View
of the United States. Agriculture, as a science, is im-

proving rapidly; and agricultural societies are established in Massachusetts, New-York, Pennsylvania, and
some other States, for the purpose of ascertaining the
modes of tillage, pasture, and grazing, best adapted to
the different districts of the Union. The chief articles of
agricultural export are wheat, flour, rice, Indian corn,
rye, beans, peas, potatoes, beef, tallow, hides, butter,
cheese, pork, &c. horses, mules, sheep, tobacco, cotton,
indigo, flax-seed, wax, &c. &c.—The following statement shows the value of agricultural exports, constituting vegetable food, in particular years, namely :

In 1802, $12,790,000; 1803, $14,080,000; 1807,
$14,432,000; 1808, $2,550,000; 1811, $20,391,000;
1814, $2,179,000; 1815, $11,234,000; 1816,
$13,150,000.

The United States far surpass Europe in navigable
capacities; their rivers are more numerous, more capacious, and navigable a greater distance. The Hudson, or North river, that ministers to the convenience
and wealth of the city of New-York, and is, by no
means, to be reckoned among the largest of the American rivers, is navigable for sizeable craft nearly two
hundred miles from the Atlantic. Some notion may
be formed of the facilities for internal navigation in this
country, by casting the eye over a map of the United
States, and tracing the course of some of the principal
rivers; for instance, *the Missouri, the Arkansas, the
Red River, the La Plate, the Ohio, the Tennessee, and,
above all, the Mississippi, the eastern extremity of
whose stream is the headwater of the Alleghany, in
Pennsylvania, about two hundred miles northwest of
Philadelphia. Its western extremity is the headwater
of Jefferson river, about 550 miles from the Pacific
ocean; making a distance between these two extreme
points of 1700 miles, in a straight line. Its northern
extremity is a branch of the Missouri, about 570 miles
west by north of the Lake of the Woods. Its southern
extremity is the south pass into the Gulf of Mexico,
about a hundred miles below New-Orleans; making a
distance, between its extreme north and south, in a

straight line, of one thousand six hundred and eighty miles. So that this river, and its branches, spread over a surface of about fifteen hundred thousand square miles, traversing, in the whole, or in part, the following States and Territories ; namely, the Territories of Mississippi, Missouri, North-west, and Illinois; and the States of Indiana, Ohio, New-York, Pennsylvania, Maryland, Virginia, the two Carolinas, Georgia, Kentucky, Tennessee, and Louisiana.

Several successful efforts have been made, and more are now in progress and in contemplation, to render the vast internal navigation of the United States still more complete by the help of canals. On this subject much valuable information may be derived from the able and luminous report of Mr. Gallatin, when Secretary of the Treasury, on public roads and canals, sent to the senate on the second of March, 1807. This Report, the substance of which will be given presently, recommends to the general government to form canals, from north to south, along the Atlantic sea-coast ; to open communications between the Atlantic and western waters, and between the Atlantic waters and those of the great lakes, and river St. Lawrence ; and, finally, to make interior canals, wherever they may be wanted, throughout the Union. The United States possess a tidewater inland navigation, secure from storms and enemies, reaching from Massachusetts to the southern extremity of Georgia, and interrupted only by four necks of land ; namely, the isthmus of Barnstable, in Massachusetts ; that part of New Jersey which extends from the Raritan to the Delaware ; the peninsula between the Delaware and the Chesapeake ; and the low marshy tract which divides the Chesapeake from Albemarle Sound.

It is needless to expatiate on the utility of such a range of internal navigation, whether in peace or war, to quicken the pace, and multiply the products of commerce ; to augment the means, and magnify the resources both of offensive and defensive warfare.

The inconveniences, complaints ; nay, dangers, resulting from a vast extent of territory, *cannot* be radically removed or prevented, except by opening speedy and easy communications through all its parts. Canals would shorten distances, facilitate commercial and personal intercourse, and unite by a still more intimate community of interests the most remote quarters of the United States. No other single operation has so direct a tendency to strengthen and perpetuate that Federal Union, which secures external independence, domestic peace, and internal liberty to the many millions of freemen that are spread over an area of territory larger than the surface of all Europe.

Impressed with the weight of these truths, the House of Representatives and Senate, in Congress assembled, in February, 1817, passed a bill, appropriating a fund for internal improvement; the principal features of which were to perfect the communication from Maine to Louisiana; to connect the Lakes with the Hudson river; to connect all the great commercial points on the Atlantic, Philadelphia, Baltimore, Washington, Richmond, Charlestown, and Savannah, with the Western States, and complete the intercourse between the west and New-Orleans. On the third of March, Mr. Madison withheld his signature, on account of his scruples, that the Federal Constitution had *not* given to Congress any power to make internal improvements in the United States; and Mr. Monroe, in his message to Congress on the second of December, 1817, after expatiating on the benefit of canals and roads, declares it to be his settled opinion that Congress has *no* power to make any such internal improvement; and advises an *amendment* to the Federal Constitution, that shall give such a power. But the committee of the House of Representatives, on this part of the President's Message, reported, on the fifteenth of December, 1817, that Congress *has* power: First. To lay out, construct, and improve *post-roads* through the several States, with the assent of the respective States. Secondly. To open, construct, and improve *military* roads, through the several States, with the assent of the respective States. Thirdly. To cut *canals* through the several States, with their assent, for promoting and giving security to internal commerce, and for the more safe and economical transportation of military stores in time of war; leaving, in all these cases, the jurisdictional right over the soil in the respective States.

If the general government cannot aid the internal navigation of the Union, it is in the power of the State governments to accomplish that important object at a comparatively small expense. For less than one hundred thousand dollars, a sloop navigation might be opened between Buffaloe and the Fond du Lac, a distance of one thousand eight hundred miles; the only interruption being the Rapids of St. Mary, between lakes Huron and Superior. The Ohio, by one of its branches, French Creek, approaches, with a navigation for boats, to within seven miles of Lake Erie; by the Connewango, to within nine; by the Muskingum to the source of the Cayahoga. The Wabash mingles its waters with those of the Miami of the Lakes; and the waters of the Illinois interweave their streams with those of Lake Michigan, whence to St. Louis boats pass without meeting with a single portage.

The Apalachian Mountains extend west of south from the forty second to the thirty-fourth degree of north latitude, approaching the sea, and washed by the tide, in the State of New-York; and thence, in their southerly course, gradually receding from the sea-shore. In breadth about one hundred and fifty miles, they present a succession of parallel ridges, following nearly the direction of the sea-coast, irregularly intersected by rivers, and divided by narrow valleys. The ridge, called Alleghany, which divides the Atlantic rivers from the western waters, preserves throughout a nearly equal distance of two hundred and fifty miles from the Atlantic ocean, and a nearly uniform elevation of three thousand feet above the level of the sea. These mountains consist of two principal chains, between which lies the fertile limestone valley, that, although occasionally interrupted by transversal ridges, and, in one place, by the dividing or

Alleghany ridge, reaches from Newburgh and Esopus, on the Hudson river, to Knoxville, on the Tennessee. The eastern and narrowest chain is the Blue Ridge of Virginia, which, in its north-east course, traverses, under various names, the States of Maryland, Pennsylvania, and New-Jersey, forms the Highlands, broken at West-point by the tide of the Hudson, and then uniting with the Green Mountains, assumes a northerly direction, and divides the waters of the Hudson and Lake Champlain from those of Connecticut river.

On the borders of Virginia and North Carolina, the Blue Ridge is united by an inferior mountain with the great western chain, and thence, to its southern extremity, becomes the principal or dividing mountain, discharging eastward the rivers Roanoke, Pedee, Santee, and Savannah, into the Atlantic Ocean; southward, the Chatahouchee, and the Alabama, into the Gulf of Mexico; and westward, the New River, and the Tennessee. The New River, taking a course northward, breaks through all the ridges of the great western chain; and, a little beyond it unites, under the name of Kanhawa, with the Ohio. The Tennessee at first runs southwest between the two chains, until having, in a course westward, turned the southern extremity of the great western chain, it takes a direction northward, and joins its waters with those of the Ohio, a few miles above its confluence with the Mississippi. The western chain, much broader and more elevated, bears the names of Cumberland and Gauly mountains, from its southern extremity, near the great bend of the Tennessee river, until it becomes, in Virginia, the principal or dividing mountain. Thence, in its northerly course, towards the State of New-York, it discharges westward the Green Brier river, which, by its junction with the New River, forms the Kanhawa, and the rivers Monongahela and Alleghany, which, from their confluence at Pittsburgh, assume the name of Ohio. Eastward, it pours into the Atlantic Ocean, James River, the Potomac, and the Susquehannah. From the northernmost and less elevated spurs of the chain, the Genessee flows into the lake Ontario; and in that quarter the northern branches of the Susquehannah appear to take their source, from among inferior ridges; and, in their course to the Chesapeake, to break through all the mountains. From the Susquehannah, the principal chain runs more eastward, and washed on the north by the lateral valley of the river Mohawk, terminates, under the name of Catskill Mountain, in view of the tidewater of the Hudson.

It is evident that a canal navigation *cannot* be carried across these mountains. The most elevated lock canal in the world is that of Languedock; and the highest ground over which it is carried is only six hundred feet above the sea. England, with all her means and appliances, has never yet completed a canal of an elevation exceeding five hundred feet above the waters united by it. The Alleghany Mountain, generally, is three thousand feet above the level of the sea. The impracticability arises from the principle of lock navigation, which, in order to effect the ascent, requires a greater supply of water in proportion to the height to be ascended, whilst the supply of water becomes less in the same proportion. Nor does the chain of mountains, through the whole extent where it divides the Atlantic from the western rivers, afford a single pond, lake, or natural reservoir. Indeed, except in the swamps along the southern sea-coast, no lake is to be found in the United States *south* of forty-one degrees of north latitude; and almost every river, *north* of forty-two degrees, issues from a lake or pond. The works necessary, therefore, to facilitate the communications from the sea-ports across the mountains to the western waters, must consist either of artificial roads, extending the whole way from tidewater to the nearest and most convenient navigable western waters, or of improvements in the navigation of the leading Atlantic rivers to the highest practicable points, connected by artificial roads across the mountains, with the nearest points from which a permanent navigation can be relied on, down the western rivers.

The undertaking may be accomplished, by making four artificial roads from the four great western rivers, the Alleghany, Monongahela, Kanhawa, and Tennessee, to the nearest corresponding Atlantic rivers, the Susquehannah, or Juniata, the Potomac, James river, and either the Santee or Savannah, and continuing the roads eastward to the nearest sea-ports. To which add the improvement of the navigation of the four Atlantic rivers, from the tidewater to the highest practicable point effected, principally by canals round the falls, and by locks, when necessary; and particularly a canal at the Falls of Ohio. And although a canal navigation, uniting the Atlantic and western waters in a direct course across the mountains, is *not* practicable, yet the mountains may be turned, either on the north, by means of the Mohawk valley and Lake Ontario, or on the south, through Georgia and the Mississippi Territory.

The country lying between the sources of the rivers Chatahouchee and Mobile and the Gulf of Mexico, is an inclined plane, regularly descending towards the sea; and, by following the proper levels, it presents no natural obstacles to opening a canal, fed by the waters of the Mobile and Chatahouchee, and extending from the tidewater on the coast of Georgia to the Mississippi. The distance in a direct line is about five hundred and fifty miles; and the design, if accomplished, would discharge the Mississippi into the Atlantic Ocean. An inland navigation, even for open boats, already exists from New-Orleans by the Canal Carondelet to Lake Pontchartrain; thence, between the coast and the adjacent islands, to the Bay of Mobile, and up its two principal rivers, the Alabama and the Tombigbee, to the head of the tide within the acknowledged boundaries of the United States.

The current of these two rivers being much less rapid than that of the Mississippi, they were for a long time contemplated, particularly the Tombigbee, as affording a better communication to the *ascending*, or *returning* trade from New-Orleans to the waters of the Tennessee, from which they are separated by short portages. The navigation of the Kanhawa and the eastern branches of the Tennessee, Monongahela, and Alleghany, in their course through the mountains, may be easily improved. From the foot of the mountains all those rivers, especially the Ohio, flow with a much gentler current than the Atlantic rivers. All those rivers, at the annual melting of the snows, rise to the height of more than forty feet, affording from the upper points, to which they are navigable, a safe navigation to the sea for any ship that can pass over the bar at the mouth of the Mississippi. And numerous vessels, from one to four hundred tons burden, are now annually built at several ship-yards on the Ohio, as high up as Pittsburg, and bringing down to New-Orleans the produce of the upper country consumed there, carry to Europe and the Atlantic ports of the United States the sugar, the cotton, and the tobacco of the States of Louisiana, Tennessee, Kentucky, Mississippi, and Indiana, and of the Missouri and Alabama Territories.

Until lately the exports far exceeded the imports of New-Orleans; such were the labour, time, and expense, necessary to ascend the rapid stream of the Mississippi, the nature of whose banks, annually overflowed on a breadth of several miles, precludes the possibility of towing paths. So that whilst the greater part of the produce of the immense country watered by the Mississippi and its tributary streams, was, of necessity, exported through the channel of New-Orleans, the importations of a considerable portion of that country were supplied from the Atlantic seaports by water and land communications. But *now* steam-boats carry merchandise and men from New-Orleans up to the Falls of Louisville, on the Ohio, a distance of seventeen hundred miles. Here a canal might be made for half a million of dollars. At present, however, there is a portage of less than two miles at the Ohio falls, whence steam-boats ply regularly to Pittsburgh, a distance of seven hundred miles; thus ensuring to the Western Country and its great outlet, New-Orleans, a rapidity of growth in wealth, power, and population, unexampled in the history of the world. It is to be noted, however, that steam-boat navigation is much more expensive than that by sloops, nearly as *ten* to *one*.

As to the communications between the Atlantic
rivers and the river St. Lawrence and the great lakes,
vessels ascend the St. Lawrence from the sea to Montreal.   The river Sorrel discharges at some distance below that town the waters of Lake George and Lake
Champlain, which penetrate southward within the
United States. From Montreal to Lake Ontario the ascent of the St. Lawrence is two hundred feet. From
the eastern extremity of Lake Ontario, an inland navigation for vessels of more than a hundred tons burden
is continued above a thousand miles, through lakes Erie,
St. Clair, and Huron, to the western and southern extremities of Lake Michigan, with no other interruption
than the falls and rapids of Niagara, between Lake Erie
and Lake Ontario. Lake Superior, the largest of those
inland seas, communicates with the northern extremity
of Lake Huron, by the river and rapids of St. Mary's.
Five Atlantic rivers approach the waters of the St.
Lawrence; namely, the Penóbscot, Kennebeck, Connecticut, the North, or Hudson river, and the Tioga
branch of the Susquehannah; which last river might
afford a useful communication with the rivers Seneca
and Genessee, that empty themselves into Lake Ontario. The Susquehannah is the only Atlantic river whose
sources approach both the western waters and those of
the St. Lawrence.

The three eastern rivers afford convenient communications with the Province of Lower Canada, but *not*
with the extensive inland navigation which penetrates
through the United States, within two hundred miles
of the Mississippi. The North river is a narrow and
long bay, which, in its course from the harbour of
New-York, breaks through or turns all the mountains,
affording a tide navigation for vessels of eighty tons to
Albany and Troy, nearly two hundred miles above New-
York. In this particular the North river differs from
all other bays and rivers in the United States; the tide
in no other ascends higher than the granite ridge, or
comes within thirty miles of the Blue Ridge, or eastern

chain of mountains. In the North river it breaks through the Blue Ridge at West-Point, and ascends above the eastern termination of the Catskill, or great western chain. A few miles above Troy, and the head of the tide, the Hudson from the North, and the Mohawk from the west, unite their waters, and form the North river. The Hudson, in its course, approaches the waters of Lake Champlain, and the Mohawk those of Lake Ontario. An inland navigation, opened by canals, between Lake Champlain and the North river, would divert to the city of New-York the trade of one-half of the State of Vermont, and of part of the State of New-York, which is now principally carried through the St. Lawrence and Province of Canada. The works necessary to effect water communications between the tide-water of the North river, the St. Lawrence, and all the lakes, except Lake Superior, would not cost more than five millions of dollars.

The principal interior canals, which have been already completed in the United States, are the Middlesex canal, uniting the waters of the Merrimack river with the harbour of Boston, and the Canal Carondelet, extending from Bayou St. John to the fortifications or ditch of New-Orleans, and opening an inland communication with Lake Pontchartrain. The uniting this canal by locks with the Mississippi, would, independently of other advantages, enable the general government to transport with facility and effect the same naval force for the defence of both the Mississippi and Lake Pontchartrain, the two great avenues by which New-Orleans may be approached from the sea.

On the 17th of April, 1816, and 15th April, 1817, the State Legislature of New-York passed acts, appropriating funds for opening navigable communications between the Lakes Erie and Champlain and the Atlantic Ocean, by means of canals connected with the Hudson river. This magnificent undertaking is already begun, and promises to make effectual progress under the auspices of Governor Clinton, who has always been its zealous promoter and patron. If ever this magnificent project shall be accomplished, and a communication actually opened by canals and locks, between Lake Erie and the navigable waters of Hudson's river, and also between Lake Champlain and those waters, the State of New-York will soon become, in itself, a powerful empire.

The completion of the projected canals would secure to the people of the United States the entire profits of this branch of home commerce, and give to the general government the security and influence connected with a thickly settled frontier, and a decided superiority of shipping on the lakes.

The State of New-York ought never to rest until it has accomplished this great object, seeing that its accomplishment will speedily multiply all her resources of territory and population. This State contains inexhaustible supplies of salt, gypsum, iron ore, and a vast variety of other valuable materials for manufacturing establishments. Its territory, containing upwards of thirty millions of acres, offers to agricultural industry a rich reward. A river navigation, scarcely paralleled in the world, for nearly two hundred miles, without interruption, and terminating on the seaboard at a port, capacious, healthy, and easy of access, at all seasons of the year; its interior boundary line passing, more than half its length, through the waters of Erie, Ontario, and Champlain; and the numerous navigable lakes included within its limits, afford the highest commercial capabilities and benefits. But the remote sections of the eastern and western districts lie neighbouring to the British provinces, and are washed by navigable waters, which flow into the Atlantic Ocean through those provinces. Facilitated by the course of their streams, and the declivity of their country, the Americans already contribute largely to their commerce. And, if not prevented, it will become permanent, and number among its agents all those who live beyond the highlands, in which our rivers, running to the north, originate, including what is now the most fertile, and what will soon be the most populous, part of the State.

In addition to recalling to the market of New-York the productions of its own soil, now alienated to Canada, the construction of these canals would draw to this State the trade of the western parts of Vermont, of a great portion of Upper Canada, and of the Northern half of all that vast region of the United States which lies west of the Alleghany mountains. The country south of the great lakes alone includes as many square miles as constitute the whole home territory of some of the first-rate European powers ; and is, perhaps, the most fertile part of the globe. That country already contains more than a million of souls, and is increasing in its population with a rapidity utterly inconceivable by the inhabitants of the old and fully peopled districts of Europe. The increase of New-England population, during the last twenty years, has averaged six per cent. annually : and the surplus thousands of this increase are continually migrating to the west. There they are joined by a numerous emigration from the Middle and Southern States, who, together with them, multiply and thrive, in proportion to the means of subsistence produced by their common industry. The projected canals will open to this immense and rapidly augmenting population a cheaper, safer, and more expeditious road to a profitable market, than they can possibly find in any other country ; and, eventually, render the city of New-York the greatest commercial emporium in the world.

The United States then exhibit a mighty empire, covering a greater extent of territory than all Europe, and held together by twenty separate State sovereignties, watching over and regulating, in their executive, legislative, and judicial departments, all its municipal and local interests ; with a Federal head, a general government, preserving and directing all its national concerns and foreign relations ; with a soil, rich in all the productions of prime necessity, of convenience, and luxury, and capable of sustaining *five hundred millions* of people ; a line of seacoast more than two thousand miles in extent, and a natural internal navigation, in itself excellent, and capable of still further

D 2

improvement, by the construction of canals, at a comparatively trifling expense; affording within its capacious bosom an asylum sufficient to receive all the distressed of Europe, and holding out the sure means of ample subsistence and perfect independence to every one who unites in his own character and conduct the qualities of industry, sobriety, perseverance, and integrity. For the best mode of location in the boundless regions of the Western States and Territories, and for the disposition of the *public* lands, held by the government in trust for the people of the United States, the reader may, profitably, consult Mr. Mellish's " Geographical Description of the United States ;" Mr. Brown's "Western Gazetteer, or Emigrant's Directory," and Mr. Darby's " Geographical Description of the State of Louisiana, the Southern part of the State of Mississippi, and Territory of Alabama:" and for the inland navigation of the United Kingdom of Great Britain and Ireland, see " Resources of the British Empire," pp. 216—223, both inclusive.

CHAPTER II.

Commerce, &c. of the United States.

SOME few years since, a theory prevailed in this country that the United States would become a more prosperous and happy nation, if they would forego, altogether and for ever, all *foreign* commerce; and, as a practical commentary upon this text, the general government, at that time wielded by Mr. Jefferson, and at his special recommendation, laid an *embargo* on all the American trade with other countries, in the month of December, 1807; and continued it with various regulations and enforcements, affecting internal commerce also, until the spring of 1809, a period of eighteen months. These "*restrictive energies*" (as they were vauntingly called by Mr. Jefferson) not only annihilated the foreign commerce, but also very materially crippled the coasting trade of the United States. The distress, misery, and ruin, produced by this great agricultural scheme, not merely to the merchants, but to the farmers also (whose interests it professed to subserve, but whose property it destroyed by taking away the markets for their produce), was so general, so deep, so intolerable, as to prove the entire fallacy of the theory; and the American people now appear universally to concur in the sentiment publicly pronounced by one of the ablest and most efficient *practical* statesmen, who now serve as ornaments and bulwarks to the commonwealth; namely, that "commerce protected by a navy, and a navy nourished by commerce," is the policy best calculated to render the United States a prosperous and powerful empire.

The aggregate commerce of the world, doubtless, is increased in consequence of the universal peace established in the year 1815 ; but, as certainly, the respective trade of the United States and Britain has been diminished by that event. Britain has lost her war monopoly, and America has ceased to be carrier for the world. They are each reduced to the level of peace competition ; and must now contend in foreign markets with the skill and ingenuity of France and Italy, the patient industry and perseverance of the United Netherlands, the rival labours of Denmark, Sweden, Russia, and the commercial parts of Germany, to which add the efforts of Spain and Portugal. Hence have arisen, during the last three years, both in the United States and in the British Isles, very general and very grievous distress, bankruptcy, and ruin, among their merchants, manufacturers, and farmers. In Britain the pressure has been more severe, on account of the enormous public expenditure, the confined territory, and crowded population of her home dominions, which allow no outlet for her people ; who must, therefore, if not directed by their government, and aided to settle in the North American colonies or the Cape of Good Hope, or New Holland, swarm out hither, to swell the rapid tide of our western emigration.

Nevertheless, so immense is her capital, so excellent her manufactures, so persevering the industry of her people, so vigorous and all pervading her government, that her *foreign* trade is rapidly improving, more particularly with the Brazils, the Baltic, Italy, and the East-Indies. In the most prosperous days her foreign commerce did *not* make an *eleventh* part of her home and colonial trade. For the gradual progress and amount of the British trade, alike in the Isles, the colonies, and all the quarters of the world, for the last hundred years, see the "Resources of the British Empire," pp. 122 —140, both inclusive; and pp. 399—450.

In the United States the pressure has been less severe than in Britain, although the bankruptcies among our merchants and manufacturers have been sufficiently numerous and distressing; and the farmers also have suffered greatly for want of a market for their produce; nevertheless, the moderate public expenditure, the comparatively scanty population, and the immense outlet for enterprising industry, in the new lands and virgin soil of the Western Country, prevent the necessity of any one, who possesses health and industry, suffering from absolute want of food, clothing, and lodging. The foreign trade of this country is, indeed, at present much less than it was previous to the embargo system; but such is the activity, skill, and enterprise of the American people, so well built, well navigated, and speedy are their ships, and so abundant the soil in valuable staples, that she must always average her full share of external commerce; and her home trade is continually increasing, by the improvement of her internal navigation, the variety of her products, and the rapid growth of her population, wealth, and intercourse. The wages of labour here average more than double their rate in England, and quadruple that in France; and land is plentiful, cheap, and fertile; so that those who are straitened and embarrassed in the large cities, have only to fall back into the country, and become industrious yeomen, and they readily provide ample sustenance for themselves, and lay a broad and permanent foundation of independence for their families.

The reader is referred to the second edition of Mr. Pitkin's Statistics for an account of the exports and imports, the home and foreign trade of the United States, and the proportions of their external commerce with different nations, during a period of nearly one hundred and twenty years, including their colonial as well as their national existence and commerce. The following tables show the amount of American foreign trade, in exports and imports, at different periods, in order to exhibit the rise and progress, and alternations of the commercial career, which this country has run, from the year 1700 down to the present time.

Years.	Exports of the United States.	Imports of the United States.
Average from 1700 to 1710,	$1,000,000	$1,100,000
1710 to 1720,	1,700,000	1,550,000
1720 to 1730,	2,600,000	1,980,000
1730 to 1740,	2,940,000	2,900,000
1740 to 1750,	3,120,000	3,630,000
1750 to 1760,	3,710,000	6,160 000
1760 to 1770,	4,670,000	7,000·000
1770 to 1780,	3,100,000	5,200,000

In 1784 - - - - - - - - - - -	4,000,000	18,000,000
1790 - - - - - - - - - -	6,000,000	17,260,000

Years.	Total Exports.	Exports of domestic origin.	Exports of foreign origin.
1791 - - - -	$19,012,041		
1795 - - - -	47,989,472		
1800 - - - -	70,971,780		
1803 - - - -	55,800,033	$42,205,961	$13,594,072
1807 - - - -	108,343,150	48,699,592	59,643,558
1808, i.e. em-bargo year,	22,430,960	9,433,546	12,997,414
1810, embar-go off	66,757,970	42,366,675	24,391,295
1814 war with England,	6,927,441	6,782,272	145,169
1815 - - - -	52,557,753	45,974,403	6,583,350
1816 - - - -	81,920,452	64,781,896	17,138,555

Of the *domestic* exports of the United States the proportions are ;—the produce of agriculture, three-fourths in value ; the produce of the forest, one-ninth ; of the sea, one-fifteenth ; and manufactures, one-twentieth.

Of the *foreign* exports, the proportions in 1807 (the greatest commercial year ever experienced by the United States) being the year immediately preceding the embargo, were $43,525,320, imported from the British Isles; $3,812,065, from France and her dependencies; and $11,318,532, from the rest of the world. During the years 1802, 1803, and 1804, the annual value of the *imports* into the United States was $75,316,937; and of the exports, $68,460,000. Of the imports the proportions were,

From Britain	$35,970,000
the northern powers, Prussia, and Germany	7,094,000
Dominions of Holland, France, Spain, and Italy	25,475,000
Dominions of Portugal	1,083,000
China, and other native powers of Asia	4,856,000
All other countries	838,000

Whence it appears that the trade between the United States and Britain is greater in amount than between the United States and all the rest of the world: which is a strong reason why the two countries, for their mutual benefit, should preserve friendly relations towards each other, in the *spirit* as well as in the letter of peace.

During the same three years, 1802, 1803, and 1804, the annual value of *domestic* exports was $39,928,000 Of which was exported to the British

dominions	20,653,000
To northern powers, Prussia, and Germany	2,918,000
Dominions of Holland, France, Spain, and Italy	12,183,000
Dominions of Portugal	1,925,000
All other countries	2,249,000

The annual value of *foreign* produce, re-exported to all parts of the world, during those three years was,

$28,533,000

Of which was exported to the British dominions	3,054,000
To northern powers, Prussia, and Germany	5,051,000
Dominions of Holland, France, Spain, and Italy	18,495,000
Dominions of Portugal	396,000
All other countries	1,537,000

Annual value of importations being . . .		75,316,000
exports—domestic		
produce	39,928,000	
foreign produce .	28,533,000	
		68,461,000

Apparent balance against the United States, $6,855,000

The imports for the year 1807 were, in value		138,574,876
exports—domestic		
produce	$48,699,592	
foreign produce .	59,643,558	
		108,343,150
Total		$246,918,026

From this great commerce with foreign nations, amounting to nearly two hundred and fifty millions of dollars in one year, together with all the wealth it poured into the country, and all the productive industry it put in motion, Mr. Jefferson's *embargo* cut off the

United States; which, in consequence of our own restrictive energies, the late war with England, and the peace diminution, have never yet nearly reached that floodtide of trade which was fertilizing and enriching every corner of the Union. For a view of the trade of the United States with each country, from the commencement of the government, distinguishing the trade of the parent country from that of her colonies and dependencies, together with a general account of the trade of America with each quarter of the world, the reader may most profitably consult Mr. Pitkin's Statistics of the United States, second edition, beginning at page 183, and continuing to page 290.

The United States, since the establishment of the Federal government in 1789, up to the commencement of commercial restrictions in December, 1807, and the war with England in 1812, increased in wealth and population with unexampled rapidity, as appears by the great increase of their exports and imports; of the duties on imports and tonnage, and of their commercial tonnage; by the accumulation of wealth in all their cities, towns, and villages; by the establishment of numerous monied institutions; by the great rise in the value of lands; and by various internal improvements, in the shape of roads, bridges, ferries, and canals; and by their annual consumption of goods increasing rapidly. For instance, the average yearly amount of merchandise, paying duties *ad valorem*, consumed, was, in

Three years, from 1790 to 1792 . . . . $19,310,801
Six years,   —   1793 to 1798   27,051,440
Three years, —   1805 to 1807   38,549,966

At least seventy millions of pounds weight of sugar are consumed in the United States. In 1810, ten millions of pounds were made in the territory of Orleans, now State of Louisiana; and about the same quantity made from the maple-tree throughout the United States.

Sugar-cane plantations are increasing in Louisiana, and twenty millions of pounds weight of sugar are supposed to have been made in 1817. In the State of Georgia, also, the sugar-cane is cultivated with success. The culture of the cane is not more laborious than that of cotton, and less liable to accidents : a moderate crop is 1000 pounds per acre ; and in a few years a sufficient quantity will, probably, be made within the limits of the United States to supply their consumption. The increase of American tonnage is unexampled in the history of the commercial world, owing to the increased quantity of bulky domestic produce exported, the increase of population, and extent of the carrying trade. The *increase* of the registered tonnage, or tonnage employed in *foreign* trade, from 1793 to 1801, was 358,815 tons, having nearly doubled in eight years. From 1793 to 1810, the increase was 616,535 tons. In 1793, the tonnage employed in the *coasting* trade was 122,070 tons ; in 1801, 274,551 tons. From 1793 to 1810, the increase was 283, 276 tons. The tonnage employed in the fisheries increased from 1793 to 1807 about 40,000 tons.

The whole tonnage of the United States, in 1810, was 1,424,780 tons, of which the different States owned the following proportions :

New-Hampshire,	*Tons* 28,817	Maryland	*Tons* 143,785
Massachusetts	495,203	Virginia	84,923
Rhode-Island	36,155	North Carolina	39,594
Connecticut	45,108	South Carolina	53,926
New-York	276,557	Georgia	15,619
New-Jersey	43,803	Ohio	*None*
Pennsylvania	125,430	New-Orleans	13,240
Delaware	8,190		

The State of Massachusetts has many hundred miles of sea-coast, with numerous inlets and harbours ; and her amount of tonnage has always been greater than that of any other State in the Union. The tonnage of the principal seaports, in 1810, was,

Of Boston . . *Tons* 149,121
   New York . . . 268,548 *Second only to that of London.*
   Philadelphia . . 125,258
   Baltimore . . . 103,444
   Charleston . . . 52,888

Now, in 1817, the whole tonnage employed in *foreign* trade is much less than it was in 1810. So much has peace all over the world lessened the external commerce of the United States. The tonnage of Britain has *not* grown with a rapidity equal to that of America; for, in 1700, it was only, 273,693 tons; in 1750, 690,798 tons; in 1800, 1,269,329 tons; in 1813, 1,579,715 tons. In 1787, France owned only 300,000 tons, in her foreign trade; in 1800, only 98,304 tons. In 1804, the nations round the Baltic, including Norway and Holstein, owned only 493,417 tons, *not* half the tonnage of the United States.

The extensive and rapidly increasing *coasting* trade, as well as the fisheries of the United States, will not only augment the wealth and comfort of the American people, but will always ensure a large body of excellent seamen for the supply of the navy, when wanted. The American navy, formerly proscribed as a burden and curse to the country, seems at length to have fought itself into favour with all parties. Its heroic achievements and splendid success, during the late war with England, and its present commanding attitude in the Mediterranean, have elevated the character of the country, and conferred an imperishable glory upon its own name; and justly claims the support and honour of the government and people, both in peace and in war, now and for ever. The American navy consists of nearly one hundred ships, brigs, and schooners, besides small sloops, and gun-boats—of which nine are rated at seventy-four, but carry ninety guns; ten forty-four guns; one thirty-eight guns; two thirty-six guns; two thirty-two guns, and thirty from twenty-eight to sixteen guns. The actual number far exceeds the rate of guns in all the classes of vessels. Congress has

made ample appropriations for the annual increase of
the navy ; so that the United States, in all probability,
will soon be able to send out fleets sufficiently numerous to cope with any European power, for the mastery
of that element, whose dominion invariably confers a
paramount influence among all the sovereignties of the
earth.   The number of naval officers, at the commencement of the last war, were thirteen captains, nine masters commanding, and seventy lieutenants.   The promotions during the war were sixteen captains, twenty-
eight masters commanding, and one hundred and
twenty lieutenants.   The promotions since the peace
have been ten captains, nineteen masters commanding,
and sixty-eight lieutenants.

   An almost universal notion prevails in this country,
that the commerce of the United States will be prodigiously benefited by the emancipation of the Spanish
American colonies, and throwing open their trade to
the world.   But this is at least problematical, because
those immense regions produce all the staples of the
United States, and many more also, and would find, in
the event of their emancipation and free trade, a more
profitable market in Britain than in the United States ;
and in return, England could supply them with manufactured goods, better in quality, more abundant in
quantity, and at a lower rate, than any other country can
possibly do.   A proof of this is to be found in the fact,
that the influx of British goods into the United States,
since the peace of 1815, has destroyed or suspended a
great portion of our American manufacturing establishments ; *a fortiori*, then, American cannot contend with
British manufactures in foreign markets, seeing that they
are beat in the unequal competition at home, upon their
own ground, although aided by protecting duties.

   It appears somewhat doubtful, whether the Spanish
colonies, *unassisted* by any other power, will be able,
eventually, to shake off the yoke of Old Spain ; for,
during nearly ten years of revolutionary movements,
they do not seem to have shown the intelligence, skill,
reflection, forecast, combination, and perseverance, re-

quisite to establish a *free* government. The hands of
England, probably, are tied up by the Treaty of Vienna;
and the United States government do not seem disposed to interfere, as they passed an Act of Congress, a
few months since, forbidding the transportation of men,
and arms, and ammunition, from our American ports to
aid the revolted colonies. The President, in his Message
of the second of December, 1817, states, that our citizens sympathize with the Spanish Americans, but the
United States government have maintained, and will
continue to maintain, a strict neutrality between the
contending parties, keeping their ports open to both,
and seeking no exclusive commercial advantage from
the colonies, if they shall become independent. Nevertheless, the United States government have ordered the
settlements on Amelia Island, at the mouth of St. Mary's
River, near the boundary of Georgia, and at Galvestown,
in the Gulf of Mexico, made by the Spanish Americans,
to be broken up by our troops ; and have sent commissioners along the southern coast of Spanish America, to
communicate with the existing authorities, and claim
redress for past and prevention of future injuries.
France and Spain both materially assisted the American
colonies in their revolt from the mother country; and,
doubtless, *any* government, whether military, or monarchical, or republican, provided the Hispano-Ameri-
cans could establish their own national sovereignty and
independence, would be infinitely preferable to the colonial system of Old Spain—a system which enslaves
both body and mind, and debases the human animal
below the condition of the brutes that perish. In all
probability, if their national independence were once
fixed, in whatever form, and under how many sovereignties soever, the felicitous contagion of liberty
would spread from the United States, and gradually
improve the spirit, and liberalize the character and
conduct of the new-born dynasties.

The reader may find considerable information on this
subject, by consulting the " Outline of the Revolution
in Spanish America, &c." by a South American, first

published in London, and republished in New-York, in November, 1817. This work gives a full and fair account of the origin, progress, and actual state of the war between Spain and Spanish America, down to the close of the year 1816. The " Letter to Mr. Monroe," on the Spanish American revolution, supposed to be written by Mr. H. Brackenridge, is an able and spirited performance; it advises our government to acknowledge the independence of the Hispano-American provinces, as soon as they become independent *de facto;* but not to go to war with Spain on their account; nor to aid them with men, money, arms, or ammunition. See also a very able article in the Quarterly Review, for November, 1817, respecting Spain and her colonies; in which the writer maintains it to be the duty of Britain, either to observe a strict neutrality, or to mediate amicably between the contending parties. This article contains much valuable information respecting Spanish America, and some profound and accurate observations on the different characteristics of its population and of that of the United States.

The advantages of the emancipation of Spanish America will pervade the whole world; but, in the first instance, will be more particularly directed towards England. The liberation of this immense region from colonial bondage has engaged the attention of some of the most distinguished statesmen, in this country and in Europe. Early in the first revolutionary war, a Jesuit, born in Arequipa, in the province of Peru, addressed the Spanish colonists, and called upon them to establish a free and independent government, which might at once secure their own prosperity and happiness, and open a liberal intercourse of reciprocal benefits with the rest of the world. This enlightened ecclesiastic, who exhibits an intimate acquaintance with the most approved principles of political philosophy, died in London, in 1798, and left his manuscript papers in the hands of the Honourable Rufus King, at that time minister in Britain, from the United States. Some part of these papers was afterward printed, through the intervention of General

Miranda, for the purpose of being distributed among his countrymen, previous to his unsuccessful expedition in 1806.

Perhaps the greatest commercial benefit, resulting from the emancipation of Spanish America, would be the formation of a navigable passage across the isthmus of Panama, the junction of the Atlantic and Pacific Oceans. The expense of such an undertaking would not exceed three or four millions sterling; and Britain could not more profitably employ twenty or thirty thousand of her distressed labourers than in executing such a task, under the superintendence of competent engineers. The completion of this navigation would give England the command of the commerce of the whole world, and soon compensate her for all the toil, and wealth, and blood, which she has expended during twenty-five years of unexampled warfare, waged for the redemption of Europe from revolutionary bondage.

In the year 1790, the scheme of Spanish American emancipation was first proposed to Mr. Pitt by General Miranda, and met with a cordial reception; but was soon afterward laid aside, on account of Britain and Spain resuming their pacific relations with each other. In the year 1797, Miranda was met at Paris by deputies and commissioners from Mexico and the other principal provinces of Spanish America, for the purpose of con-certing with him the means of emancipating their country. It was decided that Miranda should, in their name, repair to England, and communicate their pro-positions to the British government; one of which was to join the Atlantic and Pacific at the expense of the colonies, and another to cede the Floridas to the United States, the Mississippi being proposed as the boundary between the two nations; and the stipulation of a small military force, from the Anglo-Americans, to aid the es-tablishment of the proposed independence. It was also proposed to resign all the islands which belong to the Spaniards, excepting Cuba, the possession of which is rendered necessary by the situation of the Havanna, commanding the passage from the Gulf of Mexico. This document is dated at Paris, 22d of December, 1797. The proposal for the return of Miranda to England was acceded to by Mr. Pitt, with whom a conference was held in January following. It was proposed that the United States should furnish ten thousand troops; and the British government agreed to find money and ships. But Mr. Adams, then the American President, declined to transmit an immediate answer; and the measure was, in consequence, postponed. In the year 1806, Mr. Jefferson, at that time President of the United States, disavowed the expedition of Miranda to emancipate Spanish America, and actually caused Messrs. Smith and Ogden, two merchants of the city of New-York, to be indicted in the Circuit Court for this District for aiding and abetting Miranda's enterprise; but the jury found a verdict of acquittal. For a most ample and splendid account of the practicability and effects of liberating Spanish America, and joining the two oceans, see the thirteenth volume of the Edinburgh Review, pp. 277—311, both inclusive.

It appears necessary for England, now, to make some extraordinary effort to recruit her exhausted strength, and to relieve her present pressure. She has, indeed, during the lapse of five and twenty years, directed, with a daring and a steady hand, the vast resources of her mighty empire, against the common enemy of the human race: with the guardianship of presiding genius, she has aided the weak and restrained the encroachments of the strong: she has assisted the *people* of continental Europe in their patriotic efforts to trample beneath their feet the foreign domination of an invading foe; she has caused the star of Napoleon to fade into a dim tinct; she has put together the glittering fragments of disjointed Europe, and given again to that fair portion of the world the beamings of religion, the light of morals, and the beauty of social order. But her recent glories have led her to a painful pre-eminence; henceforth she is doomed to the proud but melancholy necessity of being *first* or *nothing*. The moment she recedes, the moment she bows her lofty head beneath the ascendency of any other nation, that moment she is dashed from off her wide ambitious base, and falls, like Lucifer, never to rise again. In her late protracted conflict, her frame has been shattered; her finances are dilapidated; her agriculture languishes; her manufactures droop; her commerce is diminished; her population is impoverished; and, if she hopes to sustain that high eminence which her achievements have reached, in the times of Elizabeth, of William, and of her present sovereign; achievements which have rendered her the arbitress of Europe, the bulwark of civil and religious liberty, and the tutelary angel of man; she must hasten to emancipate the Spanish American colonists, and unite the waters of the Atlantic and Pacific oceans. Unless some measures be adopted by Britain to employ and relieve her superabundant and indigent population, a much greater proportion than has ever yet left her native isles will find their way hither, to augment the number of our American citizens.

CHAPTER. III.

On the Manufactures of the United States.

THERE can be no doubt that *agriculture* has a tendency to produce a more abundant and more healthy
population than that which springs from *manufactures*;
but agriculture and manufactures act and re-act upon
each other for their mutual benefit; for the greatest
and most important branch of the commerce of every
nation is that which is carried on by the inhabitants of
the towns and cities with those of the country. The
townsmen draw from the people of the country the
rude produce, the fruits of the soil, for which they pay
by sending back into the country a part of this rude
produce manufactured and prepared for immediate use;
or, in other words, this trade between town and country consists in a given quantity of rude produce being
exchanged for a given quantity of manufactured produce. Whatever, therefore, has a tendency, in any
country, to diminish the progress of manufactures, has
also a tendency to diminish the home market, (the most
important of all markets for the rude produce of land)
and consequently to cripple the efforts of agriculture.

In young and lately established countries, however,
where the population is *not*, as yet, sufficiently numerous to answer fully the demand for labour; it is perhaps
more adviseable to confine their attention chiefly to the
raising of rude produce, to the clearing new lands, and
cultivating those already reclaimed; because they can
import manufactured goods from an old and thickly
peopled country, at a cheaper rate than they can fabri-
cate them in their own; and they will more rapidly in-

crease the number, strength, and wealth of their people
by so doing, than by consuming a larger quantity of
capital in forming manufactured goods of a worse quality, and at a higher price than that for which they can
bring them from abroad.   Besides, as the wages of
labour are so high, and land so cheap, in the United
States (and in all new countries), there is a continual
bounty offered to labourers to leave their manufacturing
masters, and go and buy land, and till it for themselves; since every man, who has any proper feeling of
independence beating at his heart, would rather toil for
himself and his family, as an uncontrolled yeoman,
than labour as a confined servant to a stranger. Whence
the manufacturers would be (as indeed they are daily
and hourly in the United States,) liable to frequent in-
terruptions in their proceedings, and suffer much prejudice in their trade, enhancing the price and deterio-
rating the quality of their wares; all which evil must
ultimately fall upon the consumers, and necessarily
entail a burdensome impediment upon the productive
exertions of the community.

The United States, therefore, it should seem, would
do well *not* anxiously to endeavour to *force* the production of manufactures by government bounties, by protecting or prohibitory duties, by monopoly prices, before an effectual demand shall be made for them by an
increased density of population along the seaboard, and
in the interior; by the more minute division of labour,
and by the more complete filling up of the other channels of trade and agriculture. Nay, perhaps it would be
wiser, for some years yet to come (until the wilderness
be reclaimed, and the population be more compact), for
the Americans to confine themselves chiefly to the raising of raw materials, and let Europe continue to be the
workshop where those raw materials might be manufactured; because experience has uniformly shown that
no nation has ever yet pushed its manufactures to any
great extent, without introducing and continuing a very
alarming quantity of misery and disease, decrepitude,
vice, and profligacy, among the lower orders of the peo-

ple; and this to the statesman, who measures the strength and greatness of a nation by the health and virtue, the prosperity and happiness, of its citizens, seems too great a price to pay for the privilege of manufacturing a few yards of broadcloth, or a few pieces of muslin. England herself is a portentous illustration of this truth: recently, and for the last five and twenty years, her *manufacturing* districts have sent forth full bands of Luddites, and Spenceans, and jacobins, and anarchists, and rebels, and assassins, that have continually put to the test the strength, and strained the nerves of her government. See the " Resources of the British Empire," pp. 140—154, for the state of British manufactures.

But as the introduction of manufactures into, and their extended increase in a country, generally promise large profits to speculators and capitalists, it is *not* to be expected that the mere circumstance of manufactures being destructive of the virtue, health, and happiness of the labourers employed in them, will ever be of sufficient weight to deter any nation from introducing and establishing these nurseries of individual wealth, and wide-spread poverty, among themselves, whenever an opportunity shall occur. The wages of labour in the United States are at least one hundred per cent. higher than in England, and quadruple those of France; and yet the agricultural products of this country find a profitable market in Europe; while the expense of erecting and continuing manufacturing establishments is such as, in many instances, to disable them from competing with those of Europe, unless protected by bounties, prohibitory duties, and a monopoly. The cause of these apparently contradictory effects is to be found in the vast quantity and low price of our new and fertile lands. One man is able to spread his agricultural labour over a much wider surface of soil in the immense regions of America, than can be done in the comparatively small and circumscribed districts into which the European farms are necessarily divided, on account of the narrow limits of territory, coupled with a crowded population.   Hence, although the system of agriculture in the United States is less perfect, and less productive on a given quantity of ground, than in some parts of Europe, yet the far wider range of land under cultivation (about three times as many acres as make up the whole superficies of the British isles) produces annually a more abundant crop, in mass, to the industry of a given number of proprietors.

Formerly, some of our leading politicians professed to think it more adviseable for the United States to prosecute the labours of agriculture, than to attempt to force manufactures into a premature and pernicious existence.   Mr. Jefferson, in his " Notes on Virginia," strenuously labours this point, and pathetically deprecates the hour when the American people shall be converted from robust and virtuous farmers into sickly and profligate manufacturers.   But he has lately altered his opinion, as appears from his recent letter to the Secretary of the Society for encouraging American manufactures, in which he seems to have forgotten all his former exclamations in favour of agriculture, and all his " Jeremiades" against manufactures.   In order to accomplish their purpose, this Society, consisting of manufacturers all over the Union, is continually beseeching and besieging Congress to exclude all foreign goods from the United States, and give them a monopoly of the American market; that is, in other words, to lay a heavy tax upon all the other classes of the community, the farmers, clergy, lawyers, merchants, physicians, and all the labouring orders, that a few manufacturers, about a *hundredth* part of the whole population, may enrich themselves by selling to their fellow-citizens bad goods, at a much greater price than they could import far better commodities from Europe.

This is, in fact, checking the growth of the wealth and population of the United States, by *at least* all the difference between the monopoly price of American manufactures and the fair competition price of imported European goods; to do which, might, indeed, be very good patriotism, but it is certainly very bad policy. The

United States having but recently commenced their
national career, and looking forward to many ages of
improvement and growth, should be, above all other
countries, particularly careful to avoid the errors of the
European mercantile system; errors which sprang up
amidst the darkness and ignorance of feudal despotism;
and which all the most distinguished political philosophers of the present age unite to condemn. The United
States, therefore, should resolutely cast from off their
shoulders all the shackles of bounties, protections, prohibitions, and monopolies, and permit agriculture,
commerce, and manufactures, to find the legitimate level
of unimpeded competition, and to employ just so much
of the productive industry and capital of the country as
individual inclination and interest might require, without any interference on the part of the government,
which ever acts the wisest part, when it suffers all the
various classes of the community to manage their own
affairs in their own way. *Laissez nous faire* was the
reply of the French merchants to M. Colbert, when he
attempted to build up the delapidated commerce of
France, by ministerial intermeddling with what no
minister can possibly either direct or understand so
well as the merchants themselves.

Besides, every free country manufactures as fast as
its wants and interests demand; because every country,
as well as every individual, prefers a *home* to a foreign
market, for the purpose of barter, sale, and purchase.
Nevertheless, the interests of agriculture are quite in-
adequate to contend with the spirit of encroachment
and monopoly so inherent in the very nature of manufacturers. Manufacturers enjoy a great advantage over
the farmers, who are scattered thinly throughout the
country, in the facility of combining together, and
acting in large bodies, so as to compel the government
to listen to their complaints. Their standing committees, and eternal clamour about the dignity of patriotism, and the necessity of not depending on foreign
nations for articles of use and convenience, are always
an overmatch for the yeomen, who, widely separated

from each other, cannot act in such close concert, nor with such efficient activity and perseverance. Add to which, many of the Members of Congress, themselves farmers, and therefore peculiarly representing the agricultural interests, are deeply engaged in manufactures and banks; whence they are not so clear-sighted to the evils of a monopoly, on the part of the manufacturers, as they otherwise might be.

During the late war with England, manufactures thrived in the United States, precisely because they had a monopoly of the home market, and compelled the consumer to pay above a hundred per cent. more for goods of an inferior quality to those which might have been imported from Europe at half the price, if our ports had been open for the admission of foreign commodities. At that period there was a capital of about £1,000,000,000 employed in carrying on American manufactures; but on the return of peace, the influx of European goods reduced the price to at least one-half, and stopped perhaps more than half of the manufacturing establishments in the Union; so that the capital now employed in American manufactories scarcely reaches the sum of five hundred millions of dollars. Nevertheless, our manufacturers are convinced that continuing this war monopoly, and compelling the American people to pay a double price for all their articles of consumption, would materially promote the national welfare of the United States. Whether or not the general government is to be borne down by this incessant clamour, and sacrifice the interests of the rest of the community to those of a very small portion of that community, remains yet to be seen. The President, in his Message of the 2d of December, says, " Our manufactures will require the continued attention of Congress: the capital employed in them is considerable, and the knowledge acquired in the machinery and fabric of all the most useful manufactures is of great value: their preservation, which depends on *due encouragement*, is connected with the high interests of the nation."

Few nations, however, can boast of skill and ingenuity in manufactures, and especially improvements in
labour-saving machinery, equal to those which have
been exhibited and discovered in the progress of the
mechanical arts in the United States. The causes of
this superior ingenuity and skill are various. The high
price of labour, and the comparative scarcity of labourers, offer a continual bounty of certain and immediate remuneration to all those who shall succeed in the
construction of any machinery that may be substituted
in the place of human labour. Add to this, the entire
freedom of vocation enjoyed by every individual in this
country. Here there are no *compulsory apprenticeships;*
no town and corporation restraints, tying each man
down to his own peculiar trade and calling, as in Europe; the whole, or nearly the whole of which still
labours under this remnant of feudal servitude. In the
United States every man follows whatever pursuit, and
in whatever place, his inclination, or opportunity, or
interest prompts or permits; and consequently a much
greater amount of active talent and enterprise is employed in individual undertakings here than in any other
country. Many men in the United States follow various
callings, either in succession or simultaneously. One
and the same person sometimes commences his career
as a farmer, and, before he dies, passes through the
several stages of a lawyer, clergyman, merchant, con-
gress-man, soldier, and diplomatist. There is also a
constant migration hither of needy and desperate talent
from Europe, which helps to swell the aggregate of
American ingenuity and invention; and the European
discoveries in art and science generally reach the United
States within a few months after they first see the light
in their own country, and soon become amalgamated
with those made by Americans themselves.

For information respecting the manufactures of the
United States, the reader is referred to General Hamilton's " Report on the subject of Manufactures," made
in the year 1791, when he was Secretary of the Trea-

sury, in consequence of an order of the House of Representatives. It is not too much to say, that this is one of the ablest State Papers which ever came from the pen of man. See also the list of American patents, published by order of Congress; Mr. Tench Coxe's "View of the United States;" Mr. Fessenden's "Register of the Arts;" Dr. Redman Coxe's "Emporium of the Arts and Sciences;" and Mr. Pitkin's "Statistics of the United States."

The following very slight summary of American manufactures is all that the limits of the present work will allow.

What the present annual value of manufactures in the United States is has not been ascertained; but, before the peace of 1815 had reduced their monopoly price, and diminished the number of manufacturing establishments, their yearly value was estimated thus :

Manufactures of Wood	$25,000,000
Leather	24,000,000
Soap and Tallow Candles	10,000,000
Spermaceti Candles & Oil	500,000
Refined Sugar	1,600,000
Cards	300,000
Hats	13,000,000
Spirituous and malt liquors	14,000,000
Iron	18,000,000
Cotton, Wool, and Flax	45,000,000
Making a Total of	$151,400,000

Of this amount nearly the whole is consumed at home, as appears from the following table of Exports :

Years.	EXPORTS OF MANUFACTURES.		
	From domestic materials.	From foreign materials.	Total of both.
1803	$ 790,000	$ 565,000	$ 1,350,000
1804	1,650,000	450,000	2,100,000
1805	1,579,000	721,000	2,300,000
1806	1,889,000	818,000	2,707,000
1807	1,652,000	468,000	2,120,000
1808	309,000	35,000	344,000
1809	1,266,000	240,000	1,506,000
1810	1,359,000	558,000	1,917,000
1811	2,062,000	314,000	2,376,000
1812	1,135,000	220,000	1,353,000
1813	372,000	18,000	390,000
1814	233,200	13,100	246,000
1815	1,321,000	232,000	1,553,000
1816	1,415,000	340,000	1,755,000

The manufactures from foreign materials are, spirits from molasses, refined sugar, chocolate, gunpowder, brass and copper, and medicines. The manufacture of *wool* is extending rapidly in the United States. The Merino breed thrives well in this climate, and their number is augmenting fast throughout the Union. The whole number of sheep already reaches nearly twenty millions, and is continually increasing. The British Isles maintain about thirty millions of sheep ; only one-third more than the American sheep, of all kinds, taken together ; and the United States can easily support twenty times their present number. In the articles of iron and hemp, and more especially hemp, the United States, probably, will soon be independent of Russia and the rest of the world. The culture of hemp succeeds in many parts of the Union, especially in Kentucky, which, in one year, produced upwards of one hundred and twenty thousand hundred-weight, valued at $700,000 and made also, in the same year, forty thousand hundred-weight of cordage, valued at

$400,000, making a million and one hundred thousand dollars for these two articles. The manufacture of cotton increases rapidly here; and the quantity consumed in the country, on the average of the years 1811, 1812, and 1813, exceeds twenty millions of pounds weight.

The manufactures of *wood* are household furniture, carriages of every kind, and ship-building, and pot and pearl ashes. The manufactures of *leather* are boots, shoes, harness, and saddles. Soap and tallow candles are manufactured both in establishments and in families. Cotton, wool, and flax, are manufactured both in establishments and in families. Iron abounds in the United States : fifty thousand tons of bar iron are consumed annually, of which forty thousand are manufactured at home, and ten thousand imported. Sheet, slit, and hoop iron, are almost wholly of home manufacture; as are cut nails, three hundred tons of which are annually exported. Cutlery, and the finer specimens of hardware and steel work, are still imported from Britain. Of the copper and brass manufactured, the zinc is chiefly, and the copper wholly, imported. Of the tin ware, the sheets are all imported. Lead is made into shot; and colours of lead, red and white lead, are imported to a large amount. Plated ware is made in large quantities in Philadelphia, New-York, Boston, Baltimore, and Charleston. The manufacture of gunpowder nearly supplies the home market, as do coarse earthen ware, window glass, glass bottles, and decanters. About a million bushels of salt are manufactured annually, and three times that quantity imported. White crockery ware is said to be made in Philadelphia of as good quality as any in England.

Saltpetre is manufactured largely in Virginia, Kentucky, Massachusetts, East and West Tennessee. Sugar from the maple tree is produced in Ohio, Kentucky, Vermont, and East Tennessee, to the amount of nearly ten millions of pounds weight annually. West Tennessee and Vermont afford abundance of good copperas. Twenty-five millions of gallons of ardent spirits are an-

nually distilled, and annually consumed in the United
States.   Four hundred water and horse-mills, working
one hundred and twenty thousand spindles, are employed in spinning cotton.   The fulling-mills amount
to two thousand ; and the number of looms exceeds
four hundred thousand ; and the number of yards of
cloth, manufactured from wool, cotton, and flax, is
about one hundred millions.   There are three hundred
gunpowder-mills ;   six hundred furnaces, forges, and
bloomeries, and two hundred paper-mills.

In the state of Vermont the chief manufactures are
of iron, lead, pipe-clay, marble, distilleries, maple-
sugar, flour, and wool.   In Massachusetts, the principal manufactures are duck, cotton, woollen, cut-
nails (by a machine invented in Newburyport, and
capable of cutting two hundred thousand in a-day),
paper, cotton and wool cards, playing cards, shoes,
silk and thread lace, wire, snuff, oil, chocolate and
powder-mills, iron-works, and slitting-mills, and mills
for sawing lumber, grinding grain, and fulling cloth,
distilleries, and glass.   In Rhode-Island are manufactured cotton, linen, and tow cloth, iron, rum, spirits, paper, wool and cotton cards, spermaceti, sugar,
machines for cutting screws, and furnaces for casting
hollow-ware.   In Connecticut are manufactured silk,
wool, card-teeth (bent and cut by a machine to the
number of eighty-six thousand in an hour), buttons,
linen, cotton, glass, snuff, powder, iron, paper, oil,
and very superior fire-arms.   In New-York are manufactured wheel carriages of all kinds, the common
manufactures, refined sugar, potter's ware, umbrellas,
musical instruments, glass, iron, and steam-boats.   In
New-Jersey are numerous tanneries, leather manufactories, iron-works, powder-mills, cotton, paper, cop-
per-mines, lead mines, stone and slate quarries.   In
Pennsylvania there are valuable colleries on the Lehigh
river, distilleries, rope-walks, sugar-houses, hair-powder
manufactories, iron founderies, shot manufactories,
steam-engines, mill machinery, the pneumatic cock for
tapping air-tight casks, hydrostatic blow-pipe, type-

founderies, improvements in printing, and a carpet manufactory. In Delaware there are cotton and bolting-cloth and powder manufactories, fulling, snuff, slitting, paper, grain, and saw-mills. In Maryland are iron-works, collieries, grist-mills, glass-works, stills, paper-mills, and cotton. In Virginia there are lead-mines, which yield abundantly, iron mines, copper mines, vast collieries, and marble quarries. In Kentucky are manufactured cotton, wire, paper, and oil. In Ohio ship-building is carried to a great extent ; indeed, in this branch of manufactures the Americans generally surpass the mechanics of all other countries. In North Carolina the pitch-pine affords excellent pitch, tar, turpentine, and lumber ; there are also iron-works, and a gold mine, which has furnished the mint of the United States with a considerable quantity of virgin gold. In South Carolina there are gold, silver, lead, black-lead, copper and iron mines, as also pellucid stones of different hues, coarse cornelian, variegated marble, nitrous stone and sand, red and yellow ochres, potter's clay, fuller's earth, and a number of die-stuffs, chalk, crude alum, sulphur, nitre, and vitriol. In Georgia the manufactures are indigo, silk, and sago. In Louisiana are manufactured cotton, wool, cordage, shot, and hair-powder.

Of the many places in the Union well adapted for manufacturing establishments, it is sufficient, at present, to notice the few following :—The town of Patterson, in the State of New Jersey, is, perhaps, as excellently situated for this purpose as any spot in the world. The falls of the Passaic river afford every convenience that water can give to put in motion machinery to any extent. In 1791, a Manufacturing Company was incorporated by the New-Jersey Legislature, with great privileges. A subscription for the encouragement of every kind of manufacture was opened, under the patronage of the Secretary of State ; five hundred thousand dollars were subscribed, and works erected at the falls of the Passaic. During the late war, the Patterson manufactures flourished, and were rendered profitable to the

proprietors by their monopoly price. Since the peace
they have declined considerably ; but there still remain
some valuable cotton and paper manufactories ; and so
admirable is the situation of the place, that manufactures cannot fail to flourish there as fast and as abundantly as the wants and inclination, and interest of the
United States demand.   The manufacture of sugar,
from the cane, thrives well ; and is increasing rapidly
in Louisiana and Georgia.

There is no part of the world, probably, where, in
proportion to its population, a greater number of ingenious mechanics may be found than in the city of Philadelphia, and its immediate neighbourhood; or where,
in proportion to the capital employed, manufactures
thrive better; and certainly, more manufacturing capital is put in motion in that than in any other city of the
Union. The town of Wilmington, and its vicinity, in
the State of Delaware, are, for their size, the greatest
seats of manufactures in the United States ; and are
capable of much improvement, the country being hilly,
and abounding with running water. The Brandywine
river might, at a comparatively small expense, be carried to the top of the hill on which Wilmington is situated, and make a fall sufficient to supply fifty mills,
in addition to those already built. The town of Pittsburgh, in the State of Pennsylvania, situated beyond
the Alleghany hills, on the confluence of the Monongahela and Alleghany rivers, where their junction forms
the Ohio, promises, in the course of a few years, to
become the Birmingham of America. It has coal in all
abundance, and of a very superior quality ; its price is
not quite three-pence sterling a bushel. It is supposed
that the whole tract of country between the Laurel
Mountain, Mississippi, and Ohio, yields coal. Pittsburgh, in addition to various other manufactures, is said
to make glass bottles, tumblers, and decanters, of equal
quality to any that are imported from Europe. It has
an inland navigation, interrupted only by the falls at
Louisville, of two thousand four hundred miles down
the Ohio and Mississippi to New-Orleans, and an inex-

haustible market for its manufactures in all the States and settlements on the borders of those mighty rivers.

But the most extraordinary, and most important manufacture in the United States, and perhaps in the world, is that of *steam-boats ;* for an interesting and instructive account of which, the reader is referred to Mr. Colden's valuable Life of Mr. Fulton. A very few facts and observations are all that can find a place here. Without entering into the dispute, respecting the mechanicians who *first* applied the force of steam to the purposes of navigation, it is certain that no one applied it *successfully* prior to Mr. Fulton; the proof of which is to be found in the fact, that since the accomplishment of this scheme in the United States, the use of steam-boats has become common in Europe ; whereas, before that period, the attempts to propel boats by steam, in that quarter of the world, were eminently vain and fruitless. Great numbers of steam-boats have been launched in Britain within a few years past; yet the principles on which they are navigated do not appear to be fully understood in that country, if we may judge from the accounts given by those who have seen and travelled in them, and by some recent publications on this subject. In the year 1807, the first steam-boat plied between the cities of New-York and Albany ; and since that time, this mode of navigation has been used with great success in many other rivers of the Union besides the Hudson : nay, steam-boats now ascend the Mississippi and Ohio rivers, hitherto nearly unnavigable, except in the direction of their currents. The facility, economy, and despatch of travelling, are all wonderfully augmented by steam navigation, the same distance being now covered in less than half the time formerly required. Albany is brought within twenty-four hours of New-York, instead of averaging three days by water, and two days by land. The following table shows the great benefit derived to the traveller from this invention ; and the cheapness of travelling, since food as well as conveyance is included.

F

	Expense.	Hours.	Miles.
From Philadelphia to New-York, by steam-boats and stages.	$10	13	96
New-York to Albany, by steam-boat	7	24	160
Albany to Whitehall, by stages . .	8	12	70
Whitehall to St. John's, by steamboat	9	26	150
St. John's to Montreal	3	4	37
Montreal to Quebec, by steam-boat	10	24	186
	$47	103	699

In the spring of 1817, a steam-boat reached Louisville, in Kentucky, from Pittsburgh, in Pennsylvania, dropping down the Ohio. She displayed her power by different tacks in the strongest current on the falls, and returned over the falls, stemming the current with ease. About the same time a large steam-boat reached Louisville from New-Orleans, laden with sugar, coffee, wines, queensware, raisins, fur, sheet lead, &c. Her freight exceeded twenty-five thousand dollars ; so that now the western waters can be ascended to any navigable point; and the commerce of the west is falling fast into its natural channel. The use of steam, applied to navigation, has so effectually removed those obstacles which the length and rapidity of the Mississippi presented to boats propelled by personal labour alone, that a voyage from Louisville to New-Orleans and back again, a distance of three thousand four hundred miles, can be performed in thirty-five or forty days ; and the property freighted is infinitely less liable to damage, and is transported at less than one-half the cost of the route across the mountains. Hence it does not seem extravagant to expect, that, in due time, steam-boats will find their way from the Atlantic Ocean into our great inland seas, by the junction of the waters of the Hudson river and Lake Erie; and, from the lakes, will carry their treasures to the Gulf of Mexico.

CHAPTER IV.

Finances, &c. of the United States.

IT is the duty of every free government to train its people gradually to bear a due weight of *internal taxation,* in order to raise an ample revenue for the purposes of national defence, of internal improvement, of rewarding long-tried, faithful public services, and the encouragement and patronage of literature, arts, and science. On extraordinary emergencies, as the sudden breaking out of war, or the necessity of sustaining a protracted conflict against a powerful enemy, a liberal use should be made of the funding system; because *a national debt,* provided it be not so great as to impede the productive labour of the community, is the best possible mode of combining immediate active and vigorous efforts on the part of a country with the means of future developement and growth ; it is, in fact, the *only* scheme by which a nation can make great present exertions without destroying its future resources. It is worse than childish, it is insane policy to trust, for the public revenue, *altogether* to the customs, or duties upon imported foreign goods (I say *imported* only, because the Federal Constitution prohibits the laying any duty on *exports* from the United States)—which a single year of maritime warfare may destroy. This is too contingent, too precarious a source of revenue on which to stake the operations of government, and to balance the movements of the public weal. The customs of England, although consisting of duties both on imports and exports, do *not* make *one-tenth* of her public revenue; she wisely leans upon internal taxation as the main prop and support of her government expenditure.

In these United States, the Washington administration, under the auspices of Hamilton as Secretary of the Treasury, as the great founder of the system of American finance, as the wise parent of public credit in this country, laid the foundation of an internal revenue by moderate and judiciously imposed taxes. The first act of Mr. Jefferson's practical ministry was to abolish the whole of this system, and leave the public revenue to rest altogether upon the customs. Mr. Madison sedulously clung to this same feeble and dastardly policy, long after the failure of revenue, the bankruptcy of the government, and the necessities of the country, had proved its entire fallacy and folly. Towards the close of the last war, his party, reluctantly and fearfully, laid some internal taxes on land, houses, and manufactures, not amounting, in the whole, to ten millions of dollars ; a considerable portion of which they have actually repealed since the peace. Mr. Munroe has a noble opportunity of being, *in fact*, a President of the United States, and not merely the leader of a dominant faction ; and if he be wise to consult the real interests of the Union, he will at once labour resolutely to establish a permanent system of internal taxation, sufficiently ample for all present purposes, and containing in itself the germs of a gradual increase, keeping equal pace with the growing resources, wealth, and population of the United States. The revenue of a state, so far as regards national power, prosperity, strength, and greatness, is emphatically *the State* ; and a government, whose income is scanty and precarious, cannot fail to become nerveless and despicable. Since this hope was expressed, Mr. Munroe has, actually, in his message of 2d December, 1817, recommended to Congress the *repeal* of all internal taxes !

There is, indeed, an awful tendency in *all* parties of the American people towards what, by a miserable misnomer, is called *economy* ; as if a system, which prevents the government from calling out the resources of the country, from rewarding its public servants, from preserving a commanding attitude in respect to foreign

potentates, were not the most pernicious prodigality !
The proceedings in Congress, during the two last
winters, were, in this point of view, portentous. The
reduction of the direct tax, from *six* to *three* millions of
dollars, and the limitation of those three millions to only
one year, are fearful omens of the entire extinction of
that tax. Nay, in the month of February last, a proposition was made to abolish *all* the internal taxes ; a
scheme, say its advocates, that failed only because it
was introduced too late in the session ; and which may
be carried into a law, by a triumphant majority, at the
next meeting of the national legislature.

The reduction of the regular army probably would
follow, as a matter of course, on the repeal of the internal taxes. Indeed, it was proposed in the Senate
last spring, on the ground that *ten thousand* soldiers are
dangerous to the liberties of the American people ; and,
therefore, should be diminished to five thousand. Britain has an army of one hundred and fifty thousand
men, stationed at home, in France, and in colonial garrisons ; besides her militia, amounting to two hundred
thousand, and her Sepoy troops in the East-Indies, rated
at a hundred and fifty thousand. And yet, no man in
his sober senses believes that the liberties of the British
people are endangered by this standing army. The
liberties of England are not about to expire under the
pressure of her military, or the encroachments of her
government ; if they are to perish, they will perish under the daggers of her democracy : if she is to be blotted
out from the list of independent and powerful nations,
she will be erased from that high scroll by the paricidal
hand of her own rabble, led on to their own and
their country's perdition by anarchial reformers, who
are alike bankrupt in fortune, reputation, character,
and principle. But we have no occasion to entertain
such fears at present ; for, while the sovereign governs
under the benignant influence of the laws ; while
the people are free ; while religion, morals, intelligence, learning, science, industry, enterprise, and
valour, continue to make England their favoured abode,

the sun of her national glory can never set, but will burn with brighter and still brighter light, until all the ages of time shall be lost in the profound of eternity. The standing army of Britain may be too numerous and too expensive for the present dilapidated state of her finances; but, in regard to the liberties of her people, it is utterly harmless and innocent.

How much more *a fortiori* then must the liberties of the American people be secure, under the presence of ten thousand men, mostly native citizens, and commanded by officers, whose courage, loyalty, and talents have been displayed on the battle-field, and have received the reward of their country's gratitude! This little army is divided and stationed in garrisons along the Atlantic coast, from the District of Maine to St. Mary's, in Georgia, a distance of nearly two thousand miles, and on the west, from the lakes to New-Orleans, a distance still greater. The American citizens are intelligent, well educated, and awake to the preservation of their liberties; every where armed, and trained to the use of arms, and comprising a militia of nearly a million of free men. Are such a country, and such a people, in jeopardy, as to their freedom, from the existence of a standing army of ten thousand men?

Upon what ground of political forecast and wisdom is it, that so many members of the Congress, and so large a portion of the people out of the national legislature, seem bent upon lessening the defences of the country; and that, too, precisely at the moment when the United States, by their rapid augmentation in greatness, and by the peculiar condition of the world, which has thrown all Europe into the hands of three or four powerful sovereigns, and which forbids the very existence of any weak or nerveless government, are more than ever exposed to disturbance in their foreign relations? Against all saving of mere money, at the expense of national dignity and strength, it behoves the American government to contend with all its influence, power, and vigilance. And, unless the government gradually train its people to bear the weight of due taxation, how

can it expect their adequate support in a fierce and
protracted struggle for national superiority, or sovereignty, or existence? Are the people of the United
States prepared, *now*, for such a conflict, as the British
people have, with so much courage, and wisdom, and
perseverance, endured for five and twenty years, and
finally conducted to so triumphant an issue? A conflict which, at the expense of seven hundred millions of
pounds sterling, and of three hundred thousand lives,
has broken down the power of revolutionary France,
and rescued Europe, America herself, and the whole
world, from impending bondage?

If not, *how* are they to acquire such habits of *enduring* patriotism and loyalty? When the danger comes,
it will be too late; it will then be in vain to appeal to
the fears and hopes of the people, to talk of forced
loans, and of conscriptions, of requisitions of men and
money. The *government alone* can inspire such high
and heroic habits into the people, by a wisely adjusted
system of internal taxation, which, increasing with the
augmenting wealth and population of the Union, will
enable government to call out, either on a sudden, or
for a continuance, all the resources of the country,
whether for the purpose of defence or offence, whenever the interests of the nation may require. Not a
moment ought to be lost in laying the foundation of
such a system; to frame which may well employ the
deepest reflection of our ablest legislators and finan-
ciers; that the taxes shall be so laid as not to obstruct
the progress of productive labour, nor divert capital
from its legitimate objects, but leave all individual effort
free to find the advantages of unrestrained competition
in every allowable pursuit.

The *banking* capital of the United States exceeds a
hundred millions of dollars. In most of the States there
are several chartered banks for the purposes of discount and deposit. The United States Bank has a
capital of thirty-five millions of dollars, of which the
general government is a stockholder to the amount of
seven millions, and appoints five out of twenty-five

directors, twenty being chosen annually by the stock-holders at large. The influence which government has over this bank will greatly facilitate all its monied operations in future, both in war and in peace. The intrinsic benefits which banking institutions afford to every commercial community are too well known to require any minute elucidation. The youthful student will find those benefits fully displayed in Sir James Stuart's Work on political economy; Dr. Smith's "Wealth of Nations," and in Mr. Thornton's admirable Treatise on Paper Credit.

The national debt of the United States at present does not amount to one hundred and twenty millions of dollars. The expense of the revolutionary war, which gave independence and sovereignty to America, was upwards of one hundred and thirty-five millions of dollars. About one-half of this expense was paid by taxes, levied and collected during the war, and the residue remained a debt due from the United and the separate States on the return of peace, in 1783. The advances made from the American Treasury were prin-cipally in paper, called Continental Money, which, ul-timately, depreciated so much that *one thousand* dollars would not buy more than *one* dollar in silver; but the specie value of the debt, independently of the paper depreciation, amounted in April, 1783, to $42,000,375, and the annual interest to $2,415,956. The interest, however, was not paid under the old confederation; and in 1790, the debt amounted to $54,124,464; and the State debts, including interest, were estimated at $25,000,000. Mr. Hamilton, the first Secretary of the Treasury, after the establishment of the Federal Con-stitution, advised the general government to assume the whole of this debt, both state and continental, amounting to $79,000,000, and bearing an annual in-terest of $4,587,444, but Congress assumed only $21,500,000, of the debts of the several States, which were appropriated to each State. On the 31st day of December, 1794, the sum total of the unredeemed debt was $76,096,468.

Provision was made by law, first for paying the interest, and then for the redemption of the capital of the debt. For the payment of the interest, the permanent duties on imported articles, the tonnage duties, and duties on spirits distilled within the United States, and on stills, after reserving $600,000 for the support of the general government and the national defence, were appropriated and pledged. The *Sinking Fund*, for the redemption of the debt, was placed under the management of the President of the Senate, the Chief Justice of the United States, the Secretary of State, the Secretary of the Treasury, and the Attorney General, for the time being, as Commissioners of the Sinking Fund, which consisted of the surplus of the duties on imports and tonnage to the end of the year 1770; the proceeds of loans, not exceeding $2,000,000; the interest on the public debt, purchased, redeemed, or paid into the Treasury, together with the surpluses of monies appropriated for interest; and, lastly, the avails of the *public* lands. The amount of debt purchased by the Commissioners of the Sinking Fund, up to the 31st of December, 1794, was $2,265,022. In March, 1795, Congress made considerable additions to the income of the Sinking Fund, and appropriated and *vested* them in the Commissioners, *in trust*, till the whole debt should be redeemed.

On the 1st of January, 1800, the total debt, funded and temporary, of the United States, amounted to $79,433,820; the debts contracted by the general government from the year 1790 to 1800, being $10,786,100, and the debts discharged during that time being $8,164,232. The causes of the augmentation of the debt were the extraordinary expenses incurred in the wars with the Indians; $1,250,000 expended in suppressing two insurrections in Pennsylvania, on account of the tax on whiskey; more than $1,500,000 spent in the transactions of the United States with Algiers and the other Barbary powers, and the still greater expenses occasioned by the disputes with revolutionary France, in 1798 and 1799. On a change of administration, in 1801, the Sinking Fund was modified anew, and on the 28th of April, 1802, Congress enacted, that $7,300,000 should be appropriated annually to the Sinking Fund; which was to be applied first to paying the interest and principal of the public debt. In 1803, the amount of debt was a little more than $70,000,000, of which $32,119,211 were owned by foreigners—by the English, $15,882,797; the Dutch, $13,693,918; other foreigners, $2,542,495. Of the residue, particular States owned $5,603,564; incorporated bodies in the United States, $10,096,398; individuals, $22,330,606.

In the purchase of Louisiana the United States paid the French government $15,000,000; of which $3,750,000 were to be paid to the American merchants, for their claims on that government, and $11,250,000 to be paid in stock, at six per cent.—the interest payable in Europe, and the principal payable in four equal annual instalments, the first becoming due in 1818. By the Act of Congress, 10th Nov. 1803, creating this stock, $700,000 annually was added to the Sinking Fund, making its income $8,000,000. After the United States had concluded peace with France, in 1800, the vast increase of their revenues, arising from duties on imports and tonnage, owing to a rapidly increasing population, and an unparalleled extension of commerce, enabled them to pay off a large proportion of the debt, which on the 1st January, 1812, was $45,154,489; the payments in redemption, from the 1st of April, 1801, to Jan. 1, 1812, being $46,022,810. During this period no additional tax was laid, except a duty of two and a half per cent. on goods imported, paying *ad valorem* duties. The sums received from 1801 to 1811, inclusive, and applicable to the payment of the interest and principal of the debt was about $90,000,000.

In the month of June, 1812, Mr. Madison and the Senate of the United States declared war against England, about the same time that Bonaparte left France with an army of five hundred thousand men, for the purpose of subjugating Russia, and completing his continental system for the destruction of the British Empire. In anticipation of their war on England, Congress, by an act of the 14th March, 1812, authorized a loan of $11,000,000, of which were obtained $10,184,700 ; certain banks loaning $2,150,000, and the residue, being $8,034,700, was funded. About half of this residue was obtained from banks, the rest from individuals. In 1813, the Sinking Fund redeemed $324,200 of this stock. On the 8th of Jan. 1813, a loan of $16,000,000 was authorized, which sum was obtained, principally from individuals, at the rate of 88 for 100 dollars ; that is, for every 88 dollars paid in money a certificate of stock for 100 dollars was issued, bearing an interest of six per cent. The stock issued for this loan amounted to $18,109,377, giving a bonus to the lenders of $20,109,377. By an act of August 2, 1813, a further loan of $7,500,000 was authorized, which was raised, by giving for every 100 dollars received stock to the amount of 113\frac{31}{100}$, at six per cent. The stock issued on this loan was $8,498,583, allowing a bonus of $998,583. On the 24th of March, 1814, a loan of $25,000,000 was authorized, of which only $11,400,000 was raised, and for which $14,262,351 of stock was issued, making a bonus of $2,852,000.

The terms of these loans were so disastrous to the government, so clearly indicating its want of credit, and the price of stocks so depressed, as to be sold at 69 and 70 for cash, a depreciation of 30 per cent., that no more was raised of the $25,000,000 loan, and Treasury Notes were issued to make up the deficiency. On all these loans, the money received by government was only $42,934,700, for which $48,905,012 of stock was issued, making a difference of $5,970,312 against the United States Treasury. In addition to this, New-York and Philadelphia lent government money, for which $1,100,009 of stock was issued, making the whole stock funded on these loans to be $50,105,022. Treasury Notes were issued to the amount of $18,452,800. The *ascertained* debt incurred by the late war, on the 20th of February, 1815, was $68,783,622, to which add the old debt of $39,905,183, and the total is $108,688,805, to which must be added outstanding debts to the amount of $13,000,000, and the whole debt of the United States is only $121,688,805. On the 24th of February, 1815, the issue of $25,000,000 of Treasury Notes was authorized; on the 3d of March, 1815, a loan of $18,452,800 was authorized to be made in the Treasury Notes previously issued.

The Sinking Fund consists of an annual appropriation of $8,000,000, arising from the *interest* of the debt redeemed, amounting in 1813 to $1,932,107 ; from the sales of *public lands*, equal in that year to $830,671, and from the duties on imports and tonnage. For the nature of the *British* Sinking Fund, and wherein it differs from that of the United States, see " The Resources of the British Empire," p. 236, *et seq.* The American Sinking Fund had redeemed of the national debt, on the 1st of January, 1814, $33,873,463. In March, 1817, the Sinking Fund income was raised to ten millions of dollars.

The *revenues* of the United States, previous to the late war against England, were derived from duties and taxes on imports, tonnage of ships and vessels, spirits distilled within the United States, and stills, postage of letters, taxes on patents, dividends on bank stock, snuff manufactured in the United States, sugar refined here, sales at auction, licenses to retail wines and distilled spirits, carriages for the conveyance of persons, stamped paper, direct taxes, and sales of public lands. The revenues have been chiefly derived from duties on imports and tonnage. Internal taxes were laid at different periods, by the Washington administration, but were *all discontinued* by an act passed in April, 1802, under the auspices of Mr. Jefferson. On the 14th of July, 1798, a direct tax of $2,000,000 was laid upon the United States, and was the only direct tax imposed previous to the late war. The customs consist of duties on imports and tonnage, and of monies for passports, clearances, light-money, &c. The *gross* amount of the customs is what accrues on the importation of merchandise; the *net* amount is what remains after deducting the drawbacks on the exportation of the same merchandise; and drawbacks on domestic spirits exported, on which a duty has been paid, and bounties and allowances for the fisheries, and on the exportation of salted provisions; *and,* after deducting the expenses of prosecution and collection, the amount is secured to government by bonds payable at different periods, according to the term of credit given to the importer.

The amount of the actual *receipts* from the Customs, from the 4th of March, 1789, the commencement of the government, to the 30th of June, 1816, was,

In 1791.........$4,399,472	In 1804.........$11,098,565
1792.......... 3,443,070	1805.......... 12,936,487
1793.......... 4,255,306	1806.......... 14,667,698
1794.......... 4,801,065	1807.......... 15,845,521
1795.......... 5,588,461	1808.......... 16,363,550
1796.......... 6,567,987	1809.......... 7,296,020
1797.......... 7,549,649	1810.......... 8,583,309
1798.......... 7,106,061	1811.......... 13,313,222
1799.......... 6,610,449	1812.......... 8,958,777
1800.......... 9,080,932	1813.......... 13,224,623
1801.......... 10,750,778	1814.......... 5,998,772
1802.......... 12,438,235	1815.......... 7,282,942
1803.......... 10,479,417	

From the 1st of January to the 30th of June, 1816, $15,426,951.

The *double* duties made the amount for 1815 so large: the Custom-house bonds became due, on an average, the year after the importation of the goods; which explains the low amount of customs for the years 1809—1810; they being the fruits of the embargo, which was suspended in 1809; and, in consequence, afforded a rich harvest to the Treasury in 1811. In 1811 the restrictive system was again enforced, and produced the famine of 1812 to the exchequer. The small amount of the year 1814 was owing to the war, commenced in June, 1812, and terminated in February, 1815. The Report of the Secretary of the Treasury, (the late Mr. Dallas,) for the year 1816, states, that on the twelfth of February, 1816, the whole of the public debt, funded and floating, was $123,630,692; but, on the first of January, 1817, did not exceed $109,748,272; reducing the debt, from the twelfth of February, 1816, to the first of January, 1817, $13,882,420.

The appropriations and payments for 1816 were

Demands on the Treasury for that year by appropriations $32,475,303

viz.—For civil department, foreign intercourse, and
   miscellaneous expenses 3,540,770
   Military department, current
    expenditure:.............. $7,794,250
   Arrearages 8,935,373
            ———— 16,729,623
   Naval establishment.................... 4,204,911
   Public debt........................ 8,000,000

Payments at the Treasury, to the 1st of August, 1816, $26,332,174

   For civil department, &c................. 1,829,015
   Military do. current expen-
    diture $4,285,236
   Arrearages............... 8,935,372
            ———— 13,220,608
   Naval department 1,977,788
   Public debt, (adding to the appropriation
    of 1816 part of the balance of appro-
    priation of 1815,)................ 9,354,752

Leaving an unexpended balance of the annual appropriation on the 1st of August, 1816, of $6,143,129
To which add the part surplus of the appropriation of 1815, used for the sinking fund 1,354,762

And the whole balance is....................... $7,497,891

The actual *receipts* of the Treasury for 1816 were,

The Cash Balance in the Treasury, (excluding Treasury Notes,) 1st January, 1816 .... $6,298,652

Customs, for seven months, from the 1st of Jan. to the last of August, 1816, without allowing for debentures on drawback, estimated at $1,829,564, 21,354,743

Direct Tax, including the assumed quotas of New-York, Ohio, South Carolina, and Georgia, for the direct tax of 1816 3,713,963

Internal duties 3,864,000

Postage, and incidental receipts 127,025

Sales of public lands, (excluding $211,440 received in the Mississippi Territory, and payable to Georgia,)........................... 676,710

Receipts in revenue, from the 1st of January to the 1st of August, 1816 .... $36,035,093

Loans, by funding and issuing Treasury Notes 9,790,825

Gross receipts from the 1st of January to the 1st of August, 1816........................,, 45,825,918

Estimated receipts, from the 1st of August to the 31st of December, 1816 19,876,710

Gross annual receipts for 1816................ $65,702,628

Probable receipts compared with probable expenditures of 1816.

The gross annual receipt for 1816 .... $65,702,631
    Appropriation for 1816 .... $32,475,303
    Excess, above the appropriation .. 6,270,395
    Unsatisfied appropriations of 1815.. 7,972,277
                                    46,717,975

    Balance of receipts for 1816 18,984,656
    Deduct Loans and Treasury Notes 9,790,821

    Ultimate surplus for 1816.................... $9,193,835

Customs from March, 1815, to July, 1816, both in-
    clusive 28,271,143
Debentures during the same period 2,624,421

Product of Customs, exclusive of collection $25,646,722

Customs from March to Dec. 1815, both inclusive, 6,916,399
Debentures during the same period............... 794,857

Product of Customs, exclusive of collection........ $6,121,542

Customs from January to July, 1816, both inclusive, 21,354,743
Debentures during the same period............... 1,829,564

Product of Customs, exclusive of collection $19,525,179

New-York Customs, from March, 1815, to July
    1816, both inclusive..................... $9,926,188
Philadelphia 5,085,206
Boston 3,579,130
Baltimore 3,339,101
Charleston........... 1,047,546
New-Orleans 732,083
Savannah 521,287
Norfolk 491,150

The duties remained nearly the same from 1802 to 1812, except the additional two and a half per cent. on merchandise imported, paying duties *ad valorem,* which constituted the Mediterranean fund : whence the great increase of duties from 1802 to the commencement of the restrictive system, was owing chiefly to the increased population and consumption of the country, and the prosperous state of American commerce, until destroyed by the embargo.   On the first of July, 1812, one hundred per cent. was added to all the permanent duties, which was to continue during the war against England, and one year thereafter.   This increased the rate of duties, *ad valorem,* to 40, 30, and 25 per cent.

Soon after the establishment of the federal government in 1789, duties on American spirits and stills were laid; other *internal taxes* were afterward laid; but were all repealed in 1802.   The sums paid on these internal taxes, from their commencement to September 30th, 1812, was $6,460,003. of which $1,048,033 were paid in 1801; and in 1812, only $4,903.   The states which paid the largest proportions of the internal taxes were Massachusetts, $232,566; New-York, $143,757; Pennsylvania, $209,545; Virginia, $115,444.   Although these internal duties were repealed in 1802, their collection has never yet been completed.   On the first of January, 1812, the balances due on the internal revenue, in the several States, amounted to $264,940.

At the first session of the thirteenth Congress, held in the summer of 1813, internal duties were laid on licences for stills and boilers, carriages for conveyance of persons, licences to retailers of foreign merchandise, wines, and spirituous liquors, on sales at auction, refined sugar, and stamped paper.   The amount of the tax was about double its former rate on most of these articles, and three times that amount on licences to retailers.   The original plan of the Treasury Department, and adopted by Congress, was *to carry on the war by loans*; and to provide no more revenue than might be sufficient to defray the *ordinary* expenses of the government, to pay the *interest* of the existing public debt, and of new loans, amounting to about $9,000,000, which were to be raised by doubling the duties on imports, and laying twenty cents a bushel on salt;

G

by sales of public lands; by direct tax of $3,000,000 ;
and $2,000,000 by a tax on stills, spirits, refined sugar,
licences to retailers, sales at auction, carriages, and
stamp paper. These taxes, however, were not permitted to commence until the first of January, 1814.
The sums raised by these internal taxes, exclusive of
the direct tax, for the two first quarters of 1814,
amounted to $2,212,491; for the two last quar-
ters, to $1,000,000. On the nineteenth of September,
1814, additional duties were laid on spirits, licences
to retailers, carriages, sales at auction, and stamped
paper.

During the same session, Congress also imposed
duties on goods, wares, and merchandise, manufactured
within the United States, as iron, candles, hats and
caps, paper, umbrellas and parasols, playing and visiting cards, saddles and bridles, boots and shoes, beer,
ale, and porter, tobacco, snuff and segars, leather, gold
and silver plated-ware, jewellery, paste-work, household furniture, and gold and silver watches.

The amount of internal duties, *accruing* in
   1814, was $3,262,197
Deduct duties, refunded or remitted   11,793
And expense of collection   148,991
The amount paid into the Treasury, in
   1814, was only   1,762,003
In 1815, the internal duties, accruing,
   amounted to .... • ..   6,242,503
Deduct duties refunded, &c. $126,769,
   and collection expense   279,227
The amount paid into the Treasury, in
   1815, was   4,697,252
The amount paid from the first of January
   to the thirtieth of June, 1816, was   3,241,427

Soon after the close of the war, in 1815, the duties
on manufactures, household furniture, gold and silver
watches, and spirits distilled within the United States,
were *repealed*, as were the *additional* duties on postage,

and retail licences. The internal duties, remaining in 1817, are duties on licences for stills and boilers, to retailers, on carriages, refined sugar, sales at auction, stamped paper, and bank notes.

Most of these internal duties, especially those on manufactures, were laid upon the articles *ad valorem ;* and both the value and quantity of the articles manufactured is made to depend, principally, on the books and *oaths* of the manufacturer, or those employed by him. The multiplication of oaths is bad policy in any government; it is, in fact, offering a perpetual bounty to one of the worst species of immorality, that of false-swearing. All the world knows what a latitude of conscience *custom-house* oaths imply in England, in France, in Holland, in these United States, and in every commercial community; and our American government now adds to this mass of evil, by a new incitement to perjury, in collecting its duties on manufactures, upon the oaths of those persons who are most directly interested to falsify the returns.

On the fourteenth of July, 1798, the first *direct* tax, amounting to $2,000,000, was laid upon the United States, and apportioned according to the provisions of the federal constitution, the fourth clause of the ninth section of the first article of which declares, that no capitation or other direct tax shall be laid, unless in proportion to the census or enumeration, directed by the third clause of the second section of the first article ; namely, representatives and direct taxes shall be apportioned among the several states, according to their respective numbers, determined by adding to the whole number of free persons, (including those bound to service for a term of years, and excluding Indians not taxed), three-fifths of all other persons ; the actual enumeration to be made once in every ten years. By marking the apportionment of direct taxes at different periods, the relative growth of the population of the several states during those periods may be distinctly ascertained. In 1798, the two millions of dollars, direct tax, were thus apportioned among the states :

New Hampshire $77,705	Delaware . . . $ 30,430
Massachusetts . 260,435	Maryland . . . 152,600
Rhode-Island . 37,504	Virginia 345,488
Connecticut . . 129,767	Kentucky . . . 37,643
Vermont 46,864	North Carolina . 193,698
New-York . . . 181,681	South Carolina . 112,997
New-Jersey . . 98,387	Georgia 38,815
Pennsylvania . . 237,178	Tennessee . . . 18,807

This tax was laid upon all dwelling-houses, lands, and slaves, between the ages of twelve and fifty, within the United States.

The number of acres, valued under the
  Act, was 163,746,688, valued at . . $479,293,264
Number of dwelling-houses, above $100,
  276,695, valued at 140,683,984

Total lands and houses $619,977,248

The slaves enumerated were 393,219. The proportion assessed upon houses was $471,989, on land, $1,327,713 ; on slaves, $196,610. In some of the states the valuations were not completed until three or four years after the tax was laid ; and from the date of its imposition to the 30th of September, 1812, a period of fourteen years, only $1,757,240 of this tax were paid into the Treasury ; and large balances are still due, now, towards the close of 1817. A second direct tax was laid on the 2nd of August, 1813, to the amount of $3,000,000 ; and thus apportioned among the states, according to the census of 1810 :

New Hampshire $ 96,793 | Maryland . . $151,624
Massachusetts . 316,271 | Virginia . . . 369,018
Rhode-Island . 34,750 | Kentucky . . 168,929
Connecticut . . 118,168 | Ohio 103,151
Vermont . . . . 98,344 | North Carolina 220,238
New-York . . . 430,142 | South Carolina 151,906
New-Jersey . . 108,872 | Tennessee . . 110,087
Pennsylvania . . 365,479 | Georgia 94,937
Delaware . . . . 32,047 | Louisiana . . . 28,925

This apportionment shows, that from 1798 to 1813, the states of New-York, Kentucky, Ohio, and Tennes- see, have made the most rapid growth in population; and that the New-England States, particularly Massa- chusetts, Rhode-Island, and Connecticut, have aug- mented their numbers very slowly. Delaware is nearly stationary; while the rest, especially Georgia, Virginia, Maryland, and Pensylvania, are increasing their num- bers with sufficient speed and force.

This tax was laid and assessed on the value of all lands and lots of ground, with their improvements, dwelling-houses and slaves; all of which articles were to be enumerated and valued by the assessors, at the rate each of them were worth in money. In the year 1814, the lands and houses of the states of New-Hamp- shire, Massachusetts, Vermont, Rhode-Island, Con- necticut, and New-York, were valued at $559,270,622; in 1799, at $283,651,885; making an increased value in fifteen years of $275,918,738 in six states. In Maryland, Delaware, North Carolina, and Tennessee, the increased value of lands, houses, and slaves, be- tween 1799 and 1814, was $365,000,000. In the whole United States the increased value exceeded $1,000,000,000. The States of New-Jersey, Pennsyl- vania, Virginia, South Carolina, Georgia, Kentucky, and Ohio, *assumed* their proportion of the tax, and were allowed a discount of fifteen per cent.

They paid into the Treasury, as their re-
spective quotas $1,159,796
The *non-assuming* states had paid up to
December 31st, 1815 1,210,000

               Total 2,369,796

Leaving an average of . . . . $ 630,204

The aggregate valuation of *houses*, *lands*, and
slaves, in the United States, under these acts,
exceeded $2,000,000,000, of which the slaves make
$400,000,000, the lands and houses more than
$1,600,000,000 ; giving an increase of one thousand
millions of dollars between 1799 and 1815. But,
doubtless, this is a very great *under-valuation*, especially
in relation to the Southern and Western States. In
New-York, the increase, during these fifteen years, has
been from *one* to *three* hundred millions of dollars ; in
Pennsylvania, from one hundred and twenty to three
hundred and seventy millions.

The average value of land per acre, including the
buildings thereon, throughout the United States, is *ten*
dollars. In particular states it varies ; as for example,
in New-Hampshire, $9 ; Massachusetts, $18 ; Rhode-
Island, $40 ; Connecticut, $35 ; Vermont, $7 ; New-
York, $17 ; New-Jersey, $35 ; Pennsylvania, $30 ;
Delaware, $13 ; Maryland, $20 ; Virginia, $5 ; North
Carolina, $3 ; South Carolina, $8 ; Georgia, $3 ; Ken-
tucky, $4 ; Tennessee, $5 ; Louisiana ,$2 ; Mississippi,
$2 ; Indiana, $2 ; Ohio, $6.

On the 9th of January, 1815, an *annual* direct tax
of $6,000,000 was laid, to be assessed, like that of
1813, but was reduced again to $3,000,000, on the
5th of March, 1816.

Since the opening of the several land-offices for the
sale of *public* lands belonging to the United States, in
1796, $8,437,531 have been received from the pro-
ceeds of those sales, up to the close of the year 1814.

The whole number of acres sold has been, during that period, 5,385,467. The whole purchase-money was $11,356,688; leaving nearly $3,000,000 due to the Treasury. There are yet unsold upwards of *five hundred millions* of acres of public lands, lying in the States of Ohio, Indiana, and Mississippi, and in the Territories of Michigan, Illinois, and Alabama, and in the Louisiana purchase. The various taxes laid in 1815 were considered as war taxes, and necessary to support public credit. The whole revenues of the United States were at that time upwards of twenty-one millions of dollars : namely, customs, $4,000,000; internal duties, $10,159,000; direct tax, $6,000,000; public lands, $1,000,000; but in 1816 they produced $1,500,000.

The *postage* of letters produces a net revenue of about $100,000 to the Treasury.

The following statement shows the estimated receipts and expenditures of the United States, at different periods, viz.

Years.	Receipts.	Expenditures.
1791	$ 4,418,913	$ 1,718,129
1795	5,954,534	4,350,596
1800	10,777,709	7,411,369
1808	17,068,661	6,504,338
1809	7,773,473	7,414,672
1818	19,550,000	18,850,000
1819	22,950,000	22,880,000
1820	22,320,000	22,910,000

The estimates of receipts and expenditure for the years 1818, 1819, and 1820, were made by the Committee of Ways and Means. The net amount of revenue received in 1815 was $50,906,106; being from customs, $37,656,486; internal duties, $5,963,225; direct tax, $5,723,152; public lands, $1,287,959; postage, &c. $275,282.

The President's Message, of the 2d December, 1817, states, that after satisfying the appropriation made by law for the support of the civil government, military and naval establishments, provision for fortifications, increase of the navy, paying interest of public debt, and extinguishing more than eighteen millions of the principal within the present year, a balance of more than six millions of dollars remains in the Treasury, applicable to the current service of the ensuing year. The estimated *receipts* for 1818, from imports and tonnage, amount to twenty millions of dollars; internal revenues, two millions and a half; public lands, a million and a half; bank dividends and incidental receipts, half a million; making a total of twenty-four millions and a half. The annual permanent expenditure for the support of the civil government, army and navy, as now established by law, amounts to eleven millions, eight hundred thousand dollars; and for the Sinking Fund, ten millions, leaving an annual excess of revenue beyond the expenditure of two millions seven hundred thousand dollars. The whole of the Louisiana debt may be redeemed in 1819; after which, if the public debt continues above par, five millions of the Sinking Fund will be annually unexpended, until 1825, when the loan of 1812, and the stock created by funding Treasury notes, will be redeemable. The Mississippi stock also will, probably, be discharged during 1819, from the proceeds of public lands; after which those proceeds will annually add to the public revenue a million and a half, making the permanent yearly revenue amount to twenty-six millions of dollars, leaving an excess of income, above the expenditure, of more than four millions of dollars.

The Secretary of the Treasury, in his report of the 5th of December, 1817, corroborates this statement, and estimates the expenditure of the year 1818 at $21,946,351; namely, civil, miscellaneous, diplomatic, and foreign intercourse, $2,069,843; military services, including arrearages of half a million, $6,265,132; naval service, including a million for the gradual increase of the navy, $3,611,376; public debt, $10,000,000; leaving a balance in the Treasury of $8,578,648, on the first of January, 1819.

The following summary, in round numbers, will convey a tolerably accurate view of the capital, income, and expenditure of the United States.

Capital, real and personal. $7,200,000,000
Income 360,000,000
Expenditure, United States $25,000,000
    The States. . . 20,000,000— 45,000,000
National debt. 100,000,000

The capital consists in reality, of
 Public lands, 500,000,000 of acres,
 at $2 per acre. $1,000,000,000
Cultivated lands, 300,000,000 of acres,
 at $10 per acre. 3,000,000,000
Dwelling-houses of all kinds. 1,000,000,000

 Total of real property. $5,000,000,000

The *personal* property of the United States consists of the national debt, which, although a debt on the part of government is,
Capital to the stockholders, who are
 American citizens $100,000,000
Banking stock.. 100,000,000
Slaves, 1,500,000, at $150 each.. . . . 225,000,000
Shipping of all kinds.. 225,000,000
Money, farming stock and utensils, manufactures, household furniture, plate, carriages, and every other species of personal property. 1,550,000,000

Total of personal property. $2,200,000,000
   real property. 5,000,000,000

Grand total of American capital*.. . . $7,200,000,000

---

* See General Hamilton's Reports " On Public Credit," and " On a National Bank;" Mr. Gallatin's " Sketches of the Finances of

Contrast this view with that of the capital, income, debt, and expenditure of any European nation, and it will instantly appear how much greater the resources of the United States are, in proportion to their population and territory, than those of the first-rate powers in Europe.   For example,

Capital, real and personal of Britain. .£18,000,000,000
Income   900,000,000
Expenditure   300,000,000
Public revenue   230,000,000
National debt £5,000,000,000, less, re-
deemed by sinking fund £1,400,000,000, 3,600,000,000

Yet, notwithstanding this alarming annual *deficit* in the public revenue of £70,000,000, the Chancellor of the Exchequer, in the last budget, (June, 1817) did not hold a desponding language, but stated, that he did not intend to reduce the interest of the national debt, nor to lessen the income of the sinking fund below the amount to which he had cut it down in 1813, which at that time was twelve millions sterling; it is now nearly fourteen.   The exchequer bills issued to supply the *deficit* bore a premium of five per cent., and an interest of only three and a-quarter, and the stocks had risen twenty per cent. during the preceding year, and the agriculture, trade, and manufactures of the whole empire were improving, so as to promise, in future, a larger public revenue, and less severe pressure upon the people.

For the facts and reasons, given at length, to show the necessity and importance of *monied institutions*, more especially the funding system, a national debt, internal taxation, and a national bank, in order to stimulate national industry, give efficiency and strength to government, and promote the prosperity and power of the

the United States;" the Treasury Reports from 1790 to 1817; Mr. Blodget's " Economica," and, *above all*, the second edition of Mr. Pitkin's " Statistics of the United States."

whole community in every free country, the reader is referred to the " Resources of the British Empire," pp. 234—306, containing a full account of the rise, progress, and present state of the financial system of England. This system, however, may be pushed too far, by stretching the public expenditure beyond the power of taxation to furnish an adequate income. This appears to have been done already in Britain, where the expenditure for 1817 was £67,817,752, and the revenue only £52,850,328, leaving a *deficit* of fifteen millions sterling, in a season of universal peace. The finance committee estimated the income of the years 1818 and 1819, at £50,000,000, and the expenditure at £65,216,657, still leaving a *deficit* of more than fifteen millions sterling annually.

How is this *deficit* to be supplied? Mr. Vansittart, in the year 1813, destroyed the progressive force of the sinking fund, by diverting all the dividends of the stock then redeemed, amounting to about nine millions sterling, to the current expenses of the year, instead of leaving it, according to Mr. Pitt's plan, for the redemption of the national debt, to swell the income of the sinking fund, which, instead of being nearly *twenty-five* millions, as it ought to have been in the year 1817, was not quite *fourteen* millions sterling. On the first of January, 1818, the outstanding or unfunded debt of Britain, will be upwards of seventy millions, making, together with the funded debt, the sum of one thousand millions, of which, nearly four hundred millions have been redeemed by the operation of the sinking fund, from the year 1786 to 1818, a period of thirty-two years ; during which time, seven hundred millions have been added to the debt. So that, by Mr. Vansittart's destroying Mr. Pitt's plan of liquidating the debt, by the continual *progression* of the sinking fund, the redemption of that debt seems to be adjourned *sine die*, since it cannot very well be accomplished by paying off *fourteen* and borrowing *fifteen* millions a-year. If England is compelled to augment her debt annually, in time of profound peace, what is she to do in the event of another war, which would immediately raise her expenditure from sixty-five to a hundred millions per annum? During the last war with revolutionary France, her Bank paper was at a discount of thirty-two per cent. which, itself, terribly enhanced her expenditure, when she had to purchase, with such depreciated paper, gold and silver for the maintenance of her armies abroad, and supplies for her services at home. Her national income from houses, lands, and every species of personal property, does not exceed two hundred millions, of which the government expends *one-third*, a proportion full as much as any people can pay, and at the same time exert their productive industry, so as to prevent the capital of the nation fron suffering a grievous annual diminution.

The following table shows the aggregate amount of the British unredeemed national debt, in October, 1817, together with the separate amount of each kind of public stock, and its holders, whether home or foreign. The reader will do well, in examining this table, to bear in mind the distinction between the value of sterling money and that of funded stock, as explained at length in the " Resources of the British Empire," pp. 232. et seq.

How disposed of	3 per cent. consols.	3 per cent. reduced.	4 per cent. consols.	5 per cent. navy.	3 per cent. 1726.	5 per cent. 1797.	3 per cent. Imperials.	Grand Total.	Long Annuities.	Imperial Annuities.
Chancery & Exchequer, Charities and Corporations	24,896,352	4,131,108	928,968	578,757	21,265	53,399	192,579	30,802,430	15,897	546
Trust and joint accounts,	8,261,862	5,559,401	681,341	784,114	25,294	3,004	305,961	15,620,977	3,068	26
Fixed property of individuals not transferred	112,019,608	19,036,229	39,910,336	25,413,502	444,332	349,006	1,509,562	198,674,605	276,878	55,803
for 2 or 3 years	141,128,025	27,606,166	42,293,756	72,246,202	384,476	489,114	3,125,818	287,275,557	878,428	156,966
Held by foreigners	11,748,870	2,685,194	888,783	1,098,234	51,142	34,316	97,045	16,599,421	5,427	941
Common national debt and reduction of land tax	29,767,308	34,398,010	....	....	....	....	1,735,822	65,291,940	....	....
Fluctuating stock transferred in the last half year	73,486,427	57,249,943	8,803,683	34,713,416	73,128	185,110	575,845	175,026,550	179,745	15,918
Grand Total	401,308,450	170,666,018	83,506,867	134,836,925	999,637	1,106,949	7,502,639	789,920,680	1,369,435	230,209

In the year 1813, the *exposè* gave the population of old France at 28,700,000 ; and of the whole empire at 42,705,000.

Capital, real and personal, at. . . .	$18,900,000,000
Income at.	945,000,000

Capital of France in 1817.	12,000,000,000
Income.	600,000,000
Public revenue.	140,000,000
Expenditure	250,000,000

A *deficit* this of $110,000,000, is so alarming in the present exhausted condition of France, as to portend either national bankruptcy, or the still greater evil of national convulsion. The dilapidated state of all the European exchequers, probably, renders it a matter of necessity for the allied sovereigns to maintain their armies of occupation at the expense of the French people. But such an annual expenditure is so far beyond the power of France, in the present depressed state of her agriculture, manufactures, and commerce, to support, as to threaten the total destruction of her ways and means ; and to create an innumerable multitude of paupers, ripened by hunger and nakedness into a state of desperation, ready for any revolution.

Russia can hardly be said to have organized any system of finance as yet; and has never been able to move her armies out of her own territories without a subsidy from England. She has, indeed, recently established a bank at Petersburgh, for the purpose of facilitating the monied operations of her immense empire. The finances of Austria, Prussia, Spain, and the United Netherlands, are in a condition truly deplorable, and require many years of peace and economy to reduce them to order, and render them productive.

It is supposed that the United States have, very recently, purchased *Florida* for five millions of dollars.

If so, they have done wisely to add a valuable territory to their southern frontier at a very small expense,
in the way of barter, which is a much easier, safer, and
better mode of acquiring dominion than that of war and
conquest. The whole purchase-money does not amount
to quite *sevenpence* sterling an acre, for the fee simple
of upwards of thirty-seven millions of acres, to say
nothing of the territorial sovereignty. The *public*
lands, as yet ungranted, will pay the price of the whole
country ten times over.

Its surface covers 58,000 square miles, and contains
not quite 10,000 people, or about one person to every
six square miles. Its sea-coast is extensive, and presents many fine harbours, and many good situations for
commercial towns. Indeed, the whole country, when
cleared, drained, and cultivated, will maintain an
abundant population.

If Florida be incorporated with the dominion of the
United States, it will very soon number a greater population than ten thousand souls. Such is the contrast
between the quickening power of popular liberty and
the benumbing influence of single despotism. Spanish
America, and the Brazils, are far superior to the United
States in all the physical advantages of soil, climate,
the products of the earth, and navigable waters; and
yet, under the weak, improvident, tyrannical administration of the Spanish and Portuguese governments,
those vast regions languish in ignorance, superstition,
poverty, weakness, and vice; while the United States
present to the eyes of an astonished world the extreme
reverse of all these bad qualities and conditions. New-
Orleans, while under the dominion of Spain, was lost in
imbecility, idleness, and folly; but now, after expe-
riencing only fourteen years of American freedom, it is
advancing rapidly towards the rank of a first-rate commercial city, by its enterprise and spirit, its growth in
wealth and population. And so will it fare with Cuba,
with Mexico, and Peru, when they become integral
parts of the United States, and exchange their present
penury and bondage for the freedom and abundance

that invariably follow the foot-tracks of a popular government.

How strange and portentous is the contrast between
the steady and progressive policy of the United States,
and the supine indifference of the British government!
Britain has lavished the life's blood of a hundred thousand of her bravest warriors, and expended uncounted
millions, in rescuing Spain from the yoke of France;
and yet she cannot, or will not, acquire a single inch of
territory, in any quarter of the globe, from the Spanish
government; while the United States, without sacrificing the life of a single citizen, and at the expense of
only twenty millions of dollars, have, within the course
of a few years, obtained from France and Spain the exclusive sovereignty over a fair and fertile dominion, at
least *twenty times* the extent of all the British isles taken
together.

Why does not England, *as part of the indemnity* due
to her from Spain, transfer to her own sceptre the
sovereignty of Cuba; seeing that the Havanna commands the passage from the Gulf of Mexico? Why does
she not take possession of Panama on the south, and
Darien on the north, and join the waters of the Atlantic
with those of the Pacific ocean, in order to resuscitate
her drooping commerce? Or is it her intention still
to slumber on, until she is awakened from the stupe-
faction of her dreams by the final fall of Spanish
America, and of her own North American provinces,
beneath the ever-widening power of the United States;
and by the floating of the Russian flag, in token of
Russian sovereignty, over the Grecian Archipelago,
and on the towers of Constantinople? Are all her national glories to be blotted out in one hemisphere, by a
power but recently emerged from the snows and barbarism of the north; and in the other hemisphere, to
be trampled into the dust by the gigantic footsteps of
her own child? Is the heathen mythology of Jupiter
and Saturn to be verified in the nineteenth century?

The island of Cuba would soon exhibit another, and
a better aspect, under the vigorous dominion of Britain,

than she now presents, under the forlorn and beggarly government of Spain. By her free and equal laws, by the weight of her capital, by the skill, industry, spirit, and enterprise of her people, Britain would soon render that island a powerful nation in itself, and a most valuable outwork of her own maritime empire. By the possession of Panama and Darien, and the junction of the Atlantic with the Pacific Ocean, England might command the commerce of the east and west, and pour such a floodtide of wealth over all her home territory as would relieve her people from the pressure of their national burdens, and give to their productive labour an unimpeded course, and an abundant recompense. Doubtless, the proposals made to the British government, in the years 1792 and 1798, by the Spanish American delegates, for the emancipation of their country, and the junction of the Atlantic and Pacific Oceans, and which have been already adverted to in a preceding chapter, on the Commerce of the United States, are to be found in the Office of the Secretary for Foreign Affairs, in London.

Notwithstanding the shattered state of the European system of finance, and the consequent weakness of the governments of Europe, it is more than ever incumbent upon the United States to lay the foundation of an ample, permanent, and growing *internal* revenue, arising from *home taxation;* because, whenever Europe becomes generally embroiled again, America will find that she *now* fills too large a space in the eye of the world to preserve her neutrality, and to keep aloof from the conflict. In spite of the apparent calm, the elements of an approaching tempest are every where visible in the European horizon. There are no symptoms of continuous health and long life in the coalition of the allied sovereigns. Russia already exhibits signs of jealousy at the naval preponderance and commercial influence of Britain; while England is alarmed at the enormous strides of the Russian government towards absolute ascendency on the continent of Europe: she refuses to join, and looks with apprehension on the Holy

H

League, whose *avowed* principles are so extremely simple, not to say childish, that they cannot fail to rouse the suspicion of every one that is acquainted with the steady, strait-forward progress by which Russia has enlarged her territory, swollen her population, and augmented her power, during the last hundred years. Austria and Prussia both tremble at the overgrown greatness of their imperial neighbour; and see, in the increase of that greatness, the forerunner of their own doom.

Meanwhile, France, whose habitual intrigue and diplomatic cunning never sleep, whatever be the form of her government, will labour incessantly to sow the seed and ripen the harvest of dissension among the coalesced sovereigns; and will strain every nerve to embroil Britain with Russia and America, that she herself may profit amidst the general confusion. The United States will be called upon to take sides in the Europeon contest; and they will, both government and people, range themselves *against* England, whom they *hate* with all their heart, and soul, and strength, as their naval and commercial rival, who must, at all events, be exterminated. They must, therefore, build up their financial system on a broad basis, in order to maintain a long and desperate struggle—since the British lion will not yield in subjection, while a drop of blood plays around and warms his heart; he will not lie down in bondage until the whole lifetide shall have been drained from out his veins.

CHAPTER V.

—

On the Government, Policy, Laws, &c. of the United States.

As all the governments of this country are purely elective, and founded upon the full sovereignty of the people, the study of *political economy* ought to make an essential part of American education; whereas, excepting in the State of Virginia, our schools and colleges generally neglect this important branch of philosophical inquiry altogether. Indeed, it is far too fashionable a doctrine in the United States, that a man may be a very profound political economist, although his ignorance on all other subjects is quite conspicuous, and his general dulness no less manifest. But, in fact, there is no royal road to this science; and although, in an hereditary aristocracy, men are *born* legislators, yet no privileges of birth can confer a knowledge of political philosophy. And I would advise those sapient personages, who insist upon the extreme facilities of this science, and that its whole compass lies within the range of the every-day exertions of ordinary understandings, to learn the individual application of the *argumentum ad modestium* to themselves, by a perusal of the political effusions of the greatest philosophers and statesmen of ancient Greece; for instance, the Treatise of Plato on the best constitution of a Republic; the elaborate work of Aristotle on Politics, and the schemes of Isocrates for obviating or preventing the external quarrels of the Greeks among themselves, by directing *a constant hostility* against foreign nations, more especially against the monarchy of Persia.

Indeed, notwithstanding their progress in civilization, and their frequent practice in war, had led the Greeks, though not to the generosity of the warfare of modern Christendom, yet to the occasional usages adopted to humanize hostility, in some degree, and to diminish the aggregate amount of its bloody horrors, still the radical imperfections of their political system, and the turbulent habits which it superinduced, led their greatest statesmen and profoundest sages to conclude that warfare was the *natural* state of man; a state which might, possibly, be regulated, but could *not* be prevented, or suspended, by any efforts of human policy. It is possible that certain popular modern writers have ever seen the works of Herodotus, Thucydides, and Xenophon? or, at least, learned from their perusal to extol Greece as the favourite land of freedom, in which that greatest of social blessings peculiarly flourished, from the age of Pisistratus to the usurpation of Philip of Macedon? Bold and frequent struggles, indeed, were made, and much private assassination, and many public butcheries, were perpetrated in the *name* of liberty, whose *spirit* seemed to be continually boiling up into fire, and smoke, and vapour; but whose substance was seldom, if ever, to be found in any of the Grecian commonwealths, whether following the fortunes, and obeying the commands of the Lacedemonian aristocracy, or those of the imperial democracy of Athens.

Could the battle of Cheronea itself, which made Philip master of Greece, be more fatal to Grecian freedom than the fields of Aigospotami and Leuctra? Xenophon, certainly, felt that his cotemporaries were *not* free ; as all his narrative writings sufficiently testify. And, if we turn from the recorded history of what actually did take place, to the observations and schemes of the ablest men who speculated upon those transactions, about the same time we find Plato, and Isocrates, and Aristotle, profound and eloquent as they were, utterly unable to propose any plan, or devise any means, by which Greece might be free. The great difficulty of mastering so complicated a science, as that of political economy, must be accepted as an apology for the system of policy recommended in that work, so much admired by the ancients, both Greek and Roman—I mean Xenophon's Cyropaideia. Fortunately for us, experience has taught *some few* of the nations of modern Christendom forms of government, beyond all comparison more favourable to private and public liberty and peace. Although successive demagogues had most wretchedly degraded the ancient Athenian constitution; yet, if there ever existed in Greece any foundation for a good government, it seems to have been in the laws, customs, and habits of Athens, as derived from the institutions of Theseus and Solon. That excellent principle—the only one on which a free government can be firmly grounded—namely, that the aggregate of *private* should make *public* good; and its practical corollary, that the rights of individuals, once established by law, should always be held sacred, seem to have been original principles, established in the kingdom of Theseus, and the republic of Solon.

But a quite different principle obtained a very general prevalence among the other Grecian commonwealths; namely, an *ideal* public good, always distinct from, and for the most part destructive of, private good; pretty much resembling the modern *jacobin* doctrine, that the true business of government is so effectually to provide for the *general* good, as most unerringly to destroy all *individual* happiness and virtue. Whereas, by the very constitution of human nature, *self-love*, or the desire of personal happiness, is implanted in the heart by God, as the primary, the perpetual spring of all human action. Man cannot love his kind, unless he first love himself. The ever-active principle of self-love is strongest in the heart of every individual; and is gradually weakened as it extends its affections throughout all the kindred charities of life—parental, conjugal, filial —throughout all the social ties of friends, neighbours, acquaintance, magistrates, country. The predominant power of the principle of self-love is implied in the very terms of that divine command, " Thou shalt love thy

neighbour as *thyself.*" Meaning, that under the
selectest influences of Christian charity man is required to give the *whole* affections of his nature to his
neighbour; that is, to every one who stands in need of
his kindness.

But turbulent, discontented, profligate men, in all
countries, trample upon the individual affections of humanity, and, in proportion as they prove themselves
faithless husbands, unnatural fathers, disobedient sons,
cruel masters, false friends, quarrelsome neighbours,
rebellious citizens, unprincipled in all their conduct, do
they arrogate to themselves the claim of being the *exclusive* champions of the public good; as if it were
possible for a wretch, steeped in all the atrocity and degradation of *private* vice, to be a real patriot, actuated by
a sincere desire to promote the welfare of his country !
Ο γαρ μισοτεκνος (says Æschines, most indignantly, in his
oration against Ctesias) και πατηρ πονηρος, ουκ αν ποτε
γενοιτο δημαγωγος χρησος, ουδε ο τα φιλματα και οικειοτατα σωματα
μη στεργων, ουδεποτε υμας περι πλειονος ποιησεται τους αλλοτριους,
ουδε γε ο ιδια πονηρος, ουκ αν ποτε γενοιτο δημοσια χρησος. "It is
impossible, that the unnatural father, the hater of his
own blood, should be an able and faithful leader of his
country; that the heart which is insensible to the intimate and touching influences of domestic affection
should be alive to the remoter impulses of patriotic feeling; that private depravity should consist with public
virtue."

One of the very first symptoms that discover the selfish and mischievous ambition of a demagogue is the
profligate disregard of individual feeling and domestic
affection. To be tenderly attached to the little, precious
circle of kindred, to feel a yearning of the heart towards
the particular subdivision of society to which we belong,
is the first principle, the radical germ of *public* affection.
It is the first link in the series of that golden chain of
love, by which we are bound, first to our families and
friends, then to our country and mankind at large.

Of all the legislators of ancient Greece, who undertook to promote the public welfare, by destroying all

private good, Lycurgus the Spartan was most successful. His first step was to make the Lacedemonians a
nation of paupers ; to destroy almost the very vestiges
of private property, under pretence of providing for
the interest of the community. Every individual was
required to sacrifice all his own pursuits, comfort, and
happiness, to whatever was called the *good of the state ;*
by which patriotic and fashionable phrase, nothing more
was in reality meant, than that all private interest
should yield, and be rendered subservient to the schemes
and views of the few ambitious men who governed the
state, and made the bodies, minds, and wills of all their
fellow-citizens the pedestal of their own exalted power.
And, as the public or national education (for no private
instruction was allowed) was chiefly directed to rendering the frame hardy and robust, to instil the necessity
of personal courage, to teach dexterity in thieving, and
skill in lying, to inculcate habits of remorseless cruelty,
the Lacedemonians, under their existing leaders, were
always prepared for the perpetration of any crimes, however dark and atrocious ; and, in consequence, were
perpetually employed, either in assassinating the *He-
lotes,* a nation of brother Greeks, whom they had reduced to slavery, or in carrying on war against, and
domineering over and oppressing, their sister republican states. Whence, all over Greece, the peaceable
and the quiet, who did not aim at political influence
or military power, but only desired peace, and security,
and civil order, were exposed to constant alarms, and
the severest sufferings.

But even the constitutions of Theseus and Solon, as
well as those of every other Grecian commonwealth,
were in want of another great political principle, spread
over many portions of modern Europe, namely, *representation,* which is, in fact, the beginning, middle, and
end of all the governments, both State and Federal, of
these United States. The essential advantage of the
principle of representation is, not merely that a great
nation can transact all its public business conveniently
by its representatives, which even a very small country

cannot do, by its assembled numbers, in wild democracy;
but also, that some responsibility may be attached to
every department of constituted power; by which provision *alone*, whatever be the name or form of government, real despotism can be obviated or prevented.
For the want of this grand improvement in modern
political science, the Grecian Legislators were quite at
a loss how to secure liberty to the great body of the
people without giving them despotic power; and thus,
in effect, the multitude became absolute and unresponsible tyrants, instead of being, what they ought to be
in every country, orderly freemen, living in obedience
to the municipal laws of the existing governments.

Those persons are either not wise, or not honest, or
neither, who pretend that political and legislative
science is easy and obvious, level to the meanest capacity, and most unlettered education; to the apprehension of the peasant who directs the plough, the artisan
who plies the loom, the carman who guides his horse,
and of all the labouring classes, whose daily toil is devoted to providing for the necessities of each passing
day. The writings of the ablest Greek philosophers
and statesmen, showing how very deficient that enlightened and illustrious nation was in many of the most
important principles of political economy, abundantly
prove how difficult and complicated that science is. Indeed, the history of all nations demonstrates by what
slow and painful steps, by what apparently accidental
circumstances, by what jarring of discordant interests,
by what violence of faction from within, by what pressure of hostility from without, by what dear-bought experience of long-continued and accumulated evils, any
advance towards perfection in the constitution and administration of government has been made. The works
of Plato and Xenophon should, in particular, be studied, in order to form an accurate notion of the imperfection of political science in their time, and of the entire inability, even of their great genius and extensive
learning, to remedy the defects, or enlarge the boundaries of that important science.

To arrive at any certain and comprehensive results in political philosophy, requires a previous patient and accurate analysis of by far the most complicated class of phenomena that can engage our attention ; namely, those effects which result from the intricate, and often imperceptible mechanism of political society. In ancient times, it was impossible to make this analysis; because, before the invention of printing, and consequent diffusion of knowledge among a large proportion of every civilized community, the human mind was compelled to waste itself in such researches, unaided and solitary ; and the difficulties attending these complicated inquiries must for ever have baffled the efforts of individual genius; since, *even now,* they yield slowly and reluctantly to the united exertions of so many successive ages, and such numerous hosts of philosophers and politicians, all combined to prosecute the same inquiries. In proportion as the experience and reasonings of different individuals, of different ages and countries, are brought to bear directly upon the same objects, and are so skilfully combined, as to illustrate, modify, and limit each other, the science of political economy assumes more and more that systematic arrangement and form, which give both encouragement and assistance to the efforts of future investigators.

In prosecuting the science of political philosophy, little is to be learned from perusing the speculations of ancient sages ; because they confine their attention to a comparison of the different forms of government, whether simple, as monarchial, aristocratic, or democratic ; or mixed, as in a combination, variously proportioned of these elemental institutions; and to examining the provisions made by each state, for perpetuating its own national existence, and extending its own military glory. It was reserved for the purer religion, and brighter philosophy of modern times, to investigate those universal principles of moral justice, which *ought,* under every form of government, to regulate the whole system of social order, and make as equitable a distribution as possible, among all the different members of a community, of the advantages and burdens of political union. In all the departments of literature, science, and art, in which genius discovers within itself the materials of its own labour, as oratory, poetry, painting, architecture, sculpture, pure geometry, and some branches of moral philosophy, the ancients have left great and finished specimens of excellence. But in physics, or natural philosophy, where the progress of improvement depends upon an immense collection of accumulated facts, and their skilful combination; and, above all, in politics, where the materials of information are scattered over the whole surface of human society, and are still more difficult to collect and arrange, the means of communication afforded by the press, have, in the lapse of the two last centuries, done infinitely more to accelerate the progress of the human mind, by the increase of substantial information, than had been accomplished in all preceding ages. *

One chief design of the legislators of antiquity was to counteract the love of money, and prevent luxury, by positive institutions, and sumptuary laws; and to perpetuate habits of frugality, and a stern severity of manners, throughout the great mass of the population. The Grecian and Roman historians and philosophers uniformly attribute the decline and fall of every nation to the destructive influence of *general wealth* upon the

---

* During the last fifty years, the most enlightened political econo-mists in Europe have laboured to improve the condition of human society, by endeavouring to inform the minds, and amend the actual policy of existing statesmen and legislators. Some of the best works on this subject are, Sir James Stuart's Treatise on Political Eco-nomy, Dr. Smith's Wealth of Nations, Mr. Malthus's Essay on Population, Mr. Brougham's Inquiry into Colonial Policy, the Earl of Selkirk's Essay on Emigration, the Chevalier Filangieris's Trea-tise on Legislation, Mr. Bentham's work on the same subject, the works of M. Turgot, and M. Quesnay, of M. Say, of the Marquis Beccaria, and of Camponanes, the Spanish philosopher, whose work on the importance of Agriculture and Commerce led him to the dungeons of the Inquisition in 1796, from which he was libe-rated, after an incarceration of twelve years, by the revolution of 1808.

national character; rendering the men idle, effeminate, dastardly, and profligate, fit only to be slaves and sycophants; and inducing the women to be immodest and vitious. But the policy of modern legislators is directly the reverse of these self-denying ordinances; so far from dreaming that poverty and beggary are the sinews of national strength, they are perpetually labouring to open new sources of individual and collective opulence, and to stimulate the active industry of all classes, by encouraging a general taste for the conveniences, comforts, and luxuries of life. And in modern Christendom, the most wealthy nations invariably exhibit a population, which exercises the greatest industry, and enjoys the most unrestrained freedom; indeed, it was the general diffusion of wealth among the lower order of the people, more especially among the burghers of the cities, which first gave birth to the spirit of personal independence and national liberty in modern Europe; and which produced in some of the governments, even on the European continent, as in Holland, the Hanse Towns, Sweden, and Switzerland, a far more equal diffusion of freedom and happiness than ever existed under the most highly vaunted constitutions of heathen antiquity.

The free governments of continental Europe, to be sure, were overthrown, and for a while destroyed by the force and fraud of revolutionary France, who, with the most rigid impartiality, restored all her vassal states to their pristine condition of poverty, barbarism, and bondage, such as shrouded the whole of Christendom in Cimmerian darkness, before commerce and wealth had poured in their streams of civilization, intelligence, and freedom. But Britain, who was enabled, by the prompt and permanent power of her government, and by the characteristic energy of her people, to ride out in safety and triumph the revolutionary storm and tempest, which scattered the wrecks of the other European governments over all the ocean of ruin, has uniformly increased in the strength of her executive, and in the liberty and refinement of her people, in proportion as private and public wealth have been diffused throughout all her dominions. The radical and fatal defect of ancient legislation appears to have been its constant aim to shape and mould, by the force of positive institutions, the order of human society, according to some preconceived, abstract notion of political expediency, without sufficiently trusting to those universal principles in the natural constitution of man, which, when allowed full scope of exertion, never fail to conduct the commonwealth to a progressive improvement in its condition, and to a continual exaltation of character.

The chief excellence in the system of modern policy, is its conformity, in some of the most important points of economics, to the order of nature ; and it is erroneous, just so far as it imposes restraints upon the natural course of human affairs, by stifling the growth or perverting the direction of individual industry and private property. Some of the most absurd and ruinous of these restraints are to be found in *mercantile monopolies*, which increase, unnecessarily, the price of all the monopoly articles ; in protecting duties on domestic manufactures, which ensures to the consumer a worse commodity at a heavier expense than a better article could be furnished by foreign importation ; in prohibitions of exportation, which operate as a check to production, by closing the avenues to competition in the markets of other nations ; in all the beggarly and despicable expedients of embargo, non-intercourse, and non-importation, the misbegotten progeny of the *restrictive* system; all of which directly tend to repress the growth of national wealth, retard the progress of population, paralyze the exertions of private enterprise, wither the sinews of public resource, render the government odious and oppressive at home, ineffectual and contemptible abroad.

The most efficient plan of policy, which any government can pursue for establishing the prosperity and advancing the greatness of its people, is carefully to follow, and steadily maintain, the order of things pointed out by Nature herself; that is to say, by allowing every one, as long as he observes the rules of justice and common honesty, to pursue his own private interest in his own way, and use his industry, talents, and capital, in the most free and unrestrained competition with the capital, talents, and industry of his fellow-citizens ; and thus to ensure a continual augmentation of the aggregate amount of national labour, intelligence, and riches. Every system of policy which endeavours, either by extraordinary encouragements to seduce towards any given species of industry a larger proportion of the capital of the country than would be naturally employed therein, if each man were left to the unbiassed employment of his own labour and property—or, by extraordinary restraints, to force from any particular species of industry some share of the capital which would otherwise be employed in it—has a direct tendency to impoverish and weaken the whole community.

A most instructive chapter on political economy might be written on the ruinous effects of those short-sighted views, which prompted our general government, some few years since, to endeavour to build up the interests of the American farmers upon the ruin of the American merchants ; whereas the well-being of agriculture and commerce is reciprocal ; they are twin-sisters ; they are born, and flourish, and fade, and die together. In modern Europe, generally, a system of policy the reverse of this has been adopted ; and one, scarcely less opposed to the order of nature, in the developement of national wealth and greatness : I mean encouraging the industry of towns and cities, at the expense of the labour of the country ; and sacrificing the interests of agriculture to those of commerce.

The mercantile system, which is now interwoven in every department of European policy, is based upon two radically erroneous principles ; namely, restraints upon importation, and encouragements to exportation ; *both* of which are unpropitious to the wealth and prosperity of the nation that imposes them.

Generally speaking, the *freer* a government is, the more it consults and provides for the personal, domestic, and social liberty and happiness of its own people, the less inclined, and less able it is to watch over, and influence the movements of other countries; and, so far it is deficient in its system of *foreign* policy. Hence arises the difficulty of constituting a system of government which shall unite in itself the threefold advantage of personal liberty, a strong executive, and an ample developement of the national mind; because the full enjoyment of individual freedom, and great power in the executive, are continually operating to thwart and counteract the efforts of each other; and, without a permanently powerful executive, it is scarcely possible to obtain a general developement of the national mind; so as to provide a regular succession of able and experienced men, in all the departments of public service, through a series of ages.

The *first* requisite, the most essential foundation of all good government, the full preservation of personal liberty, and private property, which may be considered as the sheet-anchor of human society, is provided for in a most eminent degree by *all* the American constitutions, both State and Federal. But *not one* of them all gives a sufficient scope and permanency of power to its executive, *nor* sufficiently provides for the developement of the national mind, on a scale of large and liberal information. Whence, consequently, every individual in the United States is called upon to provide, to the utmost of his ability, in his own personal vigilance over the best interests of religion and morals, for the deficient power and energy of the government. In most other countries, the government is all, and the people nothing; whence they exhibit the melancholy spectacle of capricious tyrants on the one hand, and the suffering slaves of oppression and ignorance on the other;—whereas, in the United States, it is nearly the reverse: the people are all, and the government nothing; which is the *excess* of liberty, and imposes severer obligations of duty on every free citizen to watch over the welfare of the public, the most permanent props and buttresses of which welfare are the strict preservation and general diffusion of pure religion and sound morals, throughout all the different orders of the community.

Whatever political relation subsisted between the American colonies antecedent to the revolution, in 1776, as constituent parts of the British empire, or as dependencies upon it, was completely dissolved from the moment of the declaration of American independence; for, from that moment they became, severally, independent and sovereign States, possessing all the rights, jurisdictions, and authority that other sovereign States, however constituted or named, possess; and bound by no ties, legal or political, but of their own creation, excepting those by which all other civilized nations are equally bound; and which, together, constitute the conventional and customary law of nations. The constitution, considered as a federal compact, or alliance between the several States of the Union, does not differ from other national compacts; but, considered as an original *social* compact, it is novel and unique. The American revolution gave birth to this system of polity; and in the States, generally, a *written* constitution was framed, and adopted by the people, both in their individual and sovereign capacity and character.

The advantages of a *written* constitution are many and obvious; power, when undefined, has a perpetual tendency to become absolute; and the investigation of social rights, when there is no constitutional text to consult for their explanation, is a task difficult to accomplish, and almost useless when performed. As it is necessary to the preservation of a free government, established upon the principles of a *representative republic*, that every man should know his own rights, it is also necessary to be able, on all occasions, to refer to them. Where the sovereignty is vested in the people, government is a subordinate power, and the mere creature of the people's will; it ought, therefore, to be so constructed that its operations may be the subject of constant observation and severe scrutiny. By comparing the principles of the civil polity of the United States with their effects upon the progress of the American government, and the spirit of the American people, we should be led to appreciate the municipal institutions of this country at their true value. And, perhaps, it would be adviseable to derive the elements of a legal and parliamentary education in the United States, chiefly from the history and constitutions of America herself; by which means might be imbibed the genuine principles of republican government from legitimate fountains; and the student also avoid the bias of any undue impressions derived from the artificial distinctions, the oppressive establishments, the feudal encroachments, the ecclesiastical intolerance and monopoly, which distinguish and deform almost all the nations of Europe.

Undoubtedly the British constitution, which, although not written, and therefore constructive, is yet to be learned from various precedents respecting the royal prerogative on one hand, and the privileges of the people on the other ; and in which the several powers of government are limited, though in an uncertain way, in respect to each other; and the three powers of king, lords, and commons, combined together, are without any check at all in the constitution; whence their union in parliament has been styled omnipotent, from the sovereignty of the nation residing in that body; and the municipal code of England, consisting of the common or customary, and the statute law, to an intimate acquaintance with which the American lawyers are so early, so deeply, and so constantly introduced by the prevailing course of their professional inquiries and practice, teem with invaluable principles of unstained justice, liberal equity, profound policy, and accomplished social order—principles which cannot be too generally known, studied, and received; nevertheless, it must be remembered, that many of the fundamental doctrines of the English government, and many of the maxims of English jurisprudence, are utterly subversive of an *equality* of political rights, and totally incompatible with the republican form and spirit of the American institutions and establishments. We must, therefore, care-

fully distinguish between the principles which pervade
the British, and the genius which quickens the American government; and cultivate a correct acquaintance
with republican maxims, and cherish a devoted attachment to the systems of liberty and justice, established
in these United States. This subject is elaborately
and ably unfolded by Mr. Chancellor Kent, in the Introduction to his Course of Lectures on Law, delivered
in Columbia College.

All the American Constitutions, as well those of the
separate as of the United States, are based on an
equality of civil and religious rights in all the people,
except the negro slaves, and an entire absence of all
privileged orders, and politico-religious establishments.
They differ from all other governments, ancient and
modern, in being altogether elective and representative;
and in consisting of so many different state sovereignties, with a general or federal head. The existence of
the state sovereignties, with each its separate executive,
legislative, and judicial departments, provides for all
the purposes of municipal and local regulation, and
admits of any extent of territory, and any increase of
population, without danger or inconvenience; while
the general government is organized to watch over the
national interests, to maintain due intercourse with
foreign powers, and determine the momentous questions of peace and war. Many persons in this country,
and Europeans generally, express their conviction that
the present form of our government cannot last long;
but that the American confederacy will be speedily dissolved by its own intrinsic weakness, and prodigious
extent of territory.

But a closer, and more patient inspection, probably,
would induce them to believe in the continuance of the
union, and the prepetuity of free and popular institutions. We have the authority of two distinguished
statesmen of the present day for believing in the duration of our republican institutions; the one a foreigner,
the other a native. A French philosopher, Barbé de
Marbois, in speculating upon this subject, says, "The

experience of past ages, the recollection of human revolutions, excites some disquietude in relation to the future destinies of the United States. The usual consequences are apprehended from the movements of private ambition, the inequality of fortunes, the love of conquest. But, under the peculiar circumstances in which the United States are placed, the past cannot serve as a criterion for the future. It is true, that free nations have been lost in despotism; but had those nations a precise idea of their rights and duties? Were they acquainted with the tutelary institutions of this day, the independence of the judiciary, the trial by jury, the system of representative assemblies and self taxation, the force of public opinion, now superior to all opposition? Among the ancients, liberty was but a feeling; in our times, it is both a feeling and a positive science. We all know how liberty is lost; we are all acquainted with the means of defending and preserving it. The United States have now been happy and free for nearly half a century. *Liberty* has struck deep root in the country; it is entwined with the first affections of the heart; it enters into the earliest combinations of thought; it is spun into the primitive staple of the mental frame of the Americans; it is wrought into the very stamina of all their institutions, political and social; it thoroughly pervades, and perceptibly modifies even their domestic life; it is protected by religion and the laws; it is linked with every habit, opinion, and interest; it has, in fine, become the common reason, and the want of all the American people. Propose slavery to such a people; talk to them of *unity* in the head; multiply your sophisms as you please, to prove to them the *paternity* of arbitrary power, they will never understand you. We must not suppose that the love of conquest, that fatal passion, will master or lead astray the councils of a nation, which, setting out from a line of nearly fifteen hundred leagues of coast, may spread the noble and hallowed empire of industry and the arts from the shores of the Northern Ocean to those of the Pacific."

The late Mr. Gouverneur Morris, who was one of the most able, splendid, and efficient of the statesmen that framed the Federal Constitution, in a private letter, written to a friend towards the close of his life, expresses himself thus: "Those who formed our constitution were not blind to its defects: they believed a *republican* government to be the best; they believed a *monarchial* form to be *neither solid nor durable;* they conceived it to be vigorous or feeble, active or slothful, wise or foolish, mild or cruel, just or unjust, according to the personal character of the prince. It is a dupery to cite the duration of the French monarchy at eight centuries. In that period, the provinces which lately composed it passed, by various fortune, from their subjection to Rome, through the conquests of barbarians, the ferociousness of feudal aristocracy, and the horrors of anarchy and civil war, to their union under the Bourbons. That union was not consolidated until the soaring spirit of Richlieu, and the flexible temper of Mazarin, had tamed an indignant nobility to the yoke of obedience. By the vanity, the ambition, and the talents of Louis the Fourteenth, France became the terror of Europe. By the facile immorality of the Regent, and the lasciviousness and feebleness of Louis the Fifteenth, she sunk almost into contempt. After a few years of distempered existence, under the mild and virtuous Louis the Sixteenth, the lamp of that boasted monarchy was extinguished in his blood."—There are also some very shrewd and sensible remarks, on the probable duration of our confederated republic, in "*Letters from the South*," a work lately published.

The general, or Federal Constitution of the United States was framed by a convention of deputies from the States of New-Hampshire, Massachusetts, Connecticut, New-York, New-Jersey, Pennsylvania, Delaware, Maryland, Virginia, North Carolina, South Carolina, and Georgia, at a session, begun May 25th, and ended September 17th, 1787. It first went into operation on the 4th of March, 1789. Its provisions are, in substance, these:—All *legislative* powers, granted by the Constitution, are vested in a Congress of the United States, consisting of a Senate and House of Representatives. The representatives are chosen every *second* year by the people of the several states; the electors in each state having the qualifications requisite for electors of the most numerous branch of the State Legislature. The representative must be twenty-five years old, have been a citizen of the United States seven years, and be an inhabitant of the state in which he is chosen. Representatives and direct taxes are apportioned among the several states, according to their respective numbers, determined by adding to the whole number of free persons, including those bound to service, and excluding Indians not taxed, three-fifths of all other persons. The actual enumeration of the people is to be made every ten years, in the mode directed by Congress; the number of representatives not exceeding one in thirty thousand: only, each state shall have at least one representative. When vacancies happen in the representation from any state, the State Executive issues writs of election to fill them. The House of Representatives choose their speaker, and have the sole power of impeachment.

On this portion of the Federal Constitution it may be observed, that the mode of electing the members of the lower house of Congress varies in the different states according to the various modes of electing their own representatives, established by the laws of the several states. In some, the whole number to which the state is entitled is elected by the whole people of the state; in others, they are distributed into election districts; in some, a majority of all the votes is requisite; in others, only a plurality; in some, residence of the candidate in the district is required; in others, not. The mode by districts, and plurality of votes with residence of the candidate, is most general throughout the Union.

The frequent recurrence to the people, by the frequency of elections, is a radical imperfection which pervades *all* the American constitutions, both state and federal. It has a direct tendency to make the representatives *too local* in their policy, and to induce them rather to aim at pleasing their own immediate constituents than to advance the *general* good of the nation at large ; a measure which sometimes requires an apparent sacrifice of the local interest of the peculiar district which they represent. When once seated in Congress, the members should recollect that they represent the United States, as one great empire, and not merely the little district of any particular state, whether of Virginia, or of Rhode-Island, of New-York, or of Delaware. A *triennial* election is quite frequent enough for the general government of so extensive a country, and such a rapidly-increasing population. · This frequency of election, however, is praised as the consummation of political excellence, by many writers and speakers on the art of government; yet it seems to have an immediate tendency to throw great obstacles in the way of national improvement and prosperity. The elections, both of senators and representatives, as well in the general as in the state governments, recur too often, particularly of the lower branch of the legislature. South Carolina and Tennessee are the only two states in the Union whose representatives are elected for so long a term as two years ; in Connecticut and Rhode-Island, the elections are *semi-annual* ; in all the other states, yearly.

The almost necessary consequence of these frequent elections is, that the representatives feel themselves *too dependent* upon the will of their constituents; whereas, they ought to be left entirely free to exercise the power delegated to them, at their own discretion, and to the best of their judgment, for the good of the country at large. The people also are incessantly exposed to corruption, amidst the perpetual intrigue and turmoil of frequently recurring elections; whence incapable members are too liable to be returned to the legislature. It is a notorious fact, that in many districts of the Union, unless a representative follows and obeys the current opinions, prejudices, and passions of the day, he will *not* be re-elected, owing to the running of the popular tide against him, whatever may be his other qualifications. Add to this, that in consequence of the short period of public service, it is not easy to investigate and annul spurious elections, before the session itself be at an end ; whence, there is a danger, that if a return can be obtained, no matter by what improper means, the irregular member, who takes his seat of course, shall hold it quite long enough to answer all *his* purposes of legislation. What is this in effect, but offering a high bounty by law, for the employment of electioneering intrigue and fraud, in order to obtain a return?   Such a system, having an unavoidable tendency to bewilder and corrupt the people, and to induce them to elect unworthy representatives, almost ensures the production of a legislature, *not* the best qualified by talents, learning, wealth, probity, and character, to discharge so solemn and important a duty, as that of framing laws for the well-being of an extensive, powerful, and fast-growing commonwealth.

A great part of every year, in every place throughout the Union, is literally consumed in cabals and intrigues, carried on between the candidates of the several parties and the people, in order to prepare and accomplish all the various manœuvres of electioneering tactics, which are put in constant requisition, by the frequent recurrence of elections for representatives, both of the separate and of the United States. Whence, a large portion of the time which the people ought to employ in productive industry, is expended in prosecuting the unprofitable trade of politics. The experience of history shows, that the democratic forms of government are also in themselves liable to these inconveniences ; namely, that they are too tedious in coming to any public resolution, and seldom sufficiently alert and expeditious in carrying their resolutions into effect ; that as various minds are successively employed, they are necessarily wavering and unsteady, and scarcely ever persevere to the accomplishment of the measures which they resolve to pursue ; that they are often involved in factions, which expose the nation to be made the instrument, if not the victim, of foreign powers. Now, frequent elections cannot fail of rendering a government too dilatory in its resolves; because, under such circumstances, no prudent administration would ever venture upon any important national measure, until it had felt the pulse, not only of the legislature, but of the people also.

The experience of history equally proves, that the great body of the people, in every country, are prone to be too much elated by temporary success, and too much dejected by occasional misfortune. This disposition alone renders them perpetually wavering in their opinions about affairs of state, and prevents the possibility of their ever long continuing steadily fixed to any one point. And as the House of Representatives is chosen by the voice of the general people, a choice so often renewed, almost ensures the legislature to be as wavering and unsteady in their councils, as the people themselves are in their sentiments. And it being impossible to carry on the public affairs of the executive government, without the concurrence of the lower house, the administration is always obliged to comply with the notions of the leading members of that house; and, consequently, obliged to change its measures as often as the populace change their minds. Whence, it is impossible to lay down, and steadily prosecute, any plan for the gradual developement of the national resources, and the gradual growth of the country, in prosperity, wealth, power, and influence.

Besides, in all democratic governments, faction is continually springing up from the delusions perpetually played off upon the collective wisdom of the multitude. While the essential principles of human nature remain the same, as they ever have been, there always will be, in every country, and under every possible form of government, many unquiet, turbulent, and unprincipled spirits, who can never be at rest, whether in or out of power. When in possession of the government, they require every one to submit entirely to their direction and control; in *words*, they profess to be the exclusive champions of liberty; in *action*, they are the veriest tyrants imaginable. When out of power, they are always working and intriguing against the government, without any regard to truth, justice, or common honesty, or the welfare of their country. In popular governments, where the election of representatives too frequently recurs, such pernicious men have too many opportunities of mischief, in working upon, deceiving, and corrupting the minds of the people, in order to inflame them against those who have the management of public affairs for the time being; and thus, eventually, are enabled to ripen the discontents of the deluded multitude into violent and seditious movements. Such are *some* of the evil consequences invariably resulting from the too frequent recurrence of elections, which also (it may be remarked) necessarily incapacitates the representative from acquiring an adequate acquaintance with the public business and real interests of his country, owing to the short duration of his term of service.

There are likewise some other imperfections grafted into the system of election throughout the States, which deserve notice. The voting *by ballot*, instead of *vivâ voce*, is accounted a wonderful improvement; whereas, it excludes the open, wholesome influence of talent and property at the elections; and encourages a perpetual course of intrigue and fraud, by enabling the cunning demagogue to impose upon the credulity of the weak and ignorant. Indeed, the frauds practised by the *substitution* of one set of ballots for another, in every electioneering campaign throughout the country, are in themselves innumerable and shameless; and the success of elections, generally, depends on the adroitness of intrigue exhibited by the more active political partisans.

Universal suffrage, also, is a favourite feature in our republican system, except in the State of Virginia, where a respectable property in *land* is the prescribed qualification of a voter: in some of the states, *no* proprietary qualification, either in personal or real estate, is required, and in the rest (save Virginia) much too small a possession of property, whether real or personal, is suffered to qualify the electors. Now, universal suffrage is full of evil, without any alloy of good; for it gives efficiency and perpetuity to the anti-social conspiracy of poverty against wealth, of cunning against wisdom, of knavery against integrity, and of confusion against order; the necessary tendencies of which are, to exclude the great talents, high character, and large property of the community, from the administration of government; which, under such circumstances, is too apt to exhibit a scene of folly and oppression at home, and to become an object of contempt and scorn abroad. The only stable government, which can at once secure prosperity to its own people, and command the respect of foreign nations, must lay its foundations in the preservation and *ascendency* of property. No man ought to be allowed to vote, who is not possessed of a freehold in land, that those who have the deepest stake in the soil may have the most influence in the country.

The states, however, generally require a qualification, both of property and of age, in the *elected;* which seems to be quite useless; since it is fair to presume that a man must have already acquired some considerable standing in the community before his fellow-citizens will hold him up as a candidate for election, in either branch of the legislature, whether state or federal, more especially if the electors are required to possess a proprietary qualification. Still less should there be any limitation as to *age;* for as soon as a man fairly distinguishes himself by his talents and character, demonstrating in him a capacity for public service, so soon has he the passport of God and nature to the trust and confidence of the community. How much of zeal and talent, displayed in her service, would England have lost, if Charles Fox and William Pitt had been denied admittance into the House of Commons until they had reached their thirtieth year, instead of obtaining an entrance into parliament as soon as they had passed the age of twenty-one!

It is somewhat singular, that a republic professing to establish full toleration, and give equal political rights to every religious sect, should in so many instances exclude the *clergy* from a seat in the legislature. This exclusion occurs in the constitutions of New-York, Maryland, Kentucky, North and South Carolina, Georgia, Tennessee, and Louisiana.

Mr. Smith, in his *Comparative View of the Constitutions*, makes some very sensible and spirited observations on the exclusion of the clergy from all official and legislative privileges, as well as on all the prominent features of the federal and state constitutions, which existed in the year 1796.

The disqualification of the clergy in so many states seems *either* a remnant of the old Gothic policy, transmitted from times when ecclesiastics were immured in monasteries ; though even then ecclesiastics did greatly guide the political movements of nations ; *or*, perhaps it is copied from the practice of the British government, (some years since, backed by a statute passed in order to keep Horne Tooke out of Parliament) which excludes them from a seat in the House of Commons, under pretence of their being represented in *convocation*, although both the upper and lower Houses of Convocation have been abolished for more than a century, and the bishops are allowed to sit in the House of Lords : wherefore, according to the well-known maxim, *cessante ratione, cessat et ipsa lex*, as the English clergy are *not* now represented in convocation, they ought to be represented in parliament; *or*, lastly, their disqualification in the states is the offspring of a misguided jealousy towards the clerical order, on the part of the laity.

The *expediency* of admitting into the legislature the clergy ought to be left to their own sense of propriety, to the feelings and wishes of their congregations, to the rules and ordinances of the religious body to which they belong, and to the good sense, discretion, and opinion of the electors. When the *laity* undertake to exclude the clergy by constitutional regulations, the exclusion savours strongly of political intolerance; it is, in fact, *disfranchising* the whole of a very respectable and important class of the community. The constitution of the United States contains no such exclusion; and the experience of nearly thirty years has not demonstrated either its necessity or its use. After all, perhaps the exercise of the religious duties of ecclesiastical life are *not* quite compatible with the incessant agitations of active politics; and, doubtless, the Saviour of the world himself delivered an awful lesson of denunciation against earthly avarice and ambition, when he emphatically declared, that *his* kingdom is *not* of this world. Nevertheless, the admission into the legislative councils of their country ought to be left to the individual discretion of the clergy themselves, and of those with whom they are connected: they ought *not* to be disfranchised of a great political right, to which they are justly entitled, in common with all the rest of their fellow-citizens, by any municipal regulations of a free and popular government.

The *Senate* of the United States is composed of two senators from each state, chosen by its legislature for six years: each senator has one vote. They are divided into three classes. The seats of the senators of the first class are vacated at the expiration of the second; of the second class, at the expiration of the fourth; of the third class at the expiration of the sixth year; so that one-third of the senate is chosen every second year. If any vacancy happen, during the recess of a state legislature, the state executive may make a temporary appointment, until the next meeting of the legislature, which then fills up the vacancy, either by a new appointment, or by sanctioning that of the executive. A senator must be thirty years old, have been nine years a citizen of the United States, and be an inhabitant of the state for which he is chosen. The Vice-President of the United States is president of the senate, but has no vote, unless the House is equally divided. The senate chooses its other officers, and a president *pro tempore,* in the absence of the Vice-President; or when he exercises the office of President of the United States. The senate tries all impeachments, and when so sitting is on its oath or affirmation. When the President of the United States is tried, the Chief Justice of the United States presides: the concurrence of two-thirds of the members present is necessary to conviction. In cases of impeachment, judgment only extends to removal from the existing office, and disqualification for any other office of honour, trust, or profit, under the United States; leaving the party convicted liable to indictment, trial, judgment, and punishment, according to law.

The modes of appointing the senators of the United States vary in different states: they are generally regulated by state statute. In some, one house nominates to the other till both concur; in others, both houses unite in convention, and make a joint choice; the first is called a *concurrent*, the last a *joint* vote. Both modes are either *vivâ voce*, or by *ballot*. In the first mode, the senate possesses the same equal power with the House of Representatives, which they have in every other legislative act, and of which they ought *not* to be deprived in so important a measure as this. In the last mode, their numbers being always smaller than those of the lower house, their influence is, of course, proportionally smaller. The mode by *joint* vote, and *joint* ballot, is the most prevalent; the representatives, being the more popular branch, too generally carry their point against the senate.

The duration of the senators of the United States for *six* years is well calculated to give system and stability to this important branch of the general government, more especially as it acts a *judicial* part in the trial of impeachments; and discharges *executive* functions, in appointing public officers, and in making treatise with foreign powers. In many of the state constitutions, pecuniary qualifications are required in all candidates for public office; in the federal constitution none is required, either in the representatives, senators, or president. Perhaps it would be always most prudent to throw the proprietary qualification upon the *elector*, the person who votes; because men without property, generally, not only feel less solicitude for the public tranquillity and welfare, inasmuch as they have less stake in the country, but are also more open to the seductive influence of corruption.   Whereas, it is fair to presume, that men who are sufficiently distinguished to appear as candidates for public office, when the power of voting is confined to those who have a stake of property in the soil, will be sufficiently qualified by talents and information to discern the real interests of their country, whether they themselves possess property or not.   Indeed, it is fair to infer that candidates for the federal legislature will, generally, be men of some property also, as well as men distinguished in their respective states for political talents and character.

It is of the greatest moment to the best interests of the commonwealth, that the senate should be stable in duration, and efficient in power; because it is the only proper and effectual check upon the haste and passion by which the legislative resolutions of any single assembly, derived immediately from the peo le, are liable to be influenced. The institution of a senate affords an opportunity for the deliberations of the one legislative body to correct the precipitancy of the other, not only because the legislators are divided into two separate branches; but also because the component parts of each separate branch will, probably, be different ; and, consequently, a different system and spirit will grow up from the difference of organization in the two bodies ; thus serving as a salutary constraint upon the public movements of each other.   It is to be regretted that the separate states, throughout the Union, do not in general imitate this valuable provision in the federal constitution ; for the state senates are, too frequently, either chosen for so short a time, or so immediately by the people, that they cannot exist as a legislative body, watching over, controlling, and directing, for the common good, the wayward passions and prejudices of the more uninformed portion of the community.

The state of Maryland is an honourable exception to this general and radical error in the formation of government.   By the constitution of that state, electors are appointed for the express purpose of choosing senators; and are bound by oath to select men distinguished for their wisdom, talents, and virtues. The senators are elected for *five* years. The benefits of thus, in a great measure, securing the independence of the senate upon the people, have often been felt in Maryland during the earlier years of American sovereignty. On many occasions the integrity and firmness of the senators opposed and overruled the tumultuous passions, and disorganizing shocks of the more popular branch of the legislature. There is very little resembling the wisdom of this institution in other parts of the American body politic, except the appointment, by electors, of state senators in Kentucky, of federal senators by the separate state legislatures, and of the President and Vice President of the United states by electors. In the other states of the Union, the election of senators, immediately by the people, almost necessarily ensures a perpetuity of intrigue and cabal, and renders the senators themselves too dependent upon the leading demagogues in the several districts. As the senate ought to be a salutary check upon the precipitancy and passion of the more popular branch, it should be constituted in some mode different from that of the House of Representatives—either by electors or by the people, modified and restricted in their votes by some particular proprietary qualifications.

Mr. Jefferson, in his " Notes on Virginia," condemns the constitution of that great state for having overlooked this important provision in all good government. His observations are extremely judicious, and well worthy a most attentive perusal. In Maryland and Kentucky alone, the mode of choosing senators by electors prevails. In several of the other states the voters for senators must have greater pecuniary qualifications than voters for the other branch of the legislature; and the senators themselves must possess more property than the representatives. In *other* countries, whatever be the form of government, the upper or checking branch of the legislature may emanate from some source different from the will of the people; but in the United States all political power, according to the letter and spirit of every American constitution, whether state or federal, must flow either mediately or immediately from the same fountain, the choice of the people ; in whom alone the essential sovereignty of this extended empire resides ; wherefore, in order to invigorate the senate with an adequate controlling power, it is necessary to render it less dependent upon the fluctuating will of the people than is the House of Representatives. This can only be done by one or other of the modes above suggested. The plan adopted by the states of Maryland and Kentucky appears to be the best.

The times of greatest peril to all democratic governments are derived from the contagious spreading over the House of Representatives of those violent passions which occasionally agitate the people in every free country ; and this contagious influence of popular passion and fury must be generally diffused over the representative branch of the legislature, in every place where *annual* elections prevail. If the Senate be elected immediately by the people, will it not necessarily be subject to the influence of the same popular passions, and so lose all power of effectually checking the occasional phrensy of the lower house? The *longer duration* of the senate, which exists in many of the states, in some measure counterbalances the evils necessarily attendant upon the prevailing mode of electing senators ; and the experience of the American people has, in all the recent revisions of their state constitutions, (excepting that of Georgia), induced them to increase the term of senatorial service. The Senators of the United States are elected for six years ; those of Maryland for five years; of New-York, Pennsylvania, Kentucky, Virginia, South Carolina, and Louisiana, for four years ; of Ohio for two years; and of Delaware and Mississippi for three years. In order to unite firmness, stability, and system in the upper house, together with sufficient dependence and responsibility in the senators, all these constitutions, excepting those of Maryland and

Kentucky, have established the plan of *rotation*; by which an adequate permanency is supposed to be combined with the necessary change. The mode and frequency of rotation vary in almost all the state constitutions; but the result is, in all, the same; that of periodically infusing new members into a permanent legislative body.

In the federal government there is a biennial rotation of one-third of the senators; in the state governments of New-York, Pennsylvania, Virginia, and Louisiana, an annual rotation of one-fourth; in that of Ohio and South Carolina, a biennial rotation of one-half; in those of Delaware and Mississippi, an annual rotation of one-third. In Maryland the senators sit for five years; and in Kentucky for four; but without rotation. It is worthy of notice, that in the eastern, or New-England States, *no* senatorial check upon the precipitancy of the lower house has been adopted. Their institutions are the most democratic in the whole Union. In New-Hampshire, Massachusetts, Rhode-Island, and Vermont, the senates, or councils, are elected annually, as are also the Council of New-Jersey, and the senates of North Carolina and Georgia. The habits of order and moderation, together with general diffusion of elementary intelligence, throughout the New-England states, render a check upon the popular branch of the legislature less necessary than in countries not so favourably circumstanced. It is however, dangerous to trust altogether to the influence of personal feeling and individual habit in national affairs; more especially when counteracted by the force of fixed and positive institutions.

The reason of this omission in the eastern states, in New-Jersey, and in North Carolina, probably is, that their constitutions were all, excepting that of Vermont, made during the heat and fury of the revolutionary war, when they had little experience to guide them in the formation of governments; and, above all, when the arbitrary proceedings of the *royal* councils of the mother country had created a considerable antipathy in the leaders of the infant republics, to executive councils, and senatorial branches. As to Vermont, though her constitution was made so recently as July, 1793, yet the newly settled state of the country could not be expected to furnish forth the most profound legislators, and enlightened statesmen. With respect to Georgia, the recent change in the duration of her senate, from three years to one, is not so easily accounted for. She appears to retrocede in the science of government, while her sister states are advancing in improvement. The constitutions of Connecticut and Rhode-Island are substantially the old charters, obtained from Charles the Second; those of Massachusetts, New-Jersey, and North Carolina, were framed in 1776, and 1780; those of the United States, Pennsylvania, Kentucky, South Carolina, Ohio, Tennessee, Louisiana, Indiana, and Mississippi, were established since the year 1787; those of New-York and Maryland were made during the revolutionary war in 1776 and 1777; and, considering that circumstance, it is surprising that they contain such judicious arrangements in respect to the senate.

It is to be hoped, that whenever the New-England states revise their constitutions, they will make their senate more independent of the fluctuations of the popular will, and render them more efficient checks to the occasional precipitancy of the House of Representatives. The senates of Maryland, Massachusetts, and Kentucky, have power to fill up their own vacancies. In the United States the senatorial vacancies are supplied by the state legislatures; in almost all the separate states they are filled by popular election. Thus, by the very mode of their election, and the brief term of their duration, are the senators of many of the American States almost necessarily induced to become rather the suitors of a fickle and fantastic popularity, than, as they ought to be, the steady guardians of the people's welfare; often, in direct opposition to the popular passion and clamour. Those who are entirely dependent upon the people, can seldom render any essential service to the state by the wisdom or firmness of their legislation. Such men incur the unavoidable hazard of becoming the parasites, instead of the law-givers; the instruments, not the directors of the people. Under such circumstances, if any one should happen to be so imprudently honest, as to propose a plan, which by restraining the licentiousness of anarchy, might augment the prosperity and happiness of the commonwealth, his more artful compeers would have a fine opportunity of throwing him out at the next election, by loud and long harangues upon the essential majesty, the immutable sovereignty, the collective wisdom, the immaculate virtue of the multitude. Nay, even those who profess to deceive, in order to benefit the people, must soon find, that by propagating mischievous and disorganizing doctrines, they render it impossible at any future period to induce the multitude to submit to the wholesome restraints of justice and order.

The times, places, and manner of holding elections for federal senators and representatives, are prescribed in each state, by the legislature; subject, however, to the alterations of Congress, by law, except as to the places of choosing senators. Congress must assemble at least once in every year, on the first day of December, unless they by law appoint a different day. Each house is judge of the elections, returns, and qualifications of its own members; and a majority of each constitutes a quorum to transact business; but a smaller number may adjourn from day to day, and compel the attendance of absent members, under penalties provided by each house. Each house determines the rules of its proceedings, punishes its members for disorderly behaviour, and, with the concurrence of two-thirds, expels a member. Each house keeps a journal of its proceedings, and publishes whatever it is not deemed necessary to conceal. Neither house, during the session of Congress, can, without the consent of the other, adjourn for more than three days: nor to any other place than that in which the two houses are sitting. The senators and representatives receive a compensation for their services, ascertained by law, and paid out of the treasury of the United States. They are, in all cases, excepting treason, felony, and breach of the peace, privileged from arrest during their attention at the session of their respective houses, and in going to, and returning from, the same; nor can they be questioned in any other place, for any speech, or debate, in either house.

No senator or representative can, during the time for which he is elected, be appointed to any *civil* office under the authority of the United States, which shall have been created, or the emoluments of which shall have been increased, during such time; and no person, holding any office under the United States, can be a member of either house during his continuance in office.

The excluding the executive, or cabinet-officers, from a seat in the legislature, is a favourite position in the American constitutions: its wisdom, however, may reasonably be questioned; and, perhaps, a little examination will show this scheme to be rather a subtle refinement in political theory, than a sound, practical improvement in the art of government.   For executive officers, although excluded from the legislature, must govern the whole country; and as they do actually possess the highest rank, influence, and power, in the nation, their places will always be the great objects of political ambition.   To say, that the legislature would have no concern with these men, and that the chief executive magistrate, whether president, emperor, or king, might change or appoint them at his own mere will and pleasure, without producing the least sensation in the Representative Assembly, would be idle.   The legislature would be bound by a sense of duty—(in the United States the senate is constitutionally bound) to concern itself in all such nominations; and would undoubtedly take such concern, from the still more imperative motives of personal interest, of political considerations, of the ties of blood and affection.

The only *practical* effect, produced by excluding government-officers from a seat in the legislature is, that the parliamentary debates are conducted by deputies, whom each set of ministers employ to maintain their cause, while they are themselves transacting the business of their office. Ambitious men are obliged to contend for the preservation of their places, by an inferior order of reasoners and speakers; and the ambition which ought to bring the loftiest talents of the country into open competition, on the deliberative floor of the nation, is confined, chiefly, to the more dangerous and uncontrolable intrigues of the executive cabinet; while the legislator is left to a secondary race of men, who struggle for their respective chiefs.

It is, likewise, deemed to be a marvellous improvement in the modern system of political economy, to mete out a meagre subsistence to the *public* servants of a country, and to calculate, to a single dollar, the exact amount of bodily and mental labour, for which a given salary is to be equivalent. Accordingly, there is *not* a sufficient stipend allowed to any American public officer, whether executive, or judicial, or ministerial, or naval, or military, to enable him to support the decent exterior of a gentleman. The President of the United States himself receives only a little more than *five* thousand pounds sterling a-year, the Vice-President, and Secretary of State, about *one* thousand sterling per annum; and the inferior government officers, in due descending proportion. And the officers of the separate states are worse paid than those of the United States.

This doctrine, also, is a theoretic illusion, and a practical evil; for in every civilized, opulent, and thriving society, a certain magnificence of expenditure is an indispensable part of official greatness; and, if the high places of the state do not afford sufficient means to maintain their possessor with due dignity, they are necessarily left to the acquisition of minds of an inferior order. Whence, the most important offices are likely to be filled by persons of subordinate talents; and men of genius, being virtually excluded from the helm of government, are tempted to oppose and disturb a system, which might, under a more liberal order of things, have relied upon them as its surest bulwarks of support; and, above all, this mistaken policy actually prevents the developement of great talents on a large scale, by withholding all opportunities of national exertion. So that in fact, this state parsimony is the worst of all possible state extravagance; inasmuch, as it blights the growth of intellect, and squanders away the mind of the country.

Mr. Thomas Paine, in his celebrated compendium of modern politics, called *The Rights of Man,* undertakes to demonstrate, that no free people, if they be wise, will ever give more than three thousand two hundred and fifty dollars a-year to their chief magistrate, whether called president or king; and he proceeds to prove how any nation might easily procure a discreet man, able to ride on horse-back, fully competent to discharge all the functions of executive government, for such a limited yearly stipend. It is however surmised, that the profound observations of Mr. Paine on the science of political economy are not now quite in such good odour, either in the United States, or in France, as they were towards the close of the eighteenth century. It is necessary, in order to ensure the progressive power, and permanent exaltation of a country, to affix large salaries to all the great offices of state, and to all those public situations to the discharge of whose functions it is for the common benefit that ambition should invite high talents.

It is mere insanity to say, the people can get the work done for less money, and therefore they ought to give less. No doubt, a cobler, or a retail dealer in small wares, or an attorney without practice, will patriotically consent to take upon himself the burden of governing the country, in any one of the great executive departments of state, for a small stipend; because the wages of office, though comparatively low, afford a larger income than either of these enlightened politicians can derive from the profits of his individual profession. But the business of the nation will not be well done. Nay, even in a money point of view, the nation will be a loser, by employing underlings at a small salary, to conduct the government; because such men

will actually destroy more public property, in twelve
months of mal-administration, by restraints on commerce, by bounties on manufactures, by crippling the
growth of productive industry, and by numberless other
political blunders, than would suffice to pay the most
magnificent stipends to executive officers for a hundred
years. And if we add to this the much higher considerations of the loss of national honour, and the degradation of national character—which an incapable administration always inflict upon their country—we cannot
hesitate to pronounce, that the system of *under-paying*
public officers has a direct tendency to ensure the perpetual weakness and disgrace of a community.

All bills for raising revenue in the United States
originate in the House of Representatives ; the senate
proposing, or concurring with amendments, as on other
bills. Every bill, which has passed the House of Representatives and the senate, before it becomes a law, is
presented to the President of the United States : if he
approve, he signs it ; if not, he returns it, with his objections, to the house originating the bill : that house
enters the objections on its journals, and reconsiders
the bill ; when, if two-thirds agree to pass it, the bill
is sent, with the objections, to the other house,
which also re-considers it ; and, if two-thirds of that
house approve, it becomes a law. If any bill be not
returned by the President within ten days (Sundays
excepted) after it has been presented to him, it is a
law, unless Congress prevent its return by their adjournment. The same rules are applicable to every
order, resolution, or vote of either house.

This *qualified* negative upon the proceedings of the
legislature is given to some of the state governors, by
their state constitutions, as well as to the President of
the United States, by the federal compact. In England,
the executive possesses an *absolute* negative upon legislative acts ; but in republican governments this is deemed too great a power. The royal *veto* was violently
discussed in France at the commencement of the revolution, and the discussion closed by cutting off the

king's head. M. Necker, the Genoese banker and financier, wrote a whole book upon the subject, for the express purpose of enlightening the mind of Louis the Sixteenth, who, however, did not live long enough to read it through. Thus fares it with kings, when their subjects enter into abstract discussions respecting executive prerogatives and privileges. The question, whether or not, in these United States, the executive shall have the power to obstruct altogether, or only to arrest and for a time suspend the will of a majority of the representatives of the people, assembled as a legislative body, has been variously decided in different states. In some, the executive has *no* control; in others, only a limited or qualified; in none an absolute control. The balance of opinions is in favour of a qualified negative. In 1777 the state of New-York established this principle in her constitution; but united it with a *council of revision,* composed of the governor, the chancellor, and the judges of the supreme court, to whom all bills are submitted, after they have passed both houses of the legislature.

In 1780 the constitution of Massachusetts vested the *veto* in the governor alone. In 1786 the constitution of Vermont vested in the governor and council the power not only to propose amendments to laws, but to suspend them to the next session of the legislature. In 1787 the constitution of the United States vested in the president; in 1789, and 1795, the constitution of Georgia, in 1790 that of Pennsylvania, in 1792 those of New-Hampshire and Kentucky, in 1812 that of Louisiana, in August, 1817, that of Mississippi, vested in their respective governors the power to negative all laws, unless re-considered, and passed by both houses of the legislature. In Connecticut the governor and council, forming the Upper House, possess complete legislative powers. In the states of Delaware, Tennessee, South Carolina, and Ohio, (which last constitution was framed in November, 1802,) the constitutions withhold even a qualified negative from the executive. By the constitution of South Carolina, in 1776, the governor had a full and unqualified *veto* in all cases. This power was annulled by the constitution of 1778, and even a qualified negative was refused admittance into the constitution of 1790. This seems to be a momentous error; for, whatever may be thought of the impropriety of entrusting a republican executive with an *absolute* veto upon all legislative proceedings, yet the advantages of a *qualified* negative are many and obvious.

In nearly all the states the senate is elected by the same electors who vote for representatives, and in consequence must generally be influenced by the same popular prejudices, and propelled by the same sudden and impetuous emotions; whence it *cannot* be a sufficient check upon the passions of the Lower House. When laws are passed amidst the heat and smoke of those violent impulses, which occasionally agitate every free community, it is essential to the stability and character of the government, that some external check, *dehors* the legislature, should exist, in order to arrest and allay the temporary ebullitions of legislative insanity. And in what hands so proper as those of the executive can such a power be deposited? In the event of the governor's using his qualified negative, the legislature may still pass the law, provided, upon a reconsideration of the question, two-thirds of both houses concur in thinking the bill salutary. But the mere circumstance of calling upon them again to consider the bill, laden with the deliberate objections of the executive, when time has been given for the storm of popular passion to subside, will, in general, be sufficient to prevent the passing of a very pernicious law.

In the constitution of the United States, and in those of all the states, except Virginia and North Carolina, there seems to be the same mode of trying by impeachment, the accusation proceeding from the more numerous branch of the legislature, and being heard before the other house. There are some variations in the different constitutions, as to the number of members required in both houses to constitute an accusation and conviction; in some, simple majorities being sufficient;

in others, two-thirds being required; in some a mere majority of the house may vote an impeachment, but two-thirds of the senate must convict. It might be observed that the practice of originating *money-bills* in the House of Representatives, which prevails very generally in the American Constitutions, is derived from a similar practice in the House of Commons in England, and was transplanted to this country, and engrafted into its system of colonial policy. Whatever reason there might be for such a provision in England, in order to give the Lower House some counterpoise of strength against the predominating influence of an hereditary monarchy and aristocracy, or however necessary it might have been under the colonial governments of British America, as a counterbalance to the weight of the Councils, or Upper Houses, appointed by the crown, there does *not* appear to be the same urgent necessity for adopting such a provision in the present American constitutions, since in all of them, with only three exceptions, namely, those of the United States, Maryland, and Kentucky, the senators and representatives both emanate from the same source, that of popular election; and, throughout the Union, the lower branch of the legislature has a tendency to absorb within its own vortex all the substantial powers of government, both state and federal.

Under the authority of the federal constitution Congress has power to lay and collect taxes, duties, imposts, and excises, to pay the debts, and provide for the common defence and general welfare of the United States, —all duties, imposts, and excises being uniform throughout the United States; to borrow money on the credit of the United States; to regulate commerce with foreign nations, and among the several states, and with the Indian tribes; to establish a uniform rule of naturalization, and uniform laws on the subject of bankruptcies throughout the United States; to coin money, and regulate its value and that of foreign coin, and fix the standard of weights and measures; to provide for the punishment of counterfeiting the securities and current coin of the United States; to establish post-offices and post-roads; to promote the progress of science and useful arts, by securing, for limited times, to authors and inventors, the exclusive right to their respective writings and discoveries; to constitute tribunals inferior to the supreme court; to define and punish piracies and felonies committed on the high seas, and offences against the law of nations; to declare war, grant letters of marque and reprisal, and make rules concerning captures on land and water; to raise and support armies, (no appropriation of money, however, for that use, being for a longer term than two years,) to provide and maintain a navy; to make rules for the government and regulation of the land and naval forces; to provide for calling forth the militia, to execute the laws of the Union, suppress insurrections, and repel invasions; to provide for organizing, arming, and disciplining the militia, and for governing such part of them as may be employed in the service of the United States, reserving to the states respectively the appointment of the officers, and the authority of training the militia, according to the discipline prescribed by Congress.

The federal constitution likewise empowers Congress to exercise exclusive legislation in all cases, over such district, not exceeding ten miles square, as may by cession of particular states, and the acceptance of Congress, become the seat of the government of the United States; and to exercise like authority over all places purchased by the consent of a state legislature, for the erection of forts, magazines, arsenals, dock-yards, and other needful buildings; and to make all laws necessary and proper for carrying into execution the foregoing powers, vested by the constitution in the government of the United States, or any of its departments or offices. The permanent seat of the government of the United States was established, by act of Congress, upon the river Potomac, including the town of Alexandria, in Virginia, and Georgetown, in Maryland. The laws of Virginia, with some exceptions, were declared in force in that part of the ten miles square ceded by Virginia, and those of Maryland in the part ceded by Maryland.

At present the district of Columbia is neither represented in Congress, nor in any state legislature, nor
has it any of the rights or privileges of an American
state, the supreme court of the United States having
decided that it is *not* a state under the provisions of the
federal constitution.

Notwithstanding the opinion of many very respectable persons, that the seat of the United States government at the City of Washington, in the district of Columbia, is peculiarly adapted for promoting and quickening the progress of American prosperity and strength,
it is reasonable to infer, that the location of this remote
metropolis is, of itself, too well calculated to produce an
inefficient administration of government. At present,
seventeen years after its first location, in 1800, the
federal city is, in fact, little more than a large waste,
with a few straggling houses and half-built ruins, thinly
scattered over an immense surface. A stranger is
forcibly struck with the contrast between the magnificence of the natural scenery of the place and the forlorn
appearance of the few buildings and broad streets, with
their long rows of trees, that the inhabitants call a
city. The Potomac spreads out into a vast breadth
immediately below, and is navigable up to the verge of
Washington; the back country is very extensive, and
the river affords a navigation of two hundred miles
above Georgetown. So early as the year 1798, the
members of Congress, then sitting at Philadelphia,
were repeatedly consulted respecting the assistance to
be given to the federal city, but they were nearly all
opposed to every expedient that promised to prepare the
public buildings for the reception of the general government. Whence the proprietors in the metropolis (full
half of which they had given to the government) suffered considerably. So that in 1802, fifteen hundred
lots, with their buildings, which had cost two hundred
thousand dollars, were bought in for less than twenty-
six thousand, exhibiting a depreciation of nearly seven-
eighths of their whole value.

Yet, in spite of the tardy progress, and the present

forlorn appearance of the federal city, there are not wanting politicians, who still continue to assert that this metropolis is admirably calculated, by its central situation, for the seat of American government; not only now, but also when the whole continent of North America shall be included within the boundaries of the United States, and members of Congress shall be sent to Washington, from the coast of Labrador, and the Isthmus of Darien. But notwithstanding these sublimated schemes, and Utopian visions, many of the more sober people in the United States so sensibly feel the inconvenience resulting from the seat of government being fixed at Washington, that they anxiously wish for its removal to some more civilized and habitable spot. For the accomplishment of this purpose, scarcely a session of Congress has passed since the establishment of Washington as the metropolis of America, without some attempt being made, by motion, or petition, to remove the seat of government to some less intolerable place.

The chief topics of complaint are, the desolate condition of the city itself; its remoteness from all the great commercial ports and cities of the Union, and the consequent difficulty and delay in procuring political information, respecting either foreign or domestic events; and the additional useless expense, in all the branches of government, entailed upon the nation, by their residence in Washington. To all which it has been answered, both in and out of Congress, that there must be some national metropolis; that the federal constitution empowered Congress to fix upon a permanent seat of national government, and that it has accordingly fixed upon Washington, which must therefore, " *for the honour of the nation*," continue to be the American metropolis, notwithstanding any temporary inconvenience or mischief thence resulting to the Union. Leaving the Congress to settle the point of honour among themselves, it is not difficult to prove, that much injury is derived to the United States from fixing the seat of government at Washington. All that can be alleged in favour of the American metropolis may be reduced to the following heads; namely, 1*st*. its central situation, facilitating the means of political information to the members of government. 2*ndly*. Its tendency to become populous and wealthy, by being the seat of government. 3*rdly*. Its commercial and manufacturing capabilities; and 4*thly*. Its pleasant situation, holding out strong inducements for the residence of gentlemen of independent fortunes.

First. As to its central situation, it happens that roads and navigation do not always naturally, and of necessity, radiate in straight lines from the centre to the circumference, as do light and sound; nor does the national existence of the United States depend upon being geographically metropolital. For if so, nearly all the great empires in Europe would long since have been overthrown; because, with the exception of Madrid, no great European metropolis is central; and it remains to be proved, that any particular dearth of the necessary political information prevails in Paris, London, Vienna, Berlin, or Petersburgh, merely on account of not being situated exactly in the heart of their respective territories; or that Spain is better informed, and more enlightened, than the rest of Europe, because she is blessed with a central metropolis. Besides, Washington is *not* central, since the addition of Louisiana to the Union; and will be still less so, when Florida, and Mexico likewise, shall be belted within the circle of our territorial dominion. Madrid, to be sure, *is* regulated in its position, by this supposed geographical excellence. Being nearly in the centre of the Spanish peninsula, it was deemed best fitted for the foundation of a capital. But it possesses no other local advantages; and it can never argue the most profound policy to select merely advantageous mathematical points, without regarding other and more important circumstances; but compelling the habits and conveniences of a whole nation to bend to these unpurposed notions of geographical excellence. The Spaniards, by going only thirty-five miles to the southward, might select many beautiful and advantageous situations on the banks of the Tagus, either on the plains, in the neighbourhood of Aranjuez, or on the hills of Toledo; whereas, Madrid is built on the banks of the Manzanares, which is only one of the tributary streams of the Tagus, and, during the summer months, is merely a little rivulet, crawling through a wide bed of sand. Whence, by its injudicious position, the capital of Spain is deprived of many commercial advantages.

The geographical centre of a country is *not* necessarily the focus of its power; for that power must be derived from its superior wealth, and greater population; neither of which advantages the city of Washington now possesses, or, perhaps, ever can possess, since places can only become populous and wealthy by their progress in commerce and manufactures; or by the influx of the opulent and idle, with all their apparatus of attendants, equipages, and establishments; or by the attractions of a seat of government—not one of which circumstances will apply in favour of the growth of our American metropolis; for,

Secondly, the federal government of the United States never can, by its attractions and influence, gather together a concourse of people large enough to constitute a moderately sized city. What are the attractions of the American government, that will, *alone*, ensure a great increase of wealth and population to the city of Washington? Are they inferred from the naked walls of the unfinished buildings, scattered here and there over the plain? or do they flow from the expenditure of the ample revenues, and the establishment of the magnificent households of the members of Congress, with all their menials, retainers, and dependants, that swell the train of legislative pomp and official greatness? These very congress-men, consisting of forty senators and about two hundred representatives, are, for the greater part, made up of farmers, tradesmen, mechanics, feeless physicians, and unpractising lawyers, whose wages of legislation amount to six dollars a-day (averaging less than one thousand dollars a year), during the session, while they sit brooding and engendering laws for the direction of the Union—these men, without equipages, nay, unattended by a single servant, annually wander up to Congress, from their respective districts, in steam-boats, sloops, and stages; and, during their session in the federal city, are domiciled in boarding-houses. What great and permanent influx of wealth and population can such legislators and statesmen bring into the seat of government? Nor do the executive officers of the United States, as already shown, receive salaries sufficient to support even a decent exterior to the world.

Thirdly. Great wonders, however, are expected from the extraordinary facilities of promoting *commerce* and *manufactures*, which the city of Washington possesses. But our manufactures are already carried on in districts much more favourably situated for their prosecution, on account of the superior number, wealth, and industry of their inhabitants, than Washington is, or ever can be. And the commerce of the United States naturally finds its way to the great outlets and inlets of American navigation: it never will flow, in any large streams, to the banks of the Potomac, lying at least two hundred miles from the ocean, merely because Congress sits and legislates there; while there are so many great cities in the Union, so much better calculated for all the purposes of trade; while the great seaports of Boston, New-York, Philadelphia, Baltimore, Charleston, and New-Orleans, are so admirably fitted by their natural advantages, as well as their acquired weight of capital, population, skill, and industry, to retain and increase the ample commercial operations, which they have long carried on with such immense benefit to the whole country. Besides, Alexandria, lower down on the Potomac, and nearer the sea, intercepts all the foreign trade carried on in that navigation, before it can come to Washington; and Georgetown confers upon the federal city a similar kindness, by engrossing to itself all the inland trade that is floated down the Potomac from the interior settlements and plantations of Virginia and Maryland; so that Washington is perpetually barred, by the very nature of its position, from ever becoming a great commercial or manufacturing city.

It only remains, *Fourthly*, To examine how far the pleasantness of its situation might induce the independent gentlemen of the United States to fix their residence in Washington. What seductions of pleasure are to be found in a place, which, in the summer, is too hot for any person who can fly from it to endure; and which, in winter, is remarkable for the dearness, scantiness, and badness of all kinds of accommodations and conveniences, would require much argument and more sophistry to show. And even if Washington were so pleasantly situated as to induce a desire of living in it, who are the gentlemen of independent fortune that will flock thither? Such independent gentlemen are a very rare order of beings in the United States, owing to the infancy of the nation, the form and substance of its political institutions, and more particularly to the very general custom of dividing the property, both real and personal, of a family in equal portions among all its members. Indeed, nearly every state in the Union has abolished the law of entails, and the rights of primogeniture, and adopted the English statute of distributions, for the disposition of real as well as personal estate. Almost all the men, in this country, are employed in prosecuting some profession, trade, or calling, as the means of their subsistence; whence the number of opulent men, not engaged in actual business, is very small throughout the Union. Nay, even if they were more numerous, while the separate states remain distinct and independent sovereignties, the seat of the general government never can present so many inducements to the unemployed wealthy to crowd thither, as will always be found in their own respective states, where their influence must be greater and more perceptible; and where the perpetual fluctuations of the executive and legislative bodies continually hold out objects to stimulate their ambition.

Hence, Washington *cannot*, within any reasonable period to come, grow into a large and commodious city; seeing that it holds out no attractions of residence to the opulent and unemployed; possesses no great capabilities of commerce or manufactures; is the seat of a very meagre and ill-paid government; and is *not* well situated for obtaining, speedily and correctly, the political information necessary to guide the movements of the American administration with sagacity and wisdom.

The *real*, the efficient cause of fixing, and continuing the seat of the general government in the district of Columbia, is to be found in the determination to entail upon the state of Virginia the chief sway and influence over all the rest of the Union; and to check the career of the northern and middle states, whose far superior capacities, both physical and moral, in population, wealth, industry, and intelligence, would eventually sink Virginia into the rank of a second-rate sovereignty, if the seat of the national government were on the northern line, and the northern states were permitted to avail themselves of all their agricultural and commercial advantages. Whereas now, the Virginians having the seat of government within their own territory, make it the focus of their own political intrigues; and by managing the people without doors, in the different states, they return nearly what members to Congress they please; and induce them to legislate in accordance with the scheme of Virginian policy, which never has been favourable to large and liberal views of commercial enterprise.

Indeed, it is almost impossible that there ever can be a wise and efficient administration of the American government while its seat continues at Washington, because no practical information, upon any subjects of importance to the well-being of the community, can be obtained there. If advice be wanted on any great political or commercial question, no advice can be had; for no statesmen or merchants reside at Washington; and neither public nor private libraries are to be found there: whatever wisdom is required, must be derived

L

from the members of Congress themselves. Add to this, that there is *no* weight of population, talents, property, or character, to regulate and influence the discussion of Congress, so as to restrain that venerable body from *too often* enacting absurd and oppressive laws. If the seat of government were fixed in any one of the large and populous cities, which adorn and strengthen the more civilized parts of the Union, the members of Congress would not dare to pass such acts, as they have too frequently passed, while sitting as legislators in the district of Columbia; for they would be assailed on all sides, out of doors, by the talents, information, character, and influence, of the more intelligent part of the community; and by the popular indignation of their more unthinking brethren of the multitude.

But now, the members of Congress go up from all quarters of the Union to Washington, and generally carrying with them only moderate natural capacities and no very profound acquaintance with the great political relations subsisting between the United States, and the other sovereignties of the world: they assemble together in the senate and House of Representatives, and hurry through into statutes all sorts of bills, the meaning and import of which they do not always know, and concerning the probable results of which they cannot sometimes even guess; but they obey the directions of their civil commanders, the leaders of the Virginian dynasty. And having performed these feats of legislation, the congress-men retire to their respective domiciles ; and congratulate each other upon their deliberative sagacity and wisdom, without any dread of encountering the ridicule or reproach of an intelligent human being, amidst the gross population, so thinly scattered over the naked metropolis of America. The *embargo* of 1807, 1808, and 1809, that suicidal act, which at one death-stroke cut asunder all the sinews of national industry, wealth, and reputation, was absolutely carried through the senate of the United States in the little compass of *four hours ;* the *three* readings of the

bill being forced onward, one after another, with all the
rapidity of guilt; and when the two or three really wise
and practical statesmen, who at that period happened
to be in the senate, and who foresaw the ruinous consequences of that miserable measure, requested the government party to pause, until they could obtain some
correct information as to its probable effects upon the
mercantile and agricultural interests of the country,
they were answered, that the American senate wanted
no political information; that its collective wisdom was
fully adequate to provide laws for promoting the welfare of the Union; and accordingly, the American
senate, in its collective wisdom, *did*, in the space of
four hours, take up, consider, and pass into a law, an
act laying a *perpetual* embargo on all the commerce of
the United States.

Above all, the seat of government being fixed at
Washington, gives full play and opportunity for the
exercise of *Virginian* influence to acquire complete
ascendency over the other portions of the Union. Virginia is the largest of all the United States; its laws, forbidding real property to be attached for debt; the custom of leaving the landed estates of the family to the
eldest son, in hereditary succession; the power of voting,
in proportion to the number of negro slaves upon each
plantation, (the slaves amounting to about half the population of the state;) the proprietary qualification of
a considerable freehold required in every white voter;
together with some other circumstances, in their state,
constitution, laws, and customs, all confer upon the
Virginians very great political advantages, and enable
them to act in a compact body, for the purpose of perpetuating their dominion over the middle and northern
states, throughout which they encourage the prevalence of *democracy* by every means in their power,
while they do not suffer it even to exist within the precincts of their own state; for, by excluding all freemen, who have no freehold, from voting, by themselves
possessing votes, according to the number of their

slaves ; by transmitting their landed property in hereditary succession ; and by freeing themselves from the
embarrassments attending the subjection of their lands
to attachment for debt, the planters of Virginia have
erected themselves into a *feudal aristocracy* of untitled
and unblazoned peers, and manage their affairs so
adroitly as to give laws to the rest of the Union.

By the *esprit du corps*, which actuates every Virginian landholder, and by the constitutional policy
which blends together the executive and legislative, and
in some measure the judicial departments and functions
of Virginia, that state is enabled to spread the web of
influence over all the elections, as well state as federal, in the Union, so as to secure the appointment of
proper personages, to be guided and directed by the
master-hand of its leading politicians ; whence the
congress-men generally, and a majority of the state
legislatures, have long been induced to vote and pass
laws in conformity with the political views of their Virginian lords. Well might the Virginian landholders,
therefore, so strenuously insist upon continuing the seat
of government at Washington, lest their influence over
Congress should be counteracted and defeated by the
superior intelligence, activity, and virtue, always to be
found in large and populous cities. Nay, it would not
be so easy, after a while, to induce very unqualified
men to sit in Congress, if the seat of government were
fixed in any civilized place, and the members were constantly liable to be assailed for their incapacity by the
superior sense and spirit of the inhabitants of the metropolis ; and consequently a wiser order of beings would
be selected to take upon themselves the very important
charge of legislating for millions of their fellow-men.

The next clause of the constitution is particularly
important, as relating to the abolition of the slave
trade ; it runs thus :

The migration or importation of such persons as the
states, existing at the time of framing the federal constitution, should think proper to admit, is not to be pro-

hibited by Congress prior to the year 1808 ; but a tax, not exceeding ten dollars a head, may be imposed on such importation.

In the Northern and Middle States, the slaves are few : Massachusetts has, by statute, abolished slavery altogether within her jurisdiction; New-York, New-Jersey, and Pennsylvania, have passed acts for its gradual abolition within their territories; Ohio has prohibited, by her constitution, its existence within her precincts ; Maryland, Virginia, North Carolina, South Carolina, Georgia, Louisiana, Kentucky, Tennessee, and Mississippi, keep up a large body of slaves within their respective sovereignties, amounting to about *one-third* of their whole population, and making about *one-sixth* of the population of all the United States ; namely, Maryland, 159,000 ; Virginia, 460,000 ; North Carolina, 254,000 ; South Carolina, 246,000 ; Georgia, 173,000 ; Kentucky, 238,000 ; Tennessee, 102,000 ; Louisiana, 57,000 ; Mississippi, 31,000 :— Making a total of 1,711,000.

If a Heathen poet could exclaim

" Ημισυ γαρ τ' αρετης αποαινυται ευρυοπα Ζευς
Ανερος ευτ αν μιν κατα δουλιον ημαρ ελησιν,"

what ought a Christian philosopher to think? During the session of Congress, in the winter of 1816-7, a society was established at Washington, for the purpose of colonizing the free people of colour. The citizens of the Southern States have long experienced the evils resulting from the slave system. They are kept in continual alarm and fear of an insurrection of the slaves themselves ; and the free blacks are so numerous and profligate, as to be a curse and pestilence to all our large cities. Nay, even in the Northern and Middle States, where they are better educated than in the South, their habits are so vitious, as to render them a burden on the poor-rates, and continual candidates for the state-prison. It is said, that some of the Southern planters begin to be convinced that their lands may be tilled to greater advantage by free white labourers than by negro slaves. If this conviction should spread, it may eventually lead to the abolition of slavery all over the United States. The intention, at present, on the part of the Colonization Company, is to settle as many free blacks as they can induce to go on the banks of the river Sherborough, some distance south of Sierra Leone, under the protection of England, and supply them with suitable agricultural implements, school-masters, and religious teachers. If this benevolent scheme should succeed, it may become a powerful means of christianizing and civilizing the immense continent of Africa, containing a hundred and fifty millions of Mahomedans and Pagans, steeped in igno-rance, superstition, brutality, vice, and crime. Sir James Lucas Yeo's late letter to the British Admiralty throws much light on the slave trade as it now exists, and on the state of Africa.

The nations of antiquity most celebrated for counte-nancing the system of domestic slavery were the Jews, Greeks, Romans, and ancient Germans ; but it has been of almost universal prevalence. Its beginning may be dated from the remotest periods in which there are any traces of the history of mankind. It commenced in the barbarous stages of human society ; and was retained even among nations far advanced in civilization. By the ancient Germans it was continued in the countries which they over-ran, and was thus transmitted to the various kingdoms and states that arose in Europe out of the ruins of Western Rome. In process of time, however, this species of servitude gradually fell into decay in most parts of Europe ; and, amongst the various causes which contributed to this essential alteration in the whole sys-tem of European society, none, probably, were more effectual than the uniform experience of the disadvan-tages of slavery itself; the difficulty of continuing it, amidst the growing civilization of commercial enterprise and industry, and a progressive persuasion that the oppression and cruelty, necessarily incident to its existence, were incompatible with the religious doctrines and the pure morality of the Christian dispensation.

Such was the expiring state of domestic slavery in Europe at the commencement of the sixteenth century, when the discovery of America, and of the western and eastern coasts of Africa, gave occasion to the introduction of a *new* species of slavery, which took its rise from the Portuguese, who, in order to supply the Spaniards with persons able to sustain the fatigue of cultivating their new possessions in America, particularly in the West-India islands, opened a trade between Africa and America, for the sale of negro slaves. This execrable commerce in the blood and sinews—the bones and marrow of the human species, was begun in the year 1508, when the first importation of negro slaves was made into Hispaniola, (now St. Domingo) from the Portuguese settlements on the western coasts of Africa. The employment of slaves in colonial labour was not long confined to the Spaniards, but was soon adopted by the other European nations, as they acquired possessions in America. In consequence of this general practice, negroes became a very considerable article of merchandise, in the commerce between Africa and America ; and domestic slavery struck so deep a root, that the nineteenth century had actually commenced before the powers of Christendom interfered to restrain the progress of the slave trade.

In the year 1803 the general government of the United States passed an act of Congress, prohibiting the importation of negro slaves into any part of the Union, after the commencement of the year 1808 ; in the year 1806, the British parliament abolished the importation of negro slaves into any part of the territories, home or colonial, of the empire. In 1815, Napoleon, on his return from Elba, abolished the slave trade in France; which abolition was confirmed by a subsequent decree of the present king. The Spaniards and Portuguese still continue this detestable traffic in human flesh ; and the domestic slavery of the negroes is maintained in nearly all the American colonies of Europe, whether continental or insular, and in these United States, particularly those of the south and west.

Slavery is an absolute evil, unqualified by any alloy of good: it implies an obligation of perpetual service, which nothing but the consent of the master can dissolve. It also generally gives the master an arbitrary power of administering every sort of bodily correction, however severe and inhuman, not immediately affecting the life or limb of the slave. Nay, sometimes even these are left exposed to the unrestrained will of a capricious master; or they are protected by paltry fines, and other slight punishments, too inconsiderable to prevent excessive cruelty; as was exemplified in that South Carolina master, who, in the year 1811, after lashing his negro slave most unmercifully, compelled another of his negroes (the intimate companion and friend of the person punished) to sever his head from his body with an axe, while he was held down on a block by his fellow-slaves. For this atrocious and deliberate murder the master was punished by the imposition of a small fine, prescribed by statute. If he had stolen a horse in South Carolina, and had been found guilty of the offence, the laws of that state would have hanged him; but the deliberate murder of his fellow-creature was commuted for a few dollars. God made of one blood all the nations of the earth; but the Bible is *not* often the manual of a slave-holder.

Slavery creates a legal incapacity of acquiring property, except for the master's benefit. It allows the master to transfer over, and alienate the person of the slave, in the same manner as he alienates and transfers any other species of goods and chattels. Servitude descends from parent to child, with all its severe appendages. This catalogue of misery is nothing more than a faithful description of *every* kind of personal slavery, whether existing under the municipal laws of ancient Greece and Rome, or the institution of *villenage* in feudal Europe, during the dark ages, or the present condition of negro bondmen; excepting that the remnant of *villeyn* slavery, which is altogether abolished in England and France, but still lingers, under various denominations, in some of the countries of continental Europe, particularly in Italy, Austria, and Russia, is considerably qualified in favour of the slave, by the humane provisions, and growing civilization of modern times. The bare view of the condition of slavery is sufficient to point out its pernicious consequences to those communities where it is suffered to exist. It corrupts the morals of the master, by freeing him from those legal restraints, with respect to his slave, so necessary for the control of the human passions, so beneficial in promoting the practice, and confirming the habit of virtue. It is also dangerous to the master; because his systematic oppression excites all the worst emotions of implacable resentment and hatred in the bosom of the slave; the extreme misery of whose condition continually prompts him to hazard every peril for the gratification of revenge; and his situation furnishes him with frequent opportunities of slaking his thirst of vengeance in the blood of his oppressor. Accordingly, the planters of our southern states, and of the West-Indies generally, are kept in perpetual alarm and horror, lest an insurrection of their slaves should consign them to the doom which the French masters experienced in the massacres of St. Domingo.

To the slave himself, personal bondage communicates all the afflictions of life, without affording him the recompense of a single delight, physical, intellectual, or moral. It stifles all the growth of native excellence, by denying the ordinary means and motives of human improvement. It is likewise full of peril to the commonwealth, by the radical, the *heart* corruption of those citizens on whose exertions of virtuous patriotism its prosperity so essentially depends; and by admitting within its bosom a vast multitude of persons, who, being excluded from the common benefits of its political constitution, are necessarily interested in devising the means of its destruction. In whatever light we view it, domestic slavery is a most pernicious institution; more immediately to the victim, who writhes in convulsive agony under its scorpion lash; indirectly to the master, who riots in uncontrolled dominion; and eventually to the state itself, which suffers such a leprous instilment to be poured into all the veins and arteries of the body politic.

It must, however, be remembered that the fatal tendencies of personal bondage to corrupt and destroy individua s, domestic society, and the community at large, are slackened in our southern states, by some favourable circumstances, which do *not* exist in the West-Indian colonies of the European powers. The most important of these are the much less disproportion between the number of slaves and free men, there being in many of the West-India islands ten blacks to one white; whereas, in none of our states does the black more than equal the white population;—the superior order of the permanent free inhabitants, more especially of the great planters, whose native talents are developed by liberal education, and whose manners are polished by all the refinements of well-bred society; whereas, the greater portion of West-Indian planters are needy and desperate adventurers from Europe, who pass their temporary residence in the colonies in ignorance, luxurious rioting, brutal sensuality, gaming, cruelty, and every kind of vitious indulgence, until they either perish there, or amass enough treasure from the tears and blood of their negroes to return home, and corrupt the morals of the neighbourhood where they settle;—the very superior condition and accomplishments of the female portion of our southern community, compared with that of the West-Indies, and the vicinity of sister states bound up in the same girdle of political confederacy, but steadily and systematically discouraging the existence of domestic slavery within the limits of their own territorial jurisdiction.

Nevertheless, on the score of humanity to negroes, our slave-holding states have nothing to boast; at least so far as relates to the provision of the municipal law. Our southern planters exercise the lash at their own discretion; they pay a small money-fine for the murder of their slaves, and they occasionally subject them to very severe bodily torture. The United States afford no instance of a master being capitally punished for killing his slave; yet, in the British West-Indies, some few years since, Mr. Hodge, a planter of large fortune, a magistrate, and a member of the executive council, was publicly hanged, at noon-day, after a jury of his countrymen had found him guilty of excessive cruelty to the negroes on his plantation.

In *South Carolina* the negro slaves are, by law, *burned alive* for the crimes of arson, burglary, and murder. So lately as the year 1808, two negroes were actually burned alive, over a slow fire, in the midst of the market-place in the city of Charleston. What must be the code of municipal law; what must be the state of public feeling, in respect to the wretched African race, that could suffer two human beings to be gradually consumed by fire, as a public spectacle, in the nineteenth century, in the midst of a city containing nearly twenty thousand nominal Christians, and the best of all possible republicans, who profess to look with scorn upon the tyrants, and with compassion upon the slaves of Europe!

By the provisions of the federal constitution the privilege of the writ of *habeas corpus* cannot be suspended, unless required by the public safety, in cases of rebellion or invasion. No bill of attainder, or *ex post facto* law can be passed. No capitation, or other direct tax can be laid, unless in proportion to the census or enumeration directed to be taken by a preceding provision of the constitution. No tax or duties can be laid on articles exported from any state. No preference can be given by any regulation of commerce or revenue, to the ports of one state over those of another; nor can vessels, bound to or from one state, be obliged to enter, clear, or pay duties in another. No money can be drawn from the Treasury, but in consequence of appropriations made by law; and a regular statement and account of the receipts and expenditures of all public money must be published, from time to time. No title of nobility can be granted by the United States; and no person, holding any office of profit or trust under them, can, without consent of Congress, accept any present, emolument, office, or title, from any king, prince, or foreign state. No state can enter into treaty, alliance, or confederation, grant letters of marque and reprisal, coin money, emit bills of credit, make any thing but gold and silver coin a tender in payment of debts, pass any bill of attainder, *ex post facto* law, or law impairing the obligation of contracts, or grant any title of nobility. No state can, without consent of Congress, lay any imposts, or duties on imports or exports, except what may be absolutely necessary for executing its inspection laws; and the net produce of all duties and imposts, laid by any state on imports or exports, must be for the use of the Treasury of the United States; and all such laws be subject to the revision and control of Congress. No state can, without consent of Congress, lay any duty on tonnage, keep troops, or ships of war in time of peace, enter into any agreement or compact with another state, or with a foreign power, or engage in war, unless actually invaded, or in such imminent danger as will not admit of delay.

The reader may receive much valuable information upon American affairs, relating to the government, laws, institutions, and policy of the United States, by a perusal of the following works, to the first of which, in particular, the preceding pages have been greatly indebted; namely, Mr. Smith's " Comparative View of the Constitutions of the several states with each other, and with that of the United States, exhibiting, in tables, the prominent features of each Constitution, and classing together their most important provisions, under the several heads of administration, with notes and observations." The *Federalist* was written conjointly by General Hamilton, Mr. Jay, and Mr. Maddison. Mr. Jay wrote only a few of the earlier papers; Mr. Madison wrote some of the historical essays; and the chief portion of the work was executed by General Hamilton. In depth and extent of political wisdom, in the philosophy of jurisprudence, in comprehension and elevation of national views, in high and blameless honour, in profound and luminous ratiocination, in nervous and manly eloquence, in lofty and incorruptible patriotism, the American Federalist has no superior, and very few equals, in all the volumes of political economy, containing the lucubrations of the greatest sages and statesmen of modern Europe, whether of England, France, Germany, Italy, Spain, or Holland.

Pacificus was written to defend and encourage the impartial, persevering neutrality of the United States, during the whole conflict between revolutionary France and England; a conflict that grew out of the Jacobinical insolence, intolerance, and aggression of the French revolutionary government; and for a season swept along all the continent of Europe down its tide of ruin and degradation. No higher commendation can be given of this work, than to say that it is altogether the composition of General Hamilton. *Camillus* was written to defend and explain Mr. Jay's Treaty with England, concluded in November, 1794; that treaty, to which the United States were indebted for a continual stream of prosperity and wealth, unexampled in the history of nations. The commercial part was written by Mr. Rufus King, formerly American minister near the Court of St. James's; and the political portion by General Hamilton. The whole performance displays the highest evidence of the sound judgment, extensive information, and powerful and pointed reasoning of the two distinguished statesmen who composed it. The *American Remembrancer* contains a large mass of essays, resolutions, and speeches for and against Mr. Jay's Treaty. The chief opponent of Camillus was the late Chancellor of the state of New-York, Mr. Livingston. This collection exhibits much talent and violence, both personal and legislative; and presents an ample and instructive picture of the public mind, during one of the most trying and turbulent periods in the national career of the United States.

The *American Museum* is in thirteen octavo volumes, and amidst much idle trash, and multifarious nonsense, contains a large portion of valuable information, relating to the agriculture, commerce, manufactures, politics, morals, manners, national character, natural and civil history, biography, law, and state documents of America, from the beginning of the year 1787, to the end of the year 1792, a most interesting period, during which the federal constitution was framed, and carried into practical effect. The collection of American State papers, of which ten octavo volumes have been recently published at Boston, is a most valuable addition to our stock of information, respecting the government and policy of the United States.

If the papers of the late General Hamilton were published, either in a connected narrative form; or a judicious selection of them were made, and given to the public, an immeasurable volume of light would be shed upon the internal structure, the home administration, and the foreign relations of the American government; upon the laws and polity, the commerce and manufactures of the United States; upon all that tends, directly or indirectly, to subserve the best interests, and promote the national strength, prosperity, and honour of our federative republic.

In the ancient republics of Greece and Rome, *one* man used to excel in many various departments of intellectual greatness; the same man was an illustrious warrior, statesman, lawyer, and orator. But the more minute division of labour in modern times, is satisfied with excellence in a single vocation, and we are ready to pronounce a man great, if he be a skilful general, or a profound lawyer, or a wise statesman, or an able writer, or an eloquent speaker. General Hamilton, however, united all these high characters in himself: for he was unquestionably the greatest lawyer, statesman, financier, orator, and writer of his own country, and perhaps of the age in which he lived. Hamilton was one of the Πενταθλοι, but with this distinction in his favour, that he won the prize in every contest.

On the subject of representation generally, the exclusion of cabinet ministers from the legislature, the allowing scanty stipends to public servants, and some other topics intimately connected with the wise and efficient administration of government, much very valuable instruction might be obtained by a careful perusal of the papers on parliamentary reform, scattered throughout the Edinburgh Review; and more especially the article on Cobbett's Register, in the tenth volume; a political discussion, which for depth, clearness, comprehension, and liberality, has probably never been surpassed.

The federal constitution vests the *executive* power in a President of the United States, who holds his office during the term of four years, and, *together with the Vice-President,* chosen for the same period, was originally elected thus : Each state appoints, at the discretion of its legislature, as many electors as itself has senators and representatives in Congress. But no senator or representative, or person holding any office of trust or profit under the United States, can be appointed an elector. The electors meet in their respective states, and vote by ballot for *two* persons, one of whom, at least, must not be an inhabitant of the same state with themselves. They make a list of all the persons voted for, and the number of votes for each, which they sign, certify, and transmit, sealed, to the seat of government of the United States, directed to the President of the senate, who, in the presence of the Senate and House of Representatives, opens all the certificates, and the votes are counted. He who has the greatest number of votes is President, if that number make a majority of all the electors appointed. In choosing the President, the votes are taken by states, the representation from each state having one vote ; a quorum for this purpose consists of a member or members from two-thirds of the states ; and a majority of all the states is necessary to a choice. After the choice of a President, the person having the greatest number of votes of the electors is Vice-President. Congress may determine the time of choosing electors, and the day on which they shall give their votes; the day being the same throughout the United States. The President must be a natural born citizen, or a citizen of the United States at the time of adopting the federal constitution, and be thirty-five years old, and have been fourteen years a resident within the United States. In case of the removal of the President from office, or of his death, resignation, or inability, the same devolves on the Vice-President; and Congress may, by law, provide for the case of removal, death, or inability, both of the President and Vice-President, declaring what officer shall act as President until the disability be removed, or a President elected.

By the twelfth article of the *amendments* to the federal constitution, it is provided that the electors shall *name* in their ballots the person voted for as President, and in *distinct* ballots the person voted for as Vice-President; but no one, constitutionally ineligible as President, shall be eligible as Vice-President of the United States.

This amendment is no improvement. The design of the original constitution was to put *two* efficient persons at least in nomination for the presidency; one of whom being chosen, the other would be competent to fill the office in the event of any accident befalling the President. But, because in the year 1801, Mr. Burr had nearly jostled Mr. Jefferson out of the presidency, this amendment was introduced, in order to prevent any future collision between the presidential and vice-presidential candidates. The consequence has been, that not a single efficient person has been elected to the vice-presidency since this amendment became part of the constitution. The office, ever since that time, appears to have been designated either for superannuated and decrepit men, or for persons peculiarly marked by their mental imbecility, and individual unimportance.

The constitution provides, that the President shall be elected by electors appointed by the state legislature, and prohibits *congress-men* from having either vote or influence in the matter. This provision of the constitution also Mr. Jefferson has annulled, by a practical amendment called a *caucus*. This felicitous invention is carried into full effect, by convening a meeting of all the democratic members of Congress, as well senators as representatives, *to settle among themselves*, in the city of Washington, who shall be the next President and Vice-President. Which being done, they send circulars to every state, setting forth the candidates they recommend, who, 'as a thing of course, are voted for by all the electors in the democratic states. In this manner Mr. Madison was made President; and thus, also, Mr. Munroe was chosen, although with some difficulty, as the democratic congress-men were, at first, in a majority for Mr. Crawford, of the state of Georgia. But, as Virginia could not permit a President of the United States to be produced without the pale of her own dominion, she having filled the presidential chair with her own citizens twenty-four out of the twenty-eight years which have elapsed since the establishment of the federal constitution, Mr. Crawford himself and his friends were induced, after two or three meetings of the caucus, to yield to the Virginian claims of Mr. Monroe, who was accordingly nominated; whereupon the usual circular was sent to the several states, whose legislatures accordingly appointed electors who voted for Mr. Monroe, and who was elected President.

This is, in effect, taking the election of President of the United States out of the hands of the people, and transferring it to those of an oligarchy of congress-men. In March, 1816, the senate of the United States discussed the propriety of amending the federal constitution, by establishing an uniform mode of election, by districts, of electors of President and Vice-President. The proposition was negatived; but the remarks of Mr. Rufus King, a senator from the state of New-York, and one of the members of the general convention that framed the constitution, on that question, deserve the full consideration of every sober statesman. Mr. King said, " The states may now severally direct the manner of choosing their own electors : it is proposed that the manner shall be prescribed by the constitution. This would be an important change, and an improvement. If there was any part of the constitution, deemed by its framers and advocates to be better secured than any other against the enterprises which have since occurred, it was the very provision on the subject of election to the *presidency*. The idea was, that the action of *that* particular agency, which has since controlled it, was as much displaced by the constitutional plan of electing the President and Vice-President, as could possibly be devised. The opinion had been, that all undue agency or influence was entirely guarded against ; that the men, selected by the people from their own body, would give their votes in such a manner as to afford no opportunity for a combination to change the freedom and popular character which naturally belong to the electoral bodies.

" We all know the course which this thing *has* taken. The election of a President of the United States is no longer that process which the constitution contemplated. In conformity with the original view of the authors of that instrument, I would restore, as thoroughly as possible, the freedom of election to the people ; I would make the mode of election uniform throughout the country, by throwing the whole nation into as many districts as there are electors, and let the people of each district choose one elector. Then all the people in the country would stand precisely on the same footing ; and no particular addresses could be made to the special interests and particular views of particular men, or particular sections of the country. The course *now* pursued, in this respect, is *not* entitled to that high distinction. On the contrary, our progress in government is not for the better ; it is not likely, hereafter, to be in favour of popular rights. It was with the people the constitution meant to place the election of the chief magistrate ; that being the source the least liable to be corrupt. But if, under the name of the liberty of the people, we put this power into other hands, with different interests, we place it in a situation in which the rights of the people are violated.

" With regard to the rights of the people, and the freedom of the country, no man can name a matter so important as the choice of the President of the nation. It is an infirmity in our natures, that we look for chiefs and rulers, either for their superior virtue, or their supposed subserviency to the views of those in subordinate situations. It is against the evil of the latter principle we must guard. The liberties of the people are more affected by the choice of President, than by any other ordinary political act. In this point, they are vulnerable. Here ought the rights of the people and of the states to be guarded. Our existence, and the passions of the present day, are ephemeral; public liberty should be immortal. Considering the senate should be to the people and the states not only the safe guardians of their rights, but the protectors of their liberty, I hope they will adopt a provision, so nearly connected with the perpetuation of both. All experience has shown, that the people of any country are most competent to a correct designation of their first magistrate. So far as history affords us light, it leads us to this point; that in times of difficulty and peril to a nation, when it is in the utmost need of superior talent for its high stations, no tribunal is more competent to discern, and select it, than the people. Intrigue, turbulence, and corruption, may have some sway in quiet times, when all is tranquillity, in regard to the general situation of the country; but when the ship of state is in danger, turbulence ceases, and the best men are, by an instinctive power, fixed on by the people for their governors. This has been wonderfully illustrated by history; and the best designations of magistrates have been produced in this way.

" My sober view is, that as to the election of chief magistrate of this nation, nobody is so competent as the great body of the freemen to make a proper selection. Whether, on this question, their *first* impression should be taken, is a question of great importance: there would be difficulty in making the returns of the votes: those who collected and compared the votes might defeat the choice of the peeple. Not that these objections are insuperable; and the course of things, under the *present* mode of choosing a president, is in its nature pernicious, and has a tendency to prevent the object intended by the constitution of a pure elective magistracy. Men now live, who will probably see the *end* of our government, as we now go on : terminate when it will, the termination will *not* be in favour of public liberty. For five years past, I have seen a character developing itself, the predominance of which I fear. Not a people on earth are more capable of high excitement than this people. During the excitement of the passion, to which I refer, if a contested election occurs, the gownsmen must stand aside ; another character supersedes them ; and there can be little difficulty in judging what will be the result. The march from military rule to despotism is certain, invariable. Those who think they see the probable tendency of our present system should interpose something remedial. The people in this particular are the best keepers of their own rights; and any device to remove that power from them weakens its security. I know that this proposition, if agreed to, will break down the power of the great states. I have no objection, if in curtailing their power, the same measure regulates the rights of the whole nation equally. I am willing to let the election for the presidency rest *wholly* on the people."

And in the same debate, General Harper, a senator from Maryland, said, that "as to the main proposition, he was decidedly in its favour, for this general reason, that its adoption would tend to make the elections of President less a matter of juggle and intrigue than they now are. He would not say that it would have the effect of wholly excluding intrigue ; of placing this great election on the footing on which the great men who framed the constitution vainly imagined they were placing it, of a free, unbiassed expression of the public will ; but it would bring it nearer than at present. Party arrangements and bargains would not be so easy. Bargains could not be so readily struck with one state for this great office, with another for that, as according to the present mode of election. Districting the states for electors would have a tendency to render the presidential election more free and independent; to remove it more from the grasp of party arrangements; to prevent bargains between profligate agents, and the selling of the nation for offices to the highest bidder."

The President, at stated times, receives for his services a compensation, that can neither be increased nor diminished during the period for which he is elected; nor can he receive within that period any other emolument from the United States, or any single state. Before he enters on the execution of his office, he takes the following oath or affirmation : "I do solemnly swear, (or affirm) that I will faithfully execute the office of President of the United States, and will, to the best of my ability, preserve, protect, and defend the constitution of the United States." The president is commander-in-chief of the army and navy of the United States, and of the militia of the several states, when called into the actual service of the United States. He may require the opinion in writing of the principal officers in each of the executive departments, upon any subject relating to the duties of their respective offices; and he has power to grant reprieves and pardons for offences against the United States, except in cases of impeachment. He has power, by and with the advice and consent of the senate, to make *treaties*, provided two-thirds af the senators present concur; and he nominates; and, by and with the advice and consent of the senate, appoints ambassadors and other public ministers and consuls, judges of the supreme court, and all other officers of the United States, whose appointments are not otherwise provided for in the constitution, and which are established by law. But Congress may by law vest the appointment of such inferior officers as they think proper, in the president alone, in the courts of law, or in the heads of departments.

As to the propriety of vesting the constitutional powers allotted to the President in that officer, the *Federalist* enters into a most elaborate and able discussion, more particularly upon the *treaty*-making power, which he shares with the senate. During the session of 1815-16, Congress discussed, with great ability, the propriety of confining the power of making treaties with foreign states to the president and senate, and excluding the House of Representatives from all interference on that subject. In that debate, Mr. Pinckney, late American minister in London, and now ambassador from the United States to Russia, particularly distinguished himself; and the able speeches of Messrs. Randolph, Gaston, Calhoun, Forsythe, and Hopkinson, threw great light on some of the fundamental principles of the constitution.. The right, asserted by the House of Representatives, to interpret and sanction treaties, was negatived; and properly, because the senate is a popular body of representatives, and the addition of the Lower House could furnish no new principle of safety or control. The practice of the British House of Commons, in sanctioning treaties, is no precedent for the lower branch of the American Congress; because, in England, the executive is without any check in the conclusion of treaties, except the subsequent discussion and appropriation of the inferior house of parliament. The lords have no share in the treaty-making power, although they, like the crown, are hereditary; whereas our senate, as well as our executive, is popular and elective.

The British government also, in its collective branches of king, lords, and commons, is all-powerful; and the distribution of its respective authorities very much blended together. But, under the federal constitution, the powers are precisely measured out to each branch of the general government, and the power of making treaties with foreign potentates is specifically given to the President and senate, as other powers are given separately to the House of Representatives; and others, to all the departments of government conjointly.

The President is empowered to fill up all vacancies that happen during the recess of the senate, by granting commissions, which expire at the end of their next session. He must, from time to time, give Congress information of the state of the Union, and recommend to their consideration such measures as he may judge necessary and expedient. He may, on extraordinary occasions, convene either, or both houses; and if they disagree as to the time of adjournment, he may adjourn them to what time he thinks proper. He receives ambassadors, and other public ministers; takes care that the laws are faithfully executed, and commissions all the officers of the United States. The President, Vice-President, and all civil officers of the United States, are removeable from office on impeachment for the conviction of treason, bribery, or other high crimes and misdemeanors.

In many of the states the electors of the President are chosen by the people; in some, by the state legislature. The constitution has left this point undetermined; it has only given Congress the power to determine the time of choosing the electors, and to fix a uniform day, throughout the United States, on which they shall give their votes. From the executive power to pardon, cases of impeachment, as in Britain, are excepted in all the American constitutions; and in some of the states murder and forgery are also excepted.

If there be any one principle of municipal government more imperatively important than the rest, it is that the executive should be *one and indivisible*. This position is most ably enforced and illustrated by General Hamilton, in the *Federalist*. The framers of the federal constitution were too wise to encumber the President of the United States with a constitutional council, which he is *compelled* to consult. He is only authorized to require of the principal executive officers their opinions in writing, on any subject relating to their official duties. The several states differ on this part; some having a council, established by the constitution, which the executive *must* consult, and without whose assent he cannot act; while others have no council. The general effects, resulting from the institution of a constitutional council are, that they serve as a cloak to the executive, to cover him from punishment when he does wrong; and act as obstacles to impede his motions, when he wishes to do right. It is always best that the chief magistrate of every republic should act upon his own responsibility: in difficult questions of the law he can consult the attorney-general; and on complicated political cases he can have recourse to the state secretaries, and high officers. In a multitudinous executive the subdivision of responsibility weakens the hold of public opinion and power upon the executive councils and measures; in a single executive the responsibility is concentred and operative. Wherever a constitutional council exists, every act of the executive, whether relating to appointments to office, or to qualified negatives upon the legislature, or to the pardoning of criminals, or any other matter, is done by the executive, with the advice and consent of such council.

A notion has long prevailed among a numerous body of American politicians, that a vigorous executive is inconsistent with the genius of republican government; and, accordingly, *not* a single constitution, state or federal, gives sufficient power to the executive. If the position so prevalent with us were true, republican government would be just good for nothing; because the experience of all time has shown, that energy in the executive is a leading feature in all good government, whatever be its form or substance. It is essential to the protection of the commonwealth against the assaults of foreign power; it is equally necessary to the steady administration of municipal laws to the protection of private property (the sheet-anchor of human society), from all arbitrary encroachment; to secure liberty, both personal and political, against the intrigues, enterprises, and assaults of ambition, faction, and anarchy. A feeble executive implies a feeble execution of the government: weakness in high places is never harmless, because it involves the ruin of untold millions in its career of folly. It is better for a nation that its government should be occasionally, decidedly, and vigorously wrong, than always feeble and waveringly right. A government weakly executed, whatever it may be in theory, and how beautiful soever it may appear in manuscript, or in print, on paper, or on parchment, is, for all the practical purposes of the community, as far as respects the prosperity and happiness of the nation, a *bad* government.

Unity, duration, adequate income, and competent powers, are all requisite to constitute energy in the executive. The observations, at present, must be confined to the importance of executive unity. A single executive, and a numerous legislature, are best adapted to unite vigour in the government, with deliberation and wisdom in the national councils, and the means of conciliating the confidence of the people, and of securing their privileges and interests. Now, unity is conducive to energy, because decision, activity, secrecy, and despatch, other things being equal, always characterize the proceedings of one man more than those of many men acting together; and in proportion as the number of agents is increased, will be the indecision, inactivity, want of secrecy, and positive delay in all their movements. In practice, it is of no moment whether the executive unity is destroyed by vesting the power in two or more magistrates of equal dignity and authority, or by vesting it ostensibly in one man, but subject, in whole or in part, to the control and co-operation of executive counsellors. The last mode of dividing and weakening the executive government is incorporated into many of our state constitutions. That of New-York provides a *Council of Appointment*, consisting of a senator from each of the four great districts of the state, nominated annually by the house of assembly: of this council the governor, or administering lieutenant-governor, or president of the senate, is president, and has a casting, but no other vote. This council appoints to all the offices of the state, except those provided for by the constitution itself. In New-Jersey the governor must consult his council ; but it is doubtful if their resolutions bind his judgment. In many other states the executive council has much more power over the governor than in New-York or New-Jersey.

A little reflection will show the mischief of dividing the executive in any way. Wherever, and whenever two or more men are engaged in any common pursuit, they are liable to differ in opinion. If it be a high public office, in which they claim equal dignity and power, their difference of opinion lessens the respectability, weakens the authority, distracts the plans, and slackens the operations of government. It also tends to split the community into violent and irreconcilable factions, whose mutual animosities continually disturb the public peace ; it embarrasses the execution of every measure from the commencement to its conclusion ; it counteracts, without any counterbalancing benefit, the qualities most essential to a good executive government, namely, vigour and expedition. Above all, in conducting war with a powerful enemy, executive energy is the great bulwark of national security.

In addition to this, an executive council tends directly to conceal the faults, and destroy the responsibility of government. Owing to the multiplication of the executive, it is almost impossible, amidst the mutual accusations of the governor and his council, to determine on whom the blame or punishment of any pernicious measure ought to fall. It is shifted from one to another with so much political dexterity and legerdemain, that the public is bewildered in suspense as to the real author of its calamities. In the single instance in which the governor of New-York is coupled with an executive council, the appointment to offices, every day's experience brings to light additional mischief. Without stooping to any personal crimination, it cannot be illiberal to remark that *sometimes* scandalous appointments to important offices have been made. Indeed, some cases have been so flagrant that *all* parties have concurred in censuring them; but when inquiry has been made, the blame has been laid by the governor on the members of the council, who, in return, have charged it upon the nomination of his excellency; while the people are at a loss to determine by whose flagitious influence their interests have been committed to hands so incompetent.

An executive council deprives the people of their two greatest securities for the faithful exercise of all delegated power; namely, *first,* the restraints of public opinion, which lose their efficacy alike on account of the division of censure, attached to evil measures among a number of persons, and the uncertainty on whom the blame ought to be fixed; and, *secondly,* the opportunity of discovering the actual misconduct of those whom they trust, in order to remove them from office, or subject them to merited punishment. This part of the scheme of government seems to be borrowed from England, without any analogy to warrant such a loan from a monarchy to a republic. In England the king is an hereditary, perpetual chief magistrate; and, for the sake of public peace, can do no wrong; nor is he himself accountable for the acts of his administration, and his person is sacred. Under such circumstances, it is necessary to annex to the monarch a constitutional council, responsible to the people for their advice, and for the measures of the executive government; otherwise, there would be no responsibility in the executive; and, in the place of a free government would be substituted an unqualified despotism. Yet, in England, the king is *not* bound by the resolutions of his council; although they are answerable for their advice to him. He is absolute master of his own conduct, in the exercise of his office, and may, at his sole discretion, observe or disregard the counsel offered to him.

But in a representative republic, as are these United States, where the people themselves are the only unresponsible sovereigns who can do no wrong, whose majesty is inviolable, and whose persons are sacred, *every* magistrate is, and ought to be, a servant of the public, and personally answerable to the nation for his conduct while in office; and, consequently, the reason which in the British constitution argues the necessity of an executive council is strong against the propriety of such an institution in this country. In the monarchy of England it furnishes a substitute for the prohibited responsibility of the chief magistrate; but in the American republic an executive council only serves to diminish the personal responsibility of the chief magistrate himself.

The general prevalence of an executive council in our state constitutions is also derived, in part, from that mistaken maxim of republican jealousy, which considers power as safer in the hands of many than of one; whereas the executive authority is more easily confined when single than when multitudinous. It is safer to have a single object for popular vigilance and jealousy to observe, than to distract attention by a number of such objects. All multiplication of the executive is dangerous, not friendly to social liberty. For the united credit and influence of several individuals must be more formidable than the credit and influence of either of them separately. The *thirty tyrants* of Athens, the *decemvirs* of Rome, and the *executive directory* of revolutionary France, were more terrible in their respective usurpations than any *one* of them singly could have been, and deluged Athens, Rome, and France, with *more* native blood. From either of such combinations America would have more to fear and more to suffer, than from the criminal ambition of any single president of the United States or state governor. An executive council to a magistrate, who is himself responsible for his official acts, is only a drag-chain upon his good intentions; the instrument and accomplice of his pernicious measures, and an effectual covering and defence of his evil deeds.

The power of *pardoning* lodged in the hands of the executive, and the power of punishing crimes vested in the law, must always be taken together as parts of the same municipal system. The law is fixed, as to the punishment of crime, but a discretionary power is left in the chief magistrate to moderate the punishment according to the circumstances of commission. The degree and species of punishment being fixed, best ensures the personal and political freedom of the people ; there being no slavery so miserable as where the law is uncertain in its exposition and application. " *Misera servitus, ubi jus, aut vagum, aut incognitum.*" The punishment being capital for certain crimes, best answers the purposes of terror, by its warning example to others ; whence by punishing the crime severely in one instance, its perpetration is, in many instances, prevented. And the executive power of moderating, by occasionally relaxing the severity of capital punishment, tempers justice with mercy : and while it secures the authority of the laws, does away the imputation of making crimes of different degrees of malignity equal, by inflicting death alike upon all.

In most civilized nations, the power of pardoning certain crimes has been given to the executive. It is peculiarly so in England, whence the United States have borrowed nearly all their common and much of their statute law. The king's power of pardoning is said by the old Saxon jurists to be derived " *a lege suœ dignitatis.*" As laws, in order to be just, must be general and fixed ; and as it is impossible precisely to graduate the scale of punishment to the exact proportion of crimes, on account of the incessant variation of circumstances, which renders the same generic crime more or less atrocious in degree, it is always prudent to allow a resort for pardon to the discretion of the executive, lest cases should sometimes occur to justify Cicero's observation, that " *quandoquidem, summum just est summa injuria.*" And, although laws ought not to be framed on principles of compassion to guilt, yet, according to the constitution of every free government, justice should always be administered in mercy ; and, therefore, it is the great duty required from the British executive, by his coronation oath, and the act of his government, most entirely his own and personal. In some countries the power of pardoning in the executive is not sufficiently secured. In Holland, for instance, under their old go-vernment, before the Dutch were conquered by revolu-tionary France, (what it is now, I cannot tell, having had no opportunity of examining the constitution of the United Netherlands) there was no power to pardon, unless there happened to be a Stadtholder, a magistrate, who was only an accidental part of their municipal system. Thus the Dutch republic omitted to establish in its constitution a provision essential to all sound policy, as necessary to the welfare of the community as justice itself; nay, in the opinion of some of the most celebrated jurists, giving to justice a perfection of benignity, which did not originally belong to her stern and unaccommodating nature.

In England, during all the varieties and revolutions of government, the alternations of tyranny and anarchy and well-tempered freedom, the greatest weight has always been laid upon the prerogative of pardoning lodged in the hands of the executive. Indeed, this power is a considerable abatement of the severity of what is deemed by some able jurists the harshest part of the criminal law of England, the law of *forfeiture*. Ever since the Union of the two roses, in Henry the Seventh and his queen Elizabeth, the pardoning power has generally been employed to the peace and preserv-ation of families. In the records of parliament, even in the worst times of the most tyrannical dynasties, from the reign of the Norman conqueror to the do-minion of the arbitrary Tudors and execrable Stuarts, examples of the benignant exercise of this prerogative are not wanting: and since the revolution in 1688, in the better times of well-balanced liberty, it has been peculiarly beneficial.

It is not, however, to be dissembled that this pardon-ing power has been sometimes abused in England and elsewhere. Towards the close of the seventeenth cen-tury *thirty-five thousand* criminals were pardoned at once, by a general act of grace from the republic of Venice, in order to raise a large sum of money. Francis the First of France gave Cardinal Wolsey, then on an embassy from Henry the Eighth of England, the power of pardoning *all* criminals in every French town through which he should pass. The House of Commons petitioned Edward the Third to be less liberal in pardoning malefactors, on condition of their serving him in his continental wars. With what unreflecting facility the most atrocious criminals are frequently pardoned in several of our American states, in order to make room for fresh candidates for imprisonment, is too notorious to need a comment, and too injurious to the community to be passed over in silence.

By the federal constitution, the *judicial* power of the United States is vested in one supreme court, and such other inferior courts as Congress may, from time to time, ordain and establish. The judges, both of the supreme and inferior courts, hold their offices during good behaviour; and, at stated times, receive for their services a compensation, not to be diminished during their continuance in office. The judicial power extends to all cases in law and equity arising under the constitution, the laws of the United States, and treaties made under their authority; to all cases affecting ambassadors, other public ministers, and consuls; to all cases of admiralty and maritime jurisdiction; to controversies to which the United States are a party; to controversies between two or more states, between a state and citizens of another state, between citizens of different states, between citizens of the same state claiming lands under grants of different states, and between a state or its citizens and foreign states, citizens, or subjects. The supreme court has *original* jurisdiction in all cases affecting ambassadors, other public ministers, and consuls, and those in which *a state* is a party. But, by the eleventh article of the *amendments* to the constitution, it is declared, that the judicial power of the United States shall *not* extend to any suit in law, or equity, commenced or prosecuted *against* one of the United States by citizens of another state, or by citizens or subjects of any foreign state.

In all other cases before mentioned (together with the exceptions enumerated above) the supreme court of the United States has *appellate* jurisdiction, both as to law and fact, with such exceptions and under such regulations as Congress shall see fit to make. The trial of all crimes, except in cases of impeachment, must be by jury, and the trial held in the state where such crimes have been committed; but when not committed within any state, the trial to be at such place as Congress may, by law, have directed. Treason against the United States consists only in levying war against them, or in adhering to their enemies, giving them aid and comfort. No person can be convicted of treason unless on the testimony of two witnesses to the same overt act, or on confession in open court. Congress has power to declare the punishment of treason; but no attainder of treason shall work corruption of blood or forfeiture, except during the life of the person attainted.

The American law, both state and federal, differs from that of England, in the crime of treason *not* working forfeiture of property and corruption of blood. There are some very able arguments in favour of the English doctrine of attainder, in Lord Hardwicke's "Treatise on the Law of Forfeiture," and in Bishop Warburton's "Divine Legation of Moses." Both these great men lay much stress on this punishment operating as a strong preventative against the crime, by holding up to the culprit the certainty of the extreme infamy, and absolute penury of his own immediate descendants and kindred, if he persist in perpetrating the forbidden act.

Mr. Smith, in his "Comparative View," and the present Chancellor of the state of New-York, in an introductory lecture to a course of law lectures, delivered by him in November, 1794, when professor of law in Columbia College, have given some very valuable observations on the American *Judiciary*. The substance of these observations, with such additional remarks as may occur during the discussion, will now be presented;

premising, however, that the State Constitution of New-York declares, that no judge, either of law or equity, shall hold his office after he reaches the age of *sixty* years. This seems to be a strange constitutional provision, that a man must cease to be a judge as soon as he is sixty years; because in the common course of events, provided he habitually exercises his mind by observation, reading, and reflection, he is *wiser,* and consequently better fitted to discharge the important functions of the judicial office *after* than before he reaches the age of sixty. The Spartans were so well aware of this general truth, at least practically, that they did not suffer a man to become an *Ephor,* or Judge of their highest legal tribunal, until he had actually entered his *sixty-first* year.

The State Constitution of New-Hampshire prohibits any judge from continuing in office after he attains the age of *seventy* years. This limitation as to age is undoubtedly wiser by ten years than the New-York constitutional provision, which cashiers a judge as soon as he is sixty. All limitations of this kind are foolish and cruel; because they pretend to point out the precise time when human intelligence fails; and then consign a man to absolute want, that his life may not falsily their prediction of the appointed decay of his interlect. Lord Mansfield sate on the King's Bench until he was *eighty;* and does any sound lawyer find in his decisions, during the last twenty years of his judicial career, that incapacity which our New-York constitution fixes upon a judge the moment he becomes sixty years old? At all events, if a limitation be allowable, sixty years of age is too early a period. It requires the habitual diligence of the greatest part of a man's life, together with good sound strong natural talents, to acquire the extent and depth of information, and the practical experience, which are the essential requisites of an able judge; and to disqualify him by law, at a period of life when his knowledge and experience could render him most competent to the due administration of public justice, does not exhibit a very profound degree of political sagacity or wisdom.

N

This limitation is no less cruel than absurd; for it makes no provision for the maintenance of the discarded judge. The New-York constitution, in this respect, imitates the conduct of Frederic the Second of Prussia, who boasted, " that he used men as he used oranges, he squeezed out the juice, and threw away the rind." For it casts a man destitute upon the world, precisely at a time when he is not able to provide for himself, by adopting any other calling; after it has availed itself of the youth and manhood, the time and talents, the learning and industry of him, whom it consigns to hopeless penury and barren sorrow. The least which ought in common justice to be done, is, that if our legislators will persist in cashiering a judge for no other crime than being sixty years of age, they allow an adequate pension for life to those whom they dismiss.

Perhaps no one compotent part of the American constitutions involves more momentous effects than our judiciary system. Some of the ablest papers in the Federalist are devoted to the consideration of this subject. The two chief essentials in the organization of this branch of the government, are, a proper appointment in the first instance; and an adequate independence during their judicial existence; which last implies a permanent tenure of office, and a fixed competent salary.

To secure the first object, the appointment of judges shold be vested in that branch of government which presents the greatest probability of making a good, and the most certain responsibility, in the event of making a bad choice. The executive, if single, is completely responsible: a single chief magistrate will, in general, be sufficiently interested in his own reputation, to search for able men; a multitudinous executive is under no such pressing responsibility; and a legislative body are almost entirely irresponsible ; for voting by ballot, as is the fashion of this country, their choice is that of no particular member, but every one is sheltered from accountability by the vote of every other person present. Besides, most of the members are changed either annually, or biennially; and the same body of men, which elected an unworthy magistrate, existing no longer, when his incapacity is discovered, no public shame is attached to them as a legislature. The responsibility of the executive, although lessened, is not however annihilated by assigning to a senate, or council, a negative on his nomination; and it is possible that such a negative may sometines act as a salutary check upon executive partiality; but undoubtedly, as a general rule, a divided executive is pernicious; and there is also at least an equal chance, that a senatorial, or council negative, may defeat as many proper nominations as it may prevent improper appointments.

The *independence* of the judiciary can be established only by an official tenure, during good behaviour, and by an adequate compensation for their services, not liable to diminution. A limited commission infallibly creates a dependence on the authority invested with the power of re-appointment; and a precarious compensation entails a miserable dependence upon that branch of the legislature which holds the public purse. The constitution of the United States effectually secures these advantages; for although the senate possesses a check upon the nomination of the president, yet this qualified negative is less injurious when applied to the Union at large, than in relation to a particular state; because the senators in Congress, representing their respective states, are more likely to be acquainted with the merits and character of the person nominated, than the executive, who being himself chosen from one particular state, cannot be expected to be so well informed as to the wants and wishes of the other states.

The federal judges, when once appointed, hold their offices during good behaviour, without any limitation as to age, and receive a fixed annual salary, not subject to diminution during their term of service. The salaries of these judges, like those of all other officers in the Union, whether attached to the general, or state governments, are *not* sufficient. Mr. Burke, in his " Reflections on the French Revolution," offers some pro-

found and eloquent observations on the pernicious prodigality of *underpaying* the public servants of a country.

The constitutions of Pennsylvania and Delaware
vest the appointment of the judges absolutely in the
executive; and contain every paper requisite to secure
a good judiciary, except an adequate salary; the constitution of New-York vests the choice of judges in the
council of appointment; those of New-Hampshire,
Massachusetts, and Maryland, in the governor and
council; those of Kentucky and Louisiana, in the governor, with the advice and consent of the senate; those
of Connecticut, Rhode-Island, Vermont, New-Jersey,
Virginia, North Carolina, South Carolina, Georgia, Tennessee, Ohio, and Mississippi, in the legislature. In
North Carolina, however, the governor possesses the
power of nomination.

In most of the states, the official tenure of the judges
is during good behaviour, with the exception of the limitation as to age, in New-Hampshire, and New-York;
for instance, in Massachusetts, Pennsylvania, Delaware,
Maryland, Kentucky, Virginia, North and South Carolinas, Tennessee, Louisiana, and Mississippi. In Connecticut and Rhode-Island, the judges are appointed
annually; which is a most lamentable provision, because
it renders the judges altogether dependent upon the
power which creates them; and what self-confidence can
men possess, who know that in the course of a few
months their term of office expires, and their re-appointment depends upon the mere pleasure of another body,
over whom they have neither control nor influence?
In Rhode-Island, the people have experienced the full
benefit of this absurd regulation; but the patriarchal
customs, and steady habits of Connecticut, *long* prevented her from suffering any very material injury from
this deformity in her political code; because it was a
matter of course, annually to reappoint the same man
as long as he lived, unless guilty of some flagrant misconduct. *Now,* however, Connecticut is beginning to
reap the fruit of this *ultra* democratic provision; and

bids fair to have all her institutions completely revo-
lutionized.

In Vermont, there is still greater danger of an undue
dependence of the judges on the legislature; for they
are not only elected annually, but the constitution adds,
" and *oftener*, if need be." An annual election of the
judiciary ought to satisfy democracy herself. In New-
Jersey, the judges of the superior court are chosen for
seven, and of the inferior court, for five years. By the
former constitution of Pennsylvania, the judges were
appointed for six years, but the present constitution has
had the wisdom to give them an official tenure during
good behaviour. In Georgia, the judges hold their
offices only three, in Ohio, seven years. It is, however,
matter of gratulation, that the judges of this country
are independent, as to official tenure, except in the
states of Connecticut, Rhode-Island, Vermont, New-
Jersey, Georgia, and Ohio.

The immutability of compensation, except as to increase, is essential to judicial independence. This is
secured to the judges in the constitutions of the United
States, Pennsylvania, Delaware, Kentucky, South Carolina, Georgia, Ohio, Louisiana, and Mississippi; and
indeed in every constitution made since the establishment of the federal government, in 1789, except that
of Tennessee, which only provides " that the judges
of the superior court shall, *at stated times*, receive a
compensation for their services, to be ascertained by
law;" a provision, which places the judges at the mercy
of the legislature, who, by giving or withholding an
adequate compensation, exercise a power little short of
life and death, according to the doctrine of old Shylock,
when he says, " You do take my life, if you do take the
means by which I live." The Tennessee constitution
has also another singular provision, namely, " that the
judges shall *not* charge juries with respect to matters of
fact, but may state the testimony, and declare the law."
This seems to be as much an extreme, one way, as
Lord Mansfield's doctrine of compelling the jury *not* to
intermeddle with the law at all, even when rendering a

general verdict, was an extreme the other way. At all events, the jury can never be injured by an able and dispassionate charge of an enlightened judge upon the facts of the case, more especially if they should be numerous and complicated.

In New-Hampshire and Massachusetts the judges are empowered by the constitution to give their opinion to the governor and council, on solemn occasions, and to the legislature on points of law. This provision is of doubtful policy; for it seems best that judges should never give their opinions in matters of law except from the bench. In England, indeed, they are occasionally called upon to deliver their opinions in the House of Lords; and some of the judges are themselves legislators, as temporal peers in parliament. But the separation of the great departments of government, the executive, legislative, and judicial, is not so accurately and extensively established in Britain as it ought to be. And, moreover, the occasional blending of these branches together is not so dangerous in the powerful and stable government of a constitutional and limited monarchy and an hereditary aristocracy as amidst the perpetual fluctuations of an elective democracy, where the only sure bulwark of individual liberty is to be found in the pure, unstained administration of justice to all parties in every question of property, person, and character.

In all the state constitutions, and in that of the United States, the judges are removable from their office by impeachment. In New-Hampshire, Massachusetts, Pennsylvania, Delaware, Maryland, Kentucky, Louisiana, and Mississippi, they are also removable by the governor, on an address of the legislature, for misconduct not sufficient to require impeachment. In New-Hampshire and Massachusetts the governor and council may remove, on the address of a majority of both houses; in Pennsylvania, Delaware, Maryland, Kentucky, and Mississippi, on the address of two-thirds of both houses; in Louisiana, on the address of three-fourths of both houses. During the session of Congress, in 1816-17, Mr. Sandford, a senator from the state of New-York, proposed to amend the constitution of the United States, by making the federal judges removable from office, on the vote of two-thirds of both houses of Congress, with the consent of the president.   This alarming innovation was not carried into effect.   Mr. King, senator from New-York, and Mr. Fromentin, senator from Louisiana, resisted the motion with great ability and force, and the senate negatived it by an overwhelming majority.

Such a provision endangers the independence of the judges; because, when party spirit runs high, it would not be difficult to obtain an address of a majority, or of two-thirds, or even of three-fourths of both houses of the legislature to the executive, to remove from office a judge, whose chief crime might be the belonging to a different political sect from that embraced by the dominant faction.   In general, the impeachment of the judges is framed by the Representatives, and tried before the senate or council; but in Maryland they may be removed for misbehaviour, on conviction in a court of law.   In Virginia, the impeachment of the judges of the general court is preferred by the house of delegates, and tried by the court of appeals; and that of the judges of the court of appeals is tried by the judges of the supreme court.   In North Carolina an impeachment of the judges may be framed by the assembly or grand jury, and tried by a special court appointed for the purpose.

The American judiciary, both state and federal, possesses an efficacy unknown to the courts of justice in other countries; I mean the power of bringing the validity of a law, a *statute*, passed by the legislature, whether of a single state or of the United States, to the test of the letter and spirit of a *written* constitution.   In Europe it has scarcely ever been contemplated to place any constitutional limits to the exercise of *legislative* authority.   In England, where the constitution has separated and designated the executive, legislative, and judicial departments of government, with greater precision than any other nation except the United States, the parliament is still considered paramount and absolute, and, says De Lolme, " can do every thing except make a man a woman, or a woman a man." And, although some of the judges have declared that a statute, made against natural equity, was void, yet it is generally laid down as a fundamental principle of English law, that no act of parliament can be questioned or disputed; that, in no case whatever can a judge oppose his own opinion and authority to the clear will and declaration of the legislature: his province is to interpret and obey the mandates of the supreme power of the state. Let the inconveniences of a statute be what they may, no judge, or bench of judges, can constitutionally dispense with them; their office is to expound, not make law; and, during the last hundred and fifty years, no instance has occurred of any English judge declaring an act of parliament void, on account of its being unconstitutional, or repugnant to the principles of reason or equity, or on any other ground.

But in the United States the people have established certain rights paramount to the power of the ordinary legislature; a precaution essential to security, and necessary to guard against the occasional triumph and violence of party, in a government *altogether* popular, elective, and representative. Without some such express provision settled in the original compact, as set forth in the written constitution, and constantly protected by the firmness and moderation of the judicial department, the equal rights of the minor party would probably be often disregarded in the conflicts for political power, and be sacrificed to the fury of a vindictive majority. No question can be made in these United States but that all legislative acts, contrary to the provisions of the constitution, ought to be null and void. The only inquiry is, if the legislature itself be a competent judge of its own constitutional limits; or the business of determining the constitutionality of a statute be the fit and exclusive province of the courts of justice?

If the legislature be left the unresponsible judge of its own constitutional barriers, the efficacy of this check is lost; for the legislature would incline to narrow down or explain away the provisions of the constitution, from the force of the same popular passion, or some considerations of expediency, which would lead it to overturn private rights, and invade the security of private property. The legislative *will* would then be the supreme uncontrollable law, as much with as without these constitutional limits and safeguards. Nor would the force of public opinion (the only restraint then left) be much felt or regarded; for, if public opinion were sufficient to check the tendency to mischief in governments, there would be no need of original limitations and constitutional restraints. But all experience teaches, that when powerful political rivalries prevail in the commonwealth, and parties are thoroughly disciplined and highly hostile, every measure of the legislative majority, however tyrannical and flagitious, is sure to receive the sanction of their constituents; and every step of the minor party will be equally approved of by their adherents, as well as indiscriminately rejected, misrepresented, and condemned by the voice and vote of the prevailing faction.

The courts of justice, therefore, which are organized with peculiar advantages, well calculated to exempt them, and their judicial proceedings, from the influence of faction, and to secure a steady and impartial interpretation of municipal law, are the most proper power among all the departments of government to keep the legislature within the limits of prescribed duty, and maintain inviolate the authority of the constitution. It is also an indisputable maxim in American politics, that the executive, legislative, and judicial branches should be, as far as possible, kept distinct and separate. The legislature ought not to exercise the powers of the executive or judiciary, except in clearly specified cases. An innovation upon this distribution of power tends directly to overturn the due balance of government, and introduce an unqualified despotism. But the exposition of the constitution is as much a judicial act, and requires the exercise of the same legal discretion, as the interpretation of a law, whether statute or common. The courts of justice are, indeed, bound to regard the constitution as a law of the highest nature—the supreme law of the land, to which every inferior or derivative legal regulation must conform and be obedient.

The constitution comes from the people in their character of plenary sovereignty, when defining the permanent conditions of the social alliance between the different states of the Union; and, therefore, to contend that the courts of justice must adhere implicitly to legislative acts, without regarding the provisions of the constitution, is to contend that the power of the agent exceeds that of the principal; and that the will of only one concurrent and co-ordinate department of *subordinate* authority ought to control the fundamental laws of the sovereign people. This judicial power of determining the constitutionality of statutes is necessary to preserve the equilibrium of the American government, and to prevent the usurpations of any one department upon the powers and privileges of the others. And of all the branches of government, in every free country, the legislative is most impetuous and powerful; whence the necessity of arming the executive with a negative, either absolute or qualified, upon the proceedings of the legislature. See some very ingenious reasoning in Montesquieu's Esprit des Loix, and a still abler disquisition in the Federalist, on the necessary *practical* separation of the executive, legislative, and judicial powers, from which it appears that the judicial power is the weakest of the three; and, as it is equally essential to the well-being of the commonwealth, to preserve entire the power of the judiciary, it ought *not* to be left exposed to the attacks of a popular legislature, without adequate means of a constitutional defence.

This is one reason why the judges in the state of New-York are constitutionally associated with the governor to form the Council of *Revision,* to revise all bills about to be passed into laws by the legislature; and this singular association, giving a kind of legislative power to the judiciary, renders some of the preceding observations less applicable to the constitution of New-York than to that of any other free government. Nevertheless, as a general principle of political economy, and its kindred science, municipal jurisprudence, it will be found that the right of expounding the constitution, as well as the statute law, is the most fit and effectual weapon by which the courts of justice can repel all hostile assaults, and guard against all unconstitutional encroachments upon their chartered claims and rights. Nor is there any danger that the establishment of this principle should exalt the judicial above the legislative power; for they are co-ordinate branches of government, and equally bound by the constitution; and if the judges should substitute caprice and arbitrary will for the exercise of sober discretion and rational judgment, they are *not* left, like the legislature, to the ineffectual control of public opinion; but are liable, by an express provision of the constitution, to be impeached for misconduct, and tried by the legislature; and, if convicted, removed from office.

The United States, and the separate states generally, acknowledge this power to reside in the judiciary; but, on the 29th of November, 1815, the Georgia house of representatives passed a resolution censuring their state judges for deciding the *alleviating* law; that is, a statute, passed by the Georgia legislature, prohibiting the use of any legal means for the recovery of debts, to be unconstitutional; and also denying to the judiciary the right of giving any opinion upon the constitutionality of legislative acts. This resolution is sufficiently flagrant and illegal; because it denies to a separate and co-ordinate branch of government a constitutional right, which has been acquiesced in, and *acted upon,* by the United States, by the other separate states, and by Georgia herself, heretofore; a right which, from the very nature of our republican institutions, appertains to the judiciary. But this outrageous resolution scarcely equals the usurping conduct of the Georgia senate, upon whose table, in November, 1815, was lying a bill to compel the judges to exhibit to the legislature all the rules of their courts; and to take away from the bar and judiciary the right of establishing any rules for their own government, unless they have first received the legislative sanction.

This is, at one stroke, cutting up by the roots the constitutional independence of the judiciary, and rendering the judges mere passive instruments of an arbitrary and overbearing legislature; which is, in fact, establishing the most dangerous, because the most unresponsible of all tyrannies. A single despot may be resisted, called to account, and punished; but a multitudinous despotism, composed of a numerous body of popular representatives, elected only for a short season, may, at any time, crush the liberties, and trample on all the political rights of the community, without control, and without punishment. Several of the leading members of the Georgia legislature pledged themselves never to cease their exertions until the omnipotence of the legislature was acknowledged; and they also contended that the constitution, whether state or federal, is *not* law, but merely the *will* of the people; which can only be known by the voice, resolution, and vote of its constitutional organ—the legislative assembly—which is, therefore, paramount in power and authority to every other department of government.

The judiciary of Georgia are sufficiently dependent by the tenure of their office, without any legislative encroachments upon their rights and privileges; for they are elected only for *three* years, and are removable by the governor, on the address of two-thirds of both houses. Now judges, who know that their re-election to office hinges upon the will and pleasure of their electors, at so short a distance, *cannot* feel themselves independent, and at liberty to act without regard to the opinions of those who may, or not, at their own discretion, re-appoint them to office; and the judges are equally at the mercy of the legislature, when two-thirds of the members can, by their mere address to the executive, remove them from office. It is vain, under such circumstances, to expect an impartial administration of justice. It is to be hoped that this encroachment upon the constitutional rights of the judiciary will not be imitated by any other state in the Union.

The question as to the power of trying the validity of statutes, by the provisions of the constitution, and of treaties with foreign powers, being lodged in the hands of the judiciary, could not well arise *prior* to the revolution, because the American colonies were partly governed by British statutes, the constitutionality of which the English judges themselves were not suffered to examine ; and consequently, *a fortiori*, no such authority would have been tolerated in the American judiciary. Nor were the colonial legislatures likely to permit their judges to determine the validity of statutes enacted by them. *After* the revolution, this power, although not given in express words to the judiciary, was claimed as necessarily arising out of the existence of a *written* constitution, the exposition of which, like that of any other law, can be safely entrusted only to the courts of justice. It would be destructive of all popular liberty, to permit the executive, both to explain and execute the law ; nor would it be less perilous to allow the legislature to expound as well as make laws.

The federal judiciary decide upon the validity of acts of Congress, state constitutions, and state statutes, by the provisions of the constitution, and foreign treaties ; but have no power to determine the validity of state statutes, by the provisions of state constitutions ; that power belonging exclusively to the state judiciary ; who likewise possess the right of trying the validity of state statutes and state constitutions, and acts of Congress, by the provisions of foreign treaties, and of the federal constitution. It is fair to infer, that *now*, the French and Dutch judiciary have power to try the legality of the acts of their respective legislatures, because France and the United Netherlands have each a *written* constitution ; whereas in England the judges have no such power, precisely because in that country there is no written constitution, by the letter and spirit of whose provisions the validity of acts of parliament may be examined and determined.

It is important that such a power should be lodged in the judiciary of every country ; because, although the *common law* possesses the peculiar faculty of adapting itself to the growth of the community, and of amending itself, in consequence of erroneous decisions being over-ruled by subsequent judges, or by the same judges, when better advised ; yet, a *statute*, if unrepealed, and if the statute book be never revised, makes an integral and permanent part of the municipal law ; and the experience of all history shows, that statutes are some-times passed amidst the heat and fury, the fire and smoke of party violence and wrong ; whence the neces-sity of that two-fold guard, which so happily exists in our state of New-York ; namely, the power of the judiciary to try the legality of each statute, by the provisions of the constitution ; and the occasional revi-sion of the statute book, in order to expunge those legislative acts, which the progress of time (the greatest of all innovators, as Lord Bacon calls him) the change of circumstances, and the growth of the community, might have rendered either obsolete, or impracticable, or pernicious.

The federal constitution provides, that full faith and credit shall be given in each state to the public acts, records, and judicial proceedings of every other state ; and congress may, by penal laws, prescribe the manner in which such acts, records, and proceedings shall be proved, and the effect thereof. This provision of the constitution has been seconded by an act of Congress, declaring, that the records, and judicial proceedings of each state, shall have *such* faith and credit given to them in every court within the United States, as they have by law or usage in the courts of the state whence these records are taken.

This provision of the federal constitution probably was intended gradually to reduce to one wholesome level of agreement the laws and judicial decisions of the several states of the union; in like manner as the law decisions of the different courts in England have been brought to agree, in all great legal and equitable principles, by the long-continued, and well-directed efforts of able, enlightened, and upright judges. " La diversité des loix civiles (say the distinguished jurists, who compiled the Napoleon Code,) est, comme la diversité de religion, ou de langage, une barrière, qui rend étrangers, l'un à l'autre, les peuples les plus voisins, et qui les empêche de multiplier entr'eux des transactions de tout genre, et de concourir ainsi mutuellement à l'accroissement de leur prospèrité." Indeed, nothing tends so directly to establish the whole community in social order, prosperity, and strength, as the prevalence of harmony and uniformity, in the judicial decisions of the different courts of justice throughout the country. Such a uniformity in the decisions of our courts, both state and federal, would prove the surest and firmest cement of a durable political union in the American confederacy.

The law decisions of the different English courts used to clash with each other, until the publication of the various *modern reporters* gradually brought the legal judgments of the King's Bench, Common Pleas, and Exchequer, to a salutary uniformity; which greatly augments the peace and security both of person and property; and consequently greatly increases the *national* prosperity and strength of the whole British people. Those persons who have diligently studied the law of England, as the foundation of American law, throughout all the states, know that for more than a century past, indeed ever since the complete establishment of the revolution, towards the close of the seventeenth century, a constant, deliberate, and upright administration of justice, founded upon the most rational principles, has prevailed in the different courts of the British empire.

If this provision of the constitution was intended to promote a uniformity of laws and judicial decisions throughout the United States, it has *not* succeeded; for there are actually no less than *three* different legal doctrines afloat in the different states, upon this single constitutional clause; in some states a *sister* judgment, that is, a judgment rendered in one of the sister states of the union is held to be of no more validity than a *foreign* judgment, that is, a judgment rendered in any state, or country, unconnected with our American confederacy: for example, France or England; in other states, a sister judgment is held equal to a *domestic* judgment, that is, a judgment rendered in the state, taking cognizance of the sister judgment; in other states again, a sister judgment is considered as a kind of *tertium quid*, as not quite so high as a domestic, nor quite so low as a foreign judgment.

Indeed, the discrepancy between the laws of our different states produces serious evil, by retarding and perverting the course of justice. For example, in some of the states an *attachment* law prevails, under which a person, absent from the state, may have a judgment rendered against him, that shall bind all his property all over the world, without any personal notice being given to him, or any opportunity afforded for him to defend the suit; which is a mode of proceeding contrary to the first principles of justice. This attachment law is in full force throughout all the New-England and many of the southern and western states, while the middle states hold it in abhorrence, as contrary to the principles of the common law, and endeavour to defeat its efficacy in their own tribunals. The laws in the southern and western districts of the union are generally very lax, and favour the debtor at the expense of the creditor. Nor are they very scrupulous in enforcing contracts. During the last winter, a gentleman of the city of New-York, intending to remove into the state of Kentucky, bargained with a servant, to pay his expenses of travelling thither, and a certain rate of wages for one year, the servant, on his part, contracting to remain with and serve his master faithfully during that period. On their arrival in Kentucky, the servant refused to live any longer with his master, because he could do better for himself. The master applies to the law for redress, and a Kentucky jury (which is, in truth, the judge, both of law and fact) *dissolves* the contract, on the ground that the servant was not acquainted with the nature of the western country when he made the bargain. The master was without redress, and, in addition to losing all the money expended in conveying his servant a journey of nearly one thousand miles, he was saddled with the costs of the suit instituted for the purpose of obtaining justice.

By parity of reasoning, a contract made in London or Paris ought not to be enforced in New-York, because the contracting party did not know the nature of New-York when he made the contract. Such a loose and vitious administration of municipal law argues and increases a very lax state of public morals and of public feeling in regard to the eternal distinctions between right and wrong.

A *crime* committed in one state is *not* punishable in another; for example, if a man steals a horse, or kills his neighbour, in the city of New-York, and crosses the ferry into the state of New-Jersey, he may escape punishment altogether, for the New-Jersey law takes no cognizance of a crime committed in the state of New-York, and the New-York law has no jurisdiction in the state of New-Jersey. Under such circumstances, the only chance of punishing the culprit lies in a provision of the federal constitution, which gives the citizens of each state all the privileges and immunities of citizens in the several states; and declares that a person charged in any state with treason, felony, or other crime, who flies from justice, and is found in another state, shall, on demand of the executive authority of the state whence he fled, be delivered up to be removed to the state having jurisdiction of the crime.

But so little efficacy has this constitutional provision in preventing the commission of crime, that it is the common practice of our citizens to pass from one state into another for the purpose of fighting a duel; which

O

done, the surviving parties return to the state which they had expressly left in order to commit a breach of the laws, and deride all notion of punishment. In the lapse of little more than one year, the late General Hamilton and his eldest son both crossed over the Hudson, to be killed on the New-Jersey shore, and their surviving antagonists have never been called to any legal account for destroying two of the brightest ornaments and surest bulwarks of the nation. " Thus Abner died as a fool dieth;" and the peerless Hamilton has added *his* name to swell the long and bloody muster-roll of those who have fallen victims at the shrine of the worst remnant of gothic barbarity and feudal homicide. The *Christian* requires no arguments to be urged against the prevailing practice of fashionable murder; for the Christian knows that man has no right, either to seek his fellow's life, or to throw away his own (except at his country's call), but that he is accountable alike for his own and his brother's blood to the God of the spirits of all flesh.

But to that portion of the community, which is not sufficiently under the control of religious feeling, this is a subject of deepest import. In the United States, in proportion to their population, more duels are annually fought than in any other nominally Christian country; and of these duels a greater number is fatal, owing to the superior practice and skill, and the more deliberate deadly coolness with which the Americans aim at each other's life. How many families are, at this moment, sorrowing, in hopeless misery, over the loss of a father, or a husband, or a brother, or a son, who either has been, or who might have become, not only the prop and support of his kindred house, but the defence and glory of his admiring country; who might have led her armies to victory, or shaken her senate with the thunders of his eloquence, or have built her up into a high and palmy state of national honour and strength, by the wisdom of his counsel! If the laws are ineffectual, and the guardians of those laws slumber on their post of duty, it is high time for the *moral* force of the country to be put in requisition; for the men of talents, character, property, and influence in the community to unite their efforts, to stand in the gap between the dead and the living, to stay the plague, and bid the destroying angel depart from our reformed land for ever.

It is all-important for the permanent security, repose, and prosperous condition of the United States, that the administration of justice, both civil and criminal, should be uniform and certain throughout the whole Union. Doubtless, the multiplication of our *state reporters* will, in process of time, exercise a very salutary influence in producing this desirable uniformity in the law decisions of the different state courts. But a scrupulous conformity to that clause of the constitution, which declares, " that full faith and credit shall be given to the public acts, records, and judicial proceedings of each state in any other state," would more certainly and more speedily produce this great effect; since the habit of receiving the judicial proceedings of each state in every other state, as equally binding with those of its own, would soon induce the different state courts to assimilate their law opinions, principles, and decisions with each other, as the legitimate effect of such constant and friendly intercourse. Whereas, by treating the judgments of sister states merely as foreign judgments, they necessarily tend to recede as far from any amicable assimilation with them as with the decisions of foreign courts. But nothing would so directly conduce to consolidate the strength, and prolong the duration of the American Union, as a uniformity in the legal provisions of the constitutions, statutes, and common law judgments of the several states composing that Union. Such a course of proceeding would, in the lapse of time, enable America to exhibit a more complete digest of municipal jurisprudence than the world has yet seen; because she has an opportunity of borrowing from the two great systems of legal civilization, the civil and the common law, whatever is best calculated to promote and protect the spirit of her own popular institutions, and to combine with what she thus borrows the lights of her own various and progressive experience in the different departments of human society, political, commercial, and scientific. This is the more important to strive after, because the science of *legislation* is yet, of necessity, crude and imperfect in this young and growing republic, owing to the want of long-continued political experience, and the extreme facility and latitude of empirical experiments upon the body politic, which the supreme sovereignty of so many separate independent republican states affords and encourages.

And it is full time that the people of this country should learn the necessity of *ballasting* the speculative projects of the sanguine, the credulous, the precipitate political innovator, with the cautious deliberation, the practical wisdom of the experienced, forecasting states-man, of the profound and enlightened judge. Then, indeed, might the whole federal Union be melted down into one living body of *national* peace, security, permanent prosperity, and power, by the gradual diffusion of a uniform system of municipal law over all the different confederated state sovereignties. It would not then be easy, even for the hydra-headed monster faction herself, to disentangle the warp and the woof which might be interwoven, thread upon thread, throughout all the texture of society.

The federal constitution provides, that no person held to labour or service in one state, under its laws, escaping into another, shall, in consequence of any law or regulation of that other state, be discharged from such service or labour, but shall be delivered up on claim of the party to whom such service or labour may be due. This provision enables the master of a runaway slave to claim him, even in a state, the municipal law of which has abolished or prohibited slavery, because the constitution of the United States is the supreme law of the land, to which all state laws must yield. Otherwise such fugitive slaves would be protected, because in all penal or criminal matters, municipal law permits no interference on the part of *local* law, and the *lex loci* not operating, even in civil cases, as on personal contracts, whenever its operation would clash with or contradict the provisions of municipal law. Ohio, who has prohibited the existence of slavery by her constitution, borders on all sides upon slave-holding states, from which runaway slaves often escape into her dominion ; and her reluctance, not to say absolute refusal, to give up such fugitives to their owners, has recently occasioned considerable heat and animosity between her and her neighbour Kentucky, who possesses a large body of slaves within her territory, and shows no inclination to diminish their number.

The constitution also provides, that *new* states may be admitted by Congress into the Union; but no new state formed within the jurisdiction of any other state, nor any state formed by the junction of two or more states, without the consent of the legislatures of the states concerned as well as of Congress. Congress has power to dispose of, and make all needful rules and regulations respecting the territory, or other property belonging to the United States; and nothing in the constitution shall be so construed as to produce any claims of the United States, or of any particular state. The United States shall guarantee to every state in the Union a republican form of government, and protect each of them against invasion; and on application of the legislature, or of the executive when the legislature cannot be convened, against domestic violence. Congress, whenever two-thirds of both houses shall deem it necessary, shall propose *amendments* to the constitution; or on the application of the legislatures of two-thirds of the several states, shall call a convention for proposing amendments; which in either case shall be valid, as part of the constitution, when ratified by the legislatures of three-fourths of the several states, or by conventions in three-fourths of the states as one, or other mode of ratification may be proposed by Congress; provided, that no amendment made prior to the year 1818 shall affect the provisions respecting the migration, or importation of persons into, or from the several states, and the imposition of capitation, or other direct taxes; and provided, that no state, without its consent, shall be deprived of its equal suffrage in the senate.

All debts contracted, and engagements entered into before the adoption of the constitution, shall be valid against the United States, under the constitution, as under the confederation. The constitution, and the laws of the United States, made in pursuance thereof, and all treaties made under the authority of the United States, shall be the *supreme law* of the land, and the judges in every state bound thereby, any thing in the constitution or laws of any state to the contrary notwithstanding. The senators and representatives in Congress, and the members of the several states legislatures, and all executive and judicial officers, both of the United and the several states, shall be bound by oath, or affirmation, to support the constitution; but *no religious test* shall ever be required as a qualification to any office, or public trust, under the United States.

The *amendments* already made to the constitution are, that Congress shall make no law respecting an establishment of *religion;* or prohibiting the free exercise thereof; or abridging the freedom of speech, or of the press, or the right of the people peaceably to assemble and petition government for a redress of grievances. A well regulated militia being necessary to the security of a free state, the right of the people to keep and bear arms shall not be infringed. No soldier shall in time of peace be quartered in any house without the consent of the owner; nor in time of war, but in a manner to be prescribed by law. The right of the people to be secure in their persons, houses, papers, and effects, against unreasonable searches and seizures, shall not be violated; and no warrants shall issue, but upon probable cause, supported by oath, or affirmation, and particularly describing the place to be searched, and the persons or things to be seized. No one shall be held to answer for a capital, or otherwise infamous crime, unless on a presentment, or indictment of a grand jury; except in cases arising in the land or naval forces, or militia, when in actual service, in time of war or public danger; nor shall any one be subject for the same offence to be twice put in jeopardy of life or limb; nor shall be compelled in any criminal case to be witness against himself, nor be deprived of life, liberty, or property, without due process of law; nor shall private property be taken for public use, without just compensation.

In all criminal prosecutions, the accused shall have a right to a speedy and public trial, by an impartial jury of the state and district wherein the crime was committed (which district shall have been previously ascertained by law), and be informed of the nature and cause of the accusation, be confronted with the witnesses against him, have compulsory process for obtaining witnesses in his favour, and have the assistance of counsel for his defence. In suits at common law, where the value in controversy exceeds twenty dollars, the right of trial by jury shall be preserved; and no fact tried by jury shall be otherwise re-examined in any court of the United States, than according to the rules of the common law. Excessive bail shall not be required, nor excessive fines imposed, nor cruel and unusual punishment inflicted. The enumeration in the constitution of certain rights shall *not* be construed to deny or disparage others retained by the people. The powers *not* delegated to the United States by the constitution, nor prohibited by it to the states, are reserved to the states respectively, or to the people. The judicial power of the United States shall not be construed to extend to any suit in law or equity, commenced or prosecuted *against* one of the United States, by citizens of another state, or by citizens or subjects of any foreign state. The electors shall *name* in their ballots the person voted for as President, and in *distinct* ballots the person voted for as Vice-President; but no person, constitutional ineligible to the office of President, shall be eligible to that of Vice-President of the United States.

It is a very important provision, which prescribes the mode of proposing and carrying into effect future *amendments* to the constitution, without hazarding a dissolution of the confederacy, or suspending the operation of the existing government. Accordingly, twelve additional articles were appended, as amendments to the constitution, within a few years after it first went into operation; and, in the year 1804, the amendment respecting the election of President and Vice-President was added. The amendment may be effected either on a recommendation from Congress whenever two-thirds of both houses concur in the expediency of such a measure; or by a mode which secures to the separate states an influence, in case Congress should neglect to recommend such amendments. Both these modes appear to be good: of the efficacy of the first the nation has had full experience, in the amendments already made. The second seems a fit mode, whenever the general government shall betray such symptoms of corruption as to render it expedient for the several states to exert themselves, in order to apply some radical and effectual remedy.

It is not easy to bestow too much praise upon this article of the constitution, which thus provides a safe and peaceable remedy for its own defects, as they may, from time to time, be discovered. A change of government, in *other* countries, is generally attended with convulsions that menace its entire dissolution, and portend scenes of horror and bloodshed that deter mankind from attempting to correct abuses, or remove oppressions, until they have become altogether intolerable—when a national explosion ensues that buries all the orders of the state beneath its ruins. Nor need it be apprehended that this salutary provision in the federal constitution will, *of itself*, produce instability in the general government; for the mode, both of originating and ratifying amendments directed by the constitution, must necessarily be attended with such obstacles and delays, as must prove a sufficient bar against light or frequent innovations.

Several amendments have been proposed by the States of Virginia, New-York, North Carolina, Massachusetts, New-Hampshire, Rhode-Island, and South Carolina, at different times, in convention: they are all collected in the 3d, 4th, 7th, and 8th volumes of the American Museum. Some of them appear to have been offered only *ex abundanti cautelá*, as security against misconstruction, or an undue extension of the powers vested in the federal government; while others seem to have been calculated to remedy some radical defects in the national system. Two other unsuccessful efforts to amend the constitution have been made since the publication of the American Museum; namely, one on the 12th of April, 1808, submitted by Mr. Hillhouse, a respectable senator in Congress from the state of Connecticut, to the senate of the United States. His propositions were many, and the speech enforcing them ingenious and acute. The chief amendment proposed was, in fact, a virtual abolition of the executive, as a separate branch of the American government, by reducing the President's term of service from four years to one, by lowering his salary, by transferring from him to the senate the power of appointing to and removing from office; and by annually choosing by ballot the executive from a given number of senators.

Mr. Hillhouse contended that many advantages would flow to the United States from this proposed alteration in the form and substance of their government. But, without minutely considering the various fallacies of this scheme, it is sufficient to observe, that the mere circumstance of blending together the executive and legislative departments would entail innumerable evils upon America, and speedily erect an unmitigated despotism upon the ruins of the republic. The practical as well as theoretic division of powers in a government into the three distinct departments of executive, legislative, and judicial, being the corner-stone of social liberty, and an orderly, upright administration of the commonwealth. Mr. Hillhouse's plan of amendment was rejected in the senate of the United States by a large majority.

On the 15th of December, 1814, a convention of delegates from the states of Massachusetts, Connecticut, and Rhode-Island, the counties of Cheshire and Grafton, in the state of New-Hampshire, and the county of Windham, in the state of Vermont, met at Hartford, in Connecticut, to propose amendments to the constitution. In order to accomplish which, they published a general view of the measures that they deemed essential to secure the Union against the recurrence of those difficulties and dangers which they thought arose from the radical defect of the constitution itself, aided by an unwise and impolitic administration of the general government. The amendments proposed were—*First.* That representatives and direct taxes should be apportioned among the several states included within the Union, according to their respective numbers of *free* persons, including those bound to serve for a term of years, and excluding Indians not taxed, and all other persons. *Secondly.* No new state shall be admitted into the Union by Congress, without the concurrence of two-thirds of both houses. *Thirdly.* Congress shall not have power to lay any *embargo* on the ships or vessels of the citizens of the United States, in the ports and harbours thereof, for more than sixty days. *Fourthly.* Congress shall not have power, without the concurrence of two-thirds of both houses, to interdict the commercial intercourse between the United States and any foreign nation, or its dependencies. *Fifthly.* Congress shall not make or declare war, or authorize acts of hostility against any foreign nation, without the concurrence of two-thirds of both houses, except such acts of hostility be in defence of the territory of the United States when actually invaded. *Sixthly.* No person, who shall hereafter be naturalized, shall be eligible as a member of the Senate or House of Representatives of the United States, nor capable of holding any civil office under the authority of the United States. *Seventhly.* The same person shall not be elected President of the United States a second time; nor shall the President be elected two terms in succession from the same state.

These resolutions were forwarded by the Hartford convention to the legislatures of the several states in the Union, by a majority of which they were rejected ; and, by those of New-York and Virginia, assailed with all the bitterness of reproach.

The *Federalist*, doubtless, is equal to any work, ancient or modern, in political philosophy, judicial wisdom, and profound, perspicuous, comprehensive reasoning ; but it plays the part of an *advocate* for the constitution of the United States, whose excellences it blazons forth with matchless ability, but whose radical defects it cautiously conceals from public view. The proof of this lies in the fact, that General Hamilton, the principal writer in this work, has left, in his own hand-writing, the draught of a constitution far more efficient than that which he praises so elaborately and ably, under the signature of Publius. The truth is, all the tendencies to weakness and disunion, in the frame and texture of the American governments were, from the beginning, manifest to his sagacity and genius. He had long observed that in the revolutionary war, the independence of his country was perpetually endangered by the imbecility of its government; and that for some years after the establishment of peace, in 1783, the loss of reputation, and the sacrifice of its best interests, flowed from the same source. He laboured, therefore, to erect a government of sufficient force and energy to protect and guide its own people at home, and secure reverence and honour in the eyes of foreign nations. And, in the general convention of 1787, he pressed, with all the weight of his stupendous talents, the necessity of adopting a more efficient form of government, as will fully appear if ever his most able and eloquent speech on that occasion shall be published. He drew the following outline of a plan of government for the United States, as better calculated than the present constitution to combine national strength with popular liberty.

First. The supreme *legislative* power of the United States of America to be vested in two different bodies of men ; one to be called the Assembly, the other the

Senate; who, together, shall form the legislature of the United States, with power to pass all laws whatsoever, subject to the negative hereafter mentioned. *Secondly.* The Assembly to consist of persons elected by the people to serve for *three* years. *Thirdly.* The Senate to consist of persons elected to serve *during good behaviour;* their election to be made by electors chosen for that purpose by the people; the states to be divided into election districts. On the death, removal, or resignation of any senator, his place to be filled out of the district whence he came.

Fourthly. The supreme *executive* authority of the United States to be vested in a governor, elected *during good behaviour,* by electors chosen by the people in the election districts; the governor to have a *negative* upon all laws about to be passed, and the execution of all laws passed; to have the direction of war, when authorized or begun; to have, with the advice and consent of the Senate, the power of making all treaties; to have the sole appointment of the heads or chief officers of finance and foreign affairs; to have the nomination of all other officers, including ambassadors to foreign nations, but subject to the approbation or rejection of the Senate; to have the power of pardoning all offences except treason, which he shall not pardon without the approbation of the Senate. *Fifthly.* On the death, resignation, or removal of the Governor, his authorities and functions to be exercised by the president of the Senate, until a successor be appointed. *Sixthly.* The Senate to have the sole power to declare war; the power to advise and approve all treaties; to approve or reject all appointments of officers, except the heads or chiefs of the departments of finance, war, and foreign affairs.

Seventhly. The supreme *judicial* authority of the United States to be vested in judges, to hold their office *during good behaviour,* with adequate and permanent salaries; the court to have *original* jurisdiction in all cases of capture; and an *appellate* jurisdiction in all causes, in which the revenues of the general government or the

citizens of foreign nations are concerned. *Eighthly.*
The legislature of the United States to have power to
institute courts in e ach state for the determination of
all matters of general concern. *Ninthly.* The governor,
senators, and all officers of the United States, to be
liable to impeachment for mal and corrupt conduct;
and on conviction, to be removed from office, and disqualified from holding any place of trust or profit.   All
impeachments to be tried by a court, consisting of the
chief justice or judge of the superior court of law of
each state, *provided* such judge hold his place during
good behaviour, and have a permanent salary. *Tenthly.*
All laws of the particular states, contrary to the constitution, or laws of the United States, to be void ; and
the better to prevent such laws from being passed, the
governor, or president of each state, shall be appointed by the general government ; and shall have a
negative upon the laws about to be passed in his state.
Eleventhly. No state to have any force, land or naval;
and the *militia* to be under the sole and exclusive direction of the United States ; who shall appoint and
commission the militia officers.

The chief points in which General Hamilton's scheme
differs from the present federal constitution are, the
superior permanency of the senate, the longer duration
and greater power of the executive, and the more
extensive control of the general government over the
separate states. But although General Washington approved of these provisions, as calculated to protect the
country from disorder and anarchy within, and from
impotence and contempt abroad, yet he would *not* venture to recommend so efficient a measure to the delegates assembled together in the national convention ;
and quoted the well-known saying of Solon, who, on
being asked if he had framed the best possible laws for
the Athenians ? answered, " *No,* but the best laws,
which the people of Athens, in their present temper
and situation, will bear."

The distinguishing features of all the American constitutions, as they now stand, are, that they make

every office *elective*, as contradistinguished from the *hereditary* tenures prevailing in monarchical and aristocratic forms of government; and also, that while they provide amply for the protection of personal liberty, and the property of individuals, which is, indeed, the only sure foundation of all good government, they do *not* sufficiently attend to promoting the two other great requisites of good government; namely, putting a strong and permanent disposeable force into the hands of the executive; and developing the national mind on a great scale, by instituting and encouraging large and liberal systems of general instruction. In most other countries, the government is all, and the people nothing; in the United States, the people are all, and the government nothing. The same general principle applies to all *paper* constitutions, which applies to all statute law; namely, that so perpetual is the fluctuation of human affairs, so various the modifications of which property is susceptible, so boundless the diversity of relations, which may arise in civil life, so infinite the possible combinations of events and circumstances, that they elude the power of enumeration, and mock all the efforts of human foresight. Whence, it is the duty of every wise and good government to abstain from too great a rage for multiplying statutes, and from too much minuteness in specifying the particular powers of the municipal departments. It is best, under the responsibility of impeachment for mal-conduct, to leave to the powers of government, more especially the *executive*, a sufficiently undefined latitude of authority, to enable them to adapt the necessary national measures to those exigencies which are continually arising; but which no paper constitution can possibly provide for, or foresee.

Having gone through a summary of the provisions of the United States constitution, it is proposed now to offer some general observations on the radical, the intrinsic weakness of the federal government; the necessity of gradually strengthening it, more especially in its executive branch; and, above all, the necessity of a vigorous administration of the general government upon *federal* principles, that is to say, the principles on which the constitution itself was founded and constructed. This *was* done by General Washington, throughout the whole course of his administration; and Mr. Adams appeared to begin his presidential career in the same track; but, towards its close, his policy assumed an aspect peculiarly strange and wayward, visionary and fantastic, turbulent and unsettled. Mr. Jefferson and Mr. Madison *avowedly* administered the general government altogether upon the democratic scheme, and set themselves stoutly to the task of undoing all that Washington had done; namely, disbanding the regular army, destroying the national army, annihilating the internal revenue, ruining the commerce of the country, breaking up the bank of the United States, and many other philosophical improvements in the art of misgoverning the commonwealth. Those who profess to be the intimate friends of Mr. Monroe, and to be acquainted with his sentiments, are labouring strenuously to cause the American people to believe that our new President intends to follow the good old federal plan of General Washington, and watch over the finances, encourage the commerce, nourish the navy, protect the army, cherish the liberty, prosperity, strength, and happiness of the nation at home, and secure its respect and influence abroad; that the miserable party distinctions of Federalist and Democrat are to be for ever abolished, and a political millennium to be established throughout the Union.

It is the more to be lamented, that the federal government should have been ever administered on democratic principles, because it is, in its essential conformation, *too weak* at once to balance the weight of the separate state sovereignties, to maintain its own steady dominion over all the portions of its immense Union, and to build up the nation at large, by certain steps, into a paramount power, influencing and controlling the greater potentates of the elder quarters of the globe. The great statesmen (led by Washington himself, and illumined by the transcendent genius of Hamilton) who framed the federal constitution, earnestly deprecated the notion of its being considered or conducted *as a democracy*. And many very elaborate and able arguments, founded on a careful induction from facts recorded in history, and resting on the basis of the most approved principles of political philosophy, were adduced to prove that the general government of the United States is *not* a democracy, but that care had been taken by the *General Convention*, which met at Philadelphia, in the year 1787, to infuse, as much as existing circumstances would allow, of the wisdom and energy of aristocracy, to temper and restrain the turbulence, the fluctuation, and the weakness of unbalanced democracy, which they emphatically declared to be the greatest misfortune that could be inflicted on any country.

These illustrious sages and practical politicians knew full well, that an uncontrolled democracy had destroyed Athens, and Carthage, and Rome, and the Italian republics of the middle ages, and the United Provinces of Holland: to which melancholy muster-roll of perdition may now be added the dominion of revolutionary France. They, therefore, feared that the prevalence of an *unchecked* democracy throughout the United States would consign to destruction the liberties, the wealth, the honour, the character, the happiness, the religion, the morals, the whole august fabric of public prosperity and private worth, which have, at some auspicious periods of their history, so peculiarly distinguished the national career of the confederated states of America.

It is the bounden duty of the *people* of every free country to watch over and preserve their own liberties, by keeping the declarations and measures of their rulers within the bounds of delegated dominion, prescribed by the letter and the spirit of the national constitution. And it is equally the duty of the *government* of every free country to guard against all encroachments upon the liberties of the people; to encourage the equal and impartial administration of justice; to promote the best interests of learning; to foster the arts and sciences; to quicken the activity of agriculture, manufactures, and commerce, and every species of productive industry and skill; to reverence and aid the progress of pure religion and sound morals, in all the various denominations of religious belief, and throughout all the classes of the community; in a word, to labour unremittingly to render the people prosperous and happy at home, respected, feared, and courted abroad.

In order to accomplish these great purposes, it is one, among many, of the indispensable duties of the government to *exclude* all *foreigners* from any *political* interference or influence in the affairs of the nation. They should be protected equally with the natives in all the pursuits of *private* industry and enterprise, but should never be permitted to lay their unhallowed hands upon the ark of the national government; to invade the recesses of the executive cabinet; to violate the sanctity of the temple of legislation, or to polute the ermine of justice in the tribunals of the country. All men, unless they are unsound at the heart's core, cling with fond attachment to the land that gave them birth, to its hills, and dales, and woods; to its people, government, and laws; to all the associations, physical and moral, that exercise the strongest dominion over the human mind. All *such* associations, prejudices, and predilections, every *honest* foreigner necessarily carries with him into *American* office; into the service of a country, whose social institutions, taken altogether, have no parallel in the history of the world. If a foreigner does *not* love his own native country, does not desire her well-being and prosperity, what *kind* of heart has he? Can a traitor at home be faithful abroad? Can one, who aims the assassin's knife at the vitals of his own parent country, be fitted to uphold the great national interests of a stranger land? Are unnatural hatred, dastardly revenge, and cannibal malignity, to be mistaken for lofty patriotism, comprehensive wisdom, and unblenched integrity?

It is indeed mere madness and political suicide, in *any* and in *every* country, to suffer *foreigners* to have a political vote; to permit them to elect or be elected to *any* office in the state, from that of the chief executive of the whole nation down to the lowest ministerial officer in the obscurest hamlet of an obscure district. It is quite enough that a foreigner be protected in his person, his property, his reputation, his individual efforts in his calling, by the equal administration of justice dealt out to him in common with all the other inhabitants of the community. But every country ought to be *exclusively* governed by its own *native* talent and property. In every nation that arrogates to itself the proud prerogative of being an independent substantive power, its own *native* warriors should lead their armies; its own *native* heroes should bear their naval thunders over every sea; its own *native* statesmen should guide the councils, regulate the finances, administer the government of their country; its own *native* judges should dispense the streams of law, justice, and equity throughout all the land; that the people, growing up under the shelter of the talent, property, and character of their natural guardians, may, through a long series of years, advance in prosperity, intelligence, wealth, and power, until they become the bulwark and ornament of a surrounding world. Let America, in the day of her exaltation, remember the advice of Rome's best poet:

> " Tu regere imperio populos, *Romane*, memento;
> Ilæ tibi erunt artes ; pacisque imponere Morem,
> Parcere subjectis, et debellare superbos."

General Washington administered the government of the United States with a practical efficiency and wisdom peculiarly calculated to render the country prosperous at home, and respected abroad. Owing to variofis untoward causes, the chief of which, however, was the entire inefficacy of the old *confederation of the states*, this country was in the most deplorable condition when President Washington first took upon himself the administration of the federal government, in the year 1789. The whole nation stood upon the verge of dissolution; all the national movements *at home* were full of disorder and confusion, and *abroad* full of weakness and folly; the finances were dilapidated; the commerce annihilated; the manufactures sinking; the agriculture depressed; an internal faction availed itself of and increased every domestic tumult and distress, in order to lay prostrate all the wholesome restraints of legitimate government and effective laws; the great body of the people themselves were rushing headlong into revolt and instruction against all the lawful authorities, both state and continental.

Are not the knowledge and remembrance of all these evils so many additional incitements to cling to and protect the *federal union?*—that mighty remedy which was found for the healing of all these national disorders —*that federal union* which gave form and pressure, a body and a soul, life, health, and spirit, strength, beauty, and power, to the disjointed, perishing members of these United States—*that federal union* which, if preserved, cherished, *and progressively strengthened,* cannot fail to build up the whole extent of this vast continent into imperial magnificence, wealth, and power;— protecting, exalting all its own citizens and subjects; and commanding the respect of all other nations;—*that federal union,* which, if once dissolved, ensures the breaking up of the foundations of civil order, peace, and safety, over all the range of this extensive territory; ensures a perpetuity of the anarchy, civil war, carnage, and desolation, that in the elder ages of the world deformed the fair face of the Grecian commonwealths; and which, in a more recent period, fastened upon all the Germanic empire, and on nearly the whole circumference of continental Europe, an entire century of uninterrupted hostilities, with all their train of attendant horrors and unavoidable anguish.

From the innumerable evils of its condition, this country was at that time preserved by the federal constitution, administered by the integrity and discretion of Washington; borne onward, and guided by the paramount dominion of the genius of Hamilton.

These great *practical* statesmen combined the personal liberty and security of the individual citizen with an effective administration of the national government; with an apt disposition of the public force; with the levying, discipline, and obedience of a regular army; the creation and support of an heroic navy; the collection of a productive and well-distributed internal revenue; the production and encouragement of religious ordinances and moral duties; the multiplication of the means of acquiring, preserving, and enjoying property; the general diffusion of peace and order, of civil and social habits, manners, and properties, throughout the United States.

These heroes and sages saw that no man has any *legitimate* qualification for office, except the possession of integrity, talents, and knowledge, both speculative and practical; that wherever these qualifications are found, in whatever age, or calling, or condition of life, they ought to be the unquestionable passports to all the offices of public honour, trust, and profit;—that every nation must be perilously situated, which, either through ignorance, or through the madness of party rage, shuts the gates of public service against its citizens who are most illustrious in wisdom, venerable in virtue, and respectable in wealth; which condemns for ever to the shades of retirement and privacy that weight and energy of character, so peculiarly fitted to establish, and diffuse over all the earth, their country's strength and glory; which industriously places the helm of government in the hands of men of low education, of illiberal habits, of narrow views, of sordid occupations, of visionary brains, of cold, unfeeling, selfish hearts and dispositions.

These lights and beacons of their age knew that by the fatal facility of changing the form and aspect, the body and substance of the *national* policy, as often, as much, and in as many ways as might seem expedient to the floating fancies of moon-struck, miserable politicians, the whole chain and continuity of the state must be for ever broken;—all the golden links of civilized existence, which bind together the succeeding generations of the human race, must be torn asunder for ever, and the ages of men be no more than the swarms of flies on a summer's day;—no more than the fleeting family of leaves that is scattered along the sky by the violence of the autumnal blast.

These great architects of their country's honour showed, by the whole series of their public conduct, how vastly preferable is that *practical* administration of government which builds up to that *theoretic* policy which destroys a country; that which adorns to that which deforms a nation ; that which enriches to that which impoverishes a people; that which whitens every sea with the commercial canvass to that which drains the streams, and dries up the sources of trade ; that which sends forth a navy, full freighted with Columbia's glory, to that which dismantles all the ships of war, and consigns their keels to the dry docks of destruction ; that which establishes a permanent system of finance, by a well-arranged internal taxation, to that which rests all the revenue of a nation upon the precarious basis of duties on foreign commerce.

" *Fortunati Ambo* * si quid *mea pagina possit*,
Nulla dies unquam memori vos eximet ævo."

And let it be remembered, as an additional incitement for all honest men to rampire the Union round about with their bodies, as with a living wall, and guard it from danger, that calamitous as was the state of things in this country, under the crazy auspices of the *old confederation*, the condition of the American people would be infinitely more calamitous, if the *federal union* were now to be dissevered ; and this vast continent, with its recently added dominion in the west, were to be split up, and shattered into numerous unconnected puny sovereignties, which could not fail to become the foul and fruitful sources of innumerable intestine broils. Better, far better would it be for these United States to endure an entire century of *foreign* war; or to labour fifty years

---

* Washington and Hamilton.

under the burden of *domestic maladministration*, than by severing the federal Union into a multitude of petty principalities, to entail upon all the extent of the northern continent of America the prevalence of *foreign* factions, French, Russian, and British, perpetually interfering with, and confounding all their *home* movements and measures; and, above all, to ensure a perpetuity of *feudal* anarchy and brigandage; of castellated feuds; of partisan warfare; of hereditary hostility; of arbitrary incarceration; of inquisitorial torment; of military execution; of private assassination; of public pillage; of universal oppression, and all the calamities incident to afflicted humanity, when *force* and *fraud* are the arbiters of right and wrong.

It is a *fact* which should never be forgotten, that the United States, during the period of *eight* years, under the guidance of *Washington's* administration, were raised from the lowest point of national depression, penury, and disgrace, to an exalted eminence of national elevation, riches, and honour. The *public* credit, which had been annihilated, was revived; *private* confidence, which had been extinguished, was renewed; commerce, which had long languished in indolence and despair, spread its active enterprise over the whole globe; the *national* debt, which had been considered as for ever sponged, and the public creditors, in consequence, defrauded, was funded, and in the full course of liquidation; a well-adjusted and a growing *internal* revenue was collected, without pressing upon, and impeding the progress of productive labour; industry, sobriety, good order, moral decency, and wealth, were substituted in the room of idleness, intemperance, tumult, profligacy, and poverty; *peace* was established and maintained effectually and sincerely, with all the world; *native* talents and virtue were sought for, brought forward, and raised into high official authority and trust; the national honour and influence were sustained at home, by a strict administration of justice, dealt out impartially to every individual in the community, and the national dignity was upheld abroad, by the capacity, wisdom, and courage of its diplomatic representatives in foreign courts.

America presented to the eyes of all other nations a spectacle unparalleled in the history of the human species; an infant republic, the growth of yesterday, outstripping countries white with the hoar of unnumbered ages, in population, wealth, and power; in arts and arms; in reputation, authority, and influence; and the elder sovereigns of Europe, the great, rival, primary, contending powers, vied with each other in professions of esteem, in proffers of friendship, in the wooings of alliance to the new-born dynasty of this western world.

All these wonderful achievements of national good, were the results of only *eight* years of a *wise* and *practical* administration of the federal government.

It is the more necessary to lay the foundations of government broad and deep, since every *new* government is of necessity *weak*, precisely, because it *is* new. General Hamilton was so well aware of this important truth, that he laid before the *general convention*, as stated in the preceding pages, in the year 1787, a much stronger scheme of government than the *federal constitution*, which was ultimately adopted. But Washington's prudence or timidity prevailed over the intrepid sagacity of Hamilton; and the present federal constitution was established. The rejection of Hamilton's plan, and the adoption of a feebler frame of national government, is the more to be regretted, because, every new government founded on principles of personal and social liberty, *must* be feeble; and stand in need of a very firm and vigorous administration; until time has rendered its authority venerable, and fortified its power by giving it an opportunity of growing up, and mingling with the feelings and habits of the people.

This simple but momentous truth may be illustrated by reference to the history of Britain, and of the United States. For a long period after the revolution of 1688, which placed William of Orange on the British throne, so slender was the confidence of the people of England in the stability and credit of their government, that the

Chancellor of the Exchequer of that day, *Montagu,* the father of public credit in England, could not raise a very small sum, by way of loan, without taking the Lord Mayor of London by his side, as the guarantee for government; and going, cap in hand, from house to house, and from shop to shop, requesting to borrow a hundred pounds, or even a less sum. And for the money thus laboriously raised in small parcels, their best public securities bore an interest of *twelve* per cent.; and the paper of the Bank of England was at a discount of *twenty* per cent. Whereas, for a period of twenty-five years, at the close of the 18th and beginning of the 19th century, the British government was enabled to raise loans amounting in the aggregate to *three thousand millions of dollars,* at an average of less than *five* per cent. interest; and during almost all those years, she maintained a state of unexampled warfare with nearly the whole of continental Europe, arrayed under the banners of revolutionary France.

The American government, about *forty* years after the establishment of the federal constitution, during the war with England, commenced in 1812, and closed in 1815, could *not* raise so insignificant a sum as *sixty millions of dollars,* by way of loan, although they gave in *bonus* and interest above *twenty* per cent. for what they borrowed. The paper of the southern banks was depreciated at least *twenty-five* per cent.; and the banks generally throughout the Union, excepting those at Boston, stopped paying *specie* for their own notes. Before *two years* of the war were expired, the administration of the United States were literally bankrupted, both in men and money : no one in the whole community would lend them a single dollar; nor would a single individual *voluntarily* enrol himself in their armies, so that they had actually prepared statutes for Congress to pass, enabling them to raise money by requisitions and forced loans, and to levy men by the French system of *conscription,* when the return of peace arrested these deathblows to all the popular institutions and republican liberties of the United States of America. A memorable practical comment this upon the inherent imbecility of the federal constitution; and affording a national tribute of honour to the prophetic sagacity of Hamilton.

The power of a government must always depend upon the quantity of men and money which it has at its own disposal and command; the mass or surplus capital floating in the community, and the confidence of the people in the wisdom, and their ready obedience to the directions, of their rulers; and *not* on the extent of territory, or the huge size of an immense population. The empire of China is spread over a vast surface, and supposed to contain *two hundred millions* of people; and yet so little disposable force, in men and money, has the Chinese government at command, that it exercises little or no influence over foreign nations; less, indeed, than is exercised by Holland, or Sweden, or Portugal, or any other of the smaller third and fourth-rate sovereignties of Europe. Now, influence over other potentates is the guage of a *nation's* respectability and power; in like manner as the influence of an *individual* over the interests, passions, and prejudices of his fellow-citizens, is the measure of that individual's power.

The general government of the United States has *too little* disposable force at command; it has neither an army nor a navy sufficiently numerous and extensive; its public revenue is too scanty, and too precarious; and it never can depend upon the *long-continued* support of the popular favour for enabling it to prosecute any permanent measures of enlarged and liberal policy. Being altogether a *representative republic*, it is obliged to exist too much by exciting and following the passions and prejudices of the multitude; to *control* and *regulate*, which is the bounden duty of every wise and upright government, since the ignorance and violence of the multitude have an invariable tendency to defeat the execution of every intelligent and long-sighted national scheme. If the American government oppose the hasty clamours of a misguided populace, the officers of that government will soon be converted, by dint of universal suffrage, into private citizens; and the Union is of course condemned to a perpetual oscillation of political movements.

It is *not* in the ordinary course of human affairs for such a state of things to be *permanent*; and it is to be apprehended, that the present general government of the United States will either assume a *new form*, or (what is much more desirable) will retain its *name*, but gradually become more stable and efficient, by fixing its rule upon the broad and firm foundations of *property* and *talent*; and, by progressively augmenting the power of the executive, enable it to mould the feelings, habits, and manners of the people to its own growth in strength and influence; and thus render the national government secure at home and respectable abroad. Indeed, in all popular and free governments, it is safer and better silently and gradually to devolve upon the executive those powers which experience proves it expedient to lodge there, than to confer upon it large and extensive authorities by written law; because that government is always best fitted to promote the prosperity and happiness of a nation, which has gradually grown up with and fashioned itself according to the feelings and interests of the people.

The experience of the past, in the history of nations, is the only safe guide to our reasonings upon future events; and that experience seems to teach us, that in process of time, the United States will run the same career as other sovereignties have run; that in the course of necessity and experiment they will gradually discover and adopt that system of government (*in practice* as well as in theory) which is best suited to the genius of their people, and best calculated to wield to advantage their great and growing resources. Their constitution may, eventually, be shaped in accordance with the developement of all those great and shining qualities and faculties which go to the formation of daring and elevated characters; and which call into existence the exertions of legislative wisdom, and the achievements of heroic valour;—all emanating from a system that places and permanently fixes the helm of government in the hands of the men of talent and property, as the only safe and legitimate sources and guardians of all political power.

The *materials* for making a great and powerful nation are all-abundant in the United States. They only wait the gradual growth of an energetic government, and its administration by sagacious and active statesmen. The vast extent of territory, the general salubrity of the climate, the natural fertility of the soil, and variety of its productions; the unparalleled capabilities of the country for commerce, owing to its long line of sea-coast, its numerous harbours, and its internal navigation; the intelligence, spirit, intrepidity, and enterprise of the people generally, are all admirably adapted to establish a system of political order and regulation, which, by unfolding and directing to the pursuit of their proper objects the energies of the people, in all the various classes of the community, shall render America a high and a mighty nation, protecting and rendering prosperous her citizens at home, and claiming and enforcing the respect and reverence due to her exalted moral and political rank from the other powers of the world.

The tendency of the general government to acquire strength at the expense of the state sovereignties was evident during all its different administrations, until the course of policy that eventuated in the late war began to alarm and alienate the more commercial states. When first established, the general government was looked upon as a bond of union, for certain specified purposes, between so many sovereign independent states; but the sovereignty and independence of the separate states were, by degrees, almost lost sight of, and the government, which had been collateral, came to be viewed as the principal. Men of talents, from all parts of the Union, turned their eyes to the seat of the national government as the field of their ambition, until the measures of that government reminded the separate states of their individuality, and that there were rights and powers which they had *not* surrendered. The consequence was, that the state governments immediately rose in importance, and the state legislatures, which had gradually sunk into objects of derision, received important accessions of strength in men of talents, who withdrew from the national legislature, to rally round their native states. And it more than once happened, during the late war, that the government of a single state placed itself across the path of the general government, and arrested its movements in that quarter.

The leading characteristics of the political and legal institutions of the United States at present are—*First*, The extreme elevation of the democracy or popular sovereignty of the country, and the corresponding depression of its talent and property in the scale of national influence. *Secondly*, The want of *permanency* in official station, arising from the *elective* nature of the executive and legislative, and, in some instances, of the judicial departments, and the rapid changes of the public servants. *Thirdly*, The very general diffusion of elementary intelligence, but the too scanty portion of very high or profound acquisitions throughout the community ; whence the American people, *individually*, are more adroit, more skilful, more enterprising, than the corresponding classes of society in Europe ; but the *aggregate* nation, as put in motion and directed by the government, is *not* so prompt and efficacious, because the too frequent mutations of office prevent the possibility of acquiring sufficient knowledge and power to enable the government to put in requisition, and call forth into active and *long-continued* exertion, all the resources of the commonwealth ; whereas, in Europe, although the mass of the people are, *individually*, less intelligent and less enterprising than the corresponding population of the United States, yet, in consequence of the greater permanency of office, the larger accumulation of family wealth, the more comprehensive education of the liberally instructed, and the stricter obedience and subordination of all ranks of society, the government is enabled to make a wider display and a more protracted exhibition of *national* power and strength, than it is possible for the American government to accomplish under the same or similar circumstances.

Nevertheless, it will be much easier for the American government to become as powerful and efficacious as those of Europe, and for American statesmen to acquire as much learning and political information as those of Europe, than for the European population to become as intelligent and enterprising as that of the United States; and all the world knows, that a powerful and active population is the great and effective enginery by which a statesman is enabled to aggrandize his country—is that lever of Archimedes, by which the universe itself is moved.

It is peculiarly incumbent on the people of this continually widening country, to examine the political history of the world, with a view to ascertain how far *any* nation, ancient or modern, has approximated in its social institutions towards the union of the *three* great requisites of a good government; that is to say—*First,* The personal liberty of individuals. *Secondly,* A strong and permanent power always at the disposal of the executive. *Thirdly,* An ample developement of the national mind, by a system of large and liberal education.

Such an inquiry belongs, emphatically, to the province of *political philosophy,* which is not sufficiently studied in these United States. In the most splendid era of the Athenian government the people were suffered to run riot into turbulence and anarchy, but they enjoyed *no* real liberty; the executive and effective ephemeral magistrate possessed no permanent, no effectual power; the national mind, indeed, was exhibited in most dazzling magnificence, and has left imperishable monuments of strength, elegance, taste, and splendour, in poetry, the fine arts, eloquence, history, and philosophy, for the admiration and imitation of all future ages. Republican Rome, while she continued aristocratic, preserved for several centuries a strong disposable power in the hands of her executive government, which mainly enabled her to achieve the conquest of the world; but she did *not* allow much individual liberty to the people, nor sufficiently develope the national mind, except for the purposes of *war* and *politics*. General literature and science were never pushed to any very great perfection under the Roman government, whether consular or imperial. As soon as she widened into a democracy, the whole commonwealth was torn to pieces by the fury of contending factions, whose party violence speedily paved the way for the establishment of a military despotism, that hushed into dread repose alike the voice of liberty and every effusion of exalted manly intellect.

In these United States the personal liberty of individuals is amply secured, both by the several constitutions and by the laws of the country, in its federal capacity, and in its state sovereignties ; but the power of the executive government is *not* sufficiently stable or strong, either in its federal head or in its state supremacies ; nor is the national mind sufficiently unfolded, either by liberal systems of public education, or by the discerning patronage of a munificent government. The British government is prevented from uniting in itself all the three requisites of excellence, by the remains of an hereditary feudal aristocracy, giving to a few overgrown families too much habitual influence and authority, and retarding the full expansion of intellect and power in the middle and lower orders of the people. It wants, as Lord Chatham said, a greater infusion of life's blood from the vigour of those men to whom Providence has given the intrinsic qualities of genius and courage, but from whom he has withheld the fictitious advantages of birth, rank, and fortune.

Lord Hardwicke undertakes to prove, that, although governments ought to be calculated with a view to the infirmities of those who govern, yet it is to be remembered, that *resistance* on the part of the governed should *not* be easy, and that *no form* of government can possibly be long continued, unless a high degree of confidence and power be reposed in it. Every form of government, whether monarchical, or aristocratic, or democratic, is, indeed, liable to abuse, but ought not, therefore, to be exposed to ruin. Let the form of government be ever so unrestrained, let it be a complete democracy, yet resistance to its operations ought to be difficult. For, if not, men might be inflamed by slight faults, by personal affronts, by private sufferings, to disturb the peace of their country, and involve the whole community in all the horrors of confusion, violence, and blood. A man's fears always bear proportion to his hopes; and one kind of passion, or weight of considerations, is balanced by another. In times of social order, and an upright administration of government, the *laws* ought to be sufficiently strong to deter men, moved by ambition or resentment, by private and partial affections, from erecting the standard of resistance and revolt. Nor is it to be apprehended, that in a *free* country, if the constitution be affected, if tyrannical designs be openly avowed, and supported by injustice, good men will be deterred from eventually resisting. The laws, by inspiring caution, however, will retard resistance, until it be fully ripened into action; so as to facilitate and secure its consequences; but in such a juncture of affairs, when men are roused by a love of liberty, order, and the common good, arguments addressed to private fears will *not* be able to weigh down the force of public affections.

A government should never be founded upon the notion, that those who are entrusted with power are of necessity more likely to abuse their authority than some of the particular persons, who owe it allegiance, are prone to endeavour to change or subvert that government. Such a notion is destructive of all systems of human law; because it supposes an *expediency* of weakening those strong sanctions which have been employed in every civilized country, to give them their due force and operation. The checks upon government should be altogether of *another* kind; they should consist in keeping the balance of the separate departments as even as possible; by forming every estate in the constitution, the executive, legislative, and judicial, a complete control upon each other. But it is the extreme of absurdity and danger to think of leaving the least strength or temptation to *individuals*, to resist or control the government itself.

Such a notion is also inconsistent with the nature of *law*, in two other points of view; *first*, as implying an error in *theory*; namely, that a lawgiver, when framing a scheme of government, should pay as much attention to its *possible* dissolution as to its *necessary* support; and instead of securing obedience and perpetuity to it, by the strongest sanctions which wisdom can devise or justice will admit, ought to weaken those sanctions, in order to provide for cases which are out of his reach, and which must be left to themselves; because their very happening implies a dissolution of both law and government. *Secondly*, as such a notion implies an error in *fact*; namely, that a law for punishment, or a law for indemnity, *can* operate in times of civil disorder and revolution, as in times of peace and obedience, either to create terror or afford protection. It implies, that the legislature must provide for cases of extreme necessity and dissolution; and thus, in effect, *enlarge* the right of private judgment respecting those cases, by taking off the strongest checks to private resistance. The laws of a free country should be so poised, and balanced, that a justifiable and *national* resistance, such as that of England, at the revolution of 1688, and that of the United States in the revolution of 1776, should *not* be attended with too much difficulty and terror.

Indeed, generally speaking, when those who are entrusted with the executive power have abused the design, or exceeded the limits of their trust, a weakness in the hands of government follows, which disables it from exacting the legal forfeitures that were originally established for the security of its power. The experience of all history proves, that very little protection is derived from the operation of law amidst the tumults of civil commotion; *leges inter arma silent*. When the troubles of Greece ceased by the surrender of Athens to the Lacedemonian arms, at the conclusion of the Pelopponnesian war, the *thirty* tyrants exercised cruelties against those who opposed their administration of government, unknown, not only to the municipal laws of Athens, but to those laws which cemented the general union of the Grecian states. In Rome, the proscriptions of Sylla, and of the second triumvirate, Augustus, Anthony, and Lepidus, were contrary to the genius, the ancient policy, and all the legal institutions of the commonwealth, although well accommodated to the situation and interests of those usurping demagogues, who had risen into absolute power upon the ruins of the republic. In Florence, also, the banishment and entire extirpation of numerous families were the frequent modes of proceeding, during the troubles which so perpetually shook the Italian republics in the middle ages. And in revolutionary France, the assassin's knife, and the guillotine, superseded altogether the use of the French municipal code, and of the law of nations; nay, even of the law of *nature* itself.

All these violent measures were resorted to in particular instances of civil commotion or usurpation, according as one or another faction prevailed, but were *not* derived from any permanent law of policy established in the respective countries, nor grounded upon the accustomed legal punishment of stated crimes. In fact, no correct inference *can* be drawn from the accidental severities of civil violence, against the equal, regular, and peaceable administration of justice.

Nevertheless, after all that can be said or written upon this subject, it should be remembered, that the *form* of government, like every other created thing, must always be *relative*, must always bear a close relation to the existing circumstances of the country governed. In every *free* country, the form of government must always be the result of, and adapted to, the feelings, affections, and habits of the people; who would soon break up any political establishment *opposed* to such habits, affections, and feelings; and therefore, if an hereditary monarchy, an hereditary aristocracy, and an hereditary transmission of property, have been found well suited to the feelings and habits of the people of

England, experience has fully shown than an *elective* executive, an elective senate, and a general distribution of property, are equally well suited to the affections and habits of the people of the *United States.* And as long as those habits and affections shall continue to be republican and democratic, will the government continue to be a *representative republic ;* nor would it be other than folly, and madness, and crime, in any politician to wish it different. Where are the *materials* in the republican equality of the United States to be found, out of which may be composed an hereditary sovereign, an hereditary house of peers, the vast accumulation of entailed property, throughout a series of ages; and the establishment of a national church, throughout all the ranks and gradations of a well-compacted hierarchy?

Mr. Jay, late Chief Justice of the United States, in examining the question, whether or not an American *state* can be sued in the federal courts, draws with great precision the broad line of demarcation between the nature and jurisdiction of the American and European governments. This venerable statesman and incorruptible patriot says, that "*prior* to the revolution, all the country now possessed by the United States was a part of the dominions belonging to the British crown. All the land in this country was then held, mediately or immediately, by grants from that crown, of which all the American people were subjects, and owed allegiance to the king; from whom flowed all the civil authority exercised here. They were fellow-subjects and one people; who at the revolution in 1774, appointed their general or national delegates in Congress. The declaration of Independence, in 1776, found the American people, throughout all the colonies or provinces, *already* united for *general* purposes; and at the same time providing for their more domestic concerns, by *state* conventions and other temporary arrangements.

" From the crown of Great Britain, the *sovereignty* of the United States passed to the American *people ;* and the unappropriated lands belonging to that crown passed *not* to the people of the colony, or state within whose limits they were situated, but to the *whole* people of the United States. Thirteen *state* sovereignties emerged from the principles of the revolution, combined with local convenience and considerations; but the *people* still considered themselves in a national point of view, as *one* people; and managed their national concerns accordingly. Afterward, in the hurry of war, and in the warmth of mutual confidence, they made a *confederation* of the states the basis of a general government; and more recently, in their national and collective capacity, the people established the present federal constitution; in establishing which they acted *as sovereigns* of the whole country, and declared that the *state* governments and constitutions should be bound by, and conform to, the constitution of the United States. Every *state* constitution is a compact, made by and between the citizens of a state, to govern themselves in a certain manner; and the constitution of the United States is a compact, made by the people of the United States, to govern themselves, as to general objects, in a certain manner. By this great compact, however, many prerogatives were transferred to the national government; such as making war and peace; contracting alliances; coining money, &c. The sovereignty of the nation being in the people of the nation, and the residuary sovereignty of each state being in the people of each state, a comparison of these sovereignties with those of Europe may show whether or not all the prerogatives of *European* sovereignty are essential to *American* sovereignty.

" The sovereignties in Europe, and particularly in *England*, exist on *feudal* principles, which consider the *prince* as the sovereign, and the people as his subjects, and regard his *person* as the object of allegiance, and exclude the notion of his being on an *equal* footing with a subject, either in a court of juctice or elsewhere. The feudal system contemplates the *prince* as the fountain of honour and authority, from whose grace and grant flow all franchises, immunities, and privileges; whence such a sovereign *cannot* be amenable to a court of justice, nor subjected to judicial control and actual constraint. It was of necessity, therefore, that *suability* became incompatible with sovereignty. Besides, the prince, having all the executive powers, the judgment of the court would, in fact, be only monitory, *not* mandatory to him; and a capacity to be *advised* is quite a distinct thing from a capacity to be sued. The same *feudal* notions run through all their jurisprudence, and constantly keep in view the broad line of distinction between the prince and the subject. But *no* such ideas prevail in the United States. At the revolution the *sovereignty* devolved upon the American *people,* who are truly the sovereigns of the country, but they are sovereigns *without* subjects, (unless the negro slaves are such) and have none to govern but themselves; the citizens of America are *all* equal as fellow-citizens, and as joint tenants in the national sovereignty. The differences between feudal sovereignties, and governments founded on compacts, create a difference in their respective prerogatives. Sovereignty is the right to govern; and a nation or state sovereign is the person or persons in whom that right resides.

" In Europe the sovereignty is in the prince; in the United States it rests with the people ; *there,* the sovereign actually administers the government, *here, never,* in a single instance : our state governors are only the agents of the people, and, at most, stand in the same relation to *their* sovereign in which regents in Europe stand to their sovereigns. European princes have *personal* powers, dignities, and pre-eminences, but American rulers have only *official* privileges and rank, nor do they partake in the sovereignty (whether state or national) otherwise, or in any other capacity, than as *private* citizens."

To these observations of Mr. Jay, it might be added, that in every *free* country the government runs a course similar to that of the *common law;* it has its origin in the wants, and is adapted to the conveniences and views of the community; grows with its growth, and embraces all the exigences of the nation, as it passes through its successive stages of infancy, youth, manhood, and age. As the government of a country is formed *by*, so it materially helps *to*, form the character of the people, by constant action and reaction upon each other. It is a notorious fact, that the *republican* polity of the United States, in combination with some other circumstances, has rendered the American population *superior* to that of any other country, ancient or modern. A vast extent of territory, averaging a fertile soil, and a favourable climate; a comparatively thin population; high wages of labour; an abundance of provisions; a variety of employments, in the labours of agriculture, the pursuits of commerce, the sports of the field and of the forest, all conspire to give *physical* activity and strength to the inhabitants of the United States.

The general diffusion of elementary and popular intelligence among all classes of society, more particularly in New-England, gives to the inhabitants of the United States a larger average of *mental* activity and power than falls to the lot of the mass of the people in most other countries. Indeed, with the exception of Scotland, Holland, Sweden, and the Protestant Cantons of Switzerland, no country, save America, gives to its people at large the means of acquiring the rudiments of education; and consequently the improvement and expansion of the *general* intellect of the nation are prevented. The sovereignty residing in the people, their political equality, their stake in the commonwealth, by the right of suffrage, gives to the citizens of the United States a greater *moral* elevation, a higher consciousness of self-importance, respect, and dignity, than are to be found in the people of any other country under the canopy of heaven.

Whence, in the prosecution of the arts of peace, whether at home or abroad; in agricultural toil; in mechanical skill; in mercantile enterprise, the Americans exhibit an aggregate of physical strength, activity, and perservance; of mental quickness, acuteness, and comprehension; of moral energy, loftiness, and power, surpassing that of any other *entire* nation. And in the perils of warfare, amidst the noise, and fire, and smoke, and carnage of the battle, whether on the ocean or on the land, the American squadrons do by no means yield the palm of deliberate valour, accomplished skill, and heroic patriotism, to the embodied legions of ancient Greece and Rome, nor to the well-appointed hosts of the greatest nations of modern Europe. There *must* be much of intrinsic, radical excellence in the political institutions of a country, which have lent their efficient aid to form the physical, intellectual, and moral character of *such* a people as are now spreading themselves over the vast and various territory of the United States, and daily and hourly reclaiming the waste and wilderness from the dominion of nature to the cultivation of man. And while these general causes continue to operate, the people of the United States will continue to average a physical, intellectual, and moral superiority over those of every other nation; and so long may they well continue to cherish their *present form* of government as admirably adapted to their feelings, their affections, their habits, and their interests.

It is, however, quite another and a distinct consideration, how far a government, based *altogether* in democracy, where the people, either immediately or mediately; that is to say, immediately in their own persons, or mediately through the medium of electors chosen by themselves, elect *all* their rulers, executive, senatorial, and representative; *how far* such a government would be able to sustain the pressure of an overgrown population, elbowing each other for a morsel of bread, and greatly deteriorated in their physical, intellectual, and moral qualities, as in the old and fully peopled countries of Europe. At this hour, the United States do *not* average *five* persons to a square mile; the state of New-York gives only *twenty* to every square mile, and the most populous state, Connecticut, not more than *fifty;* whereas, in England, Ireland, France, and the United Netherlands, the average is *two hundred* souls to each square mile. And it becomes a serious question for the American statesman to ponder whether or not the present form and system of government will be able to restrain and keep in order such a populace as now presses upon the respective rulers in Paris, London, and Dublin; and whether or not the many myriads, who must *then* be scantily fed, clothed, lodged, and taught, will be apt, by dint of universal suffrage, to pass an *Agrarian* law; or, by the more summary mode of sudden violence, scatter the property of the comparatively few who might then be in easy circumstances?

At all events, such a state of things opens a wide field of active enterprise to ambitious and unprincipled demagogues, inviting them to put into riotous motion the great mass of the people; and what such a mass, so put in motion, *can* do, has been fully shown by revolutionary France; the effects of whose anarchial movements are seen all over Europe at this moment, and will never cease to be felt, in every nerve and artery of man's social state, as long as the world itself endures.   Whatever other political lessons the French revolution might have taught, it has rendered perfectly intelligible *this* truth; namely, that whenever *the people* of any country choose to move in mass, they can tear up from its foundations their existing government, and scatter its fragments to the winds of heaven; and there never are wanting, perhaps, in any country, (certainly not in any country whose political institutions are cast in a popular mould,) a sufficient number of daring and turbulent spirits, who eagerly desire so to stir up and incite the populace to violence, that they themselves may ride aloft in the whirlwind, and direct the storm.   The Emperor Alexander seems to be so much alive to *this* sign of the times, that he actually appears to labour to play the part of a good democrat himself.

At the present hour, indeed, no such danger presses imminently upon the United States; nor will it, probably, so long as the *western* country opens such an immense extent of fertile soil, and favourable location, that those needy and desperate adventurers, whose pernicious habits of idleness and vice render them alike

unable and unfit to live in a state of orderly and well-
regulated society, can flock thither, and evaporate, in
reclaiming the wilderness, that factious violence, and discontented disposition, which would be much more de-
structively employed in plundering the property and
cutting the throats of their more sober-minded fellow-
citizens.   M. Talleyrand was greatly surprised to find
that in the United States, some few years after the close
of the revolutionary war, the ordinary effects of a revolution were *not* visible in the condition of the community; and he philosophizes on it thus: every *change* lays
the foundation for another, says Machiavelli; and, in
fact, without speaking of the hatreds which they perpetuate, and of the motives for vengeance which they leave
in the minds of men, *revolutions* that have shaken every
thing, and in which the whole community has taken
part, create a general restlessness of mind, a craving
after change, an indefinite eagerness for hazardous enterprises, a vague and turbulent ambition, whose tendencies are unceasingly to alter and destroy every thing
that is.

This is more emphatically true, when the revolution
has been made in the name of *liberty*;—a *free* government, says Montesquieu; that is, one *always agitated;*
and it being impossible to stop the agitation, it must be
regulated so as to exercise itself, *not* at the expense, but
for the promotion of the public happiness.   After the
crisis of revolutions, there are always many men worn
out and made old under the impression of misfortune:
such men are *not* apt to love their country, in which
they have experienced nothing but misery; and their
hatred must be guarded against, and, if possible, rendered impotent.   Time and good laws, indeed, will do
much; but establishments and outlets for such dangerous beings are necessary.   In *America*, after a revolution, very dissimilar doubtless to that of France, there
remained only slight traces of ancient animosities; but
little agitation and inquietude; few, or none, of those
symptoms which, in general, threaten every moment the

tranquillity of states newly bursting into freedom. One great cause of this strange appearance deserves consideration.

No doubt the American, like other revolutions, had left in the minds of men dispositions to excite or receive new troubles; but this *need of agitation* had been able to find a different satisfaction in a vast and new country, where adventurous projects allure the mind; where immense tracts of uncultivated lands give men a facility of employing a fresh activity, far from the scene of their first dissensions; of placing their hopes and fears in fresh speculations; of plunging themselves at once into the midst of a crowd of new schemes; of amusing themselves by frequent change of place; and eventually extinguishing, within their bosoms, the flame of the revolutionary passions.

This very facility, however, of emigration into the *western* country, raises another very important question for the contemplation of the American statesman. The direct tendency of such emigration is to enable the western territory, in the course of a few years, to outnumber, both in the senate and in the House of Representatives, the Atlantic States; which being done, the Western States, as great *inland* nations, and erroneously considering that the *commercial* policy of the Atlantic seaboard is opposed to their agricultural interests, will be apt to sacrifice that commercial policy to their own mistaken views of territorial aggrandizement. Such an alteration in the system of government would be most pernicious to New-England, the cradle of the revolution, and the efficient founder of American independence. The soil of New-England does not raise a sufficient quantity of provisions to maintain a crowded population, but its long line of sea and river coast, its numerous harbours, and the habitual enterprise of its people, give it a commercial capability, certainly never surpassed, if ever equalled by any other nation. Hence Mr. Pickering, one of the most enlightened and intrepid of her statesmen, said, in reference to his New-England fellow citizens, that their *farms* were on the *ocean*.

Great as was once the weight of New-England in the American councils, her influence of late has been borne down by the preponderance of the west. New-England, including Massachusetts and Maine, New-Hampshire, Vermont, Rhode-Island, and Connecticut, covers only a surface of little more than *sixty thousand* square miles, and contains a population of about one million and a half; whereas, the western country already counts a greater number of states—as Ohio, Kentucky, Tennessee, Mississippi, Indiani, and Louisiana, which give it a preponderance in the *senate* of the United States;—in addition to which there is an immense extent of surplus territory, out of which new states without number may be carved in the lapse of a few years. Its population already reaches between two and three millions, which enables it to vote down New-England in the House of Representatives; and it covers a surface of more than *one million five hundred thousand* square miles; that is to say, more than *fifteen* times as large as the British Isles, England, Ireland, and Scotland, put together, and averages a fertile soil, admirably adapted to sustain a very full and numerous population; a population abundantly sufficient to *outvote* not only the New-England, but all the other Atlantic States, all the states that composed the *old Union* which converted America from a British colony into an independent empire.

The *commercial* policy is necessary to the very existence of New-England, whose depopulation must follow as an inevitable result from its destruction or restriction, and its tide of emigration augments the numbers and resources of that western country, which is inclined to strike a deathblow to the prosperity of the Atlantic seaboard. There cannot well be a more erroneous political theory, than that the interests of agriculture are *opposed* to those of commerce, and conversely; for the facts and proofs that *merely* agricultural nations can never become either prosperous or powerful, and that commerce most materially forwards the improvement of agriculture itself, and of national wealth and civiliza-

tion, see " the Resources of the British Empire," pp.
383, 398, 487, 490. If the western and agricultural
policy should prevail, the Atlantic States will suffer, in
the following order; New-England most, then New-
York, New-Jersey, Delaware, and Maryland, then
Pennsylvania, which being a great manufacturing state,
depends less upon foreign commerce; then Virginia,
the two Carolinas, and Georgia, which are great planting states, their staples being tobacco, rice, and
cotton.

The tendency of all this, beyond a peradventure, is
either to break up the Federal Union, and entail a perpetuity of anarchy and civil broils throughout the whole
continent, or to crush the Atlantic States beneath the
enormous hoofs of the western mammoth.

If however, from these, or from any other causes, the
British government should suppose that the United
States are destitute of resources, and the people reluct-
ant to engage in a new war, on account of the events
of the recent conflict, it is egregiously mistaken. The
resources, territorial, intellectual, and moral, of this
country, are immense and various, and widening on all
sides with inconceivable rapidity; and the settled conviction of the American people, arising out of the cir
cumstances of the last war is, that they are decidedly
superior to the British, and can always beat them man
to man, ship to ship, gun to gun, bayonet to bayonet,
both on the flood, and in the field. And uncounted
myriads of American hearts now beat high and quick,
in eager aspirations for another contest with Britain; a
spirit which the government carefully cherishes, by
newspaper effusions, by public toasts and orations, by
congressional and state legislative speeches and resolutions; the great objects of American ambition being to
annex to their already too gigantic dominion the British
North-American colonies on the continent, and the
West-India Islands; and also the Spanish colonies bordering on the southern states.

The *general government*, indeed, was itself broken
down during the last war; it fled at Bladensburgh;

gave up Washington to the flames of a victorious enemy, and was unable to send a single recruit to its
skeleton armies, or to pour a single stiver into its exhausted treasury. But the *people* never despaired of
the republic; they always showed what feats of heroism
they were capable of performing, when directed by
competent leaders; at Plattsburgh, at Baltimore, at New-
Orleans, they rolled back the tide of invasion, and demonstrated the fatal folly of attempting to fix a hostile
army on the soil of America. On the lakes, and on
the ocean, the American stars were flying above the red-
cross flag of England; the American ships were better
built, better manned, and better fought than those of
Britain; as is natural to suppose, when of two kindred
nations equally brave, the one has an overgrown navy too
large for its population and resources; while the other
has only a few select ships, the crews of which are all
picked men and skilful seamen. The fashionable popular logic in this country is, " the British beat the
French both by sea and land, the Americans beat the
British; and therefore, the United States have nothing
to fear from European prowess; certainly not from
England, if she conducts her future wars so clumsily
as she did the last."

The American government will probably never again
exhibit such a spectacle of nerveless impotence as was
displayed during the last war. It is daily and hourly
acquiring fresh strength; its influence over the United
States bank will give it the command of the national
purse, and facilitate the raising of loans. Its military
academies throughout the Union are rendering abundant the materials of a skilful, well-disciplined, well-appointed regular army; its dock-yards and arsenals are
well-supplied, and no effort or expense spared, to create
a powerful navy, consisting of first-rate ships of the line,
large frigates, sloops, steam batteries, &c. besides the
fleets on the lakes; all which, manned by *American*
sailors, will give to the general government a formidable influence, both in peace and war, with the greatest
European sovereignties. The American rulers have

become wiser by their own experience, have profited by their own blunders, have extracted strength from a sense of their own weakness. They are *not* likely again to plunge into a war, without funds, and without men : they are now preparing, in the bosom of peace, the means of future conflict ; by building up the finances of the country, by planting every where the germs of an army, by sowing those seeds which will soon start up into bands of armed warriors, by a rapid augmentation of their navy ; and, above all, by attempting to allay the animosities of party spirit, and endeavouring to direct the whole national mind and inclination of the United States towards their aggrandizement by conquest, alike on the land and on the ocean; by adding to their present immense empire the continental possessions of Spain and England, and the British insular domains in the West Indies.

The federal government, to be sure, is radically weak in its frame and composition; but, like all other governments, it will continually increase in strength the longer it lasts, by the natural tendency of power in the hands of *all* men, whether good or bad, wise or foolish, to augment itself; by the constant growth of executive patronage and of public expenditure ; by the *latitude of construction* which ambitious ingenuity may fasten upon the words and letters of the constitution of the United States. Whence, in the course of a few years, the American government will be quite strong enough to act a very offensive part to those European powers who vainly flatter themselves with the hope that the United States are in themselves impotent, and destitute of those resources which are requisite to give a country a commanding attitude in its intercourse, pacific or belligerent, with other nations.

The great question now at issue between America and Europe, is, which of the two shall *change* its form and system of government? whether Europe shall become more democratic, or the United States more aristocratic? It is scarcely credible with what eagerness the presidential messages are read in every European court and cabinet, and among every European people. Not understanding the nature, if they know the existence of our separate *state* sovereignties, they are exceedingly surprised to find that the general government of ten millions of people is carried on at an expenditure of less than *six millions* sterling a-year, while the expenses of their own governments range from *fifty* to *one hundred millions* sterling per annum. And, as every very expensive government *must* be oppressive, because it impedes the progress of productive industry, and perpetuates the hopeless poverty of the great mass of the people, the Europeans are naturally led to desire that their own governments might approximate to that of the United States, in popular liberty and in moderation of expenditure, while the American rulers, observing that the European sovereigns have more command over the population and resources of their respective countries than they can exercise over those of the Union, as naturally desire to build up into more extensive and permanent power the system and administration of the federal government.

The probable result is, that the governments of America and Europe will approximate towards each other, *in fact*, although *in name* they may still remain different; the generality of mankind being governed by names, and very apt to be shocked and roused into tumult by their sudden change. The European governments generally, although still retaining the name of monarchies, will, perhaps, become more representative, more democratic; while the government of America, still retaining the name of a republic, will, peradventure, become more aristocratic, more powerful in its executive, and more permanent in its senate. The great difficulty, however, will be to temper the strength of the government with the personal liberty of the people; for it is a general rule, with as few exceptions as most general rules, that the freer the people the weaker the government, and conversely ; the danger therefore is, lest the American government in strengthening itself, should so far restrain the liberties of the people, as to render them in the aggregate less excellent than they now are in physical, intellectual, and moral qualities.

At present, there can be no difficulty in showing that the resources of the United States are *relatively* greater than those of Britain. The British government spends *one-third* of the whole national income of that country. Before the close of the war with France, the national income of Britain amounted to four hundred millions sterling per annum; the peace reduced the value of lands, houses, and all other productive property in that country, at least, one half, besides throwing several thousand families out of all employment. The government did *not* reduce its expenditure in the same proportion: it spends now about *seventy* millions sterling a-year, while the national income, the product of all its houses, lands, ships, manufactures, money, and every species of property, is not more than *two hundred* millions sterling; that is, giving at five per cent. a British capital, real and personal, of four thousand millions sterling. Add to this, the British national debt is above four thousand five hundred millions of dollars, of which, indeed, the Sinking Fund has redeemed about one-third, or one thousand five hundred millions of dollars; but that does *not* lessen the annual expenditure, because the government continues to receive the dividends of all the stock redeemed, which dividends are provided for by taxes taken from the people, the government having no other income than what is raised by taxation. The outstanding or unfunded debt also amounts to seventy millions sterling, and the *deficit* of revenue now, in the season of universal peace, amounts to fifteen millions sterling, or sixty-seven millions of dollars; the income this year being fifty-two millions sterling, and the expenditure upwards of sixty-seven millions. So that, unless the British government can either diminish their expenses or augment their revenue, they must soon become bankrupt; for the nation never can support a much longer continuance of loans in times of peace; or, what is tantamount to loans, the issue of Exchequer bills, which swells the aggregate of the unfunded debt.

And there is the less prospect of Britain's lightening her load of debt, on account of Mr. Vansittart having, since the year 1813, broken the progressive force of the Sinking Fund, by diverting the dividends of the stock redeemed to the current expenses of the empire, instead of permitting them to constitute a part of the income of the Sinking Fund, which was the essence of Mr. Pitt's scheme for the liquidation of the debt. The income of the Sinking Fund this year is under *fourteen* millions sterling. If Mr. Vansittart had not stopped its progress, it would have been upwards of *twenty-four* millions. A deficit of only *three* millions sterling was the proximate cause of those revolutionary movements which put the French monarchy in *obeyance* during twenty-five years.

Besides, the British Isles have no elbow-room for the spreading of an increased population; they contain only one hundred thousand square miles, or sixty-four millions of acres of land, on which twenty millions of people are crowded; whereas, the United States cover a surface of more than two millions five hundred thousand square miles, or one thousand six hundred millions of acres, over which are thinly scattered a population of ten millions. The whole annual expenditure of the United States is *not* more than *one-eight* of the national income; say, the general government spends about *six* millions sterling, and the twenty state sovereignties about *four* millions per annum, altogether making a sum total of *ten* millions; the national income, arising from the lands, houses, ships, manufactures, money, and every species of property, may be estimated at *eighty* millions sterling, or three hundred and sixty millions of dollars; that is, giving, at five per cent., a productive, real, and personal capital of sixteen hundred millions sterling, or seven thousand two hundred millions of dollars.

The national debt of America is scarcely *one hundred and twenty* millions of dollars; to set off against which, there are, at least, five hundred millions of acres of public lands; that is to sav lands held in trust by the general government for the people of the United States, and applicable to the liquidation of the debt, and to the current demands of the public expenditure. It is rating these lands much below their real value, to say they are worth *a thousand* millions of dollars. These lands consist of about two hundred millions of acres, ceded by the different states to the United States, and of the territory of Louisiana, purchased by the American government; of which all the land *not* previously granted out by the crowns of France and Spain belongs to the American government, as trustee for the American people. For it is a first principle in the law of *tenures*, that the *state*, or sovereign, whether a single person, as in a monarchy, or the whole people, as in a republic, is the only original source of titles, and possesses a sovereign right to grant lands to whom it pleases. The prodigious extent of territory yet unoccupied, but fertile, gives to the United States immense resources for future growth in population and wealth; for all the prosperity of pacific enterprise; for all the comprehensive energy and perseverance of protracted warfare. So that there can be no comparison between the capabilities and resources of *any other* country and those of the United States, provided the federal Union lasts, and increases in strength as it advances in age.

The probable approximation of the American and European governments towards each other, in effect, if not in form, is intimately connected with what may be called the *revolutionary* question; that is to say, the question first practically started by the United States, in their revolt from the mother country, and pushed to a much wider extreme by France, towards the close of the eighteenth century. The United States, indeed, only made a radical change in the form of their government, by converting an hereditary monarchy into a representative republic. They still retained, substantially, the laws, the religion, and the morals of the parent state; and, from time to time, frame and modify their municipal system according to the exigency of existing circumstances. But revolutionary France suddenly and

violently *changed* every thing ; changed its government,
religion, habits, manners, the whole frame of civil polity
and social order ; nay, the very *language* itself, giving
it an inflated, bombastic, fraudulent character, that unhappily is spreading itself all over Christendom, and
in no countries more rapidly and widely than in these
United States and England.   Every demagogue, who
breathes mischief and ruin, talks loudly, in newspapers,
and pamphlets, and club speeches, about " the high
destinies of liberty," " the liberal spirit of the age,"
" the annihilation of all prejudices in favour of religion,
morality, learning, and all the obsolete usages of ignorant antiquity ;" the whole of which means, in *his*
mouth, that all above him, whether in wealth, talent,
learning, wisdom, virtue, or character, should be pulled
down, and he himself exalted, according to *his own*
notions of his own transcendental merit.

The *revolutionary* question, as understood and enforced by its present advocates in France, Britain, and
America, is *not* a question respecting the prevalence of
any particular religious denomination, whether Papist or
Protestant, Episcopalian, or Presbyterian, Independent or
Methodist; but it is a question between religion and *no*
religion ; a flagitious attempt to carry on government,
and social and domestic life, *without* any religion of any
kind whatsoever, and consequently without any *morals;*
revelation being the basis of all moral obligation, and
every system of morals *not* so based, being easily reducible to the mere calculations of political expediency and
personal convenience; from the καλον και αγαθον of Aristotle, and the *utile et honestum* of Cicero, down to
Hume's scheme of *utility*, or Godwin's plan of *general
good;* good so very general as to destroy all individual
virtue and happiness.   Nor is the revolutionary question a question as to the relative excellence of any
particular *form* of government, whether a republic, or a
monarchy, or an aristocracy, or a democracy, or an imperial autocracy, be in itself preferable ; but it is *an assumption of fact*, that at *any* time, ambitious and unprincipled men may labour to overset the *existing* order

of things under which they live, whether as citizens or aliens, in the eager hope of raising themselves to turbulent and bloody distinction, amidst the general wreck of human society.

In a word, it is a desperate experiment, to be made by desperate, needy, profligate adventurers, of every gradation of talent, knowlege, dulness, and ignorance, in every country, particularly in every free country, that religion, government, social order, private pursuits, all that relates to man, individually or as connected with his fellows, may be always kept afloat, always fluctuate in a *revolutionary* state, and the people be perpetually fermented by appeals to their vanity, and folly, and viler passions ; that ambitious demagogues may lift themselves up to power, and be enabled to govern by fraud or force, by the bayonet and sword, or by a muzzled and perverted press. The United States, although at present blessed with free constitutions, and good codes of law, are yet revolutionary, and contain within them the seeds of those sudden changes which scatter upon the wings of ruin all the labours and products of past experience, and mock the hopes of all human expectation. France is still eminently revolutionary ; her present throne is placed upon the crater of an unextinguished volcano, whose eructations of smouldering smoke, and molten stones, and burning lava, every instant threaten it with destruction. Every step that religion and government make is made upon the reeking ashes, the still glowing embers of revolutionary fires ; those fires which are seen in fitful and portentous blaze over all the extent of continental Europe. And, unhappily, neither France nor the rest of the European continent can find a sufficient counterpoise to the revolutionary spirit, in their own governments, which do not breathe a sufficient air of freedom ; nor in their legal codes, nor in their diffusion of pure religion, and sound morality, throughout their dominions. The struggle, in that quarter of the globe, appears to be fast ripening into a conflict between indignant despotism and lawless democracy ; the collision of which two opposite extremes cannot fail to shake to its foundation the social fabric; and, whichever side ultimately prevails, to steep the victor's wreath of triumph in tears and blood.

The British government, indeed, has hitherto stood forth as the great bulwark of social order, against the ever-beating tide of revolutionary fury; but, labouring as she now is under the exhaustion of so long and terrible a conflict, so enormous a pressure of expenditure and debt, so alarming a diminution of her agriculture, manufactures, and commerce, so awful an increase of pauperism, in all the classes of her community, will she be able *long* to maintain the proud but melancholy distinction of being the solitary rock of social safety, amidst the storms and tempests of the agitated ocean; the sole remaining monument of stable rule amidst the ruins of thrones, and principalities, and powers? Even in the midst of her own home dominions, *democracy* is fast gaining ground, and insisting upon its scheme of revolutionary change; in spite of her hereditary executive, her hereditary peers, her recent orders of knighthood, her nationally established hierarchy, her close alliance between church and state.

Meanwhile her child and rival, America, is rapidly emerging into unparalleled national greatness; is flaming upwards, like a pyramid of fire; so that all the western horizon is in a blaze with the brightness of its ascending glory. Nor is the *ambition* of America less aspiring than the progress of her power is alarming. The United States, not contented with their present territory, although more than double the extent of the whole Chinese empire, lay claim to both the Floridas, and avowedly stretch their pretensions westward to the Pacific Ocean; and give very intelligible hints, through all the numberless organ-pipes of their followers, and flatterers, and servants, that they will never rest from their labours, till they have accomplished their aim, by treaty, or encroachment, or conquest; their unvarying motto being, *dolus* an *virtus, quis in hoste* requirat?

Popular governments are always sufficiently ambitious, warlike, and unresponsible; too apt to encroach upon their neighbours ; and not very prudish as to the means of aggrandizement. The United States look wistfully towards the British provinces on our North-American continent ; and the unwise act of Lord Grenville, passed through parliament in the year 1784, permitting the people of lower Canada to conduct their pleadings, and promulgate their laws, in the *French* language, has prevented them from ever becoming *British;* and so far weakened the colony as an outwork of the mother country. It has always been the policy of able conquerors, as soon as possible, to incorporate their vanquished subjects with their own citizens, by giving them their own language and laws, and not suffering them to retain those of their pristine dominion. These were among the most efficient means by which ancient Rome built up, and established her empire over the whole world ; and these were the most efficient aids by which modern France spread her dominion so rapidly over the continent of Europe. While lower Canada continues to be French in language, religion, law, habits, and manners, it is obvious that her people will *not* make good British subjects ; and Britain may most assuredly look to the speedy loss of her North-American colonies, unless she immediately sets about the establishment of an able *statesmanlike* government there, and the direction thitherward of that tide of emigration from her own loins, which now swells the strength and resources of the United States. Her North-American colonies gone, her West-India Islands will soon follow.

Indeed, it is now well understood, that if the American government had been long-sighted and wise, the United States might have been a great West India power at this moment. For Britain, during her late conflict with revolutionary France, offered either Cuba, or St. Domingo to this country ; but Mr. Jefferson suffered his own little personal feelings towards France, and against England, to prompt him to decline the offer ; and thus let slip an opportunity of aggrandizing the United States, which may never again occur under such favourable circumstances. The dominion of either of those great islands would have considerably augmented the commerce and increased the naval armaments of America; and also have given her a much higher importance in the scale of nations than she now holds. But, *diis aliter visum est*; the fears and hatreds of her executive chief have materially delayed the career of America towards the summit of national ascendency and greatness.

As for the *Spanish* colonies, they will fall, as a matter of course, to the superior energy and enterprise of the United States; for it is as natural for indolence, and ignorance, and procrastination, to yield to industry, to intelligence, and activity, as it is for the tides of the ocean to follow the phases of the moon. It is superlatively idle to suppose, that the forlorn and beggarly government of Spain, headed by a patron of the inquisition, and an embroiderer of petticoats for the Virgin Mary, will be able to resist the constant encroachments, or the direct attacks of a neighbour so enterprising, intelligent, alert, dauntless, and persevering, as the United States.

Nor let England ever lay the flattering unction to her soul, that it is possible ever to make America *her* friend. These two countries will never cease to be commercial rivals, and political enemies, until one or the other falls. As the world could not bear two suns, nor Persia two kings, so the day is fast approaching when the globe will not be able to endure the existence of these two mighty maritime empires. The maxim of *delenda est Carthago* never found more cordial advocates in the Roman senate than it now finds as applicable to Britain in the inmost recesses of every American bosom. But it behoves the United States to pause, at least *for the present*, in their strides towards territorial aggrandizement; for it is understood that the *Treaty of Vienna*, which is now the basis of national convention law in Europe, as the Treaty of Westphalia was, prior to the French revolution, stipulates, that if one European nation has any domestic quarrels, either with its colonies or within its home dominions, the high contracting parties do *not* interfere; but, if any power attacks the integral empire of any European sovereignty, the parties to the Vienna treaty protect it. Hence, Spain and her colonies are left to fight out their mutual battles, as they best can; but Portugal is forbidden to encroach upon the Spanish domains on the American continent; unless, indeed, the *Holy League*, which, under the veil of evangelical union between the contracting powers, seems to look towards planting the Russian flag upon the seven towers of Constantinople, should break in upon and derange the provisions of the Congress of Vienna.

If such be the stipulations of the Vienna pact, the United States should be wary in their attempts on the Floridas, the British Northern Provinces, and West India islands, lest they bring all Europe upon them with her numerous and well-disciplined veteran armies. It is the business of the American government to wait, and nourish the growing resources of the Union, till time and circumstance shall dissolve the present unparalleled coalition of European sovereigns, and then gradually bear down all possible opposition from any single foe. As the *disposable* force of every country must be always mainly proportioned to the *compactness* of its population, it is self-evident, that, *at present,* the United States, with only ten millions of inhabitants, spread over a territory of two millions and five hundred thousand square miles, *cannot* be very powerful for the purposes of *offensive* warfare; a circumstance, probably, which the statesmen who framed the federal constitution took into their consideration, since they so seem to have moulded that national compact as not to give the general government the power of carrying on an offensive warfare.

These great men, doubtless, desired that their native country might possess all the means of *defence,* when assailed by an invading foe; and, accordingly, they have made the most admirable provisions in the federal constitution for the accomplishment of this all-important object; their apparent design being, as much as possible, to preserve the United States free from the calamities of foreign warfare, and incite them to avail themselves of their vast *physical* capacities, and to accelerate the growth of their population and wealth, in order that America, at no distant day, might be able to rank with the *first-rate* sovereignties of the earth, in the extent, permanency, and disposable efficiency of her national resources. By *premature* efforts to aggrandize themselves by conquest, the United States will put all their present advantages in jeopardy, and endanger the dissolution of the Union, by the preservation of which they can *alone* hope to become lastingly prosperous and great. Let them remember Franklin's position, that by *patience* and *perseverance* they will be able to *outgrow* all grievances, all difficulties, and all *resistance*.

Is *Russia* now, and for the time to come, deemed formidable to Europe? Behold another and a greater Russia *here*. With a better territory, a better government, and a better people, *America* is ripening fast into a substance, an attitude of power, which will prove far more terrible to the world than it is ever possible for the warriors of the Don or the defenders of Moscow to become. Let it not, for a moment, be imagined that I seek to lean upon the exalted character, or to detract from the well-tried prowess of *Britain*. Under the blessing of Divine Providence, the world owes to *her* unrivalled exertions, to her vehement and sustained fortitude, a liberation from the most galling, base, profligate, and cruel bondage that ever stained the annals of the human race. Braver than Britons men *cannot* be. It is not in human nature to do more than affront death with cool, collected, steady, unyielding valour. Is it possible for them that are born of women to display more unbending, more triumphant heroism, than was exhibited by the British on the field of Waterloo and in the harbour of Algiers?

But it *is* meant to assert, because it can be proved, that the United States, from their territorial extent, their local situation, their political institutions, their peculiar circumstances, *do* produce a greater amount of physical, intellectual, and moral enterprise, and force in the great mass of their people, than is or *can* be produced in the aggregate population of *any other* country. Indeed, an enquiry into the condition and character of the English people would serve as the best basis on which to build the investigation of the characteristic qualities of the American population, seeing that both nations ere sprung from the same native stock, speak the same language, and exercise the same religion, are governed by similar laws, exhibit in their lives and deportments similar habits, manners, and customs. And if, under the physical and moral circumstances of England, her comparatively narrow territory, her actually crowded population, her continual wars, her frequent internal convulsions, her prodigious national expenditure, her enormous public debt, the great body of her people have been *progressively improving*, physically, intellectually, and morally, during the last entire century, and are now, as they have long been, decidedly superior to the population of every other European country—*a fortiori*, must the people of the United States during the same period have been bettered in all their qualities and conditions, by the progress of civilization diffused among a comparatively thin population, spread over a vast and various soil, by unfrequent foreign wars, by internal peace, by a small national expenditure, by a trifling public debt, by institutions, political, moral, and religious, which give the freest scope to personal activity and individual enterprise.

A late minister from the court of St. James, near the American government, *Mr. Jackson,* who had surveyed with a statesman's eye every court and every country, every cabinet and every people in Europe, both insular and continental, told me, " That he had passed through and diligently studied the states of New-York and New-England, that he had never seen such decided *materials* of national greatness as their population exhibited; that the American people were right-minded, strong-minded, sound-minded, and high-minded." And in all the soberness of solemn truth, the people of this country *have* verified the prophetic words of the departed statesman; they have, indeed, fully shown that Englishmen do *not* degenerate in the soil of America; for they have compelled the meteor-flag of England, which *had* waved in triumph on the ocean for a thousand years, to lower its ancient ensign beneath the new-born standard of her child; they have driven back from before their hardy yeomanry the conquerors of France, the deliverers of Portugal, the liberators of Spain, the emancipators of Europe; they have twined round their victorious brows wreaths of naval and of military glory, which will flourish in eternal verdure, long as the everlasting hills shall rest upon their foundations, and the stars of Heaven continue to shed their light.

In the turmoil of battle, and in the pursuits of peace, the Americans effect *more* by a given number of people than the population of any other country *can* effect. At present, indeed, the European *land* tactics are impracticable in the United States: huge masses of cavalry, numerous parks of artillery, and solid columns of infantry, cannot act in a country overgrown with trees, and bushes, and underwood, which afford means and shelter for the deadly musketry and riflemen of America, to destroy their enemy at their own leisure — themselves unseen and inaccessible. The United States must wait till their country is more cleared of its forests, particularly on their borders, before they can exhibit any military conflicts on a large and comprehensive scale. Meanwhile the *ocean* is open, and will, *ere long*, have its waters deeply died with American and British blood, contending for the exclusive dominion of that element, which is, emphatically, the cradle and the home of the mariners of both nations.

From the commencement of the French revolution, in the year 1789, to the close of the late war between America and England, in 1815, the political *parties* in the United States were opposed to each other with exceeding bitterness. Party spirit used to prevent social intercourse, and poison domestic peace. The tyranny of faction was much greater in this country than it ever has been in Britain, where it neither disturbs the harmony of families, nor trenches upon the decorum of society, either among the leaders or followers of the two great contending parties which divide, agitate, and govern that kingdom.—See the " Resources of the British Empire," pp. 351—376, for the facts and reasons to prove, that no free government can be carried on but by the agency of contending parties; and that no danger is to be apprehended either to the ministry or the people from the prevalence of party spirit. Since the peace of 1815, Mr. Monroe's tour, aided by the circumstances of the country and the times, has considerably abated the acrimony of faction in the United States, and democrats and federalists now dine at the same table without any fear of reciprocal offence.

Some of the wisest and best men of America, particularly Washington, Hamilton, and Ames, laboured to convince their fellow citizens of the necessity of extinguishing parties in our popular and elective government. President Washington's " Farewell Address" to the people of the United States, General Hamilton's Essays in the Federalist, and Mr. Fisher Ames's lucubrations scattered over all his works, contain most forcible and eloquent arguments against the mischiefs of faction. But, after all that can be said or written on the subject, a country must either be governed by the bayonet, and be enslaved; or governed by party, and be free. Parties in the United States are substantially like those in England. Two great rival sections of the people contend with each other for the exclusive administration of the government, *not* because they think themselves always right, and their opponents always wrong, but because, *on the whole*, they think they could manage the government better than their antagonists. They differ more about the *means* than the end: they both wish to exalt their country, and render her prosperous at home, and respectable abroad, however they may disagree as to the measures by which this common object can be best attained.

Indeed, *now*, the federalists and democrats do *not* differ, even as to the means; they both wish to exalt their country by the same means. For more than twenty.

years, truly, they varied most essentially in their notions
respecting the best mode of administering the government; the democrats denouncing foreign commerce,
foreign diplomacy, internal taxation, a national bank,
a regular army, and a fighting navy, as being all extremely *anti-republican*. But for the last two or three
years they seem to have outgrown these theories, and
to have begun, like other people, to take experience and
fact as the best foundation, and safest guides of political economy.

The United States are so very favourably circumstanced for a rapid growth in wealth, and population,
and national strength, that it requires only the exercise
of a little common sense to administer the *home* government, and permit the laws and institutions, which are
generally most propitious to the establishment and furtherance of popular liberty, to take their due course.
It requires, however, considerable sagacity and prudence
so to conduct our *foreign* affairs as to secure the friendship and respect of other potentates. But there is no
occasion to enter into any detail on this point, seeing
that General Washington has left a bright example of
all that a wise and upright administration of government can accomplish, for the welfare of the country ;
and our future presidents have only to follow faithfully
in his foot-tracks, in order to ensure, under Providence,
the internal prosperity, and the external respectability
of America.

In one, and that the most important department of
foreign policy, namely, *diplomacy,* the American government, under all its administrations, has exhibited great
talents and skill. In the United States there is no *corps*
of regularly bred statesmen, as in Europe ; but our
politicians generally, and more especially our diplomatists, are taken from the class of practising lawyers, who,
being men of business, shrewd observers, and well acquainted with mankind, have always been a match, and
often an overmatch, for the European ambassadors,
and plenipotentiaries, who have been systematically
trained in the routine of office, amidst all the forms and

devices of the closet.   During the last fifty years, American diplomacy has signalized itself in every court and cabinet of Europe ; and the names of Jay, Adams, Morris, King, Jefferson, Marshal, Monroe, Pinkney, and the Commissioners at Ghent, will deservedly rank as high as those of any diplomatic characters which have adorned other countries.   The peace concluded with England in 1793, by Mr. Jay, Mr. Adams, and Dr. Franklin, and the commercial treaty made with England in 1794, by Mr. Jay, are evidences of consummate diplomatic wisdom and skill.   A very slight perusal of the American State papers, lately published at Boston, will show that the American diplomatists, invariably, wield a more pointed and powerful pen than their European antagonists ; that they press their arguments with more force, place them in a greater variety of lights, and defeat, or evade, or parry, the strokes of their opponents with more adroitness and effect.   The Marquis of Wellesley, in April 1815, said in his place on the floor of the House of Lords, when discussing the negociation between the United States and Britain, respecting peace, " that the American commissioners had shown the *most astonishing superiority* over the British during the whole of the correspondence.   The noble Earl (Liverpool) opposite, probably felt sore at this observation, as no doubt the British papers were communicated from the common fund of ministers in England."

The American commissioners at Ghent were Mr. Gallatin, late Secretary of the United States Treasury, and now Ambassador to France ; Mr. John Quincy Adams, a Massachusetts lawyer, formerly minister to the courts of Berlin, Petersburgh, and London, now Secretary of State ; Mr. Bayard, a Delaware lawyer, and a senator of the United States ; Mr. Clay, a Kentucky lawyer, and Speaker of the House of Representatives in Congress ; and Mr. Jonathan Russel, formerly a merchant in New York.

Considering that diplomacy is much more effectual to permanently aggrandize a nation than war and conquest, it is astonishing that so few governments, in the history of the world, have availed themselves of its aid.   Unless we admit the United States within the circle, there are only *three* nations that have successfully seconded their efforts at extension and power by diplomatic skill; namely, ancient Rome, modern France, and Russia. The reasons why British diplomacy has been for the last five hundred years, in general, so deplorably defective, are detailed at length in " the Resources of the British Empire," pp. 333, 344.

Now, the only sound policy of every nation is to secure its independence, to augment its power, to elevate its rank.   Neither of these three great objects can be pursued singly; they are inseparably interwoven with one another.   The national independence of a state can only be secured by an unremitted *progression* in positive power, of which a greater relative rank is the necessary consequence.   It is as much the duty of states as of individuals constantly to use all honourable means of advancing themselves in wealth, character, influence, authority, and power.   All nations begin to decline from the moment they cease to rise.   *Non'progedi est regredi* is the great political axiom of human affairs. As soon as a man ceases to improve his mind by observation, study, and reflection, his intellect begins to lose ground in acuteness, strength, splendour, and comprehension.   The ambition, avarice, and ignorance of individuals allow to nations no intervals of stationary quiet, or drowsy security.

In modern times, however, the only European governments that seem to have acted on any digested system of national aggrandizement, are, that of France, since the accession of Louis the 14th, in 1643; and that of Russia, since the commencement of Peter's reign, in 1696.   These two great monarchs felt the internal strength, and appreciated the immense natural resources of their respective empires.   Although Louis did not in his own person succeed in the ultimate object of acquiring a universal French monarchy, he yet fixed the ascendency of France over the other European powers on a broad and permanent basis.   When he ascended the throne, his dominions were hemmed in, on all sides, by powerful neighbours. The House of Austria, in its two great branches, swayed the sceptres of Germany and Spain, whose territories almost surrounded France; the republic of Holland completed the line of circumvallation. Nevertheless, although, during the last thirty years of his reign, Louis was almost incessantly beaten by the allied armies of Austria, England, and Holland, he contrived, by the superior skill of French diplomacy, to enlarge his own hereditary possessions, by considerable acquisitions from Germany; to place a Bourbon on the throne of Spain, to shatter Austria, to crush Holland, to cripple England, to leave France so intrinsically powerful, as to enable her, under the augmented impulses of revolutionary action, to be an overmatch for the other powers of continental Europe, *not* merely single-handed, but for a combination of them all; so that, in 1813, 1814, and 1815, about a century after the death of Louis the Fourteenth, it required the united strength, in its full exertion, of Russia, Austria, Prussia, Sweden, Spain, and Portugal, aided by the fleets and armies of England, to rescue the whole European continent from the humiliation of French oppression.

Contrast the adroit diplomacy of France with the most miserable negotiations of England, at the peace of Amiens. So low, indeed, had England fallen under the degrading conditions of this treaty; so completely evaporated was that spirit, which, under the auspices of Marlborough, had rendered her the arbitress of Europe; that spirit which, under the presiding mind of Chatham, had smitten both branches of the House of Bourbon, and loosened the joints of the loins of France and Spain; that the Addington administration actually submitted to the mandate of Bonaparte, and indicted Mr. Peltier for a libel against Napoleon, whom he represented as a ruffian, an upstart, and an assassin. It was high time for Messrs. Addington and Company to obliterate from the memory of the English people, and to raze from the records of history all mention of the fields of Poictiers, Cressy, and Agincourt, of the battles of Blenheim,

Ramillies, and Malplaquet, and to write the name, *French department,* upon the veteran front of the British empire.

While revolutionary France was making herself complete mistress of the south-west half of continental Europe, another power of equal force (as subsequent events proved,) claimed a similar dominion over the northern and eastern sections of that district of the globe. After Austria was humbled, Prussia beaten down, the German empire broken up, Flanders, Holland, Switzerland, and Italy, conquered by the Gallic armies, the political powers and military forces of the European continent were divided between the governments of France and Russia. These two mighty empires touched each other in the beginning of the year 1812; Berlin, Vienna, and Constantinople, were only three military posts in the line of their imperial demarcation. A free and secure communication between the southern provinces of Russia, and the Mediterranean Sea, was an essential part of the system of policy established by the first Peter. This scheme of national aggrandizement has been pursued by all his successors, and is of such importance to the Russian empire, as never to be abandoned without a severe struggle.

Russia covets Candia, Negropont, and the other Greek Island in the Archipelago, as posts that might command the communication between the Black Sea and the Mediterranean. Oczakow is the key to the northern provinces of Turkey, and is to Constantinople what the Pyrenees ought always to be to Madrid. That post Russia will never relinquish; she took it from the Grand Signior in 1737, when England was mediating in favour of Turkey, with thirty-six line of battle-ships. Russia has steadily, and successfully, pursued her scheme of national aggrandizement, since the accession of Peter the First, to the present hour; in consequence of which she now possesses a territory larger than all the rest of Europe, with a brave and hardy population of more than fifty millions, four-fifths of which inhabit her European dominions. She has recently added Poland, as an outwork to her empire; and, in a few years, probably it will require nearly as powerful a coalition to stop her progress to universal dominion as was found necessary, in 1813, to reduce revolutionary France within reasonable limits. Indeed, France and Russia are the only two European powers who systematically act upon the conviction that skilful negotiation is as necessary as victory in war to augment and consolidate national dominion. The Treaty of Amiens gave more power and influence to France than she could have acquired by ten years of successful fighting.

Nay, ever since nations have fought to extend their dominions, their *progression* in power has depended *more* upon the ability of negotiators and peacemakers than upon the talents of military heroes. Every one knows that republican Rome augmented and consolidated all her military conquests by the consummate skill of her diplomacy: her whole history, during the first seven hundred years of her national existence, was little else than an alternation of successful wars, improved by dexterous negotiation, and of dexterous negotiation preparing the way for successful wars. Peter the First, the founder of Russian greatness, was a profound politician, as well as an able soldier: he knew that to conquer in war was not enough; that not to be conquered, in his turn, it was necessary *to retain, in peace,* such posts as could both guarantee the possession of his own dominions, and facilitate the acquisition of further territories. Charles the Twelfth, of Sweden, conquered Denmark and Poland; but being no statesman (only a mere soldier), he lived long enough, although he died young, to lose all his conquests, and one-half of his hereditary dominions, and the independence of his whole kingdom, which has been, ever since his death, in 1718, under the control of Russia or France.

The acquisition of Noteburg, now Schusselburgh, of Nyeskantz, now Petersburgh, and of the islands of Retusary, now Cronstadt, posts of no consideration to the

obtuser vision of the Swedish hero, has secured to Russia, for ever, the dominion of the North of Europe,
which is still more extended and magnified by her later
acquisitions in Finland and Poland. By the more recent
accessions of territory in the Crimea, and Georgia, and
in the possession of Oczakow, Constantinople, Ispahan,
and Delhi, the capitals of Turkey, Persia, and the
Great Mogul, are laid open to the arts and arms, the
legions and the diplomatists of Russia.

The war, carried on by the Grand Alliance, made in
1686, between Germany, Britain, and Holland, against
France, was one continued series of victory for *twenty-
seven* years; and yet, owing to the unskilful diplomacy
of England, the peace of Utrecht and Radstadt, in
1713-14, ruined the house of Austria, the principal
party in the alliance, subjected Holland, laid all Germany open to the inroads of France, placed a French
monarch upon the Spanish throne, and annihilated the
influence of Britain upon the continent of Europe. The
maritime war, carried on by Britain against France,
from 1759 to 1763, was a train of conquests, as was
also her land-war in the North-America colonies, during
the same period. Yet the British were so far out-manœuvred by the French negotiators, that the peace of
1763 laid the foundation of the treaty of 1783, by which
England was shorn of half her physical strength, and
all her national honour.

Had the British diplomatists at Utrecht secured, as
was then easily to be done, an independent monarchy
in Spain, and given to the United Provinces of Holland
(what, in fact, they did a century after, by the Treaty
of Paris, in 1814), a territorial basis, made by a permanent incorporation of all the Low Countries, then the
Spanish Netherlands, with the existing Dutch dominions, the independence of continental Europe probably
would not have fallen a sacrifice to revolutionary
France. And, if Britain, at the peace of 1763, had retained her conquests, made in the preceding war, she
might not have been compelled to sign away half her
empire, by the treaty of 1783; and, still less, to ac-

knowledge the paramount superiority of regicide France, by the peace of Amiens, in 1802.

One of the most triumphant issues of French diplomacy, which has already given rise to one war between the United States and England, and will probably ere long breed occasion for another conflict between these two kindred nations, was the originating and establishing the doctrine of the " *armed neutrality* ;" a doctrine which gradually grew from sufficiently large beginnings into the three sweeping propositions which Bonaparte, as the French revolutionary chief, and Mr. Madison, as our American President, laboured to compel England to receive as an improvement in the system of international law. These propositions are—*First*, Free ships make free goods. *Second*, The flag protects the crew. *Third*, No blockade is legal unless a place be invested both by sea and land.

This interpolation of national law has no other object in view than the destruction of the British maritime power. If ever acceded to, it will merge all belligerent rights in neutral pretensions. France, as a great land power, wants to annihilate England on the ocean : she has never been able to accomplish this purpose by fair fighting, in open and honourable warfare ; she, therefore, seeks to effect her object by a war in disguise, which she calls *neutrality* ; a name that these United States readily adopted under the auspices of Mr. Jefferson and Mr. Madison, in order to further their own peculiar views against Britain, as well as to second the designs of revolutionary France. A most unwise act on the part of America, because she is ripening fast into a first-rate naval power, and is therefore deeply interested in maintaining belligerent maritime rights. Examine for a moment the *practical* effect of these three neutral propositions. Britain and France are at war with each other : America remains neutral : the United States carry on all the trade of France, both foreign and coasting, in American vessels, under the eyes of the English cruisers, who have no power to annoy the trade of their enemy, because free ships make free goods.

The United States carry a body of French troops from the coast of France for the invasion of Ireland, and the British cruisers must not touch these precious transports, because the flag protects all it covers. The United States carry provisions to a French West-India Island, which a British squadron is besieging; and, of course, the impartial neutral cannot be molested, because no place is blockaded, unless it be invested with an adequate force, both by sea and land.

No doubt this doctrine is in good odour at the courts of America and France, because it gives the united advantages of war and peace to France; and to America, all the benefits of a war against England, without either its expense or danger, while it delivers up the naval power, the commerce, and the national existence of the British empire, an unresisting and helpless victim to the combined force and fraud of the United States and France.

The origin and nature of the first northern armed neutrality were forged in the diplomatic arsenals of Paris, partly for the purpose of arming the navies of Sweden, Denmark, and Holland, as a check upon the naval operations of England, and partly to prevent a confederacy between Russia and Britain. The imbecility exhibited by England, in the war that ended in the truce of Aix la Chapelle, in 1748, encouraged France to form the project of expelling the British from North America and the East Indies; to facilitate the accomplishment of which objects she endeavoured to prevent the co-operation of a Russian fleet with the English navy. Accordingly, in 1754, the French government proposed to Sweden and Denmark an *armed naval convention*, to protect the trade of the maritime States, and maintain the liberty of the Baltic. Little notice was taken of this proposal by Denmark and Sweden, until the events of the war seemed to promise success to France; when, in 1758, in hope of gaining a share of whatever commerce or naval influence England might lose, they entered into such a convention, under the sanction of France and Prussia. But the exploits of the British navy,· in 1759, and the succeeding campaigns, together with the brilliant success of the arms of old England and New England against the French North American colonies, disconcerted the measures, and suspended the effects of this armed neutrality.

The next disquisition on the mercantile rights of neutral states was brought forward by Britain herself, on some Silesian linen, which her cruisers had captured. The whole doctrine of neutral claims was fully and ably argued by Lord Mansfield, Sir Dudly Ryder, and Mr. Lee, on the part of the British government, in answer to the Prussian manifesto, delivered in 1759, by order of Frederic the Second. The British High Court of Admiralty condemned this Prussian linen as contraband of war, because it was captured on its way to France, for the supply of her naval canvass. Yet, notwithstanding the very elaborate and able report of the English crown lawyers, the British government finally paid Frederic for his cloth, and *thus* created a precedent, upon which were afterward founded the avowed pretensions of the armed neutrality in 1780. England having, at the peace of 1763, given up to France nearly all her dearly-acquired sources of maritime trade, and those strong holds in Europe, Asia, Africa, and America, which would for ever have secured her naval superiority, the French government, as might be expected, soon renewed its former project of confining the British empire to the island of Great Britain.

France at that time possessed but little influence in the Russian cabinet, and being still apprehensive of an alliance between England and Russia, in order to raise some misunderstanding between the two powers, she fawned upon the Empress Catharine, intrigued with her favourites, and caressed the ladies of her court. The French also wrote verses and sung ballads upon the heroism and legislation of Frederic of Prussia, and the patriotism and maternal affection of Juliana, Queen of Denmark; they likewise, from 1772 to 1778, gave the King of Sweden large sums of money to repair his decayed navy; all which was done, as they said, to secure

for continental Europe " *the liberty of the seas.*" The
unsuccessful campaigns of England in the United States,
in 1778 and 1779, the accession of Spain and Holland
to the American cause, together with the retreat of the
British fleet, even in her own home seas, from before
the French squadron, under d'Orviliers, seemed again
to crown the intrigue and perfidy of France with certainty of success. All the governments of Europe were
then convinced that Britain had lost America, and they
concluded, that her expulsion from the East Indies
would be the speedy consequence. The entire ruin of
the British nation was deemed to be certainly approaching, and the parcelling out of the spoils of her empire
became the subject of general discussion among the
several powers of continental Europe.

The famous convention of *armed neutrality* was,
therefore, drawn up and published ; and in 1780 acceded to by all the maritime states; even by Turkey and
Russia, together with Prussia, Sweden, Denmark,
France, Spain, and Holland ; and in 1781 was acceded
to by the United States. The Count de Florida Blanca,
then premier of Spain, at the instigation of France, de-
tained all neutral vessels in the Straits, under pretence of
the blockade of Gibraltar, and answered to the complaints of the neutral ministers at Madrid, that if their
sovereigns would resist the similar claims of England
such pretensions would be relinquished by Spain. The
doctrine of blockade, however, was *not*, at that time,
pushed to the extent for which the French and American governments afterward contended; namely, that
to constitute a legal blockade a place must be invested
with an adequate force, both by sea and land, for the
only thing required by the armed convention of 1780,
to constitute a blockaded port, was, that there should
actually be a number of enemy's ships stationed near
enough to make an entry evidently dangerous ; and the
definition in the ordinance of our American Congress,
in 1781, is to the same effect. And, in the convention
of the Baltic powers, in 1800, signed by Russia,
Sweden, and Denmark, the definition of blockade is

" where the disposition and number of ships shall be such as to render it apparently hazardous to enter." This same definition was incorporated into the convention between England and Russia in 1801 ; and the principle of that treaty has been recognised in a solemn decision of the highest legal tribunal in the state of New-York.

The *armed neutrality*, although its avowed pretension was the protection of maritime trade and indemnification for illegal captures, was, in fact, supported by the precedent which Britain herself had established in the case of the Prussian linen. All states, when once believed to be on the decline, like individual merchants, whose credit is suspected, must look for a general run or attack upon their property. It was so with Sweden, at the death of Charles the Twelfth; with Austria, at the death of Charles the Sixth; with England, on the success of the American revolution ; and with France, in the first confusion of her revolutionary struggle. To maintain the political independence of a nation, *progression* in power is necessary. The convention of 1800, between the Emperor Paul of Russia and the subordinate powers of the North, at the instigation of France, was planned and acceded to, upon principles very different from those of the former conventions: it began to assume the monstrous aspect of that new code of neutrality which was afterward promulgated by the two cabinets of St. Cloud and Washington. When Catharine broke off the commercial intercourse between Russia and revolutionary France, she signified her motives to Sweden and Denmark, and invited them to follow her example, but observed, that with the exception of France in its then rebellious state, she still adhered to the principles of a free neutral trade.

But England never acknowledged the pretensions of the armed neutrality, and persisted, during the first decade of the French revolutionary war, in capturing all neutral vessels employed in illicit commerce with her enemies. But the battle of Marengo and treaty of Luneville gave France such a decided military and political ascendency upon the European continent, that she was enabled, partly by intrigue and partly by menace, to induce Paul of Russia, Sweden, Denmark, and Prussia, to unite in getting up a second and an enlarged edition of the armed neutrality, which Nelson committed to the flames of Copenhagen, in 1801. After the peace of Tilsit, in 1807, Alexander of Russia, in obedience to the commands of Bonaparte, again insisted upon enforcing the doctrines of the armed neutrality, to which Mr. Canning, on the part of the British government, replied (18th December, 1807,) " that the King of England neither understands nor will admit the pretension of the Emperor of Russia to dictate the time or mode of his negotiations with other powers. It never will be endured by his Majesty, that *any* government shall indemnify itself for the humiliation of *serviency to France*, by the adoption of an insulting and peremptory tone towards Great Britain. England *proclaims anew* those principles of maritime law, against which the armed neutrality, under the auspices of the Empress Catharine, was originally directed, and against which the present hostilities of Russia are denounced. Those principles have been recognized, and acted upon, in the best periods of the history of Europe, and acted upon by no power with more strictness and severity than by Russia, in the reign of the Empress Catharine. Those principles it is the right of England to maintain; and, against every confederacy England is determined, under the blessing of Divine Providence, to maintain them. They have at all times contibuted essentially to the support of the maritime power of Great Britain; but they are become incalculably more valuable and important, at a period, when the maritime power of Great Britain constitutes the *sole* remaining bulwark against the overwhelming usurpations of France, the *only* refuge to which *other* nations may yet resort, in happier times, for assistance and protection.

Nevertheless, France still continued to clamour for the liberty of the seas; and in 1812, Bonaparte undertook to establish all neutral claims by the subjugation of Russia, in which, however, he did not succeed. In the same year, Mr. Maddison also, as chief of our American government, undertook, by a war against England, to compel her to acknowledge by treaty the whole of the new neutral code; to wit, that free ships make free goods; the flag protects all it covers; no blockade is legal, unless the place be strongly invested by sea and land. The war was continued by the United States for nearly three years, when, on the 24th of December, 1814, a treaty of peace was made with Britain, in which no acknowledgment, nor mention of any one of these neutral claims, was inserted; that is to say, according to the law of nations, as laid down by Grotius, Puffendorff, Vattel, and, indeed, by all the great publicists; the United States *have abandoned* these pretensions; for, whenever a nation goes to war for the avowed purpose of obtaining any given object, and makes peace without obtaining it; that object is for ever waved and relinquished.

About sixteen or seventeen years since, a little work was printed in Holland, said to be the production of the late Mr. Windham. It contains some of the most profound and comprehensive views of the nature and importance of diplomacy, together with a full developement of the diplomatic policy and career of the different nations of Europe, more particularly of France, England, and Russia, that have ever been exhibited to the world. Every page breathes the energy and wisdom of an accomplished and high-minded statesman. Whether or not the book has been republished in Britain, or has found its way to these United States, I am ignorant. It well deserves to become the manual of every political student. Many of the preceding facts and observations have been taken from it so far as it reaches; namely down to the peace of Amiens, in 1801-2, including the preliminary and definitive treaties.

The great national importance of establishing a system of skilful diplomancy will be manifest upon considering to what extreme peril the *want* of such a system reduced the whole British empire, during the second ten years of the French revolutionary war. In that awful crisis of the world, when England alone, single-handed, maintained the cause of liberty, social virtue, and civilized enjoyment, against the greater part of Europe, and its dependencies, moving under the banner of France; *even then*, the British government did *not* sufficiently consider, how they should best play for the few foreign stakes yet left in their hands; but most unwittingly threw them also into the grasp of their enemy.

It was incumbent upon England *then* to alter the general course of her accustomed diplomacy; and send out to other governments, as ambassadors, men of sound, strong, comprehensive minds, of discreet habits, and conciliatory manners; who would always pay a becoming deference to the national feelings and prejudices of the people among whom they reside, and yet justly and honourably consult and advance the real, permament interests of their own country, in their various diplomatic transactions. Above all, it was a matter of deep and serious import to England, to keep constantly in these United States a resident minister, able to comprehend the interests and relations of the two people, and of sufficient magnanimity to endeavour to unite them in the closest bonds of amity, by promoting those measures of policy and commerce, which would redound to their mutual advantage; and thus, by conjoining in the ties of friendship, the only two nations on the globe which enjoy popular liberty, and an equitable administration of justice, she might, perhaps, have *earlier* raised an effectual barrier against that unrelenting military despotism which was for so many years rolling together, as a scroll, the republics, kingdoms, and empires of the civilized world; was so long flooding out a tide of desolation, that having swept away all the ancient boundaries and land-marks of the fairer and better portions of the earth, then threatened to deluge the remainder with the waters of bitterness and death.

When it is recollected, that ambassadors furnish the intelligence, which directs all the movements of their respective governments, in relation to foreign powers, perhaps it will not be thought that too much stress has been, or well *can* be, laid upon the great importance of establishing a system of adroit and able diplomacy. In some periods of her history, Britain has seemed sensible of this momentous truth. She has availed herself of the diplomatic talents of Throgmorton, Temple, Marlborough, Walpole, Malmesbury, and Jackson. And, if she would oftener have recourse to such negotiators, she could not be so frequently overseen by France in her diplomatic pacifications and treaties; nor be so constantly exposed to the perilous necessity of standing alone, against the armed combinations of other powers, who are often blinded to their own essential interests, and duped into hostility against her by the more dexterous diplomacy of her Gallic neighbour. It must not, however, be forgotten, that the negotiations of Lord Castlereagh, which in 1814 and 1815 gave the Bourbons back to France, and restored peace to Europe, may be reckoned among the wisest and most felicitous of all the diplomatic transactions that have occurred in the history of the world.

The *character* of a nation is to be tried by the same test as that of an individual. Whoever produces the greatest results with the least means vindicates to himself the most exalted character. Now, England, with less *physical* resources and powers, that is to say, with less extent of home territory, and a smaller population, has produced greater national results than France. The British Isles cover only a surface of a hundred thousand square miles, and contain only twenty millions of souls; whereas France has a territorial basis of nearly three hundred thousand square miles, and a population of nearly thirty millions; yet, in all that constitutes permanent national strength and power; namely, a people hardy, brave, active, intelligent, and moral; productive industry, commerce, wealth, colonial possessions, all the qualities of good domestic government, in peace, in war, in high reputation for probity and honour, she is superior to France. The uniform testimony of a series of centuries proves, that whenever the British and French engage in mutual conflict, by land or on the ocean, with any thing like a parity of numbers, victory never for a moment flutters in suspense over England's national banner. Britain, therefore, in spite of the incessant errors of her diplomacy, and her being so often out-manœuvred by the more dexterous policy of France, is, *as a nation*, greater than France.

It is also to be remembered, that, although England has never yet been wise enough to *retain* in peace a *sufficient* portion of her war conquests, yet she generally holds *some* portion of them, and very seldom gives up any part of her own dominions. Whence, she is *positively* stronger in territory at the end than at the beginning of every war, although *relatively* to France she does not make herself so strong as she ought. Almost the only instance of her giving up any part of her own dominions occurred at the peace of 1783, when she signed away all that part of America which constitutes the whole of the old United States, and Louisiana, and the Floridas. Thus, by continually developing her own internal resources of intelligence, policy, trade, agriculture, and manufactures, England has gradually, in the course of ages, grown up into a first rate power, possessing, in addition to her home territory and population, nearly one-fifth of the whole habitable globe in colonial territory, containing more than one hundred millions of subjects, spread over the East and West Indies, Europe, North America, and Austral-Asia.

The causes of England's giving up so much of her conquests, at the close of every war, and her always making such miserable peace negotiations, are to be found partly in the nature of her popular government, which compels the ministry to conclude a peace on almost any terms, whenever the people, headed by the opposition in Parliament, become generally clamorous against a longer continuance of war; and partly from the ministry themselves being corrupt, or weak; *corrupt*, as at the negotiations of Utrecht, in 1715, when St. John, Lord Bolingbroke, and Harley, Lord Oxford, sacrificed the best interests of England, betrayed Holland to her ruin, deserted Austria in her hour of need, gave Spain to a Bourbon, made France the mistress of Europe; and all for what?—that a tory French faction might domineer over Marlborough, and Godolphin, and Somers, and all the disciples of William of Nassau Orange, whose wisdom and valour had rescued Europe from the iron dominion of Louis the Fourteenth, by seven and twenty years of uninterrupted victory; *corrupt* as when, in 1763, Lord Bute and the Duke of Bedford, for a beggarly sum of money, paid into their own private purse, sold all the conquests of Chatham's glorious war, in Asia, Europe, and America, for a peace which laid the foundation of the dismemberment of the British empire, in 1783; an event which the *weakness* of Lord North's administration imposed upon Britain; *weak* as when, in 1802, the Addington ministry concluded the peace of Amiens, which degraded and weakened England, and gave to revolutionary France the dominion of Europe, and extended her controlling influence over the other three quarters of the globe.

Nevertheless, in spite of these pernicious blunders in her diplomatic policy, England has, on the whole, averaged an increase of national wealth, strength, and power, during the last three centuries, from the reign of Elizabeth to the present hour, by acting on fixed principles of liberty, industry, enterprise, justice, courage, and wisdom. She is in possession now of a very large proportion of the commerce of the world; her empire in India is immense beyond a parallel; she belts the globe with her colonial dominion; she covers Europe, and Africa, and Asia, and America, with her influence. She has recently rallied the millions of Portugal, and Spain, and Holland, and Prussia, and Austria, and Russia, and Sweden, and Italy, and Germany, around her protecting banner, and led them to redemption from the most galling military and political bondage that ever bowed the spirit of man to the dust from which he sprung.

In the year 1782, Mr. Jefferson, in his " Notes on Virginia," declared that the sun of England was for ever set in darkness and in sorrow, never again to peer above the horizon ; that she was on the eve of being blotted out from the list of nations; that her liberty and glory had departed from her, and taken their flight across the Atlantic, to fix their everlasting abode in these United States. " Thy *heart* was father, *Thomas*, to that wish !" But nearly forty years have rolled their eventful tide of time, since the sage of Monticello croaked, from out his mountain cavern, this ill-omened prophecy—and the sun of England is *not* set. Nay, has it yet culminated from the equator ? Have facts accorded with the sinister forebodings of this inauspicious prophet ? Since the utterance of this oracular dirge, has she not broken down the giant strength of revolutionary France, restored the balance of empire to Europe, given peace to an exhausted world, and seated herself upon an eminence of national glory, that casts into shade all the lustre of Greek and Roman fame ?

There is no subject of pursuit more worthy the attention of the moral philosopher and statesman than a scientific investigation of human *laws*, municipal and international; which are, in fact, the historians of the justice of mankind; while the relations of political and military events are, for the most part, only the accounts of their ambition and violence. What can be more instructive than to trace out the first obscure and scanty fountains of that mighty river of jurisprudence which now waters and enriches the many nations of modern Christendom with so abundant and fertilizing a flood ? to observe the first principles of individual right, and national freedom, springing up, amidst the darkness of superstition and the pollutions of crime, to mark their progress, until the lapse of years, and a concurrence of favourable circumstances, brightened them into clearness, and unfolded them into maturity of strength ? What more instructive study than to watch the progress of the laws, their courses of deflection, of circuit, of advance ; sometimes trodden down, and apparently lost for ever, amidst the tumult and confusion of domestic anarchy and external war ; sometimes quite overruled by the hand of municipal power at home; then victorious over internal tyranny; growing eventually stronger, clearer, and more decisive, by the very violence which they have suffered; more deeply rooted by the fury of the tempest which scattered their topmost branches into the air, and covered the ground with their withered foliage; enriched even by the temporary desolation of those foreign conquests which menaced their entire destruction; softened by peace, sanctified by religion, improved, enlarged, exalted by commerce, by social intercourse, by science, and by erudition?

In addition to this course of general inquiry, the *American* student ought to obtain that information which results from an analytical investigation of the constitutions, statutes, and judicial decisions of the united and separate states; a branch of legal learning the more necessary, because the *people* of this country possess the supreme sovereign power of creating, altering, and annihilating, at their own discretion, their respective governments, whether state or federal. And, therefore, it is peculiarly incumbent on them to acquire that legal and political knowledge which will best qualify them for the judicious exercise of so important a privilege, so difficult a duty, so dangerous an experiment. By carefully examining our different constitutions, statutes, and judicial decisions, by comparing them together, and, at the same time, referring to the various degrees of order and prosperity, the condition of society, and the standard of religion and morals in each particular state, an accurate estimate might be formed of the relative excellences and defects of the different constitutions and legal codes of the Union; and a pathway of light pointed out, by which essential alterations and substantial improvements might be *gradually* introduced into the municipal systems, and political fabrics of the respective states.

Yet, notwithstanding the manifest utility of such information, and the advantages to be derived from such comparative views, however accurately the constitution and laws of any particular state may be known within its own limits, those of other states are very slightly studied beyond the boundaries of their respective territories. There are many able and learned New-York, and Massachusetts, and Pennsylvania, and Virginian lawyers; but there are very few *American* lawyers in the United States; that is to say, men acquainted with the constitutional, common, and statute laws of the several different states and of the Union. It is to be regretted, that an analytical examination of the municipal systems of the general and state governments is not made a component part of academical instruction in the colleges of the Union. Such an enquiry ought to follow a regular examination of the institutions of Lycurgus, Solon, and Numa; and an analysis of the different systems of American polity and jurisprudence ought to be considered the legitimate sequel of an investigation into the merits of the political and legal fabrics of Sparta, Athens, and Rome.

Some few attempts have been made to establish a system of legal instruction in different parts of the Union. For full thirty years past, Mr. Justice Reeve, first alone, and latterly in conjunction with Mr. Gould, an eminent lawyer and advocate, has been employed in delivering an annual course of lectures on the common law and on American jurisprudence in the State of Connecticut. These lectures have long been justly distinguished for their legal precision and learning; and have accordingly, for many years past, attracted a great number of students from all the different states.

About twenty-five years since, the present Chancellor of the State of New-York, as Professor of Law in Columbia College, delivered lectures the first session to forty students, the next to two, and the third to none, when he resigned his chair. It is no little impeachment of the good sense of the legal students of this city, that they neglected to avail themselves of the opportunity of profiting by the instruction of one of the ablest and most learned jurists of the age in which we live. In Virginia, prelections on international law are delivered by Mr. Nelson, one of the district chancellors of that state, who also fills the chair of municipal law, which was once so ably occupied by Mr. Justice Tucker, the American annotator upon Judge Blackstone's Commentaries. In Baltimore, Mr. Hoffman delivers lectures on law : he has lately published a work, entitled, " A Course of Legal Study," which is not only peculiarly serviceable to the student, but may be perused with advantage by the mature lawyer; with so much talent and skill is its various legal learning arranged and exhibited.

If the several states of Connecticut, Virginia, and Maryland, afford to their respective students such opportunities of legal instruction, is it not incumbent upon the great state of New-York, situated at the confluence of all the streams of American intelligence and enterprise, as well legal and moral, as commercial and political, *to begin* to lay the foundations of a general school of jurisprudence.

A difference of opinion exists between some of our ablest men in this country respecting the utility of *lectures ;* one party asserting that they convey *no* instruction, however composed and arranged, while another insists, that, if well digested, and clearly told, they materially aid the progress of the pupil in improvement. Lectures, on whatever subject, must, indeed, for the most part, be only a series of compilations, because no one can create *facts.* He can merely collect, by patient diligence, the experience and observations of others, wheresoever scattered in voluminous records, or floating in traditionary forms. To such a collection of materials, the lecturer must apply the analytical and synthetical processes of judgment, reasoning, selection, and combination, in order to exhibit the soul and spirit of the subjects discussed, condensed into plain and practical results. This is especially the case with those who undertake to lecture on *law ;* because, no private individual can make law, which is the result of the practical experience of the community, embodied into authority, either by judicial decisions or statutes. The teacher can only state the law to be as he finds it already determined or enacted, and thence, by induction,

T

derive general principles, applicable to similar facts and analogous particulars.

But it does *not* therefore follow that lectures are useless. Nor will it suffice to say, the student may consult the books, and compile a system for himself. Very few can possess the requisites for such a laborious and extensive undertaking. A great command of books, abundant leisure, indefatigable industry, experience to know where to search, and how to select from amidst the vast masses of unconnected particular facts and points, are all necessary. Now, *young* men cannot often be qualified to arrange and mould into shape and symmetry the huge chaos of matter that lies floating, without form and void, amidst the shoreless ocean of the law. Young gentlemen, just emancipated from the salutary restraints of academical life, are not very likely to forego the pleasures incident to that vernal season, or exchange the fascinating pursuit of classical studies and the belles lettres for the solitary task of endeavouring to thread the mazes of the legal labyrinth, with no Ariadne near to furnish a clue by which to guide their bewildered steps. But, when the preceptor's diligence has cleared away the underwood, struck out roads, and marked distances through the forest, the student will be able to journey on his way with alacrity and improvement.

He who does not study at stated times, and systematically, studies to little purpose ; and it is one great benefit of lectures, that they inculcate the necessity and furnish an example of the utility of habitual and systematic study, by pointing out the sources of general instruction, by giving practical results, by exhibiting an analysis of what is disorderly and obscure, by dealing out regular and periodical information. Besides, *new* compilations in the form of lectures are necessary on a subject so complicated, so voluminous, so constantly increasing in bulk, as the *law* must be, from its duty of habitually watching over, guiding, protecting, and punishing the circumstances, words, and actions of human society, ever fluctuating and various. Succeeding ages and multiplied researches produce new varieties of legal points and new modifications of the principles of evidence, which should be arranged and added in a sytematic form to the existing mass. The evidence, authority, and proof of law, are all of the *cumulative* kind, increasing with the increasing age, civilization, growth, prosperity, and intelligence of the community. And, by adding to the long established elementary principles of jurisprudence the discoveries and improvements of each succeeding generation, we improve the proportion, and beautify the symmetry of the legal code.

New compilations, also, are serviceable on all subjects admitting improvements and accommodation to the passing times, because all men write most successfully and intelligibly for the age in which they live. Whatever may be our admiration of the glowing sentiments and splendid eloquence of the great writers of antiquity, every day and every hour present our own age, in aspects and under circumstances, that, for all the purposes of practical utility and instruction, chains down the mind to the contemplation of the present, and causes its existing interests, passions, prejudices, habits, evils, conveniences, hopes, and fears, to predominate over those of the past ages, which are already mingled with the years before the flood. All which applies, with peculiar force, to works on *law*, because the legal code of every nation depends upon the general improvement of society for its own progression towards perfection. In proportion as the science of *metaphysics* sheds its light on the principles of evidence; as *history* unfolds the series of human actions; as *political economy* teaches the relations between government and people and the elements of international law; as *moral philosophy* points out the duties and charities of life, will the jurisprudence of a country become clear and upright in all its provisions, a shield to protect the innocent, a sword to punish the guilty, the bulwark of individual liberty, of private property, and social reputation.

It is the opinion of some very distinguished writers, that the *study of the law* invariably tends to *narrow* the faculties, to diminish and sharpen into a point of technical precision, and formal acuteness, those intellectual powers, which, under more auspicious circumstances, might explore the recondite depths of science, luxuriate in the flowery paths of literature, or range throughout the universe in quest of vast and varied information. It is assumed, as an unquestionable proposition, that a thorough lawyer is, by the very fact of understanding his own profession well, disqualified from looking upward and traversing the higher regions of intellect; the fields of metaphysical, political, moral, literary, and scientific investigation. Among these impugners of the study of the law, the most conspicuous in modern times are Mr. Burke, Mr. Canning, and the author of the Pursuits of Literature, who enforce their strictures upon its narrowing tendencies in strains of lofty and impassioned eloquence.

But Mr. Burke gives up the whole question when he says, " *except in persons very happily born.*" If these words mean men of genius, of great native talent, (and, in their context, they do not admit of any other signification) the charge against the narrowing tendency of the study of the law falls to the ground; for no man presumes that the study of the law " can open and liberalize" minds of merely ordinary capacity, because no kind of study can produce such an effect. Such minds are by their very nature incapable of comprehensive enlargement, and therefore have no business with the study of the law, *as a science.* They may, indeed, and often do, pick up an acquaintance with its minuter forms, its obscurer details, and its more subordinate technicalities. But law, in its higher and more legitimate acceptation, is to them for ever as a fountain closed, and a volume sealed. If the law *do* open and liberalize minds " happily born," that is to say, minds of great native capacity, then the narrowing tendency is *not* in the study itself, but in the mind of the student, which being by nature small and narrow, cannot be dilated nor stretched into magnitude by any intellectual process; because education can never create any new faculty, nor increase the native power of the understanding ; it can only develope, by use and exercise, those talents, whether strong and rapid, or slow and weak, which God has given to men, as the measure of their natural ability.

Mr. Canning also yields the force of his objection, when he says, " were the study of the law, indeed, conducted *as it ought*, it might well be considered as a proper preparation for the duties of a statesman," &c. But no rules of fair reasoning admit of arguing against the *use* of a thing from its *abuse*. And if a proper mode of studying the law will prepare the mind for the enlarged horizon of a statesman's view, it cannot be essential to the nature of law to narrow the understanding ; but the charge applies only to an illiberal and unwise method of studying it. And *such* a mode of studying any other science, or any department of letters, would narrow the mind, and render it bleak and barren. The proper and well-directed study of the classics, belles lettres, metaphysics, physics, politics, theology, enlarges and strengthens the intellect. But the finest capacity would become minute and paltry, were it to study any, or all of these branches of learning in the mode so justly reprobated by Mr. Canning, namely, " in order to acquire a knowledge of forms, of an ill-contrived technical jargon, and of a mass of decisions and regulations, without sufficient attention to the circumstances in which they originated, the principles on which they are founded, or their defects, and possible improvements." The law itself, therefore, is free from these objections, which can relate only to the improper mode of conducting its study.

The author of the " *Pursuits of Literature*" undertakes to prove, " that in state affairs *all* barristers are dull ;" and yet admits, that the Lords Thurlow and Loughborough were great statesmen. But Wedderburne and Thurlow were also eminent lawyers. And if the study of the law did *not* narrow their minds, it can have no natural tendency to produce such an effect in any other students. Did the study of law narrow the mind of Bacon, or Hale, or Hardwicke, or

Mansfield, or Jones, or Hamilton? The fault, then, if fault there be, lies *not* in the nature of the study, but in the *mode* of studying, or in the mind of the student. The tendency of a strong mind is to study law, as well as every other branch of intellectual inquiry, on the broad ground of general principles. To generalize, or climb, by an induction from particular facts to general results, Lord Bacon calls the proud prerogative of genius. But slow and feeble minds have no power to make general combinations. Isolated facts lie scattered up and down, singly, in their brain, like dry and withered sticks, without any bond of connexion, without any faculty of reasoning and imagination, to cause them to strike root, and branch forth into great and productive principles.

Such men, to be sure, always make formal, minute, narrow-minded *case*-lawyers. Yet it is *not* the study of the law which narrows their intellect, but their intellect which narrows the study of the law. Were they to pursue any other study than that of law they would still be narrow-minded; they would, in the pursuit of politics, or theology, or medicine, be *case*-politicians, *case*-divines, or *case*-physicians, because they are *case-men*, and must necessarily carry the groundwork of their nature into whatever calling they follow; must preserve the dowlass texture of their garment, whatever of embroidery or ornament they may heap upon it. The standard of the Persian monarchs, in their ruder ages, was a *leathern* apron. In after times, the sovereigns endeavoured to hide its unseemliness from the view, by covering it all over with barbaric pearl and gold; but it still remained, intrinsically, a leathern apron, notwithstanding its external pomp.

The following facts will show that the study of the law has no necessary tendency to narrow a strong mind. When Lord Thurlow was at the bar, and consulted on any great question, he used to make himself well acquainted with the facts of the case, and meditate on them patiently until he reached his result, by fair reasoning on the general principles of law, as applied to the question before him. He then repaired to Mr. (afterward Lord) Kenyon, the most learned common lawyer in Westminster Hall, since Sir Matthew Hale, stated to him the facts, and his own results, in order to see if his conclusions coincided with the inference of law to be drawn from judicial decisions on the same or a similar subject. And it almost invariably happened that Thurlow's result, derived from general reasoning, was in strict accordance with the inference drawn by Kenyon, from an examination of decided cases. What an eulogium does this fact convey, not only upon the comprehensive sagacity and reasoning powers of Lord Thurlow, but also on the wisdom and justice of the common law !

Lord Bacon was a profound lawyer, as sufficiently appears by his law-tracts, and more particularly his " Reading on the Statute of Uses." And, whether or not the study of the law narrowed *his* mind, may be discovered by examining his " *Novum Organum,*" and his treatise " *De Augmentis Scientiarum;*" works in which his stupendous intellect, anticipating the age in which he lived by at least a thousand years, has laid down those universal principles of investigation and reasoning, by which alone the mind can successfully regulate its search after improvement and truth :

> "——— Clarum, et venerabile nomen,
> " Gentibus, et nostro multum quod prodidit orbi."

The denunciations against the narrowing tendencies of the study of the law, pronounced by Mr. Burke, Mr. Canning, and the author of the " Pursuits of Literature," are to be found in Mr. Burke's speech on American taxation, delivered in the House of Commons, on the nineteenth of April, 1774; and in an "Answer to an Inquiry into the State of the Nation," written in 1806, in order to refute the positions of a celebrated pamphlet, written conjointly by Mr. Fox and Mr. Brougham, Mr. Canning's strictures on the study of the law were called forth, by the appointment of Lord Ellenborough, Chief Justice of the King's Bench, to a seat in the executive

cabinet. " A prefatory Epistle on the Pursuits of Literature," is exceedingly severe on all lawyers, and
especially on Lord (then Mr.) Erskine, for their incom-
petency in political affairs. All these performances
are emblazoned with splendid eloquence, and two of
them are also enlivened with keen and polished wit;
but their inferences I hope have been proved to be
fallacious.

It is objected by Mr. Bentham, in his celebrated
Treatise on Legislation, that the *common law* of England
is rude and barbarous in its origin, unfit for the present
advanced state of civilization, far inferior to the Roman
or civil law, in comprehensive wisdom, and accuracy
of detail, and radically defective in *not* being a written
code, but merely customary, and growing out of the
usages and habits of the community.

The soundness of this assertion, although urged by
such high authority, is questionable; for no individual,
no community *can* provide for, or foresee the exigencies
which are continually arising amidst the ceaseless fluctuation of human affairs; and consequently, if there
were no legal code, save what was *written,* in the shape
of ordinance, statute, or decree, society would be, at
once, too much trammelled in its movements, and without remedy in many emergencies. This is emphatically
the case in China and Hindostan, whose written codes
are prodigiously minute in their provisions, watching
over and regulating all the little details of individual
pursuit, domestic economy, and social life. Besides, in
all countries, even the most despotic, a common or customary law prevails, owing to the absolute incompe-
tence of positive enactments, legislative provisions, and
executive decrees, to regulate all the concerns of the
community. Hence, it existed among the nations of
antiquity, whether free or enslaved, as the Greeks, Per-
sians, and Romans; it exists also in the modern world,
among the bond and free; among the Hindus, Chinese,
and Turks, the nations of continental Europe, which
have adopted the civil law as the basis of their own
municipal codes, the French, Germans, Italians, Spa-

niards, and Dutch, as well as the English, Irish, and Americans, who profess to be governed almost entirely by the provisions of the common law.

This common, or customary law, implies, in its very name, as springing from the customs and habits of the country where it exists, that it is in a state of perpetual change; since the customs and habits of a people, more especially if free to follow their own inclinations, are perpetually changing. A common law prevails in all nations, but most in free communities, because in them the greatest respect is paid to the feelings, habits, manners, and customs of the people. It is impossible, by *statute*, to provide for every particular case that may arise amidst the various modifications of which property is susceptible, the diversity of relations in civil life, the many possible combinations of events and circumstances, which elude the power of enumeration, and mock the reach of all human foresight.

But whatever is not *written* is *common* law; and accordingly, in every country pretending to any administration of justice, it has been found expedient to entrust the judges with the power of deducing from the more general propositions of law, and from the habits and customs, sanctioned by usage, such practical corollaries as may most conduce to the furtherance of justice. Deductions thus formed and established, in the adjudication of particular causes, become part of the text or body of the municipal law. Succeeding judges receive them as such, and generally consider themselves as much bound by them as by the provisions of statute law. Thus grows up, gradually, a body of common or customary law. Cicero, in his "*Oratoriæ Partitiones*," expressly asserts, that in every country two sorts of law prevail; one written, the other not written, but springing up, either from the rights of nations, or the municipal customs of their ancestors. Rome and England, under their mixed governments, the one inclining to democracy in its later stages, the other pretty equally poised by the conflicting forces of monarchy, aristocracy, and democracy, have been the greatest legislators recorded in history. Rome has left the foundation, and great part of the superstructure, of her civil code, to the whole European continent—to Scotland, to the colonies of France, Spain, Holland, Sweden, and Denmark. England has, in her own island, carried the authority and government of law to a very high eminence of perfection ; and has transmitted her municipal code to Ireland, to her European, African, Asiatic, and American colonies, and to these United States.

Under both the Roman and English establishments, the common law, or known customs, and the practice and decisions of courts, acquired equal authority with positive statutes. Effectual precautions were taken for the impartial application of general rules to particular cases ; and a surprising coincidence exists in the modes of jurisdiction adopted by these two nations. In both countries the people reserved to themselves the office of judgment, and brought the decision of civil rights and criminal questions to the tribunal of peers, or *a jury*, who, in judging their fellow-citizens, prescribed a condition of life for themselves. Nay, the *term* common law, as well as the thing itself, is not confined to the law of England. Sir Heneage Finch, afterward Lord Nottingham, one of the ablest of a very long list of able English Chancellors, says, " that it is not a word new, nor strange, nor barbarous, nor proper only to England, but is common to other countries also." Euripides, more than once, makes mention of the common laws of Greece ; and Plato, in his Treatise on a republic, defines the common law to be " that which is first taken up by the common consent and usage of a country, and afterward sanctioned by judicial decisions ; he also calls it " the golden and sacred rule of reason ;" a phrase borrowed by Lord Coke, when he said, " that common law was nothing else but right reason ;" meaning, doubtless, that refined reason, the offspring of experience and wisdom, whose authority is generally obeyed by the consent of all.

The common law is peculiarly favourable to the growth and maintenance of *liberty*, both personal and political, because it cherishes and establishes those usages and customs of the people, which experience has proved to be practically beneficial; whereas, *written* law is unfavourable to freedom, by fettering the movements of social action, and by leaving no room for the growth of popular habits and customs. Hence the common law prevails most in the freest countries, whose freedom it continually augments; for example, it bears greater sway in England, and in the United States, than in any other country; because they are the most essentially free, and substantially civilized, of all nations, ancient or modern. The distinguishing characteristic of the common law is its elastic energy, accommodated to all social exigencies; alike fitted to direct and regulate the tender infancy, the aspiring youth, the matured manhood, and the venerable age of nations. Whence, its limits are in continual progression; as new exigencies arise in the community, and consequently new combinations and applications of common law principles are necessary. And, as the English and American judges, following the light of Lord Mansfield's great example, embrace the general principles of jurisprudence, the common law will travel over the dominions of equity; and that which is merely equity now, will, in the lapse of half a century, be established common law decision and practice. Within the last fifty years, the common law has embraced a considerable portion of equity jurisdiction.

In England, the common law has grown with the growth of the nation, in arts, and arms, in religion, morals, science, literature, and civilization. The English common law was rude and scanty in its origin, containing a few imperfect regulations respecting person and property, under the Anglo-Saxon and Danish dynasties; at the Norman conquest it embraced the feudal law, in relation to *real* property; afterward it incorporated the civil law, with regard to *personal* property. In the progress of its growth, it received within its capacious bosom the commercial law; and lastly, has girded within its immeasurable belt the whole system of international law, which connects together in the bonds of social intercourse all the inhabitants of the civilized world. The criminal law of England is in part Saxon, Danish, and Norman, much modified by subsequent statutes. The European codes, generally, are similar in their origin, and in much of their progress. Thus the English, Welsh, Scottish, French, Italian, Spanish, German, Danish, and Swedish codes, reflect mutual light upon each other, in all the essential points of their respective juridical systems. This is so much the case between those of France and England, that the best illustrations of the ancient French code are to be found in the earlier law writers of England; and the best commentary upon the old English law exists in the writings of the elder French jurists.

Some of the most distinguished of our American jurists are divided in opinion respecting the introduction of the common law of England into, and its authority within, the United States. On one side, it is contended that the English common law is the unwritten law of the United States, in their national or federal capacity; and that the common law of the separate states remains the same as before the revolution. While on the other side it is urged, that *no* common law exists in the courts of the United States, but their whole range is confined to taking cognizance of, and expounding the American constitutions, the acts of Congress, and treaties between the United States and foreign powers. It is, however, admitted on all sides, that the common law of England, as it existed on the breaking out of the revolution, has been incorporated into *all* the separate states, as the basis of their municipal law; subject, of course, to the control and modification of legislative provisions.

Some of the principal differences, at present existing between the American and English law, are, that our municipal code tends to scatter real property, at the death of every head of a family, whereas that of England, by the common law of descent, the statute of entails, and the custom of strict marriage settlements, tends to accumulate and perpetuate family property.

In the distribution of personal property, the American follows the English, which is derived from the civil law. Our criminal code is much milder than that of England, which is too severe, and encourages crime, by the *uncertainty* of punishment; while we augment crime by the *inadequacy* of punishment to such a degree, as to keep our state-prisons generally full, besides a continually increasing body of pardoned criminals, let loose to prey upon the public. The courts of the United States, although they disavow any binding authority in the English common law upon them, yet in fact expound their legal questions, whether civil or criminal, upon common law principles.

Upon the whole, then, the best groundwork for the earlier studies of the English and American jurists is to be found in the diligent perusal of Judge Blackstone's Commentaries, as containing an admirable outline of English law, both civil and criminal; and then the Institutes of Justinian, because the legal provisions respecting personal property, both here and in England, are almost entirely derived from the Roman code. The late General Hamilton used to say, that he had learned more of the elements and principles of jurisprudence, as a science, from the study of this than of any other work. Next in order, should be read the Book of Feuds, because the English law of real property is derived from the feudal system, and that of America (with some statute modifications), from the English law. Then Beawes's Lex Mercatoria will give an acquaintance with commercial law, as an essential part of the common law; and Vattel presents a brief outline of the law of nations, which also constitutes an integral portion of the common law. A work on national law, embracing the questions decided since the time of Vattel, is much wanted. At present, only a few miscellaneous observations can be made on some of the *defects* in our juridical system, which have been partly borrowed from England, and are in part weeds of our own growth.

In England, individual subjects, to whom the sovereign is indebted, have a remedy in the King's own courts, by *a petition of right;* whereas, in the United, and separate states, every part of the English common law relating to the sovereign was abolished by the revolution, which fixed the sovereignty in the American people. And our courts only possess so much judicial power, as is given by constitution and statute, neither of which gives an action at the suit of an individual against a state, or against the United States. Whence a creditor, whether of a separate state, or of the United States, has no other remedy than to petition the legislature to make a money appropriation to the amount of the debt due to him; which is a very precarious remedy, as appears from the fate of so many petitions to Congress, and the state legislatures, by claimants on the score of revolutionary services, during that war which gave national independence and sovereignty to the United States. There is no legal mode of compelling any one of our states to pay its just debts, whether due to its own citizens, or the citizens of other states, or the subjects of a foreign sovereign. Nay, if a state violates a treaty or an act of Congress, or any of the provisions of the federal constitution, there is no legal remedy, because the separate states are *not* amenable to the judicial authority of the United States.

The laws in this country generally favour the *debtor,* at the expense of the creditor, and so far encourage dishonesty. The number of insolvents, in every state, is prodigious, and continually increasing. They very seldom pay any part of their debts, but get discharged by the state insolvent acts with great facility, and secrete what property they please for their own use, without the creditor's being able to touch a single stiver. There is no bankrupt law in the United States, and no appeal in these matters from the state to the federal courts; whence, in every state, the insolvent acts operate as a general jail delivery of all debtors, and a permanent scheme, by which creditors are defrauded of their property. The *British* merchants and manufacturers who have trusted our people doubtless understand this.

Throughout the separate states, whatever may be the mode of appointing, or the official tenure of the superior judges, the justices and judges of the common pleas, and other inferior courts, are generally appointed during pleasure, and receive their income from the fees of office; whence litigation is grievously encouraged among the poorer classes of the community, and a horrible perversion of justice corrupts the whole body of the commonwealth.

The United and separate States have transcribed into their statute book the English laws against *usury*. All the best political philosophers unite in condemning any legislative interference with the rate of interest for the use of money; see Dr. Adam Smith, Mr. Hume, Sir James Stuart, and particularly Mr. Bentham, who demonstrates the absurdity and mischief of all usury laws most conclusively and forcibly. A single fact is sufficient to prove their inutility and folly; namely, that the *legal* always differs from the *market* rate of interest. In countries abounding with capital, the legal is above, in those deficient in capital it is below the market price. For example, in England, at this moment, the legal rate of interest is five per cent., the market price only three; in the United States the average legal rate is six per cent., and the market price varies from ten to twenty per cent. according to the rapacity of the lender, and the exigency of the borrower. In Hamburgh, where there is no usury law, the rate of interest is lower, in proportion to its capital, than if such law existed, because no premium is required for breaking it.

Some of our states, particularly that of New-York, have borrowed the English system of *poor laws*. Now, whether we adopt the theory of population laid down by Mr. Malthus, or that more recently urged by Mr. Wieland, both of whom exhibit great talent, and a most instructive display of facts, in support of their respective propositions, we must be compelled to admit, that the poor laws of England are an awful evil to that country; that they increase the indigence which they profess to relieve, and enormously augment the vice, misery, and degradation of the great mass of the English people. Whoever wishes to see the details upon this subject, may consult the discussions in the House of Commons, and the Reports on Mendicity, lately published in London; and the *causes* of the system producing such pernicious effects are unfolded with great force and clearness by Mr. Malthus, in his Essay on Population.

As yet, on account of their extensive territory, comparatively thin population, high wages of labour, abundance of employment and sustenance, the United States do not suffer so much from the system of poor laws as England. But, as far as they go, they produce substantial evil, unmingled with any good. In this city of New-York, for instance, it appears, from a memorial addressed to our state legislature, in the month of March, 1817, that, during the last winter, *fifteen thousand* paupers, that is to say, about *a seventh* of our whole population, received alms. For several years past the numbers of our poor have been increasing, and have been attended with a corresponding augmentation of profligacy and crime. When the superintendants of the New-York Sunday School Union Society, in the spring of 1816, first engaged in their labours of love, to reclaim the children of poverty, idleness, and vice, from the error of their ways to the wisdom of the just, they found the streets of the city and the habitations of the poor one living spectacle of intoxication. They were shocked to see the squalid misery, the loathsome disease, and still more loathsome moral deformity of infancy, youth, manhood, and age, all occasioned by the *habitual* use of ardent spirits among the poor, without distinction of sex or years. It is but the tribute of justice to the merits of those estimable men, to declare, that their remonstrances and efforts in the sacred cause, which they have espoused with so much zeal, charity, wisdom, and perseverance, have somewhat diminished this horrible vice, as well as lessened the profanation of the sabbath.

It is surely needless to expatiate on a fact established by the experience of all history; namely, that whenever the lower orders of the community are generally corrupted in their morals, the death-warrant of their civil and religious liberties is already signed. And, if such an event has uniformly taken place in the governments of the old world, where the people are *not* suffered to exercise any great share of political power, or enjoy any great portion of political rights and privileges, *how much more* certain and speedy must be the desolation in the United States, all of whose governments have their foundations laid broad and deep in the popular sovereignty, and all of whose institutions rest, ultimately, upon the basis of popular opinion? It requires no prophetic inspiration to foretel the rapid dissolution of a government, planted in the soil of universal suffrage, when once its electors have become deaf to the calls of duty, by the long-continued habit of iniquity, and when the mere sale of their votes to the highest bidder may be considered as one of the least dark in the long catalogue of their accustomed crimes.

The chief cause of the degradation and misery in our paupers, doubtless, is to be found in that system of poor-laws, which we have faithfully transcribed from the English statute book into our own legal code—a system by which the English poor have been materially injured in their morals, their habits of industry, their sense of character, in all that contributes to give strength and permanency to national prosperity; a system first adopted in the reign of Elizabeth, and since that time swollen, by successive statutes and innumerable judicial decisions, into a voluminous and frightful code. The same causes invariably produce the same effects, when applied to the same circumstances; and therefore, although at present, owing to our thin population, abundance of wages, provisions, and work, and the small public expenditure, the burden of the poor rates does not press with so very alarming a weight, yet it is an evil in *perpetual progression,* and will continue to eat into and gangrene the life organs of the commonwealth, precisely in proportion as the people shall continue to augment in number, and agri-

U

culture, trade, and manufactures, continue to swell the tide of individual wealth. Such *has* been the progress of this system in England, and such *must* be its course in the United States, unless the legislature, in its wisdom and mercy, see fit to annihilate or alter the whole code of poor-laws.

Man is by nature an *idle* animal; and, generally speaking, shrinks from labour, unless impelled by necessity. But the poor-law system takes away this universal impulse to industry, by relieving *all* the needy that apply for help; thus, in fact, encouraging that very idleness which is the original and hereditary sin of our common nature. Nor is idleness ever a *solitary* vice: it leads almost of necessity its votaries to intemperance, fraud, theft, and those still more atrocious crimes which shake the foundations of human society. The Spanish proverb is, "the devil tempts *other* people, but *idle* people tempt the devil." If the Spaniards would profit by the good sense of their own proverb, they would soon exhibit a beautiful and splendid contrast to the midnight darkness of *sloth and slavery* which now enshrouds their religious sentiments, their political opinions, their public liberty, their individual enterprise. The legislature of *this* country, and more particularly of our own state, is called upon by the voice of duty, as they regard the welfare of the people committed to their charge, to check the growth of an evil, whose unchecked progress must eventually convert the great mass of our community into idle, intemperate, profligate beings, and through *their instrumentality* consign our civil and religious liberties, our political and social institutions, the pride and ornament of an enlightened age, our private consolations, and public defences, the incentives to exertion, the light of hope, and the love of life, to the silence and forgetfulness of the sepulchre.

I cannot close this very slight summary of a few of the defects of our legal system, without noticing the radically imperfect organization of our New-York *Court of Errors*, which cannot be done better than in the words of Mr. Platt, now one of the judges of our supreme court, but sitting as a senator of our state, when he made the following observations, respecting our highest judicial tribunal.

The New-York State Constitution provides, that a court for the trial of impeachments, and correction of errors, shall consist of the President of the Senate, the Senators, Chancellor, and Judges of the supreme court, or the majority of them. " I cannot admit," says Mr. Justice Platt, " the doctrine of *immutability* in the decisions of this court, to the unqualified extent claimed by the plaintiff's counsel. The decisions of courts are *not* the law, but only *evidence* of law. And this evidence is stronger or weaker, according to the number and uniformity of adjudications, the unanimity or dissension of the judges, the solidity of the reasons on which the decisions are founded, and the perspicuity and precision with which those reasons are expressed. The weight and authority of judicial decisions depend also on the character and temper of the times in which they are pronounced. An adjudication at a moment when turbulent passions, or revolutionary phrensies prevail, deserves much less respect than if it were made at a season propitious to impartial inquiry and calm deliberation. The *peculiar* organization and practice of this court render it difficult to establish a system of precedents. In the supreme court, the judges confer together, compare opinions, weigh each others reasons, and elicit light from each other. If they agree, one is usually delegated by the others, not only to pronounce judgment, but to assign reasons for the whole bench. But even in that court, and in the courts of Westminster-Hall, the judges who silently acquiesce in the result do *not* consider themselves bound to recognize as law all the *dicta* of the judge who delivers the opinion of the court. In this Court of Errors, the members never hold any previous consultation together : we vote for the most part as in our *legislative* capacity. Few assign any reasons, and fewer still give written opinions, which may be reported. For these reasons, I think it would be extravagant and dangerous to consider the *dicta* and opinions of a single member, as settling definitively the law of the land, on all the points on which he chooses to give opinions, or to assign reasons."

The House of Lords in England, in relation to its being the highest legal tribunal in the empire, is liable to nearly the same objections which Mr. Justice Platt urges against the Court of Errors in this state. But in England, on every question of law, the peers, both clerical and lay, are in the habit of trusting implicitly to the opinions of the twelve judges; whereas, in New-York, our judges have *not* always the weight in the decisions of the Court of Errors which their acknowledged talents and learning ought, in all places, to command. It would be exceedingly beneficial to this state, if a convention of the people were called for the purpose of altering the constitution, at least in three particulars; namely, constituting a Court of Errors entirely of *legal* characters; abolishing the limitation as to age in the official tenure of our judges; and annihilating the Council of Appointment, that our governor might be a single, responsible, executive magistrate.

It is a common complaint, that the American bar is *overstocked.* With what?—with talent and learning. This, I believe, is *not* asserted, and would be difficult to demonstrate; since no community, in whole or in part, can be *so* overstocked, because native talent is a plant of rare growth, and still rarer cultivation, in every age and country. But our bar is overstocked with *numbers.* Grant the fact; and ask if talent and learning have any thing to fear from unnumbered combinations of dulness and ignorance. Can mere numbers of persons, who either neglect to exercise their understandings, or who have no minds to exercise, stop the progress of the combined force of talent, industry, and learning, in a profession where success so mainly depends upon the public display of genius and knowledge? Did the shades of Tartarus, the unsubstantial forms that hovered round his path, impede for a moment the march of Æneas onward to Elysium?

Whether or not our bar be overstocked with num_bers, I am ignorant, having no data on which to calcu-late with any degree of certainty and precision, if the annual increase of lawyers averages a greater propor-tion than it ought to bear to the yearly augmentation of wealth and population in the United States. But if the bar be, at present, overstocked with numbers, it is of no importance. It is merely a local and temporary incon-venience, which, when left to itself, will soon find its own remedy; for the quantity of every commodity always suits itself, ultimately, to the effectual demand of the existing market. Apply this doctrine to the law, and lawyers, and there need be no alarm as to the con-sequences of an excessive influx of students. If the bar be understocked, the practice of its members will be so abundant and lucrative, as to offer a high bounty for an immediate supply of new recruits. If it be over-stocked, the practice will be so monopolized by its abler sons, as to speak to the less efficient barristers in the very intelligible language of nakedness and hunger, that the bar is no place for them; that it opens no market for the vent of their wares; that its cardinal pillars are *not* ignorance and idleness; that its walls are *not* to be buttressed up by dulness and impudence; and that they therefore must betake themselves to some employ-ment more congenial to their nature and acquisitions, than a calling which requires the combination of na-tive talent, with patient and persevering industry.

At all events, talent and industry need never be terrified from the pursuits of law, since, by the very na-ture and condition of men and things, there never *can* be an overstock of diligence and capacity upon the face of the earth; and since *they*, when directed by prudence and discretion, cannot fail of commanding success and honour in every walk of life, and in none more certainly and more splendidly than the bar. Whichever political party be uppermost in the United States, the lawyers govern the country; they possess more influence, and exercise more power than any other power; they are emphati-cally the men of business, and as we have no separate corps of professional politicians, they engross nearly all the high offices of state, whether at home or abroad. With the exception of General Washington, every President of the United States has been a lawyer; and, without any exception, all our ablest diplomatists have been selected from the same profession.

The American bar always commands a full share of the great talent of the country; indeed, it ought and it *does* exhibit, in proportion to our whole population, as compared with that of the British isles, a larger aggregate display of intellect than is manifested by that of the United Kingdom of Great Britain and Ireland; for, in the United States, there is no other general outlet for the *first-rate* talent than the profession of the law. The nature of their political institutions forbids any hope of their statesmen ever acquiring any permanent power or extensive wealth and influence in the community, and, consequently, offers no adequate inducement for the primary talents of the country to devote themselves *exclusively* to a life of politics; whence the state seldom or never commands for her *permanent* service the first-rate abilities of her children. The *pulpits* of America are not sufficiently cherished by the national or state governments, nor sufficiently encouraged by public opinion, nor remunerated by a sufficiently ample compensation, to offer an adequate bounty to the highest order of talent. The *navy* and *army* of the United States have not yet grown up to a sufficient size and extent to vindicate to themselves the employment of any very great proportion of the first rank of American genius. These two illustrious professions must experience many years of much more active and comprehensive service than they have ever yet seen, before they can allure to their paths of peril and glory their due proportion of the dominant mind of their country.

And in no community has trade or manufacture, the plough or the loom, taken to itself *permanently* the exertions of very commanding abilities. If time and chance cast primary native genius into either of these occupations, after a few desperate struggles of agony it either seeks refuge in the tomb, or, bursting asunder the bonds of its condition, springs upward into a region of intellect more fitted to its inclination and capacity. The *bar* then is the great, the almost only repository of all the highest talents produced and reared in these United States. And the primary native genius of this extensive country, throughout all its separate state sovereignties, rushes onward to the legal standard, as offering the highest inducements of reputation, wealth, influence, authority, and power, that the commonwealth, in its present circumstances, can give.

But in Britain, her political institutions, her local situation, the circumstances of Europe, the condition of the whole world during the last fifty years, have all conspired to force her primary talents into the service of her parliament, her executive cabinet, her army, navy, church, colonial governments, and diplomatic squadrons; while her *bar* has been left to explore the mazy labyrinth of jurisprudence by the feebler lights of secondary minds. The time *has* been, indeed, when she availed herself of her first-rate capacities in the labours of the law. She *has* seen Bacon, and Hale, and Hardwicke, and Mansfield, strengthen, illumine, and dignify her seats of justice. But that was a period when these great master-spirits were wanted to build up and cope in, to the fulness of perfection, her juridical system; to reduce the decisions of her various courts of equity and law to one uniform level of wisdom, justice, and certainty, throughout all the reach of her extended empire. It was also, at a time, when her political circumstances permitted her to spare a large portion of her primary talent to rear the infancy and establish the manhood of her legal system.

But for the last fifty years, including the two great revolutions of America and France, so severe and unremitting has been the political pressure of England, that she has been compelled to pour out nearly all her first-rate intellect over the whole of her extensive dominions, in her naval, military, and civil departments.

And consequently, as primary talent is never profusely dispensed in any age or country, she has been scarcely able to spare any of it *permanently* to the service of the bar; but the moment she has discovered it to have accidentally strayed into the precincts of the forum, she has immediately called it thence into the upper regions of the state; as she did her Burke, her Pitt, her Grenville, her Canning, and her Brougham. Whence, as native genius is equally distributed over all the nations and sections of the earth, and differs only in different countries, in its developement and display, according to the circumstances in which it is placed, and as the American bar employs the first-rate talent of the United States, and the British bar uses only the secondary capacities of Britain, it follows that the American bar must average a greater intellectual power than is exhibited in the British forum, *which is undoubtedly the fact*, more especially in extemporaneous public speaking.

The Author of "Inchiquin, a Jesuit's Letters," makes some spirited and eloquent observations on the comparative merits of American and British oratory, and gives a decided preference to that of the United States, particularly in forensic speaking. He allows the English to be good reasoners, chaste writers, and classical scholars, but by no means equal to the Americans in extemporaneous elocution. The English *pulpit*, he says, is learned, didactic, phlegmatic, and never eloquent; the English *bar*, addicted to a bad style, and ungraceful elocution; and in *parliament* sober reasoning prevails over imagination and rhetoric. Chatham and Burke, he allows, and Sheridan he is inclined to admit, as orators; but they are the *only* orators which Britain has produced. The few others who were eminent, for instance, Pitt and Fox, were nothing more than adroit debaters; and the great body of public speakers in parliament, at the bar, and from the pulpit, with great good sense, and extensive acquirements, are deficient in all the properties of eloquence. To Ireland the palm of modern oratory is awarded, and Burke, Sheridan, Curran, and Grattan, held up as bright examples. A doubt is expressed if the United States have yet produced a Chatham, or a Burke; and an opinion declared that our best speakers want the finish of oratory; but it is confidently asserted that the Americans surpass all other nations in aptitude for public speaking, and in flights of bold, vigorous, and beautiful eloquence. In their public bodies, in Congress, the state assemblies, the bar of the several states, and their numerous political and academic associations, there is a much greater number of agreeable speakers than in the similar assemblies of Great Britain.

These observations of Inchiquin have been condensed for the sake of brevity, but the whole substance is preserved, and the reader is recommended to peruse the original, which abounds in spirited eloquence, and powerful efforts to vindicate the literary and national character of the United States from the aspersions so liberally bestowed upon them by Europeans. The preceding observations of Inchiquin, however, require a little modification. It appears somewhat sublimated, to exalt the public speaking in Congress, and the several state legislatures, so far above that of the British Senate, whose superior eloquence is almost necessarily implied in the fact, that the first-rate talent of England constantly directs and adorns her parliament; whereas the primary capacity of the United States *too seldom* finds its way into Congress and the state legislatures, owing to the causes already mentioned, and also to the constitutional exclusion of all office-holders from a legislative seat. And it must always be pretty much a matter of course for the *ablest* men of every dominant party to lay their *own* hands upon, and place under their own immediate guidance and control, the great offices of the executive government. Whence, consequently, in the ordinary current of events, only the eloquence of the secondary men, of that prevailing party at least, can be heard on the deliberative floor, whether of Congress, or of the twenty separate state legislatures.

It is rather extraordinary that Inchiquin should deny the meed of eloquence to Pitt and Fox, and consider them, in common with other parliamentary speakers, only as " adroit debaters." Nor is it less surprising to assert that " there are no orators *now* in the British Senate." What possible definition of an orator *can* be given that shall *exclude* the names of Canning, Welles-ley, M'Intosh, Grenville, Grey, Brougham, Lansdowne, Peel, and many others?

The *pulpit* of Britain, it must be confessed, is almost entirely destitute of pure eloquence, the poetic part of oratory, ardour of imagination, richness of sentiment, energetic and splendid expression. In speaking of the sermons of England, reference is chiefly made to *writ-ten* discourses, because her extemporaneous preachers generally lose as much in elegance and connexion as they gain in vivacity and vigour, on account of their too little previous preparation for their pulpit exercises. The sermons of England are generally characterized by purity of style, correct and luminous reasoning, simple and temperate elegance. But they seldom, if ever, aim at exciting or controlling the great master-passions of the heart; nor do they often reach the higher flights of that eloquence, which, by producing strong and perma-nent emotions, triumphs over the judgment, and chains captive the will of the audience.

It must also be acknowledged that the British *bar* generally pleads guilty to the charge urged against it, so severely and peremptorily by the Jesuit. Yet, with-in the memory of man, that bar has been led by Mans-field, Thurlow, and Wedderburne, three illustrious lawyers, who were equalled by few, and surpassed by none, in compass and variety of wisdom and eloquence. And even *now*, in her day of *secondary* lawyers, the honour of her bar has been conducted to perfection by Lord *Erskine's* felicitous combination of profound legal reasoning with splendid eloquence. Perhaps, it is not going too far to say, that Erskine's Speeches, already published, are the most finished specimens of *bar* ora-tory that any age or country has produced. This must be understood, in relation to the marked distinction between the forensic and parliamentary orations of Demosthenes and Cicero, whose *bar* speeches are not equal to those of Erskine ; although there is no assignable proportion between *his* parliamentary effusions and the legislative energy of the Greek, or the senatorial majesty of the Roman orator.

He who speaks *more* than is necessary, on any public occasion, makes his speaking an *end* ; whereas he who only speaks enough, and then ceases, uses his eloquence as the *means* of obtaining some ulterior end, some greater object ; and is the more effective practical being. Julius Cæsar always said enough; but Cicero, sometimes, said more, and was borne down by the superior weight of Cæsar's talent, efficient energy, and practical wisdom. Many other great men besides Cicero have in this respect erred, and lost sight of their object, of the business they had to perform, in their anxiety to achieve a brilliant oration. Students of law are more particularly interested in observing and acting upon this distinction ; not only because those among them who happen to possess genius, are prone, in common with all powerful minds, to give the reins to their imagination, and permit their heated enthusiasm to sweep and swing beyond the flaming bounds of time and space, *extra flammantia Mœnia Mundi* ;—but also, because the profession of the law itself can, very seldom, tolerate in a forensic speaker the bursts of deep, intense, and genuine passion ;—a rich variety of imagery, the higher flights of poetry, the finer touches of tenderness, the celestial visions of a sublimated philosophy, the majestic amplitude of a style, full, flowing, fervid, and energetic ;

> " Monte decurrens velut amnis, imbres
> " Quem super notas aluere ripas,
> " Fervet, immensusque ruit profundo
> " —————— ore."

The student should, also, remember the broad line of distinction between ancient and modern eloquence. The statesmen of antiquity made it the main business of their lives to become great proficients in public speaking; and, consequently, granting to modern orators native talents equal to those of Cicero and Demosthenes ; yet, as they do not labour so intensely on the study of their art, modern oratory *cannot* rival that of the elder time. It *must* be inferior in methodical composition, in the distribution of the subjects, in the style, elaborated to perfection by the combined efforts of study, taste, and genius ; in the mode of delivery, refined by a long course of exact discipline ; in the exquisite union of refinement with the most perfect air of simplicity, in the combination of art with nature. The proof of this may be found by comparing the deliberative orations of Demosthenes and Cicero with the parliamentary and congressional effusions of modern debaters. Yet, doubtless, the extemporaneous reasoning and declamation of modern times are better fitted for transacting the business of real life, than the more highly finished compositions of antiquity. Wherefore, as all life consists in *action*, it is perhaps wiser for public men, more particularly for lawyers and statesmen, whose whole business it is to be occupied in the transactions of real life, to accustom themselves to speaking extempore, which, although it can never render them such regular and finished orators as Greece and Rome exhibited in the best days of their high and palmy greatness, will yet better enable them to discharge, with credit to themselves and benefit to the community, those various important and difficult duties, which must ever devolve upon genius and wisdom, amidst the ceaseless activity of commercial enterprise, and the everlasting agitations of popular freedom.

It cannot be necessary to expatiate upon the benefit of an habitual study of the best recorded speeches, both ancient and modern, because they contain a vast fund of important moral, political, financial, commercial, and legal information, delivered by the ablest men of the most civilized countries in their most cultivated ages, as the last result of their happiest efforts, under the inspiration of excited genius, giving vent to its effusions, in " thoughts that breathe, and words that burn." They furnish the best models of clear, profound, and comprehensive reasoning, illumined by all the brilliancy of eloquence. They afford the finest exercise to the analytical powers of the mind, while tracing the golden links of their argumentative chain; they enlarge the understanding, and elevate the imagination, by opening the richest treasures of lofty sentiment and extensive thought, glistening in all the splendour of appropriate and copious language.

The result as to the comparative merit of American and English public speaking may be given in a few words. In the United States there is less learning and science among our clergy, less particular legal research among our lawyers, and less political information among our statesmen, than among the corresponding professions in Britain; yet, the eloquence of the American pulpit, bar, and senate, is more full of vigour and animation than that of the British church, forum, and parliament. In England, the college scholarships and fellowships, and various other munificent institutions, lend continual aid to the learning and science of her clergy; the liberal and protracted classical education, and the minute division of intellectual labour, giving to one man the single vocation of an attorney; to a second, that of solicitor; to a third, that of conveyancer; to a fourth, that of special pleader; to a fifth, that of proctor; to a sixth, that of a common lawyer; to a seventh, that of a civilian; to an eighth, that of a chancery lawyer, enable each lawyer to be more profoundly and extensively versed in the researches of his own particular department: and there being a separate class of men trained up exclusively to the pursuits of political life, who have, in fact, no other vocation than to acquire political and general information, and transact the public business, enable the British statesmen to become at once minutely and comprehensively informed of all that regards the policy of their country, both in its home government and its foreign relations.

But, in the United States, our clergy have moderate salaries; no public, and few private libraries; no fellowships nor scholarships; no learned leisure, constant preaching, and perpetual parochial duty: our lawyers

combine in one and the same personage all the various
vocations of an equity lawyer, a civilian, common lawyer, proctor, special pleader, conveyancer, solicitor,
and attorney ; and our politicians constitute no separate
class, but are taken chiefly from our practising lawyers;
whence these respective bodies have no opportunity of
acquiring so much learning and science, whether professional or general, as those of Britain. Yet, being
compelled to rely entirely on the resources of their own
minds, in their various employments, and to place their
ingenuity and vigour in a state of constant requisition,
they acquire habits of greater intellectual promptness
and energy than their British brethren who labour in
similar callings, and, leaning systematically on their numerous artificial props of multifarious information and
minute subdivision of employment, exhibit, indeed,
more learning and knowledge on the subjects which they
discuss, whether verbally or in writing; but, in general,
display less acuteness, strength, animation, and resource
of intellect than the Americans, who, having fewer
crutches, are obliged to trust the more to their own legs;
whence, in the United States, the individuals, and, in
Britain, the aggregate nation is the most powerful. At
least, this appears to be the fact to one who has had an
opportunity of observing the people of both countries,
by a residence of several years in each.

The common law reporters of the United States, and
of the separate states of New-York, Massachusetts,
Pennsylvania, Connecticut, and Virginia, are fully equal
to those of England ; and the New-York *Chancery* reports are far superior to any that Britain has ever produced. In a recent case, the two crown-lawyers of
England sent to this city a joint and decided opinion on
a very important question, involving an immense amount
of property, and requiring for its solution an intimate
acquaintance with the English common law, and with
international law in all its branches, natural, conventional, and customary. This opinion was submitted to
some of the leaders of our New-York bar, who, after
due deliberation, gave an opinion *directly contrary* to

that delivered by the attorney and solicitor general of England, and supported it by legal reference and general reasoning. When it reached England, and met the eyes of the crown-lawyers, those gentlemen were induced to reconsider the subject, the result of which was, that they finally retracted their former opinion, and acceded to that of our New-York lawyers.

In fine, those who are acquainted with both countries cannot hesitate to declare, that, although in particular departments of legal inquiry the British lawyers may be more learned, more minutely and extensively read, yet, in the exhibition of prompt, various, and vigorous talent, the bars of New-York, Philadelphia, and Boston, surpass those of London, Edinburgh, and Dublin.

CHAPTER VI.

—

On the Literature of the United States.

THE writer of a pamphlet called " The United States and England, being a Reply to the Criticism on Inchiquin's Letters, contained in the Quarterly Review for January, 1814," traces with considerable acuteness and ingenuity the causes which have retarded the progress of literature, art, and science, in this country. But the whole performance is miserably disgraced by a rancour of personal hatred, and a venom of vulgar scurrility that ought never to be admitted into literary controversy; such weapons of warfare resembling rather the tomahawk of a savage than the sword of a gentleman.

Mr. Southey is selected as the victim of the writer's spleen, and loaded with every epithet of abuse that the language of vindictive vituperation can furnish. And England, together with her institutions, religious and political, moral and social, is assailed with all the bitterness of a foiled French jacobin. It was hoped that this essence *sans-cullottism* had long since descended from all decent society, both here and in Europe, to the dregs of the populace. Besides, Mr. Southey did *not* write the Review of Inchiquin's Letters, which is said to have been the production of Dr. Ireland's pen. Whoever wrote that article, ought to have known better than to indite such execrable trash against America; and it is difficult to determine whether ignorance or scurrility be its predominant characteristic.

In a recent publication, called " Letters from the South," the American champion has glanced again at the same subject; and, if possible, has plunged into a still lower abyss of personal rancour and scurrility,

than in his former production.   The respective editors
of the Edinburgh and Quarterly Reviews are singled
out as the objects of attack : the Scottish editor is re-
prehended for his criticism on the late Dean Swift, and
compared to a " little cur dog that yelps at the carcase
of a dead lion ;" but the most envenomed shafts are levelled at the English editor, whose unpardonable crime
it is to have risen from a very humble birth, and obscure
condition, into the rank of one of the ablest writers, and
most accomplished scholars in Europe ; and to have devoted his talents and learning to the support of the
government of his country.   Among other notable discoveries, it is found that the Quarterly Review is "a low,
obscure, contemptible, Billingsgate production."   Indeed, the philosophy of these *sans-cullotte* writers appears to consist in venting low buffoonery, and the
coarsest calumnies, on all that mankind generally deem
illustrious and elevated. If a man unfortunately happen,
whether by birth or personal services, to be a prince, or
a lord, or a gentleman, he is immediately pronounced to
be both knave and fool by these profound philosophers ;
according to whose canons of judgment no one possesses
any claim to either virtue or wisdom, unless he be born
a peasant or a cobler. And the whole patriotism of
these men consists in calumniating England, certainly
without adorning or strengthening America.

It is to be lamented that any one should pervert a fine
understanding, and a fair proportion of information, by an
inveterate habit of hating and calumniating whatever has
a tendency to soften national asperity, to refine the taste,
enlarge the intellect, and exalt the character of man.

The substance of this writer's reasons for the apparently low state of letters in the United States, is, that their
learning, like their riches, is more equally distributed
than in any other country ; and although not to be found
in great masses, is diffused, in a certain degree, throughout the whole body of the people.   There are many
causes assigned why literature has not been more cultivated on this side the Atlantic ; the chief of which are,
the facility of acquiring wealth and distinction by

other means, less laborious and more certain; the hardships and dangers of the original settlers; the revolutionary war; the unsettled state of things for several years after its termination; and the origin and progress of the French revolution; all tending to divert the American mind to the love of gain, to military pursuits, to political strife, rather than to the calmer pleasures of the pen and page.

These reasons, doubtless, are correct, and are urged with considerable force, both of thought and expression. It is now, and has been for some years past, a subject of complaint among our most respectable writers, that the British are too apt to underrate the literary claims of the United States, and arrogantly condemn their productions, as being, for the most part, coarse and superficial. Mr. Walsh, in the first volume of his " American Review," expresses his indignation at this conduct, in terms pointed and eloquent; and Mr. Washington Irving, in his very interesting " Biographical Sketch of Campbell," the Scottish poet enters more largely into the subject, in a strain exquisitely touching. The complaints urged by these gentlemen have too much foundation in truth; and it would be reciprocally beneficial, if the United States and England were *both* to abstain from mutual recrimination; and to enter upon a friendly and honourable rivalry in the career of literary exertion, of scientific pursuit, and liberal praise. It may be useful, perhaps, to inquire into some of the principal causes which have influenced the progress of letters in this country; premising, however, a theory of the French philosophers respecting the nature of American intellect, and its *practical* refutation by Dr. Franklin.

The essence of this theory was, that something in the nature and constitution of the American soil and climate necessarily *diminishes* the powers, physical and intellectual, of all its inhabitants, whether human or brute. This position the Count de Buffon first advanced, in his disquisitions on Natural History; and has been followed by a numerous host of philosophers, who maintain that all our animals are smaller and weaker than those in Europe; that our dogs do not bark; that no hair grows on the bodies of our aboriginal Indians; that Europeans, who migrate hither, degenerate both in body and mind; and that their descendants are exceedingly deficient in physical activity and force, and in intellectual quickness and strength. One of these precious theorists received an adequate entertainment from the Arabs, into whose hands he fell a prisoner, during Bonaparte's expedition to Egypt, in 1798. This French *sçavant*, in order to escape manual drudgery, when questioned by his captors respecting his usual occupations, replied that he had led a *sedentary* life : the descendants of Ishmael immediately covered him with tar and feathers, and set him to hatch eggs, by preserving a sedentary posture on them in the hot sand.

Dr. Franklin, while American ambassador at Paris, undertook to refute this theory. He invited six of his own countrymen, and six Frenchmen, to dine with him. As was expected, the French gentlemen, who were all profound philosophers, began to enquire into the *causes* of the declension of nature, vegetable, animal, and moral, in America ; one said, the reason why *man*, in particular, became feebler in body and mind, was owing to the climate being too hot; another insisted that it arose from the climate being too cold ; a third assigned, as the efficient cause, the too great quantity of rain ; a fourth attributed the deficiency to too much drought ; while the two last demonstrated that both man and beast were dwarfed in America from a want of food in the country. Each Gallic disputant maintained his own side of the question with characteristic volubility for a length of time : when, at last, they all referred to Franklin, for a philosophical solution of the *cause*, why all American creatures are so inferior to Europeans in size and strength? The Doctor very gravely desired his six countrymen to stand up, side by side ; which they did, and exhibited a goodly spectacle ; for they were all stout, well-proportioned, tall, handsome men ; the half-dozen Frenchmen were then requested to stand up, side by side ; they did so, and presented a ludicrous contrast to the degenerate Americans; for they were all little, lank, yellow, shrivelled personages, resembling Java monkeys. They all peeped up at their opposite neighbours, and were silent, though not satisfied.

It is, indeed, quite philosophical to measure genius by geographical lines, and to suppose that Providence apportions talent according to degrees of latitude. The limits of the present work will not allow the discussion, or it were easy to show, both by reasoning, *a priori*, on general principles, and also by a regular induction from facts, that although *individuals* differ from each other in degrees of native talent, yet *large masses* of human beings *average* an equal aggregate amount of capacity, in all ages and countries. Indeed, when it is said there must be an average equality of talent in the whole, or in any large portions of the human race, in all ages and countries, it is only saying, in other words, that man is substantially the same being, in body, mind, and spirit, from the beginning to the end of the human creation. Whence, although individuals differ from each other in their respective proportions of talent, so that scarcely any two persons, perhaps, bring into the world precisely the same extent of capacity, the gradations of intellect being as various as the forms and countenances of men, yet the whole, or any large portion of mankind, averages an equal aggregate of talent with that of the same number in any other age or country. For instance, the ten millions of people who now, in 1817, inhabit these United States, average as large an aggregate of native genius as ten millions of French, or British, or Greeks, or Romans, or any other people, of whatever age or country, ancient or modern.

At all events, it is *too late* now to oppose any mere theory respecting the degeneracy of men in America, to the irresistible argument of contrary facts, seeing, that the Americans have, for a series of years, displayed the utmost intelligence, enterprise, spirit, and perseverance in all the occupations of peace; and likewise exhibited the most consummate skill, intrepidity, and heroism in war, whether conflicting in the field or on the ocean.

The truth is, that the great mass of the American people *surpasses* that of all other countries in shrewdness or intellect, in general intelligence, and in that versatile capacity which enables men to enter upon, and prosecute successfully, new situations and untried employments. It would be difficult for any country to show that it has produced men of greater genius, in their respective departments, than Rittenhouse, Franklin, and West.

The *causes*, therefore, why the United States have not yet equalled the most civilized European nations in the refinements of art, the improvements of science, and the splendours of erudition, are to be sought in *other* sources than those of any natural deficiency in intellectual vigour and strength. Some of these causes are now to be examined.

Compare, for a moment, the relative situation of a student in the United States and in England, and there will be no necessity of recurring to *physical* causes, in order to account for the comparative inferiority of American to British literature. In Britain the candidates for literary fame are in possession of the accumulated learning of several centuries; they have access to ample libraries, containing books written upon almost every subject of human inquiry; from the great crowding of population, they enjoy the benefit of a continual competition of talent: owing to the great opulence of the country, there is a constant demand for literary productions, which are multiplied alike by the magnificent liberality of the hereditarily wealthy, who collect together innumerable volumes, and by the spirit and intelligence of the middle orders of the people, including the learned professions, the country gentlemen, the merchants, the manufacturers, and the yeomanry, who examine for themselves into the merits of the writers they peruse; from the liberally endowed seminaries of education, both schools and colleges, a high bounty of emolument and honour is perpetually offered for the exertions of lettered men; by the extensive circulation and salutary influence of so many literary journals, replete with various information, and full of the most vigorous displays of genius, the republic of letters* in Great Britain is lopped of its luxuriance, swept of its frivolity and absurdity, cleansed of its dulness and ignorance, chastened in its strength, and brightened in its ornament. All these, and many other causes, are continually operating to excite the men of letters in Britain to a display of the most energetic and brilliant exhibitions of talent and learning; and do we therefore marvel that in every department of literature and science, the nation has produced, and still continues to produce, works of such transcendent excellence, that her philosophers, poets, orators, historians, moralists, and critics, command the applause and homage of their contemporaries, and ensure the admiration of all future ages?

But what is the case with respect to the United States? The very condition of society in this country forbids its people, *as yet*, to possess an axalted literary character. A comparatively thin population, spread over an immense surface, opposes many serious obstacles to the production and circulation of literary effusions; the infancy of its national independence, and the peculiar structure of its social institutions, do not allow a sufficient accumulation of *individual* and *family* wealth to exist in the community, so as to create an effectual demand for the costly or frequent publications of *original* works: the means of subsistence are so abundant, and so easy of attainment, and the sources of personal revenue so numerous, that nearly all the active talent in the nation is employed in prosecuting some commercial, or agricultural, or professional pursuit, instead of being devoted to the quieter and less lucrative labours of literature: the scarcity of public libraries and of private collections of books, renders any great attainments in science and erudition exceedingly toilsome and difficult: the want of literary competition, rewards, and honours, the entire absence of all government patronage, whether state or federal, together with the very generally defective means of liberal education, necessarily deter men of high talents from dedicating themselves *solely* to the occupation of letters; and consequently prevent the appearance of those finished productions, whether in verse or prose, which can *only* find an existence when the efforts of genius are aided by undisturbed leisure and extensive learning.

Such are *some* of the causes which contribute to retard the progress of literature in the United States; whence we have no right to expect, while these causes continue to operate, the appearance of many original American publications, bearing the stamp of very profound science or very comprehensive erudition. The literary taste of the generality of our readers may be inferred from inspecting the books of the *public* libraries in New-York, Philadelphia, and Boston, the three most enlightened portions of the union. The *Novels*, chiefly English, with a few bad translations from French fictions, the sweepings of the Minerva press, in Leadenhall-street, are most abundantly used, as affording the highest gratification to the lovers of literature: *Plays* and *Farces* are in the next degree of requisition: *Moral Essays* and *History* suffer a little injury in the first, less in the second, and none in the subsequent volumes; the *Classics*, elementary books on *Metaphysics*, *Political Economy*, and *Philosophical* subjects, generally sleep securely on their shelves, undusted and undisturbed by any profane hand or prying eye. Of course, this statement does *not* apply to the liberal scholars who visit these libraries—they, however, are comparatively few.

As is the generality of readers, so is that of writers, in a country; for the literary, like every other market, must always be supplied with commodities in quality and quantity proportioned to its demand for merchantable wares. If the purchasers insist upon being provided with nonsense, there will always be a sufficient supply of that article forthcoming for the use of the home consumption trade. Hence, as must ever happen in such an order of things, the press teems with those mushroom productions of folly, which are engendered by the conjunction of ignorance with impertinence. Thus, at the first dawning of the revival of letters in the south of Europe, the *Troubadors* and *Provençal*

writers deluged the land with a flood of fantastic fop&
pery and childish conceit.   Thus, in later times, even
in our own days, the minor men of letters, the *literatuli*
of the age, enter into a small conspiracy against all useful and solid information, and commit a feeble outrage
upon the efforts of genius and learning.   And as is the
case with all weak animals, these self-styled wise men,
instinctively throng together in herds, and while they
wage eternal warfare against all exalted intellect, incessantly besmear the effusions of each other's folly, with
the ignoble ordure of each other's praise.   They perpetually and reciprocally lavish the epithets of " ingenious," " learned," " acute," "illustrious," " profound,"
" philosophical," and so forth, upon the dismal lucubrations of themselves and their brethren, which afford no
light, but rather darkness visible; while at the same
time they industriously raise the cry of alarm and horror, even at the sound of the distant footsteps of sense
and knowledge.

The defenceless field animals are always gregarious;
always found in flocks and herds; but the lion ranges
alone over the extent of his undisputed dominion.   True
genius scorns the knavish arts of popular adulation: it
loves to be solitary; and when surrounded by the cack-
ling of folly, it broods over the inmost recesses of its
soul in silence, and " pines, like the melancholy eagle,
amidst the meaner domestic birds."

It is however to be remembered, that although the
condition of society forbids us, *at present*, to expect in
the United States many original writers on subjects involving an intimate acquaintance with the depths of science, and the heights of learning, yet there is *much
more* literary excellence in this country than ever meets
the public eye; because, as from the comparative thin-
ness of the population, as well as from other reasons,
authorship is *not* a distinct and separate calling, as in
some of the more crowded parts of Europe: the *best
scholars* in America are those who follow other pursuits, in addition to that of letters; namely, our professional gentlemen, the clergy, physicians, and lawyers;

and some who are not attached to either of these vocations, but are immersed in commercial enterprises, or
agricultural experiments. Among these different classes
are to be found individuals, who, on general subjects of
learning and taste, need not turn their backs to any of
the literary veterans on the other side of the Atlantic.
From the comparatively small demand for *original*
works in the United States, our ablest and best informed men seldom appear as writers; and the field of
letters is left almost entirely clear, for the exhibitions of
those who are *not* to be numbered among the most
learned, and the ablest men in America. Add to this,
that the continual influx of British literature, although
beneficial in imparting to our people new and extensive
information upon a great variety of subjects, is so far
prejudicial, as it depresses the spirit of native literature,
by creating a fastidious rage for foreign publications,
and an affectation of contempt for the productions of
our own press.

Yet notwithstanding all these unpropitious circumstances, the literary spirit has been for some years past
rising in the United States; witness the progressive increase in the importation of foreign books, in the republication of British works, and the productions of American writers. And probably, on a fair view of the subject, we may conclude the progress of letters in this
country to be *proportionally* equal to that of Britain;
considering the different states of society in the two
countries. But, perhaps, it may be useful to notice
some of the other causes which obstruct the course of
literature in the Union. Among these, is to be particularly noticed, the unfortunate practice of entering upon
active life at *too early* an age. Partly from the condition of society, and partly from the eager appetite for
wealth, which especially characterizes all young and
thinly-settled countries: divines, lawyers, physicians,
and merchants, rush into the occupations of active life,
almost before they reach that period which the wisdom
of the common law allots as the termination of infancy.
Plunging so early into the minuter details of practical

employment prevents the due developement of the intellectual faculties; and after a while renders the mind, from disuse, both unable and unwilling to direct its attention to the more abstracted pursuits of literature and science.

There is a salutary adage in the old law books, which runs thus, " In juvene theologo conscientiæ detrimentum; in juvene legistâ bursæ detrimentum; in juvene medico cæmeterii incrementum;" the consciences of his parishioners suffer by a young clergyman; the purse of his clients diminishes in the hands of a young lawyer; and the churchyard increases by the labours of a young physician. This adage, however, has *not* yet found its way into the United States, where the young people of all classes are precipitated into business during childhood. Lord Bacon complains, that in his time the full growth of mind was retarded by the pernicious custom, then prevalent in Europe, of permitting youth to enter into active life at so early an age as *thirty*. This prince of philosophers was, in common with other great men, his contemporaries, in the habit of indulging Utopian visions concerning the millennial perfection of this his " *New Atalantis*;" and the most confident predictions were hazarded, that America, rising superior to the heedlessness of European haste, would patiently unfold her national intellect, by large and liberal study; so as to produce in each particular calling the most beneficial results, and most luminous discoveries.

With such a conviction, how would Verulam be moved, could he behold with what unmeasured precipitancy this New Atalantis, this Athens of the western world, pours forth its swarms of unfledged youth to assume the responsibilities of public life, ere they have passed the little period of one and twenty years. At this unripe age, the preacher takes upon himself to expound the all-important doctrines that characterize the stupendous scheme of redemption, and to impart spiritual consolation to veteran Christians. The physician, also, is, at this early age, licensed to break the *sixth* commandment; and the lawyer is, at this premature period, allowed to practise, as master of a system, which has grown up to its present complicated perfection under the continuous efforts of the ablest men of many generations, in both the hemispheres, European and American; a system, which has reached its present maturity of wisdom as the result of the social experience of twelve hundred years. At this early age, our youth are deemed competent to prosecute the business of active commerce, and to venture gratuitous opinions upon the most difficult questions of policy, involving great national relations and interests.

The consequences of this precocious publicity are, a superficial elementary education, a perpetual pruriency of prattle upon all subjects, without a due fathoming of the depths of any one of them, and an entailed disability of fully developing the understanding, which is narrowed in early life, by being prematurely absorbed in the minute, but necessary details, incident to every practical calling. Whence, with their due proportion of genius, in common with all other nations, and with the advantage of a more general diffusion of popular intelligence than is to be found in any other community, too many of our citizens, in *all* the learned professions, begin, continue, and end their career, on much narrower ground than their native capacity, properly unfolded by previous general information, would enable them to cover.

The regular order of events, however, is providing a remedy for the intemperate haste, which has hitherto plunged beardless boys into public life. The mere pressure of a rapidly increasing population, by augmenting professional competition, must, in due time, compel the adoption of a better course of previous education. Even now a larger stock of elementary information is necessary to enable a man to distinguish himself as a divine, or physician, or lawyer, than was requisite twenty years since. And, doubtless, twenty years hence, what is now deemed a sufficiency of liberal instruction, will prove but a slender share of essential acquisitions.

Seeing then, that sufficient time and opportunity are not allowed our professional men to prosecute literary pursuits, from what fountains are the streams of American literature to spring?—from the *colleges*, scattered so profusely all over the Union? Alas! few, if any of these academical institutions are so munificently endowed, as to enable their inmates to devote the combined advantages of talent, leisure, independence, and inclination, to the service and promotion of letters. In this country there are no fellowships, no scholarships, no exhibitions, none of those situations, which, in the colleges of Europe, direct so large a portion of talents to the successful prosecution of learning. Our professors and teachers are too scantily paid, and too constantly worked, to be often able to execute original and extensive literary undertakings.

Another obstacle to the growth of literature in the United States arises from the great propensity to consume the talent of the country in the effusion of newspaper essays, and political pamphlets, instead of concentrating it in the production of some regular, consecutive work. In consequence of these desultory intellectual habits, periodical journals, as Reviews and Magazines, seldom last long. The author can obtain little or no assistance from others in his literary efforts; the persons competent to aid him in such an undertaking being comparatively few throughout the Union, and those, for the most part, actively employed in some laborious calling; and it is not in the power of any one man, however gifted with talent, adorned with knowledge, and armed with industry, to execute, *alone*, a literary journal as it ought to be executed. Add to this, the universal vice of the United States, a perpetual craving after novelty. The charge which Demosthenes brought against his own countrymen, that they were continually running about, and asking, " Is there any thing new?" is equally applicable to the Americans. This eternal restlessness, and desire of change, pervade the whole structure of our society : the same man will start into life as a clergyman, then turn lawyer, next convert himself into a farmer and land-jobber, and, taking a seat in Congress, or some state legislature, by the way, end his days as a merchant and money-broker. The people are incessantly shifting their habitations, employments, views, and schemes; the residence of a servant does not average two months in each place; the abode of a whole household is generally changed once a year, and sometimes oftener; numerous families, that have been longer settled in the elder states of New-York, Connecticut, and Massachusetts, are continually migrating into Ohio, or the territories of Alabama, Illinois, and Mississippi; the executive, the legislators, the magistrates, and officers of all kinds, are changed biennially, or annually, or half-yearly, according to the greater or less infusion of the restless spirit of democracy into our various forms of government.

Such being the temper, disposition, and habits of the people, new periodical publications are continually starting up, receive a little eager, capricious encouragement, languish a brief space, and die, leaving the same sickly course to be run by a race of successors, equally sanguine and short-lived. It is doubtful if any one of the best European journals, most distinguished for the magnificent display of genius and knowledge, were to issue from the American press, as a *native* production, it would reach the second year of its unsupported existence. Some years since, a very respectable body of men, in New-York, selected from all the three learned professions, started a periodical work, called " The American Review, and Magazine," which was ably conducted, and perished for want of patronage. The " Boston Anthology," supported by the labours of some of the best literary men of all callings in that town, some time after, shared the same fate. And, at a more recent period, the " American Review," edited by Mr. Walsh, was suffered to expire, notwithstanding the splendid talents and various erudition of its conductor.

There never was a time when the United States stood so much in need of an original, native review, as now, in order to erect a standard of independent, impartial criticism, for the benefit both of writers and readers; to animadvert upon American productions, and give some account of European literature, particularly of France, Italy, and Germany. The Edinburgh and Quarterly Reviews are republished, and widely circulated in this country; they are, unquestionably, the ablest literary journals the world has ever yet produced; they display a stupendous aggregate of genius, taste, and learning, upon almost every subject of human inquiry; and are also important to us, as exhibiting the sentiments of the two great contending parties that divide and govern the British empire. But they say little on American literature; and that little is *not* always either liberal or just. Besides, they suffer their political feelings and opinions to mingle too much with, and occasionally to pervert, their literary criticisms. An original *United States* Review, therefore, which should steer clear of the extremes of party spirit, and exhibit a fair and honest view of American literature, and such an account of European productions as might be readily obtained by a liberal correspondence with that quarter of the globe, would very materially tend to promote the cause of letters in this country, and draw out into public notice, as contributors, our ablest and best informed men, who now are the grave of their own extensive acquisitions, by reading all and writing nothing.

But, although in the higher walks of literature the United States do not yet excel, they surpass all other nations in *elementary* education; that is to say, in imparting the rudiments of instruction to the people at large. Most of the states, and especially those of New-England, have established district schools, for the instruction of the children of all the inhabitants. Whence, scarcely a native American is to be found who cannot read and write, and cast accounts; and they all read newspapers, of which there are more printed in the Union than in all the British empire, and political pamphlets, if they read nothing else. The great body of the European people are altogether *uneducated*. Holland, Sweden, the Protestant Cantons of Switzerland,

and Scotland, it is believed, are the only portions of Europe in which the *government* makes any provision for the general instruction of its population. The intellectual and moral advantages of such a system are manifest in the superior habits and character of the New-England people, when compared with the rest of the Union; in the greater sobriety and providence of the Scottish, when compared with their English and Irish neighbours; in the more regular and orderly conduct of the Dutch, Swedes, and Swiss, in comparison with the rest of continental Europe.

Yet, notwithstanding the system of parochial schools has proved so exceedingly beneficial in Scotland, the British government has *not* introduced it into England or Ireland. If the people of those two countries were as well instructed as the Scottish, the moral power of the British empire, and consequently its national strength and greatness, would be quadrupled in fifty years. Nevertheless, Britain has of late considerably increased the education of her English and Irish population, by means of the Bell and Lancaster plans, and Charity and Sunday-schools. But these operate only partially; she must establish a *national* system, if she wishes to have *all* her people instructed. The saying of George the Third, " that he hoped soon to know that every poor man, within his realm, possessed and could read the Bible," was dictated by a spirit of exalted benevolence and enlarged wisdom, better calculated to improve and render prosperous a nation, than the most splendid achievements of naval and military heroism.

Both countries would be highly benefited by borrowing from each other; England by adopting the American system of instructing *all* the people, and the United States by cultivating that higher species of learning, which has rendered the English scholars, for a series of ages, so peculiarly pre-eminent. When will the day arrive, that, in reference to *our own classical* writers, we may be able to exclaim with Callimachus?

Οιον ο τω Πολλωνος ετεισατο δαφνιδος ορπιξ!
Οια δ᾽ ολον το μελαθρον! εκας, εκας, οστις αλιτρος!
Και που δη τα θυρετρα καλω ποδι Φοιβος αρασσει.

I am afraid some considerable time will elapse before Apollo will deign to descend, and visit the temple of American inspiration, in the same manner, and to the same extent, that he has visited Greece, Rome, and England. Upon the first introduction of the Greek language into the English universities, it met with very decided opposition: the combatants divided into two companies, the one favourable to the study of the " *new* tongue," as it was called, being denominated *Greeks ;* that against it, *Trojans,* which last, whenever they saw any thing they did not understand, cried out " Græcum est, et non potest legi." For a long time, in England, the Trojans triumphed ; at last they united their forces with their opponents, and both have, ever since, contributed to augment the strength, and brighten the splendour of their country's literature. In the United States, at present, the *Trojans* are a fearful majority.

The power, wealth, and influence of every nation depends more upon the aggregate of *disposable intelligence* afloat in the community than upon its extent of territory and number of inhabitants. The progress of all nations in wealth and strength, in internal security and external influence, has been proportioned to their activity of mind and advancement in knowledge. The art of navigation, the resources of commerce, the ascendency in war, the discoveries of science, the duration of dominion, can never take up their abode permanently, excepting in countries where the paths of knowledge are incessantly explored by the various but combined efforts of numerous minds. And a general activity of intellect can only be called forth in a nation by allowing full freedom of inquiry on all religious, political, and moral subjects. A due proportion of this general activity will always be directed to the cultivation of those arts and sciences which subserve the purposes of practical life, the increase of individual convenience, and the augmentation of national power. The triumphant issue of civilized warfare is indissolubly connected with the active cultivation of mind, the wide diffusion of knowledge, the free exercise of reason, among the home population of every country. No precarious supply, no importation of talent from abroad, no partial attention to any one branch of improvement to the exclusion of the rest, can compensate for the want of general cultivation in the mind of the native inhabitants.

Of what immense benefit was the general education of their people to the United States, during their revolutionary struggle and their recent conflict with Britain, in multiplying their resources, energy, and skill! And how prodigiously has it forwarded their national career in all the arts and occupations of peace!

But although *elementary* instruction is generally diffused throughout the Union, *liberal* education is *not* sufficiently encouraged; the causes of which are rooted in the very condition of our social fabric. Some of these it may be useful to enumerate. Owing to the peculiar circumstances of America, and her great commercial capacities, a large proportion of her active talent is devoted to trade. But although trade, when considered in the aggregate, is a great engine of civilization, and very beneficial to mankind, by connecting different nations, by opening a wider field for the exertions of productive industry, and by enlarging the sphere of inquiry, yet its effect upon the understanding of the individual employed in it is *not* so beneficial. For the trader, whether a wholesale merchant, or a retail dealer, must employ his mind chiefly in detail, in attending to minute particulars and petty circumstances, which is apt to generate a habit adverse to expansion of the intellect. He, whose head is filled with commercial calculations and speculations from morning to night, will not be often inclined to peruse the pages of the historian, the philosopher, or the moralist. Under such circumstances, wealth alone will be the object of desire; and, as literature opens no such shining path to its votaries, it will become rather an object of contempt that of cultivation.

Y

In consequence of the general predominance of the trading spirit, there is a great dearth of *liberal* education throughout the United States. For no man can know the value of what he himself has never possessed; and consequently an illiterate father can never appreciate the importance of his son's being liberally educated, nor know what progress his boy makes in learning; and will be apt to imagine that it is not necessary to consume much time, or expend much money, in giving the child an opportunity of acquiring general information. Accordingly, our grammar schools are, for the most part, deplorably defective. The schoolmasters consist generally of unlettered foreign adventurers and native boys, who are themselves studying law, or physic, or divinity, and propose to teach others, that they may be able to defray the expense of their own professional probation, and then quit the trade of teaching altogether. Such schoolmasters swarm in every lane and alley of our towns and cities, and vie with each other in bold assertions, that they can carry a boy through a course of liberal education in a few months, and at a small expense. This delectable promise is swallowed by the ignorant and credulous parent, who applauds his own and the preceptor's sagacity for contriving and executing a system of instruction, which, by the expenditure of a few dollars, shall be able to counteract all the accustomed laws of human nature, falsify all human experience, operate impossibilities, and manufacture a scholar by teaching him nothing.

The use of the *grammar* is either exploded altogether, or very superficially taught, or translated into English, as some profound scholars have done with More's Greek grammar, in order to lessen the labour of education. But the basis of all valuable instruction must be laid in the necessity of intellectual toil; no mental acquisition worth possessing can be obtained without previous mental exertion. What is not known accurately is not known at all; and nothing can be known accurately without previous labour of the understanding. The only use of education is to unfold the faculties of the mind, and teach the people to think; but the superficial smattering of a few assemblages of words and phrases, badly understood, and worse delivered, can never develope any power of the mind, nor render man an animal capable of reasoning. Nevertheless, some grown-up men, who pass for scholars in the United States, profess to condemn the mode of teaching Latin and Greek by the aid of *grammar*, which they say is too abstract for the comprehension of boys; wherefore they recommend those languages to be taught " by reading a great deal, and committing the Dictionary and Lexicon to memory."

This, although a fashionable, appears to be a strange method of teaching any, especially the dead languages. Why strive to encumber a child's memory with the numberless words and phrases of a whole Dictionary, when it would be so much easier to learn and retain the comparatively few and simple rules of grammar? Besides, it is not in the nature of things that children shall read a great deal; it is necessary that their tasks be short and simple, and that they be allowed to promote their health and growth by spending a great proportion of their time in bodily exercise and amusement. Nor is it easy to perceive how the mind can be much improved by committing to memory a vast number of words and phrases to which they attach no definite meaning. Words are merely arbitrary signs to designate certain things; language is made up of words, and grammar is the reduction of language into general and fixed rules. And the universal voice of the wise and learned in all ages has required that well educated persons should speak and write with *grammatical accuracy*, in order to distinguish their effusions from those of the untaught multitude.

At first, children learn by single words, which is only endurable, while they are so young as to be only capable of receiving a few simple ideas: it would be endless to endeavour to teach a whole language by single words. The science of *grammar*, therefore, steps in, and by teaching the child a few *general* rules, together with their application, enables it to understand all the *particulars* of that language, so reduced to general rules and principles. Indeed, all sciences rest upon general rules and principles as their basis; and thus, not only render knowledge more ready at our call, and more easy of application, but also enable us continually to increase its limits. Savages teach their children by single words; and how scanty and imperfect are their languages! Infants can only be taught in detail, by single words; but as soon as the mind begins to open, and is able to rise from details to general rules, grammar is taught them, in order to facilitate, and render sure and permanent the acquisition of language.

Teaching language without the help of grammar was a favourite scheme of Mr. Locke, who, in his book on education, says, "that languages learned by rote serve well enough for the common affairs of life, and ordinary commerce." Now, allowing this to be the fact, is it such a knowledge of language as to enable a person to speak and write it correctly? If not, why discard the use of grammar? The truth is, Mr. Locke's book is a very meagre performance, not calculated to give the student enlarged and comprehensive views, but intended merely for the use of *country gentlemen;* and all the world knows what sort of philosophers the English country squires were a hundred years since. His remarks upon *poetry* and *language* are peculiarly frigid and unsatisfactory. The treatises on Education, by Dr. Knox and Dr. Barrow, contain ample refutations of all Mr. Locke's anti-classical heresies. Nay, but these very men, who explode the use of grammar in teaching boys, admit that when these boys grow up, they must study grammar, to obtain a more *critical* knowledge of the language. The whole of this boasted method then, at last, resolves itself into this, that grammar is of no use in teaching a language, but a boy must learn a dictionary by heart, and read a great deal, and after several years so spent, he must then learn the grammar, in order to understand the language.

But is it likely that boys who have been taught in so desultory and unconnected a manner will study grammar when they become men? It is better to begin at the right end, and teach the grammar in the first instance; for each general rule of grammar, by its application to a multitude of particulars, is surely a readier and more certain method of teaching a language, than by learning single words or detached phrases, without any general rules by which light can be thrown upon the different parts of the language, and by which those different parts can be conjoined, so as to constitute a *whole*, correct in its symmetry, and fair in its proportions. And requiring boys to commit the grammar to memory, and to *apply* its rules to the words and phrases that occur in the course of reading, which is called *parsing*, or analyzing the language, is a better exercise of the mind, and better calculated to unfold the reasoning powers than working a proposition in Euclid.

" The study of grammar requires more force of attention and connexion of thought than that of mathematics. Grammar unites ideas, as calculation combines figures; and its logic is as precise as that of Algebra, with the additional advantage of making at the same time a direct and powerful application to all that is alive and vigorous in the mind. Words at once denote sounds, and numbers, and images, to excite emotions in the understanding. They are subject to the strict discipline of syntax, and yet full of the native force and signification of the ideas they conventionally represent. In the metaphysics of grammar, the philosophy of language, energy of thought, and accuracy of reasoning, are intimately united."

England and Ireland have for some centuries past produced the most accomplished classical scholars in the world; and they teach Latin and Greek by the grammar. Now, it will require very strong evidence to prove the superiority of any new-fangled theory, to a method whose entire success has been established by a series of national facts for so great a length of time.

Nevertheless, we shall probably witness the abolition of grammar, as the basis of classical study in the United States ; for some of our college-professors maintain the necessity of teaching Latin and Greek without grammar, and triumphantly ask, " if children are not taught to speak and write English without the use of grammar, merely by reading and committing the dictionary to memory ?"—To which the answer is obvious, that those who have never learned grammar of any kind are *not* apt to write, if to speak English correctly ; besides, there are no opportunities of teaching a *dead*, as we can a living language, by *speaking* it.   Nor are the facilities of *reading* it so great. The utmost that this *rote*-method of teaching languages without the aid of grammar can accomplish, is to enable people to prattle in a *living* tongue, upon the ordinary topics of every-day discourse; but it *cannot* teach them to *write* correctly, even in a living tongue ; and, certainly, will give only a very superficial knowledge of the Greek and Latin languages. For undeniable witnesses to the truth of this assertion, we refer to those amongst us who have been taught the classics in this way.

In this city, the grammar-schools are as good as in any part of the Union, and there are some few excellent teachers, gentlemen who have made teaching their profession, and are themselves good classical scholars. But New-York has her full share of inefficient preceptors.

A deep conviction of the deplorable condition of our elementary schools induced the President of Columbia College, the Rev. Dr. Harris, in the year 1816, to lay before the Board of Trustees a plan for establishing a seminary of instruction, similar to the high school in Edinburgh, and attaching it to the college, as an institution that might prepare boys for entering with effect on their collegiate course; the senior form of the grammar school being, after due examination, to be transferred into the college freshman-class. This plan, the outline and details of which appear to be very judicious, has not yet been adopted by the Trustees of Columbia College.

If the grammar-schools are deficient, if the rudiments of the classics are not accurately taught ; if the boy is only crammed with a senseless jargon, conned by rote, and mechanically remembered, of course our *colleges* and *universities* cannot be calculated to produce good scholars. Where no foundation is laid no superstructure can be reared; what is never begun can never be finished. If the grammar-schools transmit to the colleges boys ignorant of the first principles of a liberal education, the colleges will, in due season, send out into the world those boys empty and uninformed, to discharge the important functions of legislating and administering government and justice for a great and rising empire. Our boys generally enter college at *fourteen*, and commence their baccalaureate at *eighteen* years of age, when they begin their studies for the profession of law, or divinity, or physic, or enter the counting-house of a merchant, where, of course, all studies excepting the ledger and the newspaper are laid aside. Nor do the professional students often prosecute classical studies to any great extent or depth. Nor is it to be expected, seeing, that in the colleges the pupils are *not* very comprehensively instructed in the classics, or belles-lettres, rhetoric, or moral philosophy, or history, or political economy, or natural philosophy, or metaphysics, or any of those great branches of knowledge peculiarly fitted to invigorate, enlarge, and adorn the intellect.

In addition to this, the American colleges generally are suffered to languish for want of sufficient funds, either from private contributions or the aid of government. Whence, they can seldom offer a bounty high enough to procure, as presidents and professors, men of talents and information sufficiently forcible and extensive to lead the minds of their pupils to literary excellence, or inspire them with an inextinguishable ardour for improvement. For men of powerful intellect generally know their own value, and cannot often be induced to starve upon a scanty stipend, when a different direction of their time, industry, and talents, might conduct them to honour and independence. The phrenzy for multiplying colleges all over the Union, and the custom of appointing illiterate men as trustees, also retard the progress of literature, by diminishing the number of students at each college, and thus lessening the means of its support, and by ensuring the appointment of absurd regulations and impracticable plans of study. Whence, altogether, Dr. Johnson's sarcasm is much more applicable to the United States than to the country at which it was originally levelled, namely, " learning *here* is like bread in a besieged town, every man has a mouthful, and no one a belly full."

There are about *fifty* colleges in the United States ; almost every state having two or three. Of these, Harvard in Massachusetts, Yale in Connecticut, and Princeton in New-Jersey, stand highest in numbers and reputation. Harvard is the most munificently endowed of all the American colleges ; the people of Boston wisely considering that the encouragement of sound literature is one of the main supports of national greatness and elevation. It has *thirteen* professorships, and affords a wider range of liberal instruction than any other college in the United States. Yale owes its high eminence to the exertions of its late president, Doctor Dwight, who, perhaps more than any man of his age, united in himself great talents, extensive learning, steady authority, affectionate regard, and practical wisdom, to discern time and circumstance, and convert every thing to the advantage of the institution which he governed, and the pupils whom he instructed. Columbia College *ought* to equal, if not surpass, every other college in the Union. Its outline of study prescribed by the statutes is excellent ; and it is situated in the heart of the most populous and opulent city in the United States at present, and which possesses the greatest capacities of future increase; and yet it numbers but one hundred students, while Princeton has two, Yale three, and Harvard four hundred.

Scarcely any systematic *lectures* on moral philosophy, metaphysics, political economy, history, belles lettres, and rhetoric, are delivered in our colleges. I know but of two instances; those of Doctor Smith, late President of Princeton, on "moral and political philosophy;" and those of Mr. John Quincy Adams, now Secretary of State, on "belles-lettres and rhetoric," when he was professor at Harvard. Mr. Adams's lectures contain an abundance of useful learning, well collected, and many able observations and inferences; but the style is occasionally too inflated and mysterious. Those of Doctor Smith are excellent so far as relates to the ethical part; but the lecturer not being either a civilian or political economist, the two great branches of political philosophy, and the law of nations, are very slightly touched. In the European colleges these subjects have employed the ablest talents; and Doctor Ferguson's "Moral Science," Dr. Smith's "Wealth of Nations," Mr. Tytler's (Lord Woodhouselee's,) "Elements of History," Professor Millar's "Origin of Ranks," and Mr. Dugald Stuart's "Elements of the Philosophy of the Human Mind;" all the substance of lectures delivered by their respective authors are among the most instructive and interesting works ever delivered to the world. Perhaps no want is more urgent in our colleges than that of a course of lectures on history; of which, whether general, as of the world at large, or of particular countries, the Americans, men, women, and children, are lamentably ignorant.

One reason, perhaps, why lectures are so seldom delivered on great general subjects, in the American colleges, is the incessant tendency of the *clergy* to monopolize the professors' chairs. This is the case with all the clerical denominations, according to their ascendency in the various colleges, whether Episcopalian, or Presbyterian, or Independent, or Baptist. During the dark ages of feudal Europe, there was some excuse for the ecclesiastical monopoly of education, because the very little learning then afloat was confined to the clergy; but as soon as the European laity had learned to read and write, this monopoly ceased; and *laymen* produced such lectures on moral philosophy, political economy, metaphysics, and history, as the combined clergy of

Christendom have never equalled. The clergy of the United States, however, can set up no such exclusive claim; because they are *not* a more generally learned body than the laity. Indeed, their education very seldom comprises within its range a very profound or extensive acquaintance with history, or political philosophy, or metaphysics; it is, for the most part, confined to the acquisition of a little Latin, and less Greek, and their own peculiar system of theology, whether Calvinistic, or Arminian, or Arian, or Unitarian, together with such miscellaneous reading as they may be able to snatch in the brief intervals of time between the composition of sermons, the details of parochial business, pastoral visits to their flock, morning calls, dining out, tea and evening parties. It is to be remembered too, that their previous preparation generally consists in going to an indifferent grammar-school, till fourteen; then entering college, which is left at eighteen; then studying divinity, and at twenty-one beginning to preach.

Besides, the clergy of the United States, for reasons given in a preceding chapter, are not often men of primary talents. Sometimes, indeed, the controlling influence of piety drives men of great talents into the church; and sometimes, perhaps, other circumstances; but, generally speaking, no one clerical denomination possesses a large proportion of the strong and active talent of the country, which is, for the most part, seduced into the law, physic, and merchandise, by the more splendid rewards of wealth, reputation, and influence, held out by those callings. Whence, in fact, the philosophical chairs in our colleges are *not* often filled; instead of a full, systematic course of moral philosophy, including the three great branches of ethics, political economy, and international law, Beattie's Syllabus, or Paley's Treatise, is given to the boys, who learn by rote, and transcribe some pages of the book, with probably here and there a remark from the professor. Conning over " Blair's Lectures," generally serves both master and pupil for a course of belles-lettres and rhetoric; and Vattel's little Outline of the Law of Nations, read, and partly transcribed, completes the circle of international law. As for metaphysics and political economy, they receive a very slender portion of regard.

The *elocution*, in the colleges, is in general extremely vitious; in addition to the common nuisance of a mouthing, monotonous rant, a *nasal* twang pervades the pronunciation. This eloquence of the nose, rather than of the mouth, prevails greatly in New-England, whose surplus population has long been spread annually over New-York and the Western States; whence this mode of elocution is continually gaining ground throughout the Union. Its origin is supposed to be traced to the county of Kent, in England, and it greatly resembles the nasal sing-song, or eternal chant of the few elder Scottish congregations, whether Covenanters or Seceders, that are yet to be found in this country. Unfortunately, our ears are saluted with these funereal sounds at the bar, from the pulpit, and *ex cathedra*, in the colleges. In common conversation also, we meet them;— and even the roseate lips of female loveliness occasionally condescend to call in the aid of the nasal organ to temper the sweetness of their silver tones.

Now, a distinct, various, well-adapted, impressive utterance, is necessary to all who desire to render their conversation instructive and pleasing. And how much of life depends upon conversation for its means of improvement and delight! how much it heightens domestic endearments, irradiates social intercourse, enforces parental instruction, deepens filial reverence, and exalts brotherly affection! In *public* life, a prompt and vigorous elocution is essential to the acquisition and maintenance of that personal influence over the feelings, opinions, passions, and actions of others; without which human communities would be deprived of their greatest cement of union, and best guide to exertion. Without the aid of felicitous delivery, in vain may the divine, the politician, lawyer, or teacher, endeavour to give to their respective sentiments, doctrines, and arguments, their due weight and efficacy. Without the accompaniments of clearness, and force of enunciation, variety and adaptation of emphasis, precision and fulness of delivery, the loftiest sentiments, the most powerful reasonings, the tenderest touches of feeling, the most animated flashes of real eloquence, are to the unfortunate audience tame and unimpressive.

The ancient Greeks and Romans, in the best days of their republics, made the study of elocution an essential part of liberal education. Many years were devoted to learning, in the schools of rhetoric, the rules and elements of appropriate and energetic delivery. Neither Demosthenes nor Cicero would have deemed himself qualified to appear as a public speaker at the bar, or in the senate, until he had diligently studied the means of obtaining a prompt, easy, apt, and forceful utterance. But the scholars, and great men of modern Christendom have, in general, been too negligent of their delivery, both in reading and speaking. Whence, it is not uncommon to hear, from the pulpit, at the bar, and in the senate, orations, full of learning, argument, and eloquence, so marred in the enunciation as nearly to destroy their effect. The public speaking and reading of the present day is too often disgraced, either by a drawling, drivelling monotony, or a quick, indistinct, sing-song cadence. The whole law of eloquence is comprised in a single sentence; " gravitas sententiarum, splendor verborum, proprietas actionis;"—weight of sense, splendour of language, and aptness of delivery. The three requisites of good delivery, or elocution, are, a clear and distinct articulation of every word, syllable, and letter; an adaptation of the various inflections and intonations of the voice to the various sense and feeling of what is spoken or read, and the following of the action or gesture, as a faithful expositor of the feeling and sense exhibited by the reader and speaker.

But what a difference is generally exhibited between the easy, various, apt, energetic, and natural tones of animated conversation, and the stiff, constrained, monotonous, vapid, and unnatural sounds emitted in public reading and speaking. Children almost universally are taught to read in a different manner, and to use different

tones, cadences, pauses, and emphases, from those which
nature dictates by the impulses of feeling and passion
in unconstrained conversation. And this artificial, unnatural method, is either inculcated or tolerated in the
recitals, public speakings, readings, and declamations of
schools and colleges. These reading and speaking
tones are seldom more than *two*; one, marking, that
the sense is not quite completed, the other, that the
sentence is closed. The first one consists of a uniform
elevation, the second of a uniform *depression* of voice.
Hence arises the unnatural and monotonous manner of
reading and speaking which is so prevalent, and which
habit only renders more inveterate and incurable. The
only effectual remedy would be, to make the study of
elocution an essential part of liberal education. At
present, the rudiments of delivery are generally taught
by unintelligent dames, and old women, or illiterate
men, who are quite ignorant of the general principles
and practical rules of elocution. And, when boys thus
initiated into the mysteries of bad reading are transferred
to the grammar-school, the matter is not mended;
for the teachers are too much absorbed in drilling their
young recruits in construing and parsing, to pay any
attention to the manner in which they read and speak
their own vernacular tongue. We are not then to marvel, that a thick and indistinct, a monotonous, drawling,
and vapid elocution is so general.

Next to the acquisition of that primary requisite of
good delivery, a clear, distinct, and forcible *articulation*,
the student should labour to obtain a proper *pronunciation*, or the most approved method of sounding words,
including the intonation and inflexion of the voice, the
accent and emphasis. An awkward pronunciation, a
bad management of the voice, the pitching too high or
too low a key-note, speaking too loudly, or feebly, to
be distinctly heard, the use of harsh intonations, of
false, uncertain, irregular cadences and emphases, are
the peculiar imperfections of particular classes of men
in every community, and spring from a faulty education,
vulgar society, low examples, inveterate habits, and

provincial barbarisms. The difference of pronunciation, between different men, relates to bodies rather than individuals, whether inhabitants of the same or different countries. For instance, the English, Irish, and Scottish, have each their own peculiar idiom in pronouncing the English tongue; and also the different provinces and countries of each of those nations have a peculiar dialect; whence, not only do the Scottish, Irish, and English differ from each other in the pronunciation of the same language, but the Aberdeen dialect is scarcely intelligible to a man of Edinburgh; that of Dublin to the people of Belfast; that of Cornwall to the cockneys in London. The great object, therefore, is to discover the *standard* pronunciation of a country. In every entire, consolidated sovereignty, the seat of government or court fixes and regulates that standard. The court at Paris is the model for all those who aspire to speak French exquisitely; the court of Madrid is the pattern of Spanish pronunciation; that of Berlin regulates the pronunciation of the north, as the cabinet of Vienna does that of the south of Germany; the government circle in London gives the tone of pronunciation to all those in the British isles who profess to be liberally educated and well-bred. All other idioms or dialects are considered as tokens of a low and defective education, and, as such, disgraceful. This standard pronunciation being, in its minuter niceties, continually fluctuating with the fluctuations of the manners and fashions of the age, cannot easily be taught by written or printed rules, but can be acquired only by habits of intercourse and conversation with those who have been thus liberally trained.

These observations, however, do *not* apply to the United States, where there is *no* standard pronunciation of the English language; for America not being a consolidated sovereignty, but a confederacy of independent states, no one state or portion of the Union can arrogate to itself the privilege of fixing the standard by which every well-bred American shall regulate his pronunciation. Massachusetts will not implicitly follow the government pronunciation of New-Orleans, or Georgia, or the Carolinas, or Virginia, or Maryland; nor will New-York pride itself in copying the court enunciation of New-Jersey, or Pennsylvania, or Ohio, or Kentucky, or Tennessee, or Indiana, or Mississippi. And still less will any of these republican sovereignties suffer the federal city of Washington to prescribe the courtly standard of pronunciation. Nor do the separate states look to their own seats of government as the models of pronunciation. The people of New-York are not anxious to adopt the mode used by their governor, senators, and representatives, convened at Albany; nor are the gentlemen of Philadelphia ambitious to copy the government enunciation of Lancaster or Harrisburgh.

Nevertheless, there is a greater uniformity in the pronunciation of English, and less diversity of dialects, idioms, and provincialisms in the United States, than in England, Ireland, or Scotland. The people of Georgia and Massachusetts, of Connecticut and Virginia, of New-York and Kentucky, approximate much nearer to each others pronunciation than do the natives of York and Devon, of Dublin and Donaghadee, of Edinburgh and Inverness. Some of the reasons for this great equality of American pronunciation are, that the United States were chiefly settled by Englishmen, in the times of Elizabeth, James the First, and the two Charleses. These first settlers, particularly in New-England, were generally people of some education, as well as of strong religious *feeling;* and therefore less likely to be infected with the peculiar dialects and provincial idioms of the places whence they emigrated. The Americans also are a very enterprising locomotive people; the inhabitants of the different states intercommunicate much with each other, and consequently assimilate in the pronunciation of that vernacular tongue common to them all. And their having no national standard induces them to look to that of England for their model; with this advantage, that whereas in England, every different county has a different dialect, the United States escape the importation of these, and follow as nearly as they

can the best English standard, by the help of approved
written rules and regulations, and the personal intercourse of some of their most intelligent citizens with
the best society in the British metropolis.

The question has been much debated, whether mc-
dern nations should pronounce Greek and Latin according to the analogies of their own living languages, or
establish a uniform pronunciation, that of the Greeks
and Romans themselves. The great objection to a plan
of universal pronunciation is, that we know very little
as to what *was* the Greek and Roman pronunciation.
Scholars, to this day, are much divided in opinion upon
this subject; and, at least, until their discussions can
be adjusted, may not the English continue their own
mode of pronouncing Greek and Latin, which is in full
accordance with the analogy of their own living tongue ;
even if it does not approximate in some few instances
so nearly to the ancient pronunciation as the Italian,
French, German, and Scottish modes? For we have
no means of ascertaining how the Greeks and Romans
actually pronounced the great proportion of their languages ; and we do know that all their idioms and
dialects, all their nicer tones and varieties of inflexion,
have perished for ever.

The Americans speak English all over the Union, yet
read Greek and Latin with the Scottish pronunciation.
The reason of this anomaly is, that although English is
their mother-tongue, yet, ever since the country has
been settled, the dead languages have been generally
taught by Scottish schoolmasters and professors, who
grafted their own mode of pronunciation upon the
native stock of English in the United States. The Scottish, as a people, are more generally educated than the
English ; and, consequently, being more enterprising,
spread themselves in greater numbers as teachers all
over the world. The most universally intelligent are
always the most enterprising and industrious nations.
The Scottish pronunciation of Greek and Latin more
nearly resembles that of the French, Italians, Spaniards,
and continental Europeans, generally, than does the

English, because the Scottish mode of pronouncing English bears a greater resemblance to the vernacular pronunciation of the European continent; which mode is supposed also to approximate nearer than that of the English to the pronunciation of the ancient Greeks and Romans.

But there appears to be no good reason why the Americans, who in general pronounce the English language in greater purity than the people of England, should violate all the analogies of their own living pronunciation, and engraft into their classical utterance a foreign tone and accent, borrowed from the Scottish, whose idioms, intonations, and inflexions, are altogether alien from their own. Nor can this habit long continue in the United States; for they will soon cease to look to Scotland for teachers of the dead languages. And when American scholars instruct the youth of this country, they will, of course, follow the genius and character of their own language, whose analogies will eventually eradicate all the vestiges of Scottish pronunciation; which, even now, does *not* pervade the union; for at the colleges of Schenectady, in New-York, Princeton, in New-Jersey, and of New-England, generally, the students are taught to read and speak the classics after the English mode.

The object to be acquired is, to ascertain the English quantity with which the vowels and consonants of the Greek and Latin languages are to be pronounced; and then give utterance to these learned tongues, with the same distinct and manly articulation, the same bold and impressive intonations, the same force of emphasis and variety of cadence, with which the best English poets and prose writers are read and spoken. This, however, cannot be accomplished by the mere knowledge of the dead languages, but by an intimate acquaintance with the general analogies and floating usages of our own mother-tongue. And in the nature of things, and the radical conformation of the human mind, these analogies must always enter largely into the scholar's pronunciation of the dead languages. And, in fact, every nation

z

does pursue this course. The Scottish, French, Italians, Germans, and Spaniards all pronounce Greek and Latin according to the analogies of their own living tongues; and what reason can be assigned why the Americans and English, who both speak one common language, whose mother tongue is neither Spanish nor German, nor Italian, nor French, nor Scottish, should not be permitted to follow the same law of nature, reason, and liberty, in pronouncing the dead languages, according to the analogies of their own living idiom? On what principle should a Frenchman or Scotchman undertake to teach an American or Englishman to read and speak Latin and Greek, with a French or Scottish pronunciation, which would not equally justify teaching the pupil to read and speak English with a French or Scottish pronunciation? Let then a Scotchman and Frenchman, as long as they continue to talk Scottish and French, follow the analogies of their own living tongues in pronouncing the dead languages, and also let the numerous and growing millions of America and England pronounce the classical tongues according to the general analogies and best usages of their own living language, and cherish that English pronunciation which has taken deep root, and sprung up aloft in their own native soil; which is congenial to the frame and character of their language, which owes its origin to the habits and manners, the ideas, opinions, and sentiments, the peculiarities, views, intelligence, and national achievements of the people.

The *custom* which regulates the pronunciation of all living languages is *not* made up altogether of the usage of the mere multitude of speakers in a community, counted numerically, and suffered to vote, *per capita*, for the standard of national utterance; nor does it spring entirely from the usages of the studious, in the recesses of their halls and colleges; nor does it owe its origin to the unmingled efforts and effusions of the affluent, gay, and fashionable portion of society; but is compounded of the usages of all these three classes of men. The learning of the scholars acts as a restraint and balance-wheel, alike upon the frivolous affectation and ever-shifting caprice of the wealthy and fashionable, and upon the illiterateness and ignorance of the multitude: the refinement and delicacy of the well-bred and po-lished curb and diminish the pedantry of the mere scholar, and soften the rude forward vulgarity of the uneducated and uninformed, while the plain, strong, home-bred, practical common sense of the industrious orders, erects a barrier of equal force against the light and airy incursions of fashion, and the ponderous attacks of laborious scholarship. The Latin and Greek infusions of the schools, the nicer peculiarities of polished life, and the native provincialisms of the irregularly educated, must all be received and tolerated by each other, for a long time, and to a great extent, before they can grow up into that permanent general use, which constitutes an established custom of pronunciation.

The *si vis me flere*, etc. of Horace is as applicable to teaching as to dramatic enunciation; and no lecturer will ever be able to render his labours either interesting or instructive to his pupils, if his manner be dull, cold, and formal, and his elocution monotonous, drawling, nasal, and vapid. The ingenious ardour, or, as the an-cients call it, the sacred fire of youth, can only be kept alive, and fanned into a brighter flame, by the kindred enthusiasm of the teacher, whose *example*, as well as precept, is necessary to inspire the student with a love for letters. The enthusiasm of the head is genius, the enthusiasm of the heart is virtue; and both lie at the foundation of all real greatness. The paramount ex-cellence of every instructor consists in the ability, so happily to temper and combine the three several in-fluences of *duty, necessity,* and *ambition,* as to make them all co-operate in their respective stations and powers, to produce in his pupils *confirmed habits* of intellectual diligence. This once accomplished, *his* work is effectu-ally done, for *they* will ever after continue to enlarge the limits of their understanding, by vigilant observa-tion, by systematic reading, by patient reflection, by ra-tional conversation, so that all which they see, observe, read, and hear, shall directly tend to sharpen the sense of *perception*, strengthen the power of *association*, quicken and render more retentive the *memory*, exercise and invigorate the *judgment*, deepen and enlarge the faculty of *reasoning*, and kindle all the fires of the *imagination* into a brighter and steadier blaze.

The course of lectures on *belles-lettres* and *rhetoric* should contain an inquiry into the elements of criticism on metaphysical principles, by which Aristotle's Poetics, the fragment of Longinus on the sublime, and Quinctilian's institutes, should be examined and tried. A critical code of general rules should be established, and illustrated by selections of passages remarkable for their sentiment, or expression, or both, from the best poets and prose writers, in the Greek, Latin, English, French, Italian, and Spanish languages.

The course of lectures on *moral philosophy* should demonstrate, that all the systems of ethics, whether ancient or modern, which are *not* based on revelation, are reducible to a calculation of individual expediency, for want of a sufficient sanction to enforce the observance of their rules and precepts; whereas the moral code revealed in the Scriptures is applicable to all the conditions and circumstances of human life, individual, domestic, and social. This should constitute the first great division of the subject; the second should consist of an outline of *political philosophy*, and the attention be particularly directed towards an investigation of the means best adapted to render a nation permanently prosperous and powerful. The third division should comprehend an inquiry into the *law of nations*, as founded on the law of nature, on conventional, or treaty law, and on common, or customary law. It would require the labour of several years, employed in general reading, and patient thought, to improve and complete two such courses of lectures, which would find very imperfect substitutes in the daily or weekly dole of a few pages of Blair, Beattie, and Vattel.

The few following might be some of the subjects which would admit of profitable discussion; namely, *first*, that the *moral* impulses and *intellectual* capacities of every human being are *by nature* co-equal, and co-ordinate ; that is to say, the sensibilities of the heart, and powers of the head, in every being, are naturally equal in strength ; a dull man having by the very constitution of his nature slow and blunt feelings ; and genius being by nature endowed with quick and ardent sensibilities; and so, proportionally, through all the gradations of intellect, from the highest to the lowest order of minds. In *after* life, the moral and mental co-equality is seldom preserved, owing to some persons cultivating their feelings more than their understandings ; while others improve their minds to the neglect, or at the expense of their moral impulses and emotions ; and, consequently, as all the human powers, whether physical, or intellectual, or moral, grow in strength, or decay in weakness, as they are exercised or disused, the *natural* coequality of feeling and mind is deranged by the subsequent cultivation of the one, in an undue and disproportionate preference to the other.

Secondly. That the possession and display of great intellect does *not* necessarily imply the exercise or possession of moral virtue. For, if it did, individuals and nations would be just and upright, precisely in proportion to the quantity of their talent and information ; and communities and persons would be vicious and profligate in the direct ratio of their dulness and ignorance ; propositions which are contradicted by the uniform experience of fact and history.

Thirdly. An inquiry should be made into the *comparative* mind of the ancients and moderns. This question has been agitated by the learned in Europe ever since the revival of letters. One sect of scholars has contended that the ancients excel the moderns in all the attributes of genius, while another maintains the superiority of the moderns. In the last century a third heresy sprung up amidst the European philosophers and scholars, who, at that time, as they supposed, discovered the secret of man's *perfectibility;* which doctrine, if true, decides the question; for if the human race be growing wiser and wiser, every succeeding generation, in its progress towards perfection, of course the ancients were mere children, as to talents and acquisitions, in comparison with modern wise men ; and the politicians, warriors, poets, historians, orators, and philosophers of Greece and Rome, are, by several centuries, inferior to the corresponding classes of men who protect, adorn, and guide the present era of illumination. By pushing the two first theories to their legitimate extremes, their inconclusiveness will appear : for, on the supposition that the ancients were superior in capacity to the moderns, the world has only to grow to a certain age, when all the human beings in it will be mere drills and changelings, if mind diminishes every succeeding generation ; and on the supposition that the moderns excel the ancients in talent, the converse result will be produced, and the nearer we travel up to the commencement of the creation, the more certainly we approximate to a race of ideots and dunces.

It should therefore be shewn, both by reasoning, *a priori*, from certain undisputed elementary principles of metaphysics, and also by a general induction from particular facts, that neither of these three opinions is correct ; but, that although individuals differ from each other in the amount of native talent, yet large masses of men, as whole communities, average an equality of natural capacity, in all ages and countries. How far that natural capacity shall be developed into active power and display, must, of course, depend upon the existing circumstances of the age and country in which it appears ; as the form and spirit of government, systems of education, character of the people, and all those predominating influences which stamp the family features, and direct the destinies of nations. In examining this question, an inquiry should be made into the best means of securing for the public service a *succession*, regularly continued from age to age, of able men, in all the high departments of the state, political, military, and literary. And, in particular, should be explored the causes which accelerate or retard the growth of mind in these United

States, so far as it is employed in the pursuit of politics, literature, art, and science.

Fourthly. An analysis of the political history of the world should be made, with a view to ascertain how far any nation, ancient or modern, has approximated in its social institutions towards the union of the three great requisites of a good government; namely, the personal liberty of the people, strong and permanent power in the hands of the executive, and an ample developement of the national mind, by a system of comprehensive, liberal education.

Fifthly. An inquiry should be made into the elementary principles and practical exhibition of eloquence, both oral and written; in the course of which, the best writers of Greece, Rome, Italy, France, and England, should be analyzed, and their happiest effusions pointed out, as illustrations of the general rules laid down. These few subjects, with some others which might be named, if properly discussed and exemplified, would very materially tend to lay the foundation of intellectual excellence, broad and deep, in the student's mind.

In our colleges, the mathematics are generally well taught; but *not* so either the classics or metaphysics, or belles-lettres and rhetoric, or moral philosophy, including the three branches of ethics, political economy, and national law.

The study of *metaphysics* is eminently useful in sharpening, brightening, and strengthening the faculties of the mind, by accustoming it to the process of analysis, the exercise of abstraction, recollection, arrangement, careful inquiry into the springs and sources of human passions, character, and conduct. And, in addition to opening the best roads for the judicious direction and management of the understanding, the science of mind is kindred to, and prepares the way for the investigation of other important sciences. The only certain foundation of *philology* and *criticism* rests upon a knowlege of metaphysics, which enable us to examine and classify the ideas that words represent, to give precision and force to language, and to ascertain the sources of the emotions raised within our bosoms by the contemplation of sublime or beautiful objects, whether belonging to the material world, or the offspring of moral magnificence and loveliness. *Moral philosophy* owes its existence to metaphysical investigation, which explores and analyzes those feelings, affections, passions, and sentiments of the heart, which it is the business of morals to regulate and guide. No moral writer can clear even the threshold of his science, without the aid of metaphysics. Even *political economy* derives light and direction in its pursuits, and endeavours to promote the well-being of states from the insight which metaphysics afford into the nature of individual man, seeing that the multiplication of these individuals constitutes the living materials of that state which the political economist labours to adorn and aggrandize.

Neither the *mathematics* nor the *physical sciences* are well adapted to develope the faculties of youth. In early life the study of mathematics exercises only the mechanism of the understanding; and children who are early doomed to the drudgery of casting calculations, and eternally working in figures and algebraic signs, bury in everlasting forgetfulness all the fine and fertile seeds of imagination, which in that vernal season of existence, under a more liberal culture, would spring up into a lofty stem, wave its luxuriant branches in the air, display the rich beauty of its blossoms, and ripen into an abundance of fragrant fruit. Nor are the destruction of all fancy and the prevention of all taste counterbalanced by any transcendent accuracy of mind: for arithmetic, algebra, and mathematics, only make us acquainted, in many different forms, with a few simple propositions always the same. Demonstrated truths do not show us the way to those that are probable and contingent, and which alone can direct our steps in the active business of practical life, in the prosecution of the arts, in the intercourse of society. This doubtless applies only to the common labours in the mathematical trenches : for invention in this science, as in every other pursuit, is the felicitous result of excited genius. But of the thousands, who pore over the beaten track of mathematics, how many exhibit either sense or reason in the important transactions of life? To those who are *not* inventors, this study affords the means of unfolding only one faculty, that of reasoning closely and conclusively upon *given* premises; it confers no power of taking ground, and laying down premises on which to build up a system of prompt, various, inductive reasoning. A *dull* man may make a good mathematician, but by no possibility a good classical scholar.

It is the province of liberal education to develope and improve *all* the faculties of the mind, and to cultivate and improve the whole moral being; which desirable purpose is best accomplished by the study of *language*, as the chief object of instruction, attended, indeed, and aided by the cultivation of the arts and sciences, but itself the primary pursuit. The study of language is peculiarly fitted to render the faculty of associating similar and simple ideas, or of combining various and dissimilar images more facile and rapid. By attributing definite ideas to arbitrary signs and conventional sounds, and by forming abstract and general, when particular and definite notions cannot be obtained, the powers of association and imagination, like all the other faculties, must, by exercise and use, be greatly strengthened. Add to which, by increasing the rapidity and strength of the associative faculty, the study of language improves the capacity of reasoning, increases the brilliancy of wit, and brightens the blaze of imagination; whence all the mental powers are enabled to work with greater promptness and effect upon every subject of human inquiry submitted to their cognizance and consideration.

But, above all the *dead* languages, the Greek and Latin tongues should be more especially studied, as conducive to the great end of liberal education; not only because they contain some of the highest flights of genius, but also because they have a greater accuracy, a more philosophical precision than any living, floating,

continually-shifting language can possess. By paying
particular attention to the study of these two inestimable
languages, from the first dawning of academic instruction to the close of life, the mind is quickened,
strengthened, and rendered clear and luminous in all
its views. It is from the long experience of their utility that the study of these languages has been made
the basis of all the establishments of liberal education
which have trained up so many profound and accomplished scholars in Europe.

All the qualities and elements united in language are
gradually comprehended by the student while engaged
in translating from one tongue into another. All his
faculties are improved by the process of mastering the
peculiar idioms of two different languages at the same
time. He is compelled, by the very nature of his study,
to make himself acquainted with the several ideas presented by the words he reads in regular succession; to
compare and combine different sorts of analogies and
probabilities offered to his consideration in the opinions,
sentiments, and propositions that he peruses. The
number of faculties which this study awakens at the
same time ensures it the pre-eminence over *every other*
species of instruction. It quickens the power of perception, by accustoming the mind to discern the nicer
peculiarities of idiomatical language in different tongues;
it gives speed and force to the faculty of association, by
presenting various shades of difference in the ideas
expressed by words, similar or synonymous, in different
languages; it renders the memory strong and retentive,
by exercising it constantly in the recollection of new
words and images; it deepens and strengthens the
judgment, by continually soliciting its decisions on the
more exquisite models of taste and beauty in composition which the great writers of antiquity have left; it
invigorates and enlarges the capacity of reasoning, by
perpetually requiring a train of argument upon the various questions in ethics and politics, started by the
ancients, under very peculiar aspects of the human
mind; it brightens and renders more intensely splendid

the imagination, by introducing it to an intimate acquaintance with the finest specimens of poetry and eloquence, precisely at that period in the history of man when they were most eagerly and successfully cultivated.

But further, the appropriate subject of the best portion of *classical* learning, the study of the poets, historians, orators, and philosophers of Greece and Rome, is the investigation and improvement of our *moral* nature; the feelings, passions, plans of action, hidden springs, and various movements of our being. The most exalted wisdom, the most sound, practical common sense of social life, in its highest refinement, is drawn from the springs of Helicon and the fountains of Parnassus, from the groves of Academus, and from the schools of the Portico and Lyceum. All narrow and single systems of education are bad ; but if any one branch of learning deserves pre-eminence, it is that which induces an habitual contemplation of ourselves and of our common nature, in a close acquaintance with which men must always feel a deeper interest and possess a larger stake, than in the lines and diagrams of the mathematician, the retorts and alembics of the chymist, or any combination of material substances which the natural philosopher may explore. It is far better, however, that the study of the classics should be accompanied with that of all the sciences, in order to impart a course of full and accomplished education.

It might, perhaps, be of some utility to sketch a very brief outline of the system of instruction pursued in the schools and colleges of England, that the people of the United States might know how far classical literature is prized in the land of their fathers, and learn, themselves, to set a higher value upon it than they have hitherto done. Let us instance the three great public schools of *Eton, Westminster, and Winchester*, as leading the van of English liberal education. At these schools a boy stays until he is *eighteen* ; before he reaches which period he is expected to be able to read, *ad aperturam libri*, Virgil, Horace, Terence, Cicero, and Livy ; Homer, Demosthenes, Longinus, Aristophanes, and the Greek tragedians, to compose, readily, and abundantly, and constantly, in English verse and prose, and in Latin verse and prose; and, occasionally, in Greek verse and prose ; to make Latin epigrams extempore, to declaim in Latin, to write Latin critiques on a given book of Homer, or play in Aristophanes, or Æschylus, or Sophocles, or Euripides ; to have the finest passages of the Greek and Latin classics always afloat in the memory, and ready for apt citation and allusion. In the English universities these studies are prosecuted on a wider scale, and with the additional pursuits of mathematics, natural philosophy, history, moral philosophy, logic, belles-lettres, rhetoric, and municipal law. Cambridge is supposed to be peculiarly partial to mathematical, and Oxford to classical studies ; but at both, the system of instruction is ample and highly liberal. At *two and twenty* they graduate, and *after* this, (except in the church, whose order of deacon is taken at *three and twenty*), they begin to study for the learned professions of law and physic. This is the general course in England and Ireland, which produce the most finished scholars in Europe. Trinity College in Dublin has long been celebrated for its great proficiency in all classical attainments. The English and Irish, generally, continue their acquaintance with the classics in after-life.

In Scotland the boys learn no Greek at school, which they leave at twelve, when they enter the university, and graduate at sixteen; so that classical literature is not much cultivated. A few years since, indeed, the study of prosody, and the composition of Latin verse, were introduced into the high school of Edinburgh. But the principal studies among the Scottish are moral philosophy, political economy, public law, and metaphysics.

It is an old objection of Mr. Locke, but bandied about the United States with as much eager triumph as if it were both novel and wise, " that it is foolish to require boys to compose in verse, if we do not wish to make them poets." The answer is—that boys are required to make verses, *not* in order to become poets, but to obtain a more complete acquaintance with, and dominion over the language in which they compose. Let any one make the experiment, and he will find that he must pass more thought through his brain, and a greater abundance and selection of expression in composing twenty lines of verse, in whatever language, than in writing four times the same quantity of prose. Lord Mansfield was not disqualified for being one of the greatest lawyers, statesmen, and orators, the world ever saw, because, all his life, even *after he was eighty*, he used to write Latin verses in the various rythms, nearly equal to the best poetry of the Augustan age. Nor was Sir William Jones a less profound jurist and philosopher because he was an accomplished versifier in the English, Latin, and Greek languages.

It is too prevalent a fashion in the United States to consider all *classical*, nay, all general education, *at an end*, as soon as a boy leaves college at the age of eighteen, when he begins to prepare himself for becoming a merchant, who is supposed not to stand in need of any literature; or a clergyman, or physician, or lawyer, who are deemed to want nothing more than a mere knowledge of theology, medicine, or law. In addition to which, it is thought prodigious wisdom to rail at all studious habits, and talk loudly about trusting to the energies of native genius, which must not be stifled by poring over books. The consequence is, that the Latin of our college boys soon becomes threadbare, and their Greek quite worn out.

When Demosthenes was reproached by a fopling of his day, that his orations smelt of the lamp, he replied, " true, there is some difference between what you and I do by lamp-light." To derive all from native genius, to owe nothing to others, to scorn to look at objects through the spectacles of books, is the praise which many men who think little and talk much delight to bestow upon themselves and their kindred favourites. But no one in his senses would wish to exclude the student from an acquaintance with the works of others ; for if it were possible, and men were forbidden to avail themselves of the labours of their predecessors, each succeeding generation would be obliged to begin anew their researches into the first rudiments of knowledge; and mankind for ever remain in merely an infantile state, as to all the purposer of improvement: that man being, as Cicero observes, only a child in understanding, who is ignorant of the transactions and events, the opinions and discoveries, of those who have gone before him. The truth is, the repeated perusal of the heroes of literature, as Longinus calls them, is of absolute necessity in the first years of study, and of immense importance in after life. Nor will it enfeeble the mind and prevent its exhibition of originality. Invention, doubtless, is the great characteristic of genius; but men learn to invent by being conversant with the inventions of others, as they learn to think by reading the thoughts of others.

Whoever has so far formed his taste as to contemplate with delight, and feel deeply the excellences of great writers, has already studied to considerable effect. Quinctilian says, that to take real pleasure in reading Cicero, is one of the most unequivocal marks of genius a student can exhibit. For, merely from a consciousness of delighting in what is excellent, the mind is elevated, and roused to an effort at resembling what it admires. The inventions of preceding writers are not only the best nourishment of infant genius, but also the most substantial supply of energy and animation to mature talents. The most powerful mind is in itself but a barren soil, soon exhausted, if left to repeat often the periodical growth of its own native vegetation; a soil which will produce only a few scanty crops, unless continually fertilized with the abundant addition of foreign manure.

Nevertheless, it is gravely asserted by many, and practically enforced by the example of more, that classical literature and general information are injurious to professional men; that those make the best divines who know nothing but the peculiarities of their own sectarian theology; that those are the most expert physicians who peruse only the prevailing systems of the nosology of the day; that those are the soundest lawyers whose whole reading is confined to the points, cases, and practice of law.   But error has *her* gray hairs as well as truth.   The *real* inference is, that he who professes to know nothing but his own scheme of divinity, or the existing system of medicine, or the mere technicalities of law, is *not* a sound theologian, or able physician, or profound lawyer,   because it displays either dulness or idleness,   or both,   for one to pass through life without acquiring general information.   Indeed, *idleness* long continued produces nearly the same effects as dulness, by blunting the powers of genius itself; since man holds all his natural faculties, physical, intellectual, and moral, only upon this conditional tenure, that *by exercise* they are all strengthened and enlarged, *by disuse* all weakened and diminished.

Were Luther, and Calvin, and Horseley, less profoundly skilled in their own peculiar systems of theology than the most ignorant clergymen of their respec tive sects, because they were also learned in all the learning of their times? Were Friend, and Boerhaave, and Haller, and Heberden, less expert in the healing art than the most ignorant, impudent, and murderous empiric, because they were eminently distinguished as general scholars, in addition to being most accomplished physicians? Were Bacon, and Hale, and Mansfield, and Jones, less able, and less profound, as jurists, than the most illiterate, narrow-minded, pettifogging attorney, because they had assiduously strengthened and adorned the stupendous power of their original genius by a vast and varied acquaintance with the recondite depths of science, the exquisite refinements of art, and the dazzling splendours of erudition? It were indeed a consummation devoutly to be wished, that our American students, following the foot-tracks of these illustrious examples, would prefer to herding in the dark and dismal abodes of the antagonists of learning, to whatever profession they may belong, the directing of their devoted, though distant, gaze and admiration towards the regions of the sun, where shine in unborrowed lustre the great poets, historians, orators, statesmen, and philosophers of the world :

> "———— οθι τ' Ηους ηριγενιας
> " Οιχια, και χοροι εισι, και αντολαι Ηελιοιο."

In *every* profession various kinds of learning are eminently useful, although to common, slow understandings they do not appear to bear any very close relation to their particular calling; and various general information always tends to quicken the power of penetration, and strengthen the judgment. A mind, liberally cultivated, has an extensive intellectual grasp, which seizes at once, as by intuition, every argument that bears fairly on the question, and thus ensures accuracy and stability to all its serious deliberations and mature conclusions. But a narrow understanding (and all ignorance in its very nature, and *ex vi termini*, implies narrowness of the understanding,) being unacquainted with elementary principles and general truths, is confused and perplexed by every ordinary occurrence, and is busied only in managing little points, and raising quibbling objections that cannot stand a moment against the direct artillery of that able, well-applied, comprehensive reasoning, which is ever the legitimate result and sure reward of time diligently employed in laying the broad basis of a liberal education.

Ignorance is the greatest of all evils, because it tends to augment and perpetuate every other evil, by precluding the possible entrance of all good. . Its fatal influence not only indisposes the mind to exertions for its own deliverance, but also excites a malignant opposition to every effort to enlighten mankind. Men love this darkness rather than light, because it conceals the dimensions of danger, favours the slumber of indolence, and soothes the dreams of folly. And so completely does *long-continued* ignorance tend to disqualify the mind for improvement, that it is only in the earlier stages of life that it is capable of being trained by the patient process of education, to *habits of intelligence.* It is vain to endeavour to operate any great moral change, or intellectual improvement, on the full-grown population of any community. Their characters are fixed; their faculties have ceased to be progressive; the range of their ideas has already taken the form and pressure, the hue, and colouring, and direction, of their previous education; and cannot tolerate any innovation upon their long cherished prejudices and circumscribed customs. It is with youth, nay, with childhood, the labours of the preceptor must begin; for to them, in a great measure, is the successful prosecution of intellectual and moral culture confined. "He (observes Dr. Johnson) who voluntarily continues in ignorance, when he *may* be instructed, is guilty of all the crimes and follies which ignorance produces; as to him who extinguishes the night fires of a beacon, are justly to be imputed all the calamities of the shipwreck occasioned by the darkness." It is by the diffusion of general information alone that the understanding can be improved in all its faculties; that the thoughts, which now only occasionally appear to the secluded speculations of a few solitary thinkers, can be communicated from intellect to intellect, concentrated in strength, and brightened in reflected splendour; so that an uninterrupted chain of progressive improvement may unite together all the intelligent minds of an enlightened community.

The *rythm* of the Latin language is entirely disregarded; and in this free country we murder *prosody ad libitum.* Our gravest divines, most learned physicians, profound lawyers, and celebrated professors, talk familiarly of "*Aristides*," of "*Herodotus*," of suing "*in formâ pauperis*," of the writ "*facias habere possessionem*," and so forth. The excuse for this systematic rebellion against all metre was for a long time found in the fact that our Scottish teachers neglected all prosody: this apology must cease now, because some years since the proper metrical pronunciation of the classics was introduced, as part of its system of education, into the high school at Edinburgh; and that celebrated seminary now produces prize poems in Latin Hexameters. Mr. Burke might have thundered his " magnum vectīgal est parsimonia" into the ears of an American administration, without offending their nicer classical organs, or hearing both from the treasury and the opposition benches, the portentous sound of "tīgal, tīgal," echoing through all the house, until his premeditated speech was prematurely brought to a close.

It would be considered a sure token of a low and vulgar education, if an American were to mis-pronounce every English word he uttered, and make all the long syllables short, and all the short syllables long; and it is not less offensive to hear the Latin and Greek languages treated in the same barbarous manner; to observe the quantity of every word in Homer and Virgil, in Demosthenes and Cicero, regularly assassinated by men who call themselves scholars. To confess the truth, however, our free-born citizens are apt to take as much liberty with the rythm of their mother tongue as with that of the dead languages; and we daily hear, from the pulpit, in the senate, and at the bar, of " peremptōry," "territōry," " dormitōry," "legīslăture," "genuīne," "sanguīne," &c.* The late Mr. Gouverneur Morris, one of the ablest and most eloquent men whom the world has produced, in an inaugural discourse to the New-York Historical Society, condescended to use some splendid sophistry, in order to prove that poetry and rythm are unworthy the attention of America, because steam-boats are useful to the community. The language of the orator is lofty, but we might ask whether or not *his* judgment would have been as sound, and *his* imagination as well disciplined, if he himself had been a classical scholar; and whether or not England

---

* Note, that this page, instancing the neglect of prosody, was handed to me without a single mark to denote the quantity of the syllables which our American scholars so regularly mis-pronounce. Upon inquiring the cause, I was informed, that they had no such marks, and the press was stopped till the type-founder could cast them. And this printing-office is one of the first and most respectable in the United States.

is inferior to other nations in the inventions of art, and the discoveries of science, because she excels them all in literature?

The United States have produced scarcely a single *learned* writer, in the strict acceptation of that term; indeed, I do not know one American work on classical literature, or that betrays any intimate acquaintance with the classics. And, excepting Cicero's works, printed accurately and well by Wells and Lilley, at Boston, the only classical productions of the American press are the republication of a few common schoolbooks. Nor, I believe, have the United States produced any *elementary* work on ethics, or political economy, or metaphysics. The great mass of our native publications consists of newspaper essays, and party pamphlets. There are several respectable state and local histories, as those of New-York and New-Jersey, by Smith, Trumbull's History of Connecticut, Ramsay's History of South-Carolina, to which add his Account of the United States, and Holmes's Annals, M'Call's Georgia, Darby's Louisiana, and Stoddart's Account of that State, Jefferson's Notes on Virginia, Borman's Maryland, Prud's Pennsylvania, Williams's Vermont, Belknap's New-Hampshire, Hutchinson's Massachusetts, Sullivan's Maine, Minot's History of Shay's Rebellion, and Drake's History of Cincinnati, in Ohio; together with divers accounts of the late war, mostly written in that crusading style which revolutionary France has rendered current throughout the world.

Of native *novels* we have no great stock, and none good; our democratic institutions placing all the people on a dead level of political equality; and the pretty equal diffusion of property throughout the country affords but little room for varieties, and contrasts of character; nor is there much scope for fiction, as the country is quite new, and all that has happened from its first settlement to the present hour, respecting it, is known to every one. There is, to be sure, some traditionary romance about the Indians; but a novel describing these miserable barbarians, their squaws, and papooses, would not be very interesting to the present race of American readers.

Our *poetry* is neither abundant nor excellent; the state of society is not favourable to its production; there is not much individual wealth to afford patronage,. nor any collegiate endowments bestowing learned leisure: the trading spirit pervades the whole community, and the merchant's ledger and the muses do not make very suitable companions. The aspect of nature, in the United States, presents magnificence and beauty in all profusion; but hill and dale, and wood and stream, are not alone sufficient to breathe the inspirations of poetry, unless seconded by the habits and manners, the feeling, taste, and character of the inhabitants. Besides, the best English poets are as much read here as in Britain; and Milton, Cowper, Burns, Scott, Southey, Byron, Campbell, and Moore, are formidable rivals to our American bards, who must either follow some other more substantial vocation than poesy, or soon mingle, as spirits, with the inhabitants of the ethereal world; for, beyond all peradventure, the most exalted genius, aided by the most extensive learning, if dependent on literary pursuits alone for subsistence, would be permitted to starve by our good republican Mæcænates. The late president Dwight, when quite a young man, wrote two respectable poems, called "The Conquest of Canaan," and "Greenfield Hill." Mr. Barlow's "Columbiad," though full of hard words, and loud-sounding lines, has many magnificent descriptions of natural scenery, and some most fantastic visions of crude philosophy, and still cruder politics. Mr. Sargeant, of Boston, has written some very spirited national lyrics; and Mr. Pierpoint's "Airs of Palestine" are an elegant and popular performance. "*The Bridal of Vaumond*" is in a much higher strain; and the writer, though evidently young and unexperienced, has swept the chords of his lyre with a master's hand, and gives token of an energy of intellect, reach of thought, and variety of information, which, if well directed, and steadily impelled, cannot fail to conduct him eventually to the heights of our com-

munity. Possibly this little poem may not be a favourite with those profounder critics who read by the finger
rather than the ear, on account of its various rythm ;
but those to whom the happier effusions of genius, taste,
and feeling are dear, cannot fail to appreciate its high excellence. *Woodworth's* poems, lately published in New-
York, are manifestly the production of an uneducated
mind; but they evince a vigour of talent, a depth of
feeling, and, in many instances, a purity of taste, that
ought to carry their possessor up from the drudgery of
a mere mechanical employment into a purer and a more
congenial atmosphere. The too scanty biographical
sketch of the author, prefixed to these poems, contains
an interesting account of the struggles of unassisted genius with early penury, and a protracted period of unpropitious circumstances. A hint is thrown out in this
sketch of the publication of a second volume of Mr.
Woodworth's poems: if this be done, it is adviseable for
the author to bestow some additional care upon the
rythm, the rhymes, and the general structure and finish-
ing of his verses.

The greatest national work which the United States
have produced, is Chief Justice Marshall's " Life of
Washington." The character of Mr. Marshall, for great
talents and sound information, has been long thoroughly
established. When young, his reputation as an advocate was great. Some years since, in 1797-8, he displayed his dexterity, judgment, and decision, as a diplomatist, in his well-known negotiation with M. Talleyrand; and now, as Chief Justice of the United States,
he maintains, with masterly ability, firmness, and dignity, the best interests of liberty and law ; which, indeed, are always inseparable. The work, however,
bears evident marks of haste and negligence, which,
indeed, is confessed by the author ; but

" Ου χρη παννυχιον ευδειν βουληφορον ανδρα ;"

a *judge* should never be *too indolent*. Nevertheless, the
book is written in a clear, manly, and vigorous style,

and contains an admirable outline of the history of the British North American colonies from their first settlement to the breaking out of the revolutionary war. Full justice is done to the exalted character of Washington, and to his illustrious compatriots; an ample and instructive account is given of the origin and progress of political parties in the United States; and the notes contain disquisitions, replete with profound reasoning and philosophical analysis.

Of *periodical* works we have some few that exhibit considerable talent, and contain much valuable information. The *Port Folio* is conducted by its present editor, Mr. John E. Hall, with great ability, taste, and judgment, and displays many admirable specimens of elegant and finished composition, and of sound, manly criticism. This journal was originally established by the late Mr. Dennie, who is called the American Addison, nearly twenty years since, and is the only periodical work in the United States to which so long a life has been accorded. Mr. Dennie was the first gentleman in this country who devoted himself, *exclusively*, to the pursuit of letters, which he cultivated to the last hour of his earthly pilgrimage; and received from his benevolent fellow-citizens, as a recompence for his felicitous effusions of genius, taste, feeling, tenderness, eloquence, wit, and humour – *permission to starve.*

For general ability, and various information, the " *North American Review*," edited at Boston, is probably the most conspicuous of all the periodical publications in the United States.

In the *Analectic Magazine* there are able original essays, well written biography, and some judicious criticism. The *Portico* displays a vigour of thought, a boldness of originality, and a manly eloquence, that deserve much more than the languishing support, balancing between life and death, which it receives from the opulent citizens of Baltimore. *The American Magazine and Review*, recently floated in New-York, contains much valuable information respecting the proceedings of the various learned societies in the United

States; but its critical department stands altogether on a false foundation, namely, that criticism consists in finding fault. "He is a very great critic," says Sheridan, sarcastically, "for nothing pleases him." It requires, however, much more talent and learning, as well as more good temper, to praise judiciously than to blame indiscriminately. The *Neologist* is a periodical paper, of which nearly one hundred numbers have appeared in the New-York Daily Advertiser, which still continues to publish its lucubrations twice a-week. It is, evidently, the production of young persons, who have, as yet, but little experience in the affairs of the world, or the social habits of our great cities; but, beyond all doubt, the United States have *not*, hitherto, produced essays equal to those of the Neologist, in real genius, learned criticism, ethical disquisition, fine taste, sound thought, chaste composition, various erudition, and touching eloquence. And we trust, as it is widely circulated through the medium of the newspapers in New-York and Boston, that it will serve to correct and restrain the pruriency of our little master-misses and literary foplings to prattle incontinently upon the merits of a minute ballad, or small song, or new *pas seul;* and teach them, either to be silent, or learn to direct their attention to some more profitable employment: perhaps the *Neologist* may teach them the meaning of the proverb, " *ne sutor ultra crepidam.*"

Mr. Trumbull's *M'Fingal,* written to ridicule the tories during the revolution, exhibits much of the wit, and some of the learning, of Butler's Hudibras. Mr. Washington Irving's *Salmagundi* and *History of Knickerbocker,* need not shrink from competition with any European performance, in the felicitous combination of good humoured wit, delicate irony, dexterous delineation of character, skilful exposition of the fashionable follies prevalent in the United States, with the occasional relief of exquisitely finished composition, full of tenderness, melancholy, pathos, and eloquence. Mr. Irving's *Sketch of the Life of Campbell,* the Scottish poet, is an admirable union of sound philosophy, delicate taste, judicious criticism, fine feeling, and elegant writing.

Mr. Wirt has long been known as one of the most eloquent speakers and writers in the union : as an advocate, he is considered the first at the Virginia bar, a bar fertile in powerful and animated oratory. His *Old Bachelor*, a collection of essays on various subjects, first stamped his excellence as a writer, and is become deservedly popular all over the country : its chief objects are to vindicate the American character and intellect from European aspersions, to rouse the martial spirit of his countrymen, and excite a love of letters in the United States. His *British Spy* exhibits the finer characteristics of American eloquence, alike in the author's own composition, and in his delineations of some of our first-rate oratory. His *Sketches of the Life of Patrick Henry* gives a most interesting, instructive, and eloquent account of Henry, who is considered as one of the greatest orators and profoundest statesmen that Virginia has produced. And also it exhibits the origin and progress of the chief actors who brought about the independence of the United States.

It is quite enough to say of the late Fisher Ames, that he is denominated by his fellow citizens *the Burke* of America.

Mr. Colden's *Life of Fulton* is a very instructive and valuable work. It is, however, manifestly the production of one more accustomed to public speaking than to closet-composition ; and it is well known, that some of the most eloquent speakers in the senate, and at the bar, both in Britain and in the United States, *for want of practice,* do not write with so much precision, fluency, and force, as their undoubted talents and information would naturally lead us to expect. Rousseau used to say, " that with whatever faculties a man might be born, that of writing well was not one ; for that can only be attained by long and constant exercise, and habitual imitation of the best models." And when Dr. Johnson was once shown a book written by an eminent British statesman, he said, " this book, Sir, is written with great ability: it displays vast reach of thought and variety of erudition; and the style, considering the gentleman has not been used to write, is excellent."

It is not, of course, intended to notice all the writers who have by their talents and information shed a lustre on the United States, but merely to mark out a few examples of different species of literary excellence. It would, however, be quite unpardonable to omit the name of Mr. *Walsh*, who is, confessedly, the first man of letters we have on this side of the Atlantic. His information on general literature, politics, and history, is copious and accurate. His style of writing is elaborate, vigorous, splendid, and eloquent; with, perhaps, rather too frequent a use of the *sesquipedalia verba*, and of French words and phrases, which weaken the strength, and mar the uniformity of the composition. The English language is sufficiently comprehensive and energetic to give adequate expression to any sentiment, however sublime, or tender, or indignant, or pathetic: the whole compass of the human heart and head may be struck upon its chords, and every tone made to discourse most excellent music. Dr. Johnson, in animadverting upon the gallicisms of Mr. Hume, said, " that if they were suffered to gain ground, England would soon be reduced to babble a dialect of France." What is now said is by no means said for the purpose of depressing or detracting from the great merits of Mr. Walsh, from whose writings, (to use a strong expression of Lord Bacon,) " he who does not receive instruction and delight, must be more than man, or less than beast." And, might I be permitted to add, that splendid and vigorous as are the writings of Mr. Walsh, his *conversation* is still more rich, instructive, and interesting?

The United States ought to cherish the efforts of a man so gifted and so adorned, who devotes to the prosecution of letters talents and learning, that, otherwise directed, would command any height of exaltation and influence which our community can give. Mr. Walsh's *Lettter on the character and genius of the French govern-*

ment is a peculiarly splendid production, and contains some very valuable information, altogether new, when promulgated, on the finances and internal administration of the imperial revolutionary government. It was profusely praised by both the Edinburgh and Quarterly Reviews, and cited with great applause by Lord Chief Justice Ellenborough, from his seat in the King's Bench. Mr. Walsh's *American Review*, in four octavo volumes, contain much very interesting information on the state of society and manners, in France and England, which ought to be published in a separate form, as a most acceptable boon to every reader. This review also exhibits some sound criticism on American productions, and considerable information on foreign literature, particularly the French, German, and Italian; and, above all, a lofty and sustained effort to raise the tone of literature in the United States, and make his country sensible, that no nation ever can become really great and permanently prosperous, until it protects and cultivates letters. In his correspondence with General Harper, on the probable result of the conflict between revolutionary France and the rest of Europe, the same characteristics of copious information and splendid eloquence appear: his remarks on the portentous power of Russia, doubtless, the European sovereigns *now* feel to be true and just.

In his *American Register*, of which two octavo volumes have appeared, he takes a wider range, as may be seen by a reference to his very admirable introduction to the first volume. He gives an able and interesting bird's-eye view of the political state of Europe, the domestic occurrences of the United States, the congressional and parliamentary debates on the most important topics of finance, navigation, and general policy; and exhibits a fine panorama of American and European literature. He particularly presses upon his countrymen the necessity and importance of a wider system of education, and a more extended circle of literature: his observations on the benefits of a *national university* are replete with wisdom and eloquence.

Sufficient juctice has *not* been rendered to Mr. Walsh's literary efforts in the United States; in Britain he is better appreciated. *There* they demanded *four* editions of his Letter on the French government in a few weeks; whereas *here* his own countrymen have suffered a *second* edition to languish uncirculated through the space of several years. It was a duty to say thus much of one, from whose lucubrations I have received so much pleasure and instruction; and I have nothing further to add, than to express my warmest wishes for the continuance of his literary career, in the words of his own favourite poet:

" I, decus, I, nostrum, et *melioribus* utere fatis !"

Medical science appears to have made by far the greatest improvement of any intellectual pursuit in the United States; and the schools of New-York, Philadelphia, Boston, and Baltimore, are so well supplied with able professors and lecturers, as to supersede the necessity of our medical students resorting to Edinburgh, London, or Paris, for instruction in any one branch of the healing art. A medical school has also been recently established in Kentucky, under the most favourable auspices of able teachers, and a strong inclination on the part of the western states to support the institution with funds, and supply it with pupils. Several able medical periodical works are continually issuing from the American press.

With regard to the *fine arts*, our *sculpture* extends but little beyond chisseling grave-stones for a church-yard; and our *painting*, for want of individual wealth, is chiefly confined to miniatures, portraits, and landscapes: the only splendid exceptions, are Mr. Trumbull's historical paintings of the *Battle of Bunker's Hill, the Death of Montgomery*, the *Sortie from Gibraltar;* together with some Scripture pieces, and the great national pictures which he is now preparing for the capitol at Washington. But American genius is equal to that of Europe for the fine arts, as is evident from the United States having produced West, Trumbull, Stuart, Copeley, Alston, and Leslie. The Academies of the fine arts, at New-York and Philadelphia, contain some fine paintings, and a few good pieces of sculpture, imported from Europe. Boston, New York, Philadelphia, and Washington, contain some very handsome public buildings; the city-hall of New-York, a marble edifice, probably surpasses in magnificence and beauty every European building out of Italy.

Mr. Walsh, in the second volume of his *Register*, in translating M. de Marbois's preliminary discourse, says, " Hitherto the Americans have *not* made great progress in the elegant arts: their public libraries, their museums, would not in Europe be thought worthy to decorate the mansion of an opulent amateur. They style the edifices in which their legislators assemble *capitols ;* and this appellation, which is now held ambitious, will one day appear quite modest. They have no cirques, amphitheatres, nor mock sea-fights. It will never perhaps be necessary for them to construct citadels, or environ their towns with ditches and ramparts. There will not be seen among them, either pyramids, or proud mausoleums, or basilicks, or temples, like those of Ephesus and Rome. Ages must revolve before they will erect those edifices, of which the idle and barren magnificence imposes heavy sacrifices on the present generation, diverts their industry towards objects of mere parade, and entails wretchedness on posterity. The time of the Americans is wisely divided between permanently useful labours and necessary repose. They employ themselves in preparing their fields for the production of food; in rendering their dwellings commodious, in opening roads, and digging canals. Commerce and navigation already supply them with wealth; the arts of real utility embellish their cities ; and Europe, which so long stood single, as the country of the sciences and human wisdom, now shares with America this noble distinction."

The genius of America is peculiarly distinguished for its invention in the useful mechanics arts: in allusion to this, the late Mr. Gouverneur Morris, a few months before his lamented death, said, " there are persons of some eminence in Europe, who look contemptuously at our country, in the persuasion that all creatures, not excepting man, degenerate here. They triumphantly call on us to exhibit a list of our scholars, poets, heroes, and statesmen. Be this the care of posterity. But, admitting we had no proud names to show, is it reasonable to make such heavy demand on so recent a people? Could the culture of science be expected from those, who, in cultivating the earth, were obliged, while they held a plough in one hand, to grasp a sword in the other? Let those who depreciate their brethren of the west remember that our forests, though widely spread, gave no academic shade. In the century succeeding Hudson's voyage, the great poets of England flourished, while we were compelled to earn our daily bread by our daily labour. The ground, therefore, was occupied before we had leisure to make our approach. The various chords of our mother tongue have, long since, been touched to all their tones, by minstrels, beneath whose master hand it has resounded every sound, from the roar of thunder rolling along the vault of heaven, to ' the lascivious pleasings of a lute.' British genius and taste have already given to all ' the ideal forms that imagination can body forth, a local habitation and a name.' Nothing then remains for the present age but to repeat their just thoughts in their pure style. Those, who on either side of the Atlantic, are too proud to perform this plagiary task, must convey false thoughts in the old classic diction, or clothe in frippery phrase the correct conceptions of their predecessors. But *other* paths remain to be trodden, *other* fields to be cultivated, *other* regions to be explored. The fertile earth is not yet wholly peopled : the raging ocean is not yet quite subdued. Be it *ours* to boast, that the first vessel successfully propelled by steam was launched on the bosom of Hudson's river. It was here that *American* genius, seizing the arm of European science, bent to the purpose of our favourite parent art the wildest and most devouring element. This invention is spreading fast through the civilized world; and though excluded, as yet, from Russia, will, ere long, be extended to that vast empire. A bird hatched on the Hudson will soon people the floods of the Wolga; and cygnets descended from an American swan, glide along the surface of the Caspian Sea. Then the hoary genius of Asia, high throned on the peaks of Caucasus, his moist eye glistening while it glances over the ruins of Babylon, Persepolis, Jerusalem, and Palmyra, shall bow with grateful reverence to the inventive spirit of this western world."

The *remedies* to be applied for the removal of those impediments which obstruct the progress of literature in the United States are *not* very difficult of access, since no material causes of defect exist to render the intellect of America incapable of any improvement within the compass of human genius to attain.

The *trading* spirit, indeed, cannot be extinguished by the anathemas of the priest, or the declamations of the moralist. Massilon may preach, and Boileau may satyrize, yet the merchant will continue to speculate, and count his gains. Nor is it desirable, if it were possible, to exterminate the trading spirit, which is indelibly and beneficially written on the human heart, and renders man, by nature, a trading animal. It can, however, and *ought* to be modified and restrained, lest it become excessive, and absorb all honour, intellect, virtue, propriety, and feeling into its insatiable gulph. *So* fell Tyre, and Sidon, and Carthage, and Venice, and Holland. *This* spirit requires restraint in the United States. The beginning of the remedy must be found in meliorating our systems of *elementary* education; in rendering them seminaries where the morals of youth may be purified and exalted, and their understandings invigorated and expanded. If this be once done, the colleges, of course, must adopt a larger and more liberal plan of instruction; whence, the absorbing tendency of the trading spirit will be restrained and counterpoised, the love of literature flourish, literary competition spring into existence, literary rewards and honours

create an effectual demand for the exertions of genius
and learning, large private collections of books and
ample public libraries be gathered together, and the
whole nation rise in the scale of power and dignity, by
having the life's-blood of intellect and knowledge in-
fused into all its veins and arteries, from the source of circulation, the heart.   Then, indeed, may we expect the
refinements of art, and science, and letters, to follow in
the train of opulence, and purify it from its grossness.

The means of literary competition must be provided
and multiplied.   Men of genius must be roused to
exertion by the collision of kindred genius.   " Give me
kings to run with, and I will start," said Alexander,
when urged to contend at the Olympic games.   Men
of great talents, if they see no high standard of literary
excellence raised in the country, either pursue some
other vocation, or sink into indolence and ease.   This
desirable purpose may be accomplished by properly
constructed *Literary Societies*, where men meet together to contribute, each his share, to the common
stock of intellect, and mutually watch over, collide with,
and invigorate each other's understanding.   A remarkable illustration of their utility is furnished by the
French Academy, founded in 1635, by Cardinal Richlieu,
to improve the French language, grammar, poetry, and
eloquence.   This academy published an excellent Dictionary, and exceedingly improved the style of French
composition.   In its first harangues, the style is cold,
barren, feeble, insipid, and uninteresting.   As we advance in the perusal of its volumes, the language becomes richer, more splendid, and, occasionally, elegant
and vigorous; and the concluding dissertations are full
of the happiest sentiment, conveyed into language brilliant, energetic, and eloquent.

In a literary society, *properly constituted and well
conducted*, every member is continually incited to diligence in the composition of his writings, because he
knows that they will undergo a strict examination from
his fellows, whose criticisms will enable him to correct
what is erroneous, brighten what is obscure, lop what

is superfluous, invigorate his sentiments, and chasten his language. Such institutions also diffuse an honourable spirit of literary ambition over the community, by holding up an object of esteem, towards which men of genius may press for enrolment among its members, by giving to the public its lucubrations, to form a literary repository; and, by creating models of good writing, to strengthen the understanding, and refine the taste of the nation into which they breathe the spirit of their intelligence. And such an institution is exceedingly beneficial to the members, in enlarging their knowledge, and po lishing their taste by the collision of intellect in their literary conferences. In such a republic of letters, men bear sway in proportion to their superior mind. To the opinions of such men on matters of literary investigation attention is always paid, and rewarded by corresponding improvement. Men of equal or similar talents and acquisitions contend in this amicable conflict, and from the reciprocal contest results mutual instruction, and the growth of wisdom and information is rapidly increased by the continual application of the most powerful incitements to intellectual exertion; namely, the authority of the already celebrated, the contradiction of aspiring candidates for literary renown, the desire of praise so generally prevalent, the dread of ridicule, which so much more generally prevails, and finally, by the elevated wish to become useful to our country and to the world.

There are learned societies in Boston, New-York, and Philadelphia, which have contributed, and are continually contributing, much to the growth of intellect and information in the United States. The *Historial,* and the *Literary and Philosophical* Societies of New-York, have been peculiarly serviceable in promoting the progress of letters and science. Some of their members have read able and instructive papers: the orations of the late Mr. Gouverneur Morris were compositions peculiarly splendid and finished; and Mr. Clinton's Introductory discourse to the Literary and Philosophical Society covers a vast and various extent of science and erudition. Indeed, Governor Clinton has always approved himself the warm friend and patron of art, literature, and science, as the means best calculated to make his country permanently illustrious and powerful; as well as rendered them essential service by his own personal contributions. The *Corporation* of the city of New-York deserve all praise for their magnificent appropriation of an extensive range of buildings, to the exclusive use of literary and scientific societies.

But, perhaps, the most effectual means of promoting the progress of learning in the United States would be the establishment of a *National University*. Mr. Blodget, in his *Economica*, details at length General Washington's views and wishes respecting this important subject. Mr. Walsh, in the Introduction to the first volume of his *Register*, has lent all the aid of his talents and eloquence, to set forth the vast advantages of such a measure. And the President, in his Message of the 2d of December, 1817, suggests to Congress " the propriety of recommending to the states an *amendment* of the federal constitution, giving to Congress power to institute seminaries of learning, for the all-important purpose of diffusing knowledge among our fellow-citizens throughout the United States."

So early as the year 1775, at the very commencement of the revolutionary struggle, General Washington, while in camp at Cambridge, near Boston, looked forward to the establishment of a national university. Not being able, when living, to effect this object, he left, by his will, stock equal to twenty-five thousand dollars, towards establishing such an institution in the federal city, and invited the subscriptions of his fellow-citizens for the same purpose. He directs the annual proceeds of his own legacy to be invested at compound interest until the fund, together with other subscriptions, should be sufficient to accomplish the whole plan proposed. If ever a national university, liberally endowed, and well sustained by the talents and learning of its professors, shall be established, it will do more towards promoting the progress of letters in the United Sates than any single institution which has yet been planted. In such a national seminary, the whole circle of the arts, and sciences, and erudition, should be taught; the *classics*, both Greek and Latin, thoroughly, as the best basis of all liberal education ; to which add the mathematics and natural philosophy, and regular courses of lectures on moral philosophy, political economy, belles-lettres and rhetoric, elocution, metaphysical science, municipal jurisprudence, and the law of nature and nations. It would be a patriotic duty for all classes of society, the people at large, the men of leisure, the men of business, the physicians, the lawyers, the statesmen, and the divines of America, to unite their powerful efforts to create and maintain such a national institution ; another Athens in this western orb, which, under their guardian auspices, may long flourish, as the general repository of learning ; and eventually render these United States at once the bulwark and ornament of literature within their own extensive dominions, and the permanent object of esteem and admiration to the whole surrounding world.

The following observations of Mr. Walsh, in relation to this subject, cannot be too often repeated, nor too widely circulated.

" Sovereigns and governments alone can raise up institutions for education, of the amplitude and mechanism required to give energy and efficacy to all the human faculties. Without such institutions we *cannot*, in the United States, expect to display *that perfection of individual and social being* which the European nations have nearly attained, and which we are, *in other respects*, beyond the rest of the world, privileged to reach. It is to the *national government* that we must look for the means of becoming the rivals of Europe in the pursuits which give *most* honour and happiness to our species. The *state*-governments have not the ability, and are not likely to have the inclination, to create those means. We are a great commercial, and are to be a great military people, only through the federal system ; we can become a literary and philosophical people by the same agency alone. *All* these qualifications are necessary to constitute national greatness, upon the scale which suits our unrivalled opportunities. We must be Greece, Rome, and Carthage, at once; or, what is more modern, Italy, France, and England, in the same frame."

Generally speaking, our systems of education for *girls* are practically better than those for boys; and accordingly, our women generally are more intelligent and conversible than the men. In some of our larger cities, it is fashionable for the young ladies to learn the elements of botany and chymistry, in addition to the common rudiments of female instruction. In our own city of New-York, Mr. Griscom, a celebrated teacher, has established a course of lectures on natural philosophy for young ladies, who attend him in great numbers, from our most respectable families. Such a course of instruction, combined with suitable reading and reflection at home, would lay the basis of solid and substantial information, as the means of utility and delight throughout the whole of life.

Miss Hannah More's "*Strictures on the Modern System of Female Education*" are admirably adapted to render women sensible, well-bred, and excellent in all the various relations and charities of life. They teach, that *domestic* virtue is woman's chiefest ornament and praise, and more likely to be found in a liberally educated than in an unintelligent female. Her observations on this point are peculiarly good; there is, at present, room only for the few following sentences. "Since, then, there is a season, when the youthful must cease to be young, and the beautiful to excite admiration, to learn how *to grow old gracefully*, is, perhaps, one of the rarest and most valuable arts which can be taught to woman. And, it must be confessed, it is a most severe trial for those women to be called to lay down beauty, who have nothing else to take up. It is for this sober season of life, that education should lay up its rich resources. However disregarded they may hitherto have been, they will be wanted now. When admirers fall away, and flatterers become mute, the mind will be driven to retire into itself; and if it find no entertainment at home, it will be driven back again upon the world with increased force. Yet, forgetting this, do we not seem to educate our daughters *exclusively* for the transient period of youth, when it is to maturer life we ought to advert? Do we not educate them for a crowd, forgetting that they are to live at home? For the world, and not for themselves? For show, and not for use? For time, and not for eternity?

" The chief end to be proposed in cultivating the understandings of women, is to qualify them for the *practical* purposes of life. Their knowledge is not often, like the learning of men, to be reproduced in some literary composition, nor even in any learned profession; but it is to come out in *conduct*. It is to be exhibited in life and manners. A lady studies, not that she may qualify herself to become an orator or a pleader; not that she may learn to debate, but to act. She is to read the best books, not so much as to enable her to talk of them, as to bring the improvement which they furnish to the rectification of her principles, and the formation of her habits. The great uses of study to a woman are, to enable her to regulate her own mind, and to be instrumental to the good of others. To woman, therefore, *whatever be her rank*, I would recommend a predominance of those more sober studies, which, *not* having display for their object, may make her wise without vanity, happy without witnesses, and content without panegyrists; the exercise of which will not bring celebrity, but improve usefulness."

The American ladies have learned, that it is *not* altogether the *business* of their lives to administer to the mere pleasure of man, as the plaything of his hours of relaxation from the toils of ambition, or the cravings of wealth; to be entirely absorbed in the pursuits of ephemeral fashion, and "when God has given them one face, to make unto themselves another, to jig, to amble, and lisp, and nickname God's creatures, and make their wantonness their ignorance." They have discovered, that God has given them such high capacities of excellence, such acute perception, such exquisite feeling, such ardent affection, for the purpose of becoming man's companion and guide; the soother of his sorrows and heightener of his joys; the object of his proud submission, his dignified obedience, his chivalrous worship; the being whose smile forms the joy of his life, the sunshine of his existence.

> " Till *Hymen* brought his love-delighted hour,
> There dwelt no joy in Eden's roseate bower.
> In vain the viewless seraph, lingering there,
> At starry midnight charm'd the silent air;
> In vain the wild-bird caroll'd from the steep,
> To hail the sun slow wheeling from the deep;
> In vain, to soothe the solitary shade,
> Aërial notes in mingling measure play'd;
> The summer wind that shook the spangled tree,
> The whispering wave, the murmuring of the bee,
> Still slowly passed the melancholy day,
> And still the stranger wist not where to stray;
> The world was sad, the garden was a wild,
> And man, the hermit, sigh'd *till woman smil'd.*"

CHAPTER VII.

On the Habits, Manners, and Character of the United States.

THAT *foreigners,* who do *not* speak the same language as the people of this country, should be extremely ignorant of the resources and character of the Americans, is not a subject of surprise: the very circumstance of their speaking in a different tongue, added to the general prevalence of despotism in their respective governments, and want of information in their subjects, will sufficiently account for *their* unacquaintance with the past history, the present situation, the future prospects of the United States. But *Britain* can find no such excuse for *her* portentous ignorance of this country: *her* blood flows in every vein, and quickens every artery of the giant offspring, sprung from her teeming loins; *her* language, laws, religion, habits, manners, and pursuits, have reproduced *another* Britain in this western world, on a far more extended scale of capacity, magnificence, and power, than its venerable mother can ever hope to attain; cooped and cabined in as she is, by the narrow dimensions of her own territorial dominions.

Indeed, the general, not to say universal ignorance which prevails in Britain, alike in the government and in the people, respecting all the essential qualities, and national characteristics of these United States, is almost incredible to those who have not attentively examined the subject. Perhaps it is chiefly owing to the intercourse between the two countries being almost exclusively *commercial;* for in general merchants are not apt to investigate a country, either very comprehensively, or very accurately, beyond the states of its markets, and the course of its prices current. And, until it shall become the fashion for the gentlemen and men of education, *both* of America and of Britain, to travel over, and explore each other's country, the two nations must, and will remain in profound ignorance of their reciprocal relation, character, and interest.

In addition to all this, the British government has *not* been sufficiently careful to send out able and intelligent *ambassadors* and ministers to the United States.

The reasons *why* the British diplomacy is in general defective; and why, in particular, so few able ambassadors have been sent out by her to these United States, are detailed at length in " *The Resources of the British Empire,*" from p. 332 to 351; containing also, the causes of Britain's general unacquaintance with the movements and dispositions of foreign nations, and of her neglecting to avail herself of the *presses* of other countries, in order to tell her own story, and to justify her own measures to the world.

This is the more to be regretted, as it regards the United States and Britain, because the interests of both countries are similar; and their mutual peace, good understanding, and friendship, redound so much to the essential benefit of both. *M. Talleyrand,* first a bishop under the old regime, then a citizen sans-culotte, then a revolutionary and imperial prince, and finally, a Bourbon prime minister, was so well aware of the reciprocal interests of America and Britain, that in a memoir read to the National Institute, he proposed the fixing a powerful *French* establishment in the United States, as the *only* means of counteracting the peaceful and amicable tendencies of two nations sprung from the same stock, speaking the same language, living under the same or similar laws, using the same religion, and exhibiting the same habits and manners.

The clerical citizen prince complains grievously of the existence of *any* commercial or friendly intercourse between America and Britain; when, after the revolutionary struggle, in which the French so effectually aided their new allies, and the United States had thrown off the dominion of the English, every reason seemed to indicate a *dissolution* of those mercantile connexions which had before subsisted between two portions of the same people. The chief of these reasons were—the recollection of the evils produced by a seven years' war; a defiance and hatred of Britain, and attachment to France, as their companion in arms, and their liberator from colonial vassalage; attachment, most forcibly manifested at the breaking out of the war between France and England, in the year 1793; at which period the conversation and actions of the American people, their newspapers and pamphlets, their town-meetings and public speeches, their illuminations and clamour, almost drove the administration of Washington himself to manifest, by joining the French revolutionary republic, in its war against Britain, the strong inclination towards France, and the equally deadly hatred towards England, which then pervaded so large a portion of the United States.

These, and other reasons, it was hoped would, for ever, turn the tide of American commerce from its accustomed channel; or, if it should happen to incline a little towards the shores of England, it would require a very trifling exertion, on the part of *France*, to divert it entirely to *her own* dominions. Closer, and more accurate observation, however, will soon detect the fallacy of all such conclusions, and point out the helplessness of an artificial and circuitous policy to resist the universal efficiency of nature herself when she appeals to the human heart, in the accents of a kindred tongue, and with the all-prevailing voice of manifest advantage. *Individuals* may sometimes, and under certain circumstances, feel the impulses of *gratitude*, and act under a deep and permanent sense of kindness shown and benefits received; a great proportion of individuals, however, like Milton's hero, consider it to be a debt, " so burdensome, still paying, still to owe," that they are eager to cast it off for ever, by returning the recompence of hatred and calumny into the bosom of their benefactor. *Nations,* large masses of men, being a body in continual flux, liable to perpetual change in opinions, sentiments, relations, and actions, *never can be* capable of gratitude to other nations. It is idle, therefore, for France to insist upon a grateful return from the United States, on account of her aiding them in their revolutionary war; and equally idle for Britain to request that the American people shall cease to revile and calumniate all her institutions and proceedings, because *her* capital and credit have enabled the United States to render themselves opulent and powerful in an extensive commerce, in growing manufactures, in a widening agriculture, in a variety of thriving moneyed establishments. *Interest* and *ambition* are the pole-star and magnet of nations; gratitude and affection the incentives of individual, not of national action. Besides, the gratitude of America was due to Louis XVI. personally, and was fully cancelled by his subsequent regret that he had ever assisted the United States, and by the efforts of his cabinet, in the year 1783, to prevent England from acknowledging their independence, to exclude them from the Newfoundland fisheries, and to confine their territory to the eastward of the Alleghany mountains; all showing that the object of France was *not* regard to the United States, but a desire to weaken both America and Britain, by protracting the conflict between them.

Whoever has well observed America, cannot doubt that she still remains *essentially English,* in language, habits, laws, customs, manners, morals, and religion; that her ancient commerce with England increased, many fold, instead of declining in activity and extent, subsequent to the independence of the United States; and that, consequently, so far as relates to commercial intercourse, the independence of America has been beneficial to Britain. *M. Talleyrand,* indeed, labours to prove that the inconsiderate conduct of the old French government (as contradistinguished from the revolutionary system) laid the foundation of the commercial success of England with the United States. He thinks, that if, after the peace which secured the independence of America, France had been sufficiently sensible of the full advantage of her existing position, she would have continued and sought to multiply exceedingly, those political, commercial, and social relations, which, during the revolutionary war, had been established between her and her Transatlantic Allies; and which had been forcibly, and bloodily broken off with Britain. If this had been done, the ancient habits and relations between America and England being almost forgotten, France could have contended with peculiar advantages against every thing which had the least tendency to reconcile the Americans with the English, so as to prevent the possibility of any cordial and permanent friendship ever existing between the two nations.

But the French court was fearful, that the same principles of *democracy*, which she had protected and encouraged by her arms in America, should introduce themselves, and be disseminated among her own people; and therefore, at the conclusion of the war in 1783, she did not sufficiently continue, and promote her political and commercial connexions with the United States. Whereas England wisely forgot, and subdued the bitterness of her resentments; she immediately re-opened her channels of communication both social and mercantile with America, and rendered them still more active than at any period prior to the Revolution. By such conduct she directed the attention of the United States towards a profitable market; and thus increased the obstacles to the ascendency of French influence. For the will of man is always powerfully swayed by inclination and interest; and notwithstanding the occurrence of a long and sanguinary war, and all the efforts of political faction, the Americans have a natural bias towards England, to whose kindred people all their own habits assimilate them.

Identity of language itself, as M. Talleyrand observes, is a fundamental relation between different individuals and different countries; upon which the political moralist, and the moral philosopher, cannot too patiently, and too profoundly meditate. This very

identity of tongue establishes between the two nations,
America and England, a common character, which will
always enable, nay, induce them to recognize and con-
sort with each other.   They mutually feel themselves
at home, whenever they travel into each other's territory, they give and receive reciprocal pleasure in the
interchange of sentiment and thought, in the discussion
of their various opinions, views, and interests. But an
insurmountable barrier is raised up between two different people, who speak two different languages; and
who, therefore, cannot utter a single word, without
being compelled to remember that they do *not* belong
to the same country; between whom every solitary
transmission of sentiment and thought is irksome labour, and not a social enjoyment; who never can be
made to understand each other thoroughly; and with
whom the result of conversation, after the fatigue of un-
availing efforts to be reciprocally intelligible, is to find
themselves reciprocally ridiculous.   This of course applies to the mass of a people ; there are well educated
individuals in most countries, who can converse with
each other fully in a tongue not common to both
speakers.

Accordingly, notwithstanding the *government* of
France, both under the Bourbons during the old
regime and under the revolutionary regicides, whether
democratic, directorial, consular, or imperial, always
exercised considerable influence over the government of
America; which so far from being influenced by, was
always prone to suspect and take offence at every act
of the British government, however harmless or well
intended ; yet, in every part of the United States, individual Englishmen feel themselves to be Americans ;
and individual Frenchmen find themselves to be as
completely strangers as if they were animals of different species at least; even if they might be considered generically the same.

Nor is it any marvel to see this natural, necessary,
habitual assimilation towards England, in a country
where, in addition to the identity of language in both,
the great distinguishing and characteristic features of

the form of government, and of the system of municipal law, whether in the federal union, or in the separate state-sovereignties, are impressed with so strong a family resemblance to the leading lineaments of the British constitution. The personal liberty of the individual citizen in the United States rests upon precisely the same foundations as those which support the personal freedom of the British subject; namely, the *habeas corpus act*, and *trial by jury*. Whoever attends the sittings of Congress, and the state-legislatures, and listens to the discussions respecting the framing of laws, whether for the Union, or for the separate states, will hear all their quotations, analogies, and examples, taken from the laws, the history, the customs, the parliamentary rules and usages of England. In the American courts of justice, the authorities cited are the statutes, the judgments, the decrees, the reported decisions of the English courts; in familiar and friendly accompaniment with those of the American tribunals.

In the higher and more cultivated classes of society in both countries, there is also a community of taste and sentiment on subjects of literature, and a common feeling of pride in the great poets, philosophers, historians, and general writers of the mother country, that forms a strong bond of union.

Now, if a people so trained and so circumstanced, have no natural, no habitual bias and inclination towards England, we must renounce all belief and trust in the controlling influences of language, laws, habits, manners, customs and usages, upon the opinions, feelings, passions, actions, and character of men; we must deny that man receives any effectual impressions, any permanent modifications, from surrounding circumstances; from all that he sees, hears, reads, observes, and is engaged in, from the cradle to the grave. It is, comparatively, of little moment, that the *names* of a republic and a monarchy appear to place between the two governments distinctions which cannot be confounded, and obstacles which cannot be surmounted. For, in fact, there are strong republican features in the representative portion of the

English constitution; and there are monarchial lineaments distinctly visible in the executive branches of the American constitutions, both state and federal. This was more peculiary the case, as long as the presidency of General Washington continued; for the force of public opinion and sentiment, attached to his *person* throughout the whole of the United States, bore a striking resemblance to that kind of magical power and illusion, which many most distinguished political writers attribute to the pervading influences of monarchy, under the name of *loyalty* to the reigning sovereign.

This sentiment, however, did *not* survive the executive magistracy of Washington; the strange and wayward conduct of President Adams, together with the schism in the federal party during his administration, forbade all personal attachment to him. And Mr. Jefferson and Mr. Madison avowedly administered the federal government altogether on *democratic* principles and views, which cut up by the root all possibility of personal attachment, stifle every generous feeling of enthusiasm and reverence, and degrade the government of a country from the high eminence of a national administration, into the deep abyss of the dominion of a faction. Mr. Monroe, indeed, has lately been making progress through the United States, and " buying golden opinions from all sorts of men," with the hope of rekindling that flame of loyalty and national attachment to their executive chief, which glowed in the bosoms of the American people for the illustrious Washington, " first in war, first in peace, and first in the hearts of his fellow-citizens."

It is surprising, that M. Talleyrand, who has made so many profound remarks, and drawn such wise and comprehensive inferences, in his *Memoir* to the National Institute, should so egregiously have mistaken the *character* of the Americans. He says, that as a people newly constituted and formed of different elements, their national character is not yet decided. They remain English from ancient habit; and because they have not yet had time to become completely Americans.

Their climate is not yet formed: their character still less. If we consider those populous cities filled with English, Germans, Irish, and Dutch, as well as with their indigenous inhabitants; those remote towns so distant from each other; those vast uncultivated tracts of soil, traversed rather than inhabited by men who belong to no country, what common bond can we conceive in the midst of so many incongruities? It is a novel sight to the traveller, who, setting out from a principal city where society is in perfection, passes in succession through all the degrees of civilization and industry, which he constantly finds growing weaker and weaker, until in a few days he arrives at a misshapen and rude cabin, formed of the trunks of trees lately cut down.

Such a journey is a sort of practical and living analysis of the origin of people and states: we set out from the most compounded mixture, to arrive at the most simple ingredients: at the end of every day we lose sight of some of those inventions which our wants, as they have increased, have rendered necessary; and it appears as if we travelled backwards in the history of the progress of the human mind. If such a sight lays a strong hold upon the imagination; if we please ourselves by finding in the succession of space what appears to belong only to the succession of time, we must make up our minds to behold but few social connexions, and no common character amongst men, who appear so little to belong to the same association. In many districts the sea and the woods have formed fishermen and wood-cutters. Now, such men have *no* country; and their social morality is reduced within a very small compass. Man is the disciple of that which surrounds him. Hence, he whose bounds are circumscribed by nothing but deserts, cannot receive lessons with regard to the social comforts of life. The idea of the need which men have of each other does not exist in him; and it is merely by decomposing the trade which he exercises, that one can find out the principles of his affections and the sum of his morality.

The American wood-cutter does *not* interest himself in any thing; every sensible idea is remote from him. Those branches so agreeably disposed by nature, beautiful foliage, the bright colour which enlivens one part of the wood, the darker green which gives a melancholy shade to another; these things are nothing to him; he pays them no attention; the number of strokes of his axe required to fell a tree fills all his thoughts. He never planted; he knows not its pleasures. A tree of his own planting would be good for nothing in his estimation, for it would never during his life be large enough to fell. It is by destruction he lives; he is a destroyer wherever he goes. Thus, every place is equally good in his eyes; he has no attachment to the spot on which he has spent his labour, for his labour is only fatigue, and unconnected with any idea of pleasure. In the effects of his toil he has not witnessed those gradual increases of growth so captivating to the planter; he regards not the destination of his productions; he knows not the charm of new attempts; and if, in quitting the abode of many years, he does not by chance forget his axe, he leaves no regret behind him.

The vocation of an American fisherman begets an apathy almost equal to that of the wood-cutter. His affections, his interest, his life, are on the side of that society to which it is thought he belongs. But it would be a prejudice to suppose him *a useful* member. For we must *not* compare these fishermen to those of Europe, and think that the fisheries here are, like them, a nursery for seamen. In America, with the exception of the inhabitants of Nantucket, who fish for whales, fishing is an *idle* employment! Two leagues from the coast, when they have no dread of foul weather; a single mile, when the weather is uncertain; is the sum of the *courage* which they display; and the line is the only instrument of which they know the practical use. Thus their knowledge is but a trifling trick; and their action, which consists in constantly hanging one arm over the side of the boat, is little short of idleness. They are attached to no place; their only connexion with the land is by means of a wretched house which they inhabit. The sea affords them nourishment; and a few cod-fish, more or less determine their country. If their number seems to diminish in any particular quarter, they emigrate in search of another country, where they are more abundant. The remark, that fishing is a sort of agriculture, is not solid; all the qualities and virtues attached to agriculture are wanting in him who lives by fishing. Agriculture produces a patriot, in the truest acceptation of the word; fishing can only form a cosmopolite.

So that it is not only by reason of their origin, language, and interest, the Americans so constantly find themselves to be Englishmen; an observation which applies more especially to the cities. When one looks upon the people wandering among the woods, upon the shores of the sea, and by the banks of the rivers, the general observation is strengthened with regard to them, by that *indolence*, and want of *native character*, which renders this class of Americans more ready to receive and preserve a *foreign* impression. Doubtless, this will grow weaker, and altogether disappear, when the constantly increasing population shall, by the culture of so many desert lands, have brought the inhabitants nearer together. As for the *other* causes, they have taken such deep root, that it would require a *French establishment* in the United States to successfully counteract their ascendency. Undoubtedly, such a political project should not be overlooked by the government of France. No confutation of such positions can be necessary.

M. Talleyrand, however, has discovered his usual sagacity in tracing the settlement of colonies, and the sources of their population, when he says, the different causes which gave rise to colonial establishments have been seldom pure. Thus, ambition and the ardour of conquests carried the first colonies of the Phœnicians and Egyptians into Greece: violence, that of the Tyrians to Carthage; the misfortunes of war, that of the fugitive Trojans to Italy; commerce, and the love of riches, those of the Carthaginians to the isles of the Mediterranean, and the coasts of Spain and Africa; necessity, those of the Athenians into Asia Minor, the people becoming too numerous for their limited and barren territory; prudence, that of the Lacedemonians to Tarentum, to deliver themselves from some turbulent citizens; and urgent policy, the numerous small and unimportant colonies of the Romans, who showed their wisdom in giving up to their colonists a portion of the conquered countries; because they appeased the people, who incessantly demanded a new division of the land, and because they thus formed of the discontented themselves a sure guard in the countries which they had subdued. The ardour for plunder, and the fury of war, much more than the excess of population, sent the colonies, or rather irruptions of the people of the north into the Roman empire; and a romantic piety, greedy of conquest, those of the European croisaders into Asia.

After the discovery of *America,* the folly, injustice, and avarice of individuals thirsting after gold, threw them upon the first countries to which their barks conveyed them. The more rapacious they were, the more they separated; they wished not to cultivate, but to lay waste. Those, indeed, were *not* true colonists. Some time afterward, religious dissensions gave birth to more regular establishments; thus the puritans took refuge in the north of America; the English catholics in Maryland; the quakers in Pennsylvania; whence Dr. Smith concludes, that the *vices,* not the wisdom of European governments, peopled the new world. Other great emigrations likewise, were owing to a gloomy policy, falsely called religious. Thus Spain rejected the Moors from her bosom; France the protestants; almost all governments the Jews; and every where the error which had dictated such deplorable counsels was recognized too late. They had discontented subjects, and they made them enemies who might have served, but were forced to injure, their country.

The inhabitants of the United States consist of Europeans and their descendants, African negroes and

c c

their descendants, and the Aboriginal Indians,—of which last it is not intended to treat, as they are verging rapidly to extinction, under the pressure of American encroachment, which Mr. Monroe, in his Message of the 2d of December, 1817, maintains to be quite proper, and says, " The hunter state can exist only in the vast uncultivated desert.   It yields to the more dense and compact form, and greater force of civilized population; and, of right, it *ought* to yield, for the earth was given to mankind, to support the greatest number of which it is capable, and no tribe or people have a right to withhold from the wants of others more than is necessary for their own support and comfort."

The great mass of our people is of *English* origin, and *not* made up, originally, of convicts, mendicants, and vagabonds, according to the vulgar, but erroneous opinion.   The first settlers in this country were, for the most part, of respectable families and good character, who came hither under the guidance of intelligent and distinguished leaders, and laid the basis of an innumerable people in the best principles and habits of religious toleration, political independence, and social virtue.   These early colonists fled from civil and religious persecution in their native country, to find an asylum in the western world, and have given birth to a people who still retain the puritanical precision, the stern republicanism, and the daring intrepidity of their ancestors.   New-England was settled altogether by Englishmen, except an Irish colony in the hilly part of one county of Massachusetts, and a few Scottish and Irish settlements in New-Hampshire.   With these exceptions, the New-England population is, at this hour, entirely of English origin.   The same source also supplies a great majority of the people in the middle, and a still larger proportion in the southern states.   The Germans make about a fourth of the population of Pennsylvania, and a part of the inhabitants of New-York and New-Jersey.   They are, however, fast yielding their language, habits, and customs to the predominance of the English.   The same may be said of the Dutch

settled in New-York, New-Jersey, and Pennsylvania.
A few French protestants settled at New Rochelle and
Staten-Island, in the state of New-York, and in Charleston, South-Carolina. The Irish emigrants are found
chiefly in Pennsylvania and Maryland; and many are
scattered over New-York, New-Jersey, Kentucky, and
some other states. Those who are papists, from the
middle and south of Ireland, compose the bulk of the
day labourers in our large cities; the protestants from
the north of Ireland generally become agriculturists in
the interior of the country.

The Scottish, who are generally intelligent, industrious, good citizens, have settlements in New-Hampshire, New-York, New-Jersey, Pennsylvania, and
North-Carolina. Some Swedes are found in New-
Jersey, Pennsylvania, and Maryland; and some Swiss
are settled in the state of Indiana. Some small Welsh
settlements have been made in Pennsylvania and New-
York. The new states, which are continually rising,
like exhalations from the earth, in the western country,
and denoting a growth of population rapid and gigantic, beyond all parallel in the history of nations, are
supplied with settlers chiefly from the annual surplus of
New-England, which indeed has been for many years
the *officina gentium* to the states of New-York, Ohio,
Kentucky, and all the interminable regions of the west.

The accessions from *foreign* countries make but a
small proportion of the aggregate of American population. From 1785 to 1815, the annual importation of
foreigners into the United States did *not* exceed five
thousand. Since that period the European migrations
hither have been more abundant. Of these, the French,
in great numbers, direct their steps to the Alabama
territory; and the Irish are endeavouring, under the
auspices of Mr. Emmet, of New-York, to get up an
Hibernian colony in the Illinois country. Many of our
imported foreigners are the lees and dregs, the refuse,
the vilest specimens of Irish and English population,
who reside chiefly in the large cities on our seaboard,
and show forth their patriotism by incessantly vilifying

all the institutions of their native country, and by violating the laws of their adopted nation. The proportion of these imported politicians, however, to the whole community, is not great. The New-England States, throughout, are unpolluted with the mixture of foreign population; and our yeomanry, generally, all over the Union, are native Americans.

Full *one million seven hundred thousand* negroes are held *as slaves* in the United States, which also contain upwards of two hundred thousand *free* people of colour. Both these classes, however, acquire occasionally an admixture of the blood of the white portion of our population, and the *mestizos* are gaining fast in number upon the blacks. The great body of American negroes are to be found in our southern states.

The experience of all history proves that the structure of society in *slave-holding* countries is unfavourable to internal security and peace at all times; and still more so to security and strength in the season of foreign warfare. Indeed, all moral evil possesses a dreadful power of perpetuating and augmenting its own atrocity; whence, the evil of slavery, once established, scarcely admits of remedy; because the *emancipation* of slaves in large masses is nearly, if not quite impracticable; the difference between the habits of a slave and those of a free citizen being wide as the poles asunder. A slave is ignorant of the very elements of *industry*, which is the basis of all social prosperity. While in bondage he only obeys the impulse of another's will, he is actuated by no other motive than the dread of the lash; whereas, when made free, he must think, will, plan, provide for himself and family, and perform all the duties of a citizen. It is necessary to make a slave a man, an animal capable of thought and reflection, before he is made a free man. The slave, recently liberated, has experienced only the most laborious and irksome of the occupations of a citizen, and not having learned any forecast, is unwilling to toil when free. The negroes of St. Domingo at first knew only the two extremes of slavery and rebellion; afterward they experienced the blessings of military despotism, under the pressure of which they at this hour bend and groan ; and it is not easy to determine from which of these three miserable states the transition to the social and orderly rank of a free citizen is most difficult.

Besides, our slaves are in a very uncivilized state; and, as is peculiarly exemplified in our aboriginal Indians, the industry of a savage, his habits of voluntary obedience, his perception of political rights, his capacity of becoming the citizen of a regular community, is still lower than that of a mere slave. He is quite ignorant of the necessity of voluntary exertion and peaceable submission, which forms the strongest cement of civilized society. Savages know no medium between the extremes of unlimited servility and uncontrolled despotism ; among them it is the lot of the slave to obey and toil, the privilege of the master to command and be idle. This is manifested all over the coast of Africa, where the sable chiefs exercise absolute sway over their wretched subjects, or slaves. We are not, therefore, to expect that a body of emancipated slaves, whether emancipated by manumission or rebellion, can be converted into a community of free citizens, living under a regular government and equitable laws. Much instruction on this point may be derived from a careful perusal of Mr. Brougham's very able and learned work on " *Colonial Policy* ; and Sir James Lucas Yeo's recent letter to Mr. Croker contains some very interesting information respecting the condition and conduct of the free negro colony at Sierra Leone.

The experience of St. Domingo, for nearly twenty-five years past, proves that revolted slaves are incapable of receiving and enjoying the blessings of free institutions, for they have only exchanged the horrors of civil bondage for those of military despotism. And the emancipated Negroes of Massachusetts prove that such an order of beings have not the capacity of availing themselves of the benefits of civil liberty. For in that state, where slavery is abolished by law, and which consequently opens an asylum to fugitive slaves from neighbouring states, the negroes do *not* keep up their stock of population, by the help both of native breeding and runaway importation; so improvident, so helpless, so wanting in all those habits of steady and useful industry, which are essentially necessary to enable the citizens of a free community to obtain a competent support for themselves and a growing family, have they been rendered by a long continuance of slavery, either in their own persons, or in those of their immediate progenitors, and by their almost total destitution even of the rudest elements of civilization and culture.

This incapacity for receiving and profiting by the precious boon of liberty, would be still more visible in the event of emancipating the slaves of our southern states, because *their* negroes are much more numerous, and have always been more harshly treated than those of Massachusetts; for the peculiar situation of the negroes under such circumstances would tend very little to promote their contentment, or peaceable demeanor, or regular industry. They would form the lowest part of the community, destitute of property, and therefore unable to enjoy some of the most essential political privileges, and toiling for a bare subsistence. It is to be feared, therefore, that our southern negroes, while labouring under the double curse of slavery and want of civilization, can only be kept in subjection by their white masters so long as they are kept in chains. The day that breaks the fetters of a slave destroys the authority, and endangers the security of his lord. Whilst the slave-holding system exists, the division of the negroes, the vigilance of the overseer, the fear of the driver's lash, and the horrible torments inflicted upon servile contumacy, may prevent the blacks from uniting and extirpating their masters. Although Mr. John Randolph, on the floor of Congress, declared, that even now, whenever the midnight bell tolls the alarm of fire in any of the towns or cities of Virginia, every mother clasps her infant to her bosom in agonizing expectation that the tocsin is sounding the cry of a general negro insurrection, and warning the devoted victims of the near approach of indiscriminate pillage, rape, murder, and conflagration.

Thus the modern system of *negro slavery*, as it prevails in the European colonies, and in this free republic, is one entire circle of evil. It not only creates an enormous mass of physical suffering and moral guilt, during the continuance of the negroes in the fetters of personal bondage; but also, by brutalizing their bodies, by darkening their understanding, by corrupting their hearts, it incapacitates them for receiving and using the privileges and blessings of civil and religious liberty, whence this system, as it now flourishes among nations calling themselves Christian, provides, by the very atrocity and vast aggregate amount of its own guilt for its own frightful perpetuity.

In our southern states the slaves are not often allowed to profit by religious instruction, their masters having an absolute property in their bodies, are apt to consider their *souls* as thrown into the bargain, and seldom suffer the mild light of revelation to irradiate the gloom of their desolate condition. The *free* blacks which swarm in our northern and middle states are generally idle, vitious, and profligate, with very little sense of moral obligation to deter them from lying, thieving, and still more atrocious crimes. For some winters past, a gang of free blacks used to amuse themselves in the city of New-York, by setting fire to whole rows of houses, for the purpose of pilfering amidst the confusion and horror of the flames. In the winter of 1816-17, a negro was hanged for this crime, and fires have been proportionally scarce in New-York ever since. A hint this, which might be rendered profitable, if our state legislature would strengthen the criminal code, and recommend our *house-breakers, highway-robbers,* and *forgers,* to the gallows, instead of providing them with a comfortable domicile in the state prison for a season, and then letting them out to renew their depredations upon the public.

Of late, however, some philanthropists, among whom the *Friends,* or Quakers (as they always do in every work of benevolence and usefulness) bear a distinguished part, have endeavoured to meliorate the moral condition of the free blacks in the northern and middle states. In consequence of which, African schools and churches have risen up, and black teachers and preachers have shown themselves as competent to perform their important functions as their white brethren. Doubtless, the only possible means of rendering these negroes honest, industrious, and provident, are to be found in the general diffusion of religious and moral instruction among them. And it is certainly high time to refute, by practical proof, the assertion of Mr. Jefferson, in his Notes on Virginia, that the negroes are a race of animals inferior to man. A few ages of civil liberty and general education would silence this cavil of infidelity against the scriptural doctrine, that God made of *one* blood all the nations of the earth.

As *religion* is the great basis of national character, it is necessary to examine its effects in relation to the United States. In the " Resources of the British Empire," beginning at page 377, are adduced reasons to show the intimate connexion between the piety and prosperity of nations, and conversely; the necessity and importance of *national*, as contradistinguished from personal, religion, that is to say, the acknowledgment of God as the Governor of the world, by the state or government, as the representative of the community; and the inestimable benefits resulting from a general diffusion of individual or personal religion.

Indeed, the voice of all history, which is emphatically the voice of philosophy speaking by example, warns us, that every nation which has broken asunder the bonds of religion, whether founded on the light of natural conscience, inherent in the heart of every man, or upon the clearer light of Revelation from Heaven, has invariably given itself up to every species of profligacy; untying all the ligaments of social virtue, and stifling in lust and blood every dear relation, every domestic charity of parental, conjugal, and filial duty. When ancient *Persia* departed from the simplicity and purity of the religious institutions of the elder Cyrus, she fell headlong into all the corruptions of effeminate immorality; and sunk in the dastardly enervation of universal vice, yielded her extended empire to the yoke of a foreign conqueror. When the ancient Republics of *Greece* exchanged the simple maxims of their pristine religion for the general prevalence of philosophical unbelief, they degenerated into universal sensualism; and all classes of the community, setting themselves in open sale to the highest bidder, followed their clamorous and ignorant demagogues throughout all the gradations of domestic anarchy, weakness, and corruption, into the sepulchral sleep of external despotism. When *Rome*, despising the religious reverence of her republican ancestors, ceased to regard the obligations of an oath, and cultivating generally the atheistic materialism of her infidel philosophers, practised with unblushing impudence every crime of violence and fraud, she fell from her high estate of national glory, into the despicable meanness of unrestrained democracy; whence, by an easy, quick, and natural transition, she passed into the kindred bondage of single military tyranny; and finally bowed her imperial head beneath the sterner morality and superior prowess of the Barbarians of the north.

In later times, *Continental Europe* has read a memorable lesson to all nations and ages, of the inevitable ruin attached to a wilful departure from the doctrines and duties of Heaven's last best gift to man, *revealed* religion. During the greater part of the *eighteenth* century, the kings and princes, the nobles and ambassadors, the politicians, writers, and people of almost every nation on the European continent, strove in wretched rivalry for a vile pre-eminence in the guilt of rejecting the Scriptures of God, and calumniating the religion of Christ. As the necessary consequence of this universal speculative unbelief, as universal a deluge of immorality, baseness, and corruption, private and public, national as well as individual, flooded their foul and feculent streams of pollution over all the surface of continental Europe. And what has been the great practical commentary which Jehovah himself has given upon the impious text of this *new* philosophy? For the space of five-and-twenty years every nominally Christian nation on the European continent has been wasted by fire, and sword, and pestilence; by famine, and internal broil, and foreign invasion; not a single country within the verge of continental European Christendom has escaped the terrible lustration of human blood.

And have these *United States* no cause of similar alarm? Cannot they read the same handwriting upon the wall, which declared to the kindred nations of Europe, that they had been weighed in the balance, and were found wanting? When the purer light of Christianity is corrupted and darkened in the eastern section of our Union, and the Revelation of God too generally rejected in the southern and western extremities of the commonwealth, have we any right to expect that *this* country will escape those national visitations, which the European continent has so abundantly reaped in a full harvest of agony and ruin? The late president Dwight declared, in 1812, that there were *three millions* of souls in the United States entirely destitute of all religious ordinances and worship. It is also asserted, by good authority, that in the southern and western states societies exist, built on the model of the Transalpine clubs in Italy, and the atheistic assemblies of France and Germany, and, like them, incessantly labouring to root out every vestige of Christianity. So that, in the lapse of a few years, we are in danger of being overrun with unbaptized infidels, the most atrocious and remorseless banditti that infest and desolate human society.

Indeed, many serious people doubt the permanence of the federal constitution, because in that national compact there is *no* reference to the Providence of God: " *We the people,*" being the constitutional substitute of Jehovah. Of *national* religion we have not much to boast; a few of our state governments, particularly in New-England, and recently in New-York, do acknowledge God as the governor among the nations, and occasionally *recommend* (for they have no power to appoint) days to be set apart for general fasting, and prayer, and thanksgiving. But the greater number of the states declare it to be *unconstitutional* to refer to the Providence of God in any of their public acts; and *Virginia* carries this doctrine so far, as not to allow any *chaplain* to officiate in her state legislature; giving as a reason, by an overwhelming majority of her representatives, in December, 1817, that the constitution permits no one religious sect to have preference to any other; and therefore, as a chaplain must belong to *some* sect, it would be unconstitutional for the Virginian legislators to listen to his preaching or prayers.

In the winter of 1814-15, the legislature of Louisiana rejected, by an immense majority, a bill " For the better observance of the Sabbath; for punishing the crime of sodomy; for preventing the defacing of the church-yards; for shutting the theatres and stores on Sunday; and for other purposes." The chief opposer of the bill declaring, on the legislative floor, "that such *persecuting intolerance* might well suit the New-England puritans, who were descended from the bigoted fanatics of old England, who were great readers of the Bible, and, *consequently*, ignorant, prejudiced, cold-blooded, false, and cruel; but could never be fastened on the more enlightened, liberal, and philosophical inhabitants of Louisiana, the descendants of Frenchmen."

In this respect the Louisianians have shown their kindred to the regenerated citizens of modern France, who have compelled Louis the Eighteenth to *repeal* his decree for enforcing a decent respect to the Sabbath; and the Sunday now is, as it was during the revolution, a day of business, or pleasure, without any regard or reference to the divine founder of the Christian dispensation.

It was reserved for the illumined sages of the eighteenth century of the Christian era to discover that *religion* was the cause of all the political evils which deform human society. The Egyptian, Persian, Grecian, and Roman legislators, all deemed it necessary to lay the foundation of their municipal codes upon the

broad basis of religious sanction.   Not a single philosopher, statesman, or sovereign, is to be found in all the
records of heathen antiquity, who ever for a moment
doubted that some higher bond of obligation, than can
possibly be derived from the exterior ligaments of human law, is indispensable to connect together communities of men in firm and lasting ties.   They knew full
well, that without a direct appeal to the tribunal of
natural conscience, without the religious obligation of
an oath, without the internal safeguard of an habitual
watch over the thoughts of the heart, regulating an
innumerable multitude of words and deeds, which no
human laws can touch, but which, according to their
good or evil direction, either adorn or dishonour the
aggregate of life, no community of men can long flourish
in personal virtue, or national prosperity.   What human
laws can regulate the intercourse of benevolence and
gratitude between the rich and poor, or measure out
the affection that ought to be shown to a parent, wife,
or child?   Or prescribe the limits of friendship, or graduate the scale of punishment to the numberless tres-
passes against the duties of affection and charity?   In
all these, and countless other instances, religion alone
can bind the obligation and measure of duty upon the
heart.   Where the authority and power of man reach
not, the arm of God alone can guide the footsteps of
human conduct.

Revolutionary France possesses the execrable honour
of having first reduced individual and national atheism
to a regular system.   In the beginning of the 18th century, Mr. Bayle, who had escaped from the fangs of
the Doctors of the Sorbonne, at Paris, into the marshes
of Holland, undertook to teach Europe that *a nation of*
atheists must, infallibly, be better governed than a country of Christians ; because, being freed from all the
restraints of religious prejudice, they would be at liberty
to follow the pure impulses of a virtuous and unimpeded
nature.   Bishop Warburton, in his *Divine Legation,*
and President Montesquieu, in his *Esprit des Loix,* both
laboured, in opposition to Bayle's doctrine, to prove

that a society of atheists could *not* be held together, for want of a bond of mutual obligation alike binding upon all; for an atheist, not allowing the authority of any higher tribunal than his own estimate of his own self-interest, will break any human law, whenever, according to his own calculations, it would be advantageous to *him*, and provided also he could elude personal punishment. But the disciples of Bayle, the metaphysical and political doctors of the French revolution, Helvetius, Raynal, D'Alembert, Condorcet, Diderot, and all the rest of those brilliant banditti, who set fire to the four corners of the world, improving on their master's hint, united all the force of perverted genius, misapplied learning, ill-directed science, dazzling declamation, glittering wit, and habitual sophistry, in order to persuade men, that all the political evils which disfigure the earth, flowed immediately from the existence and support of the *Christian Religion;* and that mankind could not fail of enjoying uninterrupted beatitude, if they would only eradicate every vestige of Christianity from the human heart and conduct.

Revolutionary France tried the grand experiment; she abolished Christianity, declared death to be an eternal sleep, passed a decree denouncing terrible vengeance against all who believed in the existence of a God, worshipped the perfection of human reason in the person of a prostitute, and placed her on that same altar which had been reared by the hand of adoration to the Lord Jesus Christ himself; pronounced marriage an unholy monopoly, and stigmatized all the feelings and affections of parents, brethren, and children, as vulgar and unphilosophical prejudices. From July, 1792, to March, 1796, it was *death* by law in France for any one to pronounce the name of God or Christ, except in execration; and during this period, many thousands of men, women, and children, were actually murdered by law, for the crime of professing themselves to be Christians. Acting upon these enlightened views, and original discoveries, the French nation proceeded to murder their lawful sovereign, to butcher their ancient nobility, and established clergy; to proclaim and enforce an indiscriminate pillage of all public and private property, to bathe their hands in each other's life, to exalt a midnight assassin to an imperial throne, to cradle the new-born dynasty of an upstart ruffian in tears and blood, to convert all France into one universal brothel, one universal slaughter-house.

As the other nations of continental Europe followed with too fatal a facility the footsteps of French illumination, jacobin and atheistic France, finding a bosom friend in the atheism and jacobinism of the rest of the European continent, was soon enabled by the poison of fraud, and the force of arms, to triumph over all the religious, moral, and social establishments of Christendom. Thrones were overturned, and the altars of God trampled down beneath the cloven hoof of impiety; the rich were despoiled of their possessions, and all the people in one undistinguished mass crushed beneath the great nether millstone of an oppression unparalleled in the annals of remorseless tyranny. Nor was the tide of Gallic invasion ever rolled back, nor its career of victory checked, until the princes and people of continental Europe had been lashed by the scorpion whip of long continued calamity and insult, into the full conviction that the *new* philosophy is the unerring road to personal and national ruin. Accordingly, when they had been sufficiently disciplined in the severe, but salutary school of suffering, the European nations, from the north and from the south, from the east and from the west, of their populous continent, returned to the good old way of reverence to God, integrity towards man, and high-hearted loyalty to their native land; and rallying from all quarters under the banners of a legitimate patriotism, routed the hordes of Gallic philosophy, drove them back confounded within the borders of their own dominions, and in the heart of France stifled jacobinism in its own life's blood.

At the advent of the Messiah, the greater portion of the known world was under the dominion of one empire. Knowledge and civilization had reached a higher point of excellence than at any preceding period. This general and excessive intellectual culture was accompanied with a correspondingly general and excessive immorality—a fact in itself amounting to a demonstration, that the mere improvement of the mind can do nothing towards removing or amending the natural depravity of the human heart. At this time the Greek and Latin languages had reached their summit of perfection. They divided between themselves the intellectual dominions of the whole empire. The Latin predominated over the western, the Greek over the eastern section of imperial Rome. The ancient dialects of Italy, the languages of Africa, Spain, Gaul, Britain, and Pannonia, had all retired before the use of the Roman tongue. The Greek was the language of science and literature, the Latin that of all public transactions, laws, ordinances, and institutions of government. Well educated men were alike conversant with both. All the knowledge then afloat in the world was concentrated in one focus of brightness by the best writers of Greece and Rome. Art, and nature, and science, were ransacked, explored, exhausted; to furnish the poet with splendid imagery, to emblazon the eloquence of the orator, to sharpen the weapons of the dialectician; to point the sting of the satyrist, to round the period of the philosopher, to swell the pomp of learning.

But in the midst of all this blaze of intellectual glory, what was the condition of the human heart? The heart of man was at this time darker and more hideous than the sepulchre of death. The barriers of moral decency were broken down; every crime and every abomination was either perpetrated, or tolerated; public profligacy and private vice had converted the whole earth into one vast charnel-house of atrocity and horror. All the profane historians and annalists of that period bear testimony to the charges against the heathen world, which the holy Spirit of God puts into the mouth of the apostle of the Gentiles.

Such was the deplorable condition of the moral world, when the Sun of Righteousness arose with healing in his wings, and the darkest recesses of the human heart were illumined with the light of life. Wherever Christianity has prevailed in its purity, and precisely in proportion to the evangelism of its doctrines, setting forth the fall of man from his primeval innocence, the original and natural depravity of the human heart, the justification of sinners by Jesus Christ, the sanctification of the human spirit by the Holy Ghost, the Godhead of the three Divine Persons in one mysterious Trinity, have individual purity of morals, and national prosperity and happiness uniformly flourished. Wherever *Christianity* spread its mild and benignant light, the waste and wilderness of life began to bloom as the paradise of God; the nations of the earth became purified and exalted in all their moral and intellectual faculties, they were freed from the fetters of political, social, and domestic slavery; they were more advanced in skill and knowledge, more deeply versed in science, more accomplished in literature, more alive to industry and enterprise, more refined in all social intercourse, more adorned with every nobler virtue, and every polished grace, more benevolent to man, more devoted to God.

But the dawning of this brightest day was soon overcast with clouds and thick darkness; *superstition* soon poisoned the waters of life in their springs, and in their sources; a superstition which lulled to rest all fears of future punishment, while it sanctioned and encouraged the commission of every crime; which held out incitements to the most profligate ambition, and provided for the indulgence of the most sensual sloth; a superstition, whose imposing ceremonies were interwoven with all the institutions of society; and whose spirit of delusion was diffused throughout all the principles of civil government. The *corruptions* of Christianity soon began to darken, and gradually to extinguish the lights of the understanding, and the sensibilities of the heart; so that a greater and more stupendous mass of ignorance and

iniquity, than had ever yet oppressed the earth, was exhibited in the moral and intellectual death of ten successive centuries. The whole circumference of Christendom was veiled in the darkest pall of civil and
religious bondage; the human conscience was benighted
amidst the terrors of the dungeon, the rack, the gibbet,
and the flame; and the persons of men were delivered
over a prey to the perpetuity of feudal anarchy and
horror.

In the midst of this noon of night, it pleased Divine
Providence again to interpose for the benefit of human
kind : the Spirit of God again moved upon the moral
and intellectual chaos, and in the fulness of his own appointed time, he raised up Luther, and Calvin, and
Knox, and an innumerable army of saints and martyrs,
at the era of the *Reformation*, to bring back the children of disobedience from the error of their ways to the
wisdom of the just; to teach men the pure doctrines of
revelation, to be the means of enlightening the mind,
and amending the heart of all the forlorn beings that were
slumbering in the confines of darkness, or trembling
under the shadow of death. Then, indeed, arose a new
order of things; the human heart swelled with the sub-
limest raptures of spiritual devotion; all the charities
of father, husband, son, and brother, were mingled in
every life-throb of the bosom: substantial integrity and
habitual courtesy at once supported and embellished the
whole fabric of society: the mind of man sprang upward like a pyramid of fire, and by its blaze of intellectual light, dissipated the Stygian darkness of the middle
ages, and an uninterrupted chain of progressive improvement united together all the intelligent minds of
re-illumined Christendom.

But man, weak, frail, unsubstantial man, the chang-
ling of an hour, ever prone to pass from one into the
other extreme, soon vibrated from the grossest superstition into the most obdurate unbelief. And we, who now
live upon the earth, are doomed to witness this last and
most dreadful of all the eras of human depravity, that

of general profligate *infidelity.* The light of religion being quenched, that of moral philosophy is speedily swallowed up in the surrounding darkness ; all the duties of moral obligation having no other basis than the will of God revealed to man in his inspired word. All political studies are proscribed, lest they should point out the path to civil and religious liberty. No moral culture is encouraged, and no intellectual improvement permitted, save that which teaches the more speedy accomplishment of the works of blood and desolation, which makes war more frequent, more extensive, more murderous. Whence, a few ages of *infidelity* would roll back the nations of the earth into all the barbarism of universal ignorance, into all the abominations of universal iniquity. To this most deplorable condition was the European continent verging rapidly, under the *infidel* dominion of revolutionary France.

Let us pause a moment, and re-survey the threefold progressive augmentation of heavenly light, accompanied with a threefold progressive deterioration of human depravity.

When man had only the *lesser* light of natural conscience to guide his uncertain steps through the mazes of moral duty, the Pagan world, although partially illumined in intellect, was immersed in the grossness and profligacy of vice. Yet were the heathens superior, both in doctrine and practice, to the grand corrupters of Christianity, whose superstition polluted the *greater* light of revelation, and approximated the human animal nearer to the brute beast in understanding, and to the fiend in iniquity. But the total *rejection* of the greater light of revelation produces a more impenetrable darkness of the understanding, and a more entire depravity of the heart than ever arose from the united efforts of the corruption of Christianity and perversion of the natural conscience. So that the world now presents the spectacle of the greatest light of mind and most unspotted purity of heart in those countries where the unsophisticated Gospel is believed, contrasted with the midnight of the intellect and the loathsome iniquity of those regions which have cast off all allegiance to God and to his Christ.

The influence of *infidelity*, like the baneful Upas, lays the hand of death upon all that it touches; it corrupts the morals, debases the intellect, perverts the resources, tarnishes the character, annihilates the honour of every people whom it enfolds in the harlotry of its embrace; it rolls together as a scroll all the rights and liberties of civilized society; it casts that scroll into the fire of hell, feeding upon the misery of man; it cuts off every retreat from virtue and happiness into human intercourse; it lays for ever low in an untimely tomb all that dignity, tenderness, wisdom, charity, affection, and confidence, can add of lustre and of love to the children of mortality; it has never failed, wheresoever it has rolled its waters of bitterness and of death, to sweep away all the ancient boundaries and landmarks of human improvement; it *has* rolled its stream of ruin over all the art and pride of Egypt, Greece, and Italy, and every other region, waste or cultivated, wholesome or poisonous, in the earth; it *has* polluted the shades of learning and science, laid open and desolate the properties of men, levelled the temples, and destroyed the altars of the living God; scattered to the wild fury of the winds every hope and every production of nature that looks upward to the Heavens: and after undermining all the props and buttresses of social order that have been reared and strengthened by the labours of hereditary ages, after washing down into the mire of desolation kingdoms, and nations, and empires, and people, and languages, so that before it the earth was as the Garden of Eden, and behind it a deserted waste, it plunges itself, together with all that it encircles, into the gulph of remediless perdition.

In the *present* state of the world, infidelity is closely allied with the *revolutionary* question; and, generally speaking, those who are eager to revolutionize all existing governments, under the ostensible pretence of promoting the *liberty* and *property* of mankind, are alike infidels in precept and in practice. But these patriotic politicians widely mistake the matter; for all past experience shows, that civil liberty and national prosperity always flourish most where pure Christianity prevails ; and that despotism is the most unrestrained and cruel, and public happiness most completely stifled where unbelief predominates. This was strongly exemplified in the contrasted condition of Britain and France, during the revolutionary conflict. *France,* during that awful period, was a prey to the worst species of desolation ; her whole people, let loose from the salutary restraints of religious and moral obligation, presented the hideous spectacle of one entire mass of systematic and legalized corruption ; her agriculture was neglected, her external commerce annihilated, her internal trade stagnant, her manufactures drooping, her science and literature darkened almost to extinction; her whole community groaned under the most sanguinary and remorseless tyranny that ever crushed the heart of man to the earth ; her sons were dragged in chains to whiten with their bones and moisten with their blood the soil of far-distant lands, while her own deserted widows and fatherless babes lay mouldering in unburied heaps throughout every nook and corner of her swollen and overgrown empire. During this same period, the *British* people were protected in their equal rights by the unstained administration of equal justice ; the full security of life, liberty, and property, was preserved to all; a continual accumulation of wealth pervaded all the departments of her dominions, which exhibited an improved and improving system of agriculture, an extensive and extending commerce, manufactures thriving and increasing, the arts liberally patronized, science and literature in all their branches promoted ; their lands, canals, houses, rivers, presenting the most unequivocal proofs of progressive industry and prosperity; the people advancing in pure religion and sound morals, steady in their habits and manners; whence resulted the enlargement of their territorial possessions by honourable conquest; their inexhaustible stock of talents, the living genius of freedom and intelligence, which explored the powers and recesses of nature, to abridge the labours and embellish the productions of art; rendering knowledge tributary to the wants, the comforts, and the enjoyments, not only of their own offspring, but also of the whole human race.

M. Talleyrand observes, that he was particularly struck with the *calmness*, in relation to religion, evidenced in the United States, so contrary to the zeal and enthusiasm displayed in England; and he attributes it to a variety of causes, some of which it may be well to mention. He supposes that the first and most important consideration in a *new* country is *to increase its riches;* that the proof of such a disposition manifests itself every where in America; and that we find evidence of it in every part of their conduct; and that the customs, with regard to religion itself, are strongly tinctured with this prevailing disposition. In *England* religion has always exercised a powerful influence over the national mind and character of the people; in that country the greatest philosophers and profoundest sages have cast the sanctity of religion over their most intense and various intellectual pursuits. Since the age in which Luther first peered above the horizon, as the morning star of the Reformation, numerous sects and denominations of Christianity have either sprung up in England, or found their way thither from other countries. And, although in general the great national establishment of the church, together with nearly a full toleration of other persuasions, has maintained a general current of tranquillity and peace within the bosom of the British isles; yet, occasionally, the temporary ascendency and fierce fanaticism of some of the other denominations have wrought sudden and great political changes in that nation.

All these various Christian denominations have been transplanted into America; and several of the separate states actually owe their political origin to the exclusive emigrations of some of these sects. It was, therefore, to be expected that these religious emigrants would, after their transmigration, continue to maintain their original state and character, and frequently convulse and agitate the American body politic. But, although for a time religion appeared to give a cast of national character to the original pilgrims, and their immediate descendants, yet those distinguishing features gradually disappeared, and religion in the United States has gradually settled down into the level of a mere personal, portable secret, instead of continuing to be what it yet remains in England – a kindred fire, flaming with electrical diffusion, from heart to heart, and lighting up the glow of general enthusiasm among the people. In the United States all the various religious sects seem to co-exist in a calm, unruffled atmosphere. It is not very uncommon for the father, mother, and children of the same family, each to follow, without opposition, their respective modes of worship; a spectacle that seldom occurs in Europe, where religion, when it operates at all, actuates not only individuals, but masses of men, in their joint views and combined exertions.

Hence, no leader of any religious persuasion in the United States, however ardent may be his own zeal, and however vigorous and incessant his own efforts, can induce his followers to labour to aggrandize that sect, with as much effectual exertion as he could, under the same circumstances, induce a similar body in Europe to co-operate with him. On the days of public worship, in this country, the individuals of the same family set out together; each goes to hear the minister of his own sect, and they afterward return home to employ themselves, in common, in their domestic concerns. This diversity of religious opinion does not seem to produce any contradiction or discordance in their sentiments as to other things. Whence, if there happens to arrive here, from Europe, an ambitious sectary, eager to afford a triumph to his own particular tenets, by inflaming the passions of men, so far from finding, as in other countries, multitudes disposed to enlist under his banners, and ready to second his violence, his very existence is scarcely perceived by his nearest neighbours; his individual enthusiasm is neither attractive, nor interesting, nor contagious; he inspires neither love, nor hatred, nor curiosity; but is suffered to die away into nothing, beneath the frozen pole of universal indifference.

This was peculiarly exemplified in Dr. Priestley. This heresiarch, and veteran trumpeter of sedition, had openly menaced the hierarchy of England and the British constitution with speedy destruction. His partisans followed him, eagerly and blindly, throughout all the numberless changes of his ever-shifting religious and political creeds; they poured out at his feet their time, their property, their obedience, their acclamation; they enabled him to publish, and circulate widely, his pestilent heresies, and malignant invectives against the church and government of England. He sate, like a demi-god, snuffing up the incense of adulation from the Socinian democrats of Great Britain. But how reversed the picture, when he exchanged an English for an American home! A meagre deputation of obscure clergymen in our city of New-York welcomed him to the United States with an absurd speech, full of jacobin bombast and fustian. He afterward repaired to Philadelphia, where he preached a few frigorific sermons to thin and drowsy audiences; he then retired to Northumberland, in Pennsylvania, where he passed the remainder of his life in making small experiments amidst his alembics, crucibles, and retorts, for the result of which no one expressed the least interest; and he also occasionally ushered from the press religious and political pamphlets, which no one ever read. His death excited little, if any more sensation among the Pennsylvanian patriots than they are wont to exhibit at the dissolution of a German farmer, or a German farmer's horse.

In the United States every one follows, pretty much according to his own inclination, his religious opinions, and pursues with undivided eagerness his temporal concerns. This apparent apathy perhaps arises partly from the universal equality of all religious denominations. In America no form of worship is prescribed, no religious ordinances are established by law; whence, every individual is left at liberty to follow his own will; to neglect or cultivate religion as he sees fit. Almost all the ardour of the moment that is passing is employed in devising the means of acquiring wealth, and promoting the success of the political party, in which the active individuals are enrolled. Hence result a general calmness and composure in the American community, with regard to the personal feelings and universal diffusion of religion; and it *sometimes* happens that Jehovah himself is shouldered from the altar peculiarly dedicated to his solemn services, by the devotedness of the whole heart to the shrine of mammon, or to the pursuits and calculations of political intrigue.

In the United States there is no national church established, no lay-patronage, no system of tithes. The people call and support their minister; few churches having sufficient funds to dispense with the necessity of contribution by the congregation. The law enforces the contract between the pastor and his flock, and requires the people to pay the stipulated salary so long as the clergyman preaches and performs his parochial duty, according to the agreement between him and his parishioners. In Massachusetts, Vermont, New-Hampshire, and Connecticut, the law requires each town to provide, by taxation, for the support of religious worship; but leaves it optional with every individual to choose his own sect. The general government has no power to interfere with or regulate the religion of the Union, and the states, generally, have not legislated farther than to incorporate, with certain restrictions, such religious bodies as have applied for charters. In consequence of this entire indifference on the part of the state governments, full *one-third* of our whole population are destitute of all religious ordinances, and a much greater proportion in our southern and western districts. It is quite just and proper that no one sect should have any preference, either religious or political, over the others; but the state-governments ought, at least, to interfere so far as New-England has done, and enforce by law the maintenance of religious worship in every town, leaving the choice of his denomination to each individual.

The not interfering at all is a culpable extreme one way, as the English system of an exclusive national church, shutting out the other sects from equal political privileges, is a mischievous extreme the other. In the United Netherlands, in Prussia, in Russia, and even in France, all the religious denominations stand on equal political ground; and cannot Britain learn to augment her intellectual and moral power, by repealing her *test* and *corporation* acts, and permitting *all* her people to serve her to the full extent of their capacity, in her civil and military functions? During the time when Russia broke down the military strength of revolutionary France, the commander-in-chief of all her armies belonged to the Greek Church, her minister of finance was a Protestant, and her premier was a Papist. Her affairs were not the worse conducted because she disfranchises none of her sects of their political rights, on account of their religious opinions. The prominent evils of the English Church system are the *ministerial* and *lay patronage*, and the *tithes*. Suppose, for example (as was actually the fact when Lord Bolingbroke served Queen Anne,) the British prime minister is an *avowed infidel*, what kind of clergy would he be apt to place in the crown livings? Evangelical men, or careless irreligious clerks? The *lay* patrons, also, whether noble or gentle, put into the livings, in their gift, pastors, in whose call the people have no voice, but are, nevertheless, required to sit under their ministration. Now, if the lay patron be not religious, the probability is that his clergyman shall not be too well acquainted with the stupendous scheme of revelation. And, perhaps, few things are better calculated to foster the growth of infidelity in a country than putting into *any* church men who dole out only a little thin, diluted Sabbatical morality once in seven days, instead of expounding the great statute book of Christianity, and inculcating the characteristic, distinguishing doctrines of the Bible.

" Meanwhile, the hungry sheep look up, and are *not* fed," and yet grave personages profess to marvel at the rapid growth of other denominations, whose pastors, on moderate stipends, perform faithfully the duties of the highest, the holiest, the most important, and the most interesting vocation that can be accorded to man.

The system of *tithes* is perhaps the very worst possible mode of providing for the clergy that could be devised. They impede the progress of agriculture, and create perpetual dissensions between the pastor and his own people; and keep in a state of incessant exasperation all those other sects, who dissent from the doctrines and government of episcopacy. The tithes take a tenth part of the *gross* produce of the land, and consequently operate as a tax, oppressive in proportion to the amount *expended* in cultivating, and not to the *net profits* of the land produce; whence, they grow more and more intolerable, as a country expends more and more capital in agriculture; and are a much greater grievance in England now, when so vast an aggregate of farming capital is employed, than when agriculture consisted chiefly in pasture, and very little money was expended in culture, or tillage. Unless the British government shall commute the tithe system for some other mode of maintaining the national clergy, it will continue an evil, as pernicious as the *poor laws,* the *public debt,* or the *game laws,* all of which are, in their nature and amount, singularly oppressive, and two of them tend directly to produce immorality and vice. The tithes amount to nearly *one-fourth* of the rental of England and Ireland; to at least ten millions sterling a year; to which add church lands, and other property, five millions more, and it gives an annual expenditure of fifteen millions sterling, or *sixty-seven* millions of dollars, for the maintenance of the established church ; to which add ten millions for poor rates, forty-four millions for the interest of the national debt, and twenty-one millions for government expenditure, amounting in all to ninety millions sterling, or *four hundred and five* millions of dollars a-year; an awful burden of expenditure on twenty millions of people ;

averaging nearly five pounds, or at least twenty dollars
a head for each inhabitant of the British Isles ; whereas,
in the United States the whole public expenditure of
the general government, twenty state governments, the
poor laws, corporations, and counties, scarcely amount
to fifty millions of dollars, or five dollars a head for each
individual of ten millions of people who are rapidly increasing in number, and whose immense land resources
are rising in value every hour.

In *Ireland*, the tithe system is still more oppressive
than in England. *Four-fifths* of the population are
papists. In many parishes *all* the people are papists,.
having no protestant minister, but the *nominal* parson
resides either in England or France, or elsewhere, as
suits him, and the *tithe proctor* grinds down the Irish
farmer and peasant, and perpetuates their abject hopeless
poverty.

Our different sects dispute here verbally, and by
writing, pretty much as they do in Europe. But the
liberal piety of the age, its philosophical spirit and genius, the circumstances of Christendom, the prevalence
of Bible and Missionary Societies and Sunday Schools,
all conspire to approximate the different religious persuasions towards each other in the labours of love, and
in the beauty of harmony ; to break down the partition
wall of sectarianism, and to unite all denominations in
their blessed efforts to spread the light of revealed truth
over the remotest corners of the globe. It is in vain
for *any* church to attempt to uphold its exclusive pretensions against the social institutions, feelings, and habits,
of the country where it is placed ; and still more vain
to endeavour to revive now, in these United States, the
intolerant bigotry, which disgraced Europe in the seventeenth century. Lord Clarendon, in his *Life* of *himself*, makes some very sagacious observations on the
manner in which Archbishop Laud, by straining his
ecclesiastical pretensions too far, and indulging an unbounded lust of clerical domination, brought his royal
master to the block, and ruined that very church which
he so zealously laboured to exalt.

The prevailing religious sects in the United States are, the Presbyterians, the Independents, the Episcopalians, Methodists, and Baptists; of which last persuasion there are 2,600 settled, and 1,000 unsettled congregations.   Pure Episcopacy is in fact an ecclesiastical monarchy, the bishop being the executive chief over all the clergy of his diocess. It is, however, in this country more adapted to the genius of our republican institutions than it ever was in England, even before the houses of convocation were abolished; for with us, the annual state convention consists of *lay* delegates as well as clergy, the bishop presiding; and the general convention, which meets once in three years, is composed of all the bishops in the Union, who form the upper house, and of lay delegates and clergy from all the different diocesses, who constitute the lower house.   Indeed, every church must of necessity conform its government and discipline in some measure to the spirit and substance of the social institutions of the country where it is fixed. Yet, notwithstanding our republican polity and habits, the bishops exercise great authority over their diocesan clergy, and possess very considerable power in regulating and governing the church.

Presbyterianism, in its government, is a representative republic; its ecclesiastical tribunals throughout all their gradations of church sessions, presbyteries, synods, and general assemblies, are composed of an equal number of clergy and lay elders, whose votes have all equal efficacy, and who transact their business on their deliberative floor, much in the same manner as do our Congress and state legislatures.   In the Independent Congregational churches all is carried by universal suffrage in each separate congregation, there being no general ecclesiastical tribunal to which may be referred the graver matters of doctrine and discipline, but all being submitted, finally and without appeal, to the votes, male and female, of each single audience.   In such a system it is almost impossible to prevent the departure from old, and the introduction of new doctrines; and, accordingly, both in old and New England, many of the Independent churches have passed gradually from Calvinism, through the intermediate stages of Arminianism, Arianism, and Semi-Arianism, into Socinianism, or Unitarianism, or, as Priestley calls it, Humanitarianism, because it denies the divinity of Jesus Christ, and considers him merely " as a frail, peccable, erring man."

The great body of the Congregationalists are to be found in New-England, and some of their churches are scattered through the middle and southern states, which are, however, chiefly occupied by the Presbyterians. Episcopacy prevails most in New-York, Pennsylvania, Maryland, Virginia, and South-Carolina, and is supposed to be gaining ground in some parts of New-England. The Friends, or Quakers, are most numerous in the middle states; they are here, as in Europe, and every where else, peculiarly active in all works of benevolence. For example, in promoting peace, discouraging war, aiding the progress of Bible Societies and Sunday Schools, and the abolition of slavery. The Methodists occupy chiefly the interior of the southern states, although they have churches scattered over the greatest part of the Union. The Baptists abound most in the western states. The Papists are most numerous in Maryland, and in the large cities on our sea-board; their numbers are continually augmented by European importation; but they seldom make proselytes from other sects. The Dutch Reformed Church is principally confined to New-York and New-Jersey. Jews are scattered in small numbers all over the Union, excepting New-England, where a veritable Israelite is no more able to live than in Scotland.

The American clergy of all denominations are in general decorous in their exterior, and faithful in the discharge of their pulpit and parochial duties. There is, however, in some of our cities a custom, which diminishes their usefulness; namely, the *collegiate* system, which makes three or four churches common to as many or more clergymen. In New-York, the Presbyterians have wisely abandoned this scheme; the Episcopalians and Dutch still retain it. Instead of giving one regular pastor to each separate congregation, the essence of the collegiate system is, not to suffer the same clergyman to preach twice successively in the same church; whence, there can be no regular exposition of the scriptures, without which no congregation can be built up in Christian instruction; mere single unconnected sermons, or sabbatical essays, never did, and never will, teach a people the scheme of Revelation. The collegiate system also does not admit of pastoral duty and parochial visitation, without which the real religion of a church can never be kept up or established. A minister of moderate talents and learning, if he be the stated pastor of a single church, will be able to do much more good by regular preaching and exposition of the scriptures, and parochial visitation, than a man of the first-rate capacity can possibly effect by occasional preaching in a church in common with talents and learning of every various gradation. No order of ability and information can compensate for a radical deficiency of system.

Notwithstanding so large a portion of our population is altogether without religious ordinances, yet, of late, religion has been, unquestionably, gaining ground in the United States; and that cold-blooded compound of irreligion, irony, selfishness, and sarcasm, which the French call *persiflage*, is not so rife now as formerly. Religion is becoming *fashionable* among us, which is a strong proof of the existence of a great mass of real piety in the country. Some of our *soi-disant* philosophers, however, profess to ridicule this fashion, and to deride the *cant* and *hypocrisy* of the present day, which they liken to the fanaticism of the puritans, who converted the English monarchy into a protectorate.

But the *extent* of hypocrisy must always be regulated by that of true religion. If religion be not generally spread over the community, there can be no effectual demand for extensive hypocrisy; which, in itself, is never any thing more than the homage of vice to virtue. If the great body of the people do not highly value religion, it can never be worth the while of leading *statesmen* to play the hypocrite, and affect to be pious, in order to become acceptable in the eyes of the nation. If the politicians of revolutionary France, and of our southern and western states, do *not* find it necessary to conceal their disregard for all seriousness and religion, but can *afford* to avow their impious tenets of speculative and practical infidelity, it only proves that there is *too little* religion in their respective communities, to compel them to wear the mask of hypocrisy, and assume the semblance of that piety which is generally diffused. It only proves, that the host of infidels are *now* become more numerous, and more daring in Christendom, than they were in some former ages. In Britain, religion is so pravalent among all sects and denominations, that her leading politicians *dare not*, whatever may be their private opinions, openly avow themselves to be infidels, whether Deists or Atheists.

The rapid spread of *Sunday Schools*, and of *Missionary* and *Bible Societies*, affords a most consolatory proof of the increase of religion in the United States. Two years have not yet elapsed, since their first institution in this country, and they have already considerably diminished the ignorance, poverty, and vice of our larger cities. Many of our most respectable families, both ladies and gentlemen, gratuitously engage in the labour of teaching the Sunday scholars, black and white, old and young. Their exertions have caused the Sabbath to be respected by the poor, the idle, and the profligate; and have quickened the growth of piety, order, industry, and cleanliness amidst the habitations of filth, indolence, confusion, and iniquity. The *reports* of the various Sunday School Societies are peculiarly interesting, for their mass of important facts, their strain of manly religion and benevolence, the ability and eloquence of their composition.

The *Missionary* Societies are established for the purpose of converting those Indians who are not yet exterminated by the sword of American encroachment; and also to supply with religious instruction the millions of our own people, who are altogether destitude of religious ordinances. The labours of these societies have been singularly beneficial, and are daily and hourly augmenting in usefulness.

Both the Sunday Schools and Missions unite their excellent efforts to aid the progress of *Bible* Societies, which, perhaps, constitute the most important and most comprehensively useful institution that has ever blessed the human race, since the day-star of the *Reformation* first dawned upon a benighted world. The most effectual means probably, that, under the blessing of Divine Providence, can be devised to oppose an effectual obstacle to the general progress of unbelief and immorality, are to be found in the extensive and judicious distribution of the sacred Scriptures. The study of the Bible facilitates access to the fountain of life; prepares the way for the instructions of the living teacher; opens the widest road to all moral and intellectual improvement; axalts the whole nature of man to a higher eminence in the scale of rational and spiritual being. If you wish to know what is in man; what his nature, and what his conduct, under every form of society, political as well as religious; what his character in every individual condition, savage or civilized, give your days and nights to the study of the Scriptures. They were dictated by the Holy Spirit of that Almighty God who created man, and who, therefore, is most intimately acquainted with the nature of his creature. That nature is most clearly depicted throughout all the pages of the inspired volume; which, indeed, affords the largest range of contemplation to those enlightened and sagacious minds that are earnestly bent upon directing successfully their inquiries into the inmost recesses of the human heart; because it is upon *his own* entire knowledge of the nature and character of man, that the Divine Saviour of the world has so strikingly accommodated *his* scheme of religion to the wants and relief of that being for whose means of eternal salvation Christianity was promulgated.

What has been already affected by the efforts of the *Bible Societies,* scattered over so large a portion of Christendom, in removing the darkness of the understanding, and purifying the corruptions of the heart, (or, at least, in rendering the exterior morals more decorous, for the heart of man can only be cleansed from its unrighteousness by the inspiration of the Spirit of God,) is a sufficient pledge to encourage the unremitted exertions of every real Christian, of whatever name, sect, or persuasion, to persevere in this labour of love. *Fourteen* years have not yet elapsed since the first establishment of the *British and Foreign Bible Society* ; and in this little period the sacred Scriptures have been spread over all the home dominions of Great Britain ; have been translated in whole, or in part, into more than a hundred different languages, and dispersed over almost all the habitable globe ; over the whole of continental Europe, a part of Africa, a considerable portion of Asia; nay, have even penetrated the habitations of the aboriginal barbarians of our American wilderness.

The Reverend Mr. Owen's *History of the British and Foreign Bible Society* is one of the most able, eloquent, instructive, and interesting books which has ever proceeded from the pen of man.

Since the establishment of this primary institution, Bible Societies have sprung up in unnumbered multitudes, partly branching off from the parent trunk, partly self-created and independent, but all in Christian harmony and accord with each other, wheresoever scattered over the distant regions of the earth. In Britain the affiliated societies are augmented beyond all power of count, and furnish a continual supply of the word of life to those vast masses of the poor and destitute, which are always to be found in old and fully peopled countries. On continental Europe these blessed institutions, in some measure, allayed even the horrors of universal warfare; and where the ravages of earthly desolation continued to spread themselves, the revealed word of God taught the sufferers to lift their hearts above this perishing scene of things, and direct their views towards those mansions of eternal joy, " where the wicked cease from troubling, and the weary are at rest." In Russia, more especially, and to an immense extent ; in Sweden, Den-

E e

mark, Saxony, Bohemia, Hungary, the United Netherlands, Prussia, Switzerland, and many other parts of the
European continent, Bible Societies, aided by the munificent donations of the British and Foreign Institution, are perpetually diffusing the word of God.   May
Divine Providence enable these societies to stem the
torrent of general infidelity, which has been infecting
the nations of continental Europe with the taint of death
during the lapse of an entire century !

Nor have these United States, in proportion to their
population and means, fallen short of their Christian
brethren in Europe in well-directed efforts to dissemi-
nate the sacred Scriptures.   In almost every state of
the Union, north, east, west, and south, and in many
separate districts of some of the states, have Bible Societies started up, under the auspices of zeal and wisdom.   The *American Bible Society*, a national institution, established so recently as in May, 1816, has
already about a hundred and fifty auxiliary branches ;
besides which there are some few independent Bible
Associations, and a considerable number of *Bible and
Common Prayer-book* societies.   The old and young,
the rich and poor, of every Christian denomination, have
sprung forward with alacrity and ardour to enrol themselves under the banners of the Cross ; to do personal
suit and service to the great Captain of their salvation,
by distributing *His* glad tidings of present peace, and
future hope, and eternal safety, among all those who
have hitherto lived without God in the world.

Neither can it be said, that America does not stand
in need of every individual, every social effort, to distri-
bute the sacred oracles among her children.   The savage tribes of Indians, who prowl around our frontiers,
or who roam over the pathless wilderness, remain still
benighted in all the original darkness of pagan ignorance
and superstition.   Nay, even our own fellow-citizens in
the United States require all the assistance that can be
given to facilitate their access to the means of eternal
life.   Full *three millions* of our people are altogether
destitute of Christian ordinances ; and as the population

of this country increases with a rapidity hitherto unexampled in the history of nations, unless some effectual means be adopted to spread the light of the gospel over those sections of the Union, which now lie prostrate in all the darkness of unregenerated depravity, before half a century shall have elapsed, our federative republic will number within its bosom more than twenty millions of *unbaptized infidels.*

The voice of duty, therefore, and of humanity, and Christian charity, calls loudly upon us to strain every sinew, to stretch every nerve, in strenuous and unremitted exertion, to circulate the Holy Scriptures among all the orders and classes of our community. This soul-ennobling duty is the more incumbent upon Bible Societies, because it is *their* peculiar privilege to be a Christian Society, instituted for truly Christian purposes : with *them,* engaged as they are in one common labour of philanthropy, every partition wall of sectarian bigotry is broken down ; every denomination of all Christian persuasions is met together with one heart, and with one accord. *They* leave to graceless zealots the miserable consolation of worrying each other, and disgracing themselves by the fiercest contentions about the paltry shibboleths of puny polemics ; *their* sole object is to give a free course, a wider circulation to the unsophisticated word of God ; and I trust that they will never for one moment slacken their exertions of time, talent, knowledge, substance, opportunity, body, soul, and spirit, their universal nature, in this great, this interesting service, while a single section of our country, a single town, village, or hamlet, nay, a single family, or individual, within the whole circumference of our vast and rapidly widening republic, is to be found, to whom the sacred Scriptures are as a fountain closed, and a volume sealed.

The *morals, manners,* and *character* of every country are based upon its religious and social institutions, which in the United States are framed in the fulness of individual liberty, leaving every one to think, speak, and act, according to his own inclination and views, provided, however, that he keeps (as Shakspeare calls it) on the windy side of the law.

The great body of the American people are of English origin, and resemble their parent country in morals, manners, and character, modified, indeed, by the diversities of government, soil, climate, and condition of society. Being, however, all under the influences of the same language, religion, laws, and policy, the several states which compose the Union present substantially the same character, with only a few shades of local variety. All our governments are elective and popular, the plenary sovereignty residing in the people, who therefore feel a sense of personal importance and elevation unknown to the mass of population in any other country. To which add their general intelligence, abundance, enterprise, and spirit, and we see a *people* superior to those of every other nation in physical, intellectual, and moral capacity and power.

In *New-England* property is more equally divided than in any other civilized country. There are but few overgrown capitalists, and still fewer plunged into the depths of indigence. Those states are alike free from the insolence of wealth on one hand, and the servility of pauperism on the other. They exhibit a more perfect equality in means, morals, manners, and character than has ever elsewhere been found. With the exception of Rhode-Island, they all support religion by law; their numerous parish priests, all chosen by the people themselves, moderately paid, and, in general, well informed and pious, are continually employed on the sabbaths, and during the week days, in the instruction and amendment of their respective congregations; their elementary schools are established in every township, and perhaps not a native of New-England is to be found who cannot read, and write, and cast accounts. They live universally in villages, or moderately sized towns, and carry on their commercial, manufacturing, and agricultural operations by the voluntary labour of freemen, and not by the compelled toil of slaves. In sobriety of morals and manners, in intelligence, spirit, and enterprise, the New-England men and the Scottish are very much alike. Dr. Currie, in his profound and elegant biography of Burns, enters at length into the causes which have rendered the great body of the Scottish people so very superior to those of any other European country; the result of his reasoning is, that this national superiority is owing to the combined efforts of the system of *parish schools,* giving to *all* the means of elementary education, and of a moderately paid, able, and well-informed clergy, coming into constant contact with, and instructing and regulating the people; to which he adds, as no small auxiliary, the absence of those *poor laws* which have impoverished, and deteriorated, and corrupted the whole people of England.

In this country we have unfortunately adopted the English poor-law system; which, so far as it yet operates, is a cankerworm knawing at the heart's core of our national morals, prosperity, and strength. The American people, however, possess one decided advantage over those of Scotland and every other country; namely, that of the *political sovereignty* residing in them; whence they exhibit in their own persons a moral fearlessness, confidence, and elevation, unknown and unimagined elsewhere. A native free-born American knows no superior on earth; from the cradle to the grave he is taught to believe that his magistrates are his servants: and while in all other countries the people are continually flattering and praising their governors, *our* government is compelled to be eternally playing the sycophant and acting the parasite to the majesty of the people. It may, on the whole, be safely asserted that the New-England population surpasses that of all the rest of the world in steady habits, dauntless courage, intelligence, enterprise, perseverance—in all the qualities necessary to render a nation first in war and first in peace. Upon inquiry, I was informed by one of our southern generals, who particularly distinguished himself on our northern frontiers during the last war, that the New-England regiment in his brigade was peculiarly conspicuous for its exact discipline, its patient endurance of fatigue and privation, its steady, unyielding valour in the field, while his own native Virginians were more careless, more reckless, more inflammatory, more fit for a forlorn hope, or some desperate impracticable enterprise. He added, that he regularly found that all the *rum* dealt out as rations to his New-England soldiers had glided down the throats of his Virginian regiment, whose *pay*, in return, had been regularly transferred to the pockets of the more prudent eastern warriors.

In the *middle* states the population is not so national and unmixed as in New-England, whose inhabitants are altogether of English origin. They do *not* support religion by law; and a considerable portion of their people are destitute of clergymen, even in the state of New-York, and a still greater proportion in some of the other middle states. In some of them, elementary schools are not numerous, particularly in Pennsylvania, many of whose people can neither write nor read. Property is not so equally divided, and the distinction of rich and poor is more broadly marked than in New-England. Many of their settlements are more recent, and exhibit the physical, intellectual, and moral disadvantages of new settlements, in the privations, ignorance, and irreligion of the settlers, who were composed of many different nations, having no one common object in view, either in regard to religious, or moral, or social institutions. The English, Dutch, Germans, French, Irish, Scottish, Swiss, have not yet had time and opportunity to be all melted down into one homogeneous national mass of *American* character. The *slaves* in this section of the Union are more numerous than in New-England, and in Maryland sufficiently so to influence and deteriorate the character of the people. The moral habits of the middle states, generally, are more lax than those of New-England. New-York, indeed, partly from proximity of situation, but chiefly from its continual acquisition of emigrants from the eastern states, is rapidly assuming a New-England character and aspect.

In the *southern* states, religion receives no support from the law; and a very large proportion of the inha-

bitants are destitute of regular preaching and religious
instruction. The elementary schools are few, and in
general not well administered; many of the white inhabitants cannot even read. Labour on the seaboard
is performed chiefly by slaves; and slavery here, as
every where else, has corrupted the public morals.
The mulattoes are increasing very rapidly; and, perhaps,
in the lapse of years, the black, white, and yellow population will be melted down into one common mass.
Duelling and gaming are very prevalent; and, together
with other vices, require the restraining power of religion and morality to check their progress towards national ruin.

When speaking of the gradual relaxation of morals
in the United States, as we pass from the north and
east to the south and west, it is to be understood that
the American ladies are *not* included in this geographical deterioration. In no country under the canopy of
heaven do female virtue and purity hold a higher rank
than in the Union. We have no instances among us of
those domestic infidelities which dishonour so many families in Europe, and even stain the national character
of Britain herself, high as she peers over all the other
European nations in pure religion and sound morality.
Our American ladies make virtuous and affectionate
wives, kind and indulgent mothers; are, in general,
easy, affable, intelligent, and well-bred; their manners
presenting a happy medium between the two distant
reserve and coldness of the English, and the too obvious,
too obtrusive behaviour of the French women. Their
manners have a strong resemblance to those of the Irish
and Scottish ladies.

The public morals, however, of the female population of our southern and western states are materially
injured by the existence of the slave system. Even Mr.
Morris Birkbeck, whose *ultra whiggism* has led him in
his old age to fly with horror from the despotism of
Britain, because she overthrew his friend Napoleon, the
great patron saint of liberty in Europe; even he expresses grave doubts if the condition of his enslaved

countrymen be quite so bad as that of the negroes in Virginia ; and he runs a philosophical parallel, very much after the manner of Plutarch, between the situation of the English peasantry and that of the Virginian slaves, balancing their respective evils under various heads of inquiry ; and, upon the whole, seems inclined to think that the British people are *not yet* reduced so low in the scale of oppression and suffering as the black inhabitants of our " *Ancient Dominion.*" Indeed, the sensibilities of this veteran reformer were so much awakened, he says, as actually to cause him to shed tears when he saw some slaves sold in Richmond, the capital of Virginia ; and he does not hesitate to affirm, that the superior morals of those states which have abolished slavery proves servitude to be, in truth, the bane of society.

Mr. Birkbeck says, that in May, 1817, he was at Petersburgh, on his way to Indiana, where he is now endeavouring to lay the foundations of a colony, to be peopled by English, who, like himself, are too virtuous and too wise to live under the British government, whose wickedness and tyranny are consummating its speedy perdition. He says he found a Virginian tavern like a French hotel, but more filthy, without its culinary excellence, and dearer than an English inn. The daily number of guests at its ordinary was fifty, consisting of travellers, shopkeepers, lawyers, and doctors. He found the Virginian planter a republican in politics, and full of high-spirited independence, but a slave-master, irascible, lax in morals, and wearing a dirk. He never saw in England an assemblage of countrymen who *averaged* so well in dress and manners. Their conversation gave him a high opinion of their intelligence—the prevailing topic was *negro slavery*, an evil which all professed to deplore, many were anxious to fly from, but for which none could devise a remedy.

One gentleman, an invalid, was wretched at the thought of his family being left, for a single night, without his protection from his own slaves. He was himself labouring under the effects of a poisonous potion, administered to him by a negro, his own personal servant, to whom he had been particularly kind and generous, and who thus recompensed his indulgence. It was stated, that severe and rigorous masters seldom suffer from the resentment of their slaves. On the 10th of May, 1817, Mr. Birkbeck saw two female slaves and their children sold by auction in the street at Richmond; a spectacle which exceedingly shocked him; he could scarcely endure to see them handled and examined like cattle, and when he heard their sobs, and saw the tears roll down their cheeks, at the thought of being separated, he could not refrain from weeping with them. Such is the consistency of an English patriot, who laments that his own native country was not enslaved by that virtuous republican, Bonaparte!

In selling slaves, our southern planters and dealers pay no regard to parting nearest relations, to separating parents and children, or tearing asunder husbands and wives. Virginia prides itself on the comparative mildness with which its slaves are treated; and yet, in the first volume of the *American Museum* there is a heart-rending account of a slave being, for some offence, put into an iron cage, suspended to the branches of a lofty tree, and left to perish by famine and thirst, unless the birds of prey, to admit which the bars of the cage stood at intervals sufficiently wide, could terminate his life sooner, by plunging their beaks and talons into his vitals. In the mean time the eagle, the vulture, and the raven feasted upon the quivering flesh of the living victim, whose body they mangled at their own leisure; and the high-spirited republicans of the ancient dominion were gratified by knowing that the air was tainted by the putrefaction, and loaded with the expiring cries and groans of an agonized fellow-man, doomed to die by protracted torture.

Virginia supplies, annually, with slaves of her own growth, the states farther south, where the treatment of the negroes is said to be much more severe and more destructive of life. There are regular dealers, who buy up slaves, and drive them in gangs, chained to-

gether, and more than half naked, to a southern market.
Few weeks pass without some of these wretched creatures being marched through Richmond, on their southward course: a few months since nearly two hundred
were sold by auction in the street, and filled all the
region round with their cries, and shrieks, and lamenta-
tions.   Mr. Birkbeck observes, that he found in Virginia the condition of the negroes more miserable, and
the tone of moral feeling in their owners much higher
than he had anticipated; that he is confirmed in his
detestation of slavery, both in principle and practice,
and that he esteems the general character of the Virginians.

The *western* states participate in the morals, manners, and character of those sections of the Union by
which they are peopled, namely, the southern and middle, and, above all, the New-England States.   Mr.
Birkbeck's account of the emigration westward, and of
his own progress through the new settlements, is interesting and instructive: from his narrative I shall borrow such facts as may illustrate the present inquiry.
Indeed, all America appears to be moving to the west.
The political consequences of this migration will soon
be portentous.   During the revolutionary war, and for
some years after its termination, the influence of New-
England predominated in our national councils, and
Washington's administration established the prosperity
and glory of the country on a solid basis.   Afterward
Virginia contrived, by managing the southern and middle states, to render New-England nearly a political
cypher in the Union.   And now, the rapid growth of
the western states, in population, wealth, and strength,
threaten, ere long, to give them a preponderance over
all the Atlantic sections of the United States, and to
entail upon us a system of *tramontane* policy, but little
accordant with our commercial views and interests.
The first step of decided western legislation probably
will be the removal of the seat of general government
from Washington across the Alleghany mountains, to
some place near the Pacific Ocean.

On the great route towards the Ohio, the traveller has constantly in view groups of emigrants, directing their steps towards the land of promise; some with a little light waggon, covered with a sheet or blanket, and containing bedding, utensils, provisions, and a colony of children, drawn by one or two small horses, and perhaps accompanied by a cow. A few silver dollars also are carried for the purchase of public land, at two dollars an acre, one-fourth of the purchase-money to be paid immediately, upon entering the claim at the land-office of the district where the purchase is located. The New-England pilgrims are said to be known by the light step and cheerful air of the women, marching in front of the family caravan; the New-Jersey wanderers by being quietly housed under the tilt of the waggon; while the Pennsylvanian emigrants creep loitering behind, with melancholy gait, and slow. A cart with one horse, or a single horse and pack-saddle, transports a family from the eastern to the western section of the Union, a distance of between two and three thousand miles; and, not unfrequently, the adventurer carries all his fortunes on his staff, while his wife, barefooted, follows, bearing on her shoulders the treasure of the cradle.

The Americans are unquestionably the most locomotive, migrating people in the world. Even when doing well in the northern, or middle, or southern states, they will break up their establishment, and move westward with an alacrity and vigor that nothing but the necessity of adverse circumstances could induce in any other population. In the year 1817, nearly twenty thousand waggons, averaging a burden of forty hundred weight each, travelled between Baltimore and Philadelphia, on one side, and Pittsburgh on the other side of the Alleghany mountains. The freight, or carriage of the goods thus conveyed exceeded two millions of dollars; to which add numberless well loaded stages and mails, travellers in waggons, on horses, and on foot, and some notion may be formed of the incessant line of march over these three hundred miles of the western road.

Travellers from the eastern districts often leave their horses at Pittsburgh, and go down the Ohio to their place of destination; while those from the west, proceed eastward in stages. Even elderly women make long journeys on horseback, for instance, from Tennessee to Pittsburgh, a distance of twelve hundred miles; nay, sometimes the lady will carry an infant on the horse, in addition to herself, a blanket above and beneath the saddle, a pair of saddle-bags, a great coat, and an umbrella. Mr. Birkbeck, in June, 1817, when at Washington, in Pennsylvania, saw a farmer and his wife well mounted and equipt: they had ridden from the neighbourhood of Cincinnati, in Ohio, and were proceeding on horseback to visit their friends at New York and Philadelphia, a distance of seven hundred miles. They had left Cincinnati six days before, had travelled two hundred and seventy-two miles, and their horses were quite fresh; a conclusive proof of their excellence.

Mr. Birkbeck gives the history of a farmer and tavern-keeper, about twenty miles from Washington, as an example of the rapid appreciation of property in the western country. The man is thirty, has a wife and three fine children. His father is a farmer in the neighbourhood, and gave him five hundred dollars to begin the world with, which he did by taking a cargo of flour to New-Orleans, distant about two thousand miles. In 1815, he had increased his property to nine hundred dollars, and bought two hundred and fifty acres of land, sixty-five of which are cleared, and laid down to grass, for three thousand five hundred dollars, of which three thousand are already paid. His property is now worth seven thousand dollars, having grown half that sum in value in two years, with a full prospect of a much greater appreciation in future. In many parts of Ohio land is now worth from twenty to thirty dollars an acre; an advance in value of *a thousand* per cent in the last ten years.

Nevertheless, Mr. Birkbeck admits, that emigrants with small capitals, particularly if from Europe, are liable to great inconveniences. For money, although abun-

dantly competent to the purchase of land, is soon consumed in the expenses of travelling, which are great.
The settlers in the new country are generally needy
adventurers, and exposed to difficulties, which, in addition to unhealthy situations, shorten life. The public
land intended for sale is laid out in the government
surveys in quarter sections of 160 acres each, or one-
fourth of a square mile. The whole is set up at auction,
and what remains unsold may be bought at the district
land office, at two dollars an acre; one-fourth to be
paid down, and the residue in instalments, to be completed in five years. The emigrant having paid his
eighty dollars for a quarter section, is often left penny-
less, and repairs to his purchase in a waggon, containing
his wife and children, a few blankets, a skillet, a rifle,
and an axe. After erecting a little log hut, he clears,
with intense labour, a plot of ground for Indian corn, as
his next year's subsistence, depending, in the mean-
time, on his gun for food. In pursuit of game, he
must often, after his day's work, wade through the
evening dews up to the waist, in long grass or bushes,
and returning, lie on a bear's skin, spread on the damp
ground, exposed to every blast through the open sides,
and to every shower through the open roof of his dwell-
ing, which is never attempted to be closed until the approach of winter, and often not then. Under such extreme toil and exposure, many of the settlers speedily
perish.

Sometimes he has to carry his grain fifty miles to a
mill to be ground, and wait there some days till his
turn comes. These difficulties of course diminish as
the settlements thicken; and the number of emigrants
increases each successive year with incredible rapidity.
Land cleared, commands from twenty to thirty dollars
an acre; and thus, in the course of the last fifteen years,
a tract of country four times as large as the British
Isles has been *decupled* in value. The towns in the
western country, as is particularly the case with Zanes-
ville, Lancaster, and Chilicothe, in Ohio, are often situated without any regard to the health of the inhabitants,

provided they be well located for profit; gain being the chief object of pursuit with our American adventurers. Cincinnati itself stands too low on the banks of the Ohio; its lower parts being within reach of the spring floods. But it has grown as by enchantment, and promises soon to become one of the first cities of the west. Within the little space of five years the greatest part of its present dimensions and wealth has been produced.

It exhibits now, where, within the memory of man, stood only one rude cabin, several hundreds of commodious handsome brick houses, spacious and busy markets, substantial public buildings, thousands of industrious thriving inhabitants, gay carriages, and elegant females, shoals of craft on the river, incessant enlarging and improvement of the town, a perpetual influx of strangers and travellers; all sprung up from the bosom of the woods, as it were but yesterday. Twenty years since, the immense region, comprising the states of Ohio and Indiana, numbered only thirty thousand souls, less than are now contained in the little county of Hamilton, in which Cincinnati stands.

Probably the time is not far distant when the chief intercourse with Europe will no longer be through the Atlantic States, but be carried on through the great rivers, which communicate by the Mississippi with the ocean, at New-Orleans; in consequence of the ascending navigation of these streams being subdued by the power of steam.

Full two thousand boatmen are regularly employed on the Ohio, and are proverbially ferocious and profligate. The settlers along the line of this great navigation exhibit similar habits; and profligacy and fierceness appear to characterize the population on the banks of these mighty rivers. Indiana is more recently settled than Ohio, and its settlers superior in rank and character; the first founders of Ohio being very needy adventurers. The inhabitants of Indiana have generally brought with them from their parent states habits of comfort, and the means of procuring the conveniences of life. They are orderly, peaceable citizens, respect and obey the laws, are kind and neighbourly to each other, and hospitable to strangers. The mere hunters, who rely for subsistence on their rifle, and a scanty cultivation of corn, and live in a state of poverty and privation nearly equal to that of the Indians, always retire at the approach of the regular settlers, and keep themselves on the outside of the cultivated farms.

There is no striking difference in the general deportment and appearance of the great body of Americans *in the towns,* from Norfolk in Virginia, to Madison in Indiana. The same well-looking, well-dressed, tall, stout men, appear every where pretty much at their ease, shrewd and intelligent, and not too industrious. When asked why they do not employ themselves? they answer, " we live in freedom, we need not work like the English; as if idleness itself were not the worst species of slavery. In the *country* are to be found several backwoodmen, who are savage and fierce, and view newcomers as intruders. They, however, must quickly yield to the rapid growth of civilization. The great body of the western settlers are, beyond all comparison, superior to the European farmers and peasantry in manners and habits, in physical capacity, and abundance, and above all, in intelligence and political independence.

The activity and enterprise of the Americans far exceed those of any other people. Travellers continually are setting out on journeys of two or three thousand miles, by boats, on horses, or on foot, without any apparent anxiety or deliberation. Nearly a thousand persons every summer pass down the Ohio as traders or boatmen, and return on foot; a distance by water of seventeen hundred, by land, of a thousand miles.

Many go down to New-Orleans from Pittsburgh, an additional five hundred miles, by water, and three hundred by land. The store or shop-keepers of the western towns resort to Baltimore, New-York, and Philadelphia, once a year, to lay in their goods. But in a short time, probably, these journeyings eastward will be exchanged for visits down the Ohio and Mississippi to New-Orleans. The vast and growing produce

of the western states, in grain, flour, cotton, sugar, tobacco, peltry, lumber, &c. which finds a ready market
at New-Orleans, will, by means of steam-boat navigation,
be returned through the same channel in the manufactures and luxuries of Europe and Asia, to supply the
constantly-increasing demands of the west, and render
New-Orleans one of the greatest commercial cities in
the universe.

Learning, taste, and science, of course, have not yet
made much headway in the west; their reading is, in
general, confined to newspapers and political pamphlets,
a little history, and less religion; but their intellects are
keen, vigorous, and active. The following observations
of Mr. Walsh, in the first volume of the *American Register*, are expressed in his usual style of felicitous splendour:—" In inspecting the schools of our western
country we are alarmed lest the population should im-
measurably outgrow the means of instruction, and their
intellectual fall far short of their numerical weight in
our national councils. But the apprehension vanishes,
in a great degree, before the activity, the emulation, and
the sagacity which characterize our tramontane brethren. The force with which the mind *vegetates* among
them can be best illustrated by the growth of their
plants in a virgin loam. All the faculties knit, spread,
and luxuriate, vigorously and wildly, as the branches
of their sycamore. This intense vitality of the intellect,
when fed by science, and the knowledge of mankind,
must give the most splendid results. We may judge
from the specimens of the ore which we have seen in
Congress what the metal will be after sublimation. I
must confess that I was lost in admiration at the prospects which open in that quarter upon the pride of human intelligence and power; it is a perspective of which
the magnificence can be credible only to those who
have made their examination at leisure upon the spot,
and with a recollection of what history relates as to the
adolescence of the mightiest communities mentioned in
its annals. At a distance hardly a suspicion is entertain-
ed of the promise—I should say, rather, the impending

maturity of the west. It is a great empire, lying, as it were, in ambush for mankind, and destined to explore all parts of the intellectual world. *Liberal* education, by which I mean the systematic tuition of the sciences and classics, is there exceedingly backward; but the rudiments of mere English education are almost universal."

Having thus, very summarily, glanced at the morals, habits, and manners, of the four great sections of the Union, a few remarks will be hazarded as applicable to the Americans, generally, in their national capacity and character.

The high wages of labour, the abundance of every kind of manual and mechanical employment, the plenty of provisions, the vast quantity and low price of land, all contribute to produce a healthy, strong, and vigorous population. Four-fifths of our people are engaged in agricultural pursuits, and the great majority of these are proprietors of the soil which they cultivate. In the intervals of toil their amusements consist chiefly of hunting and shooting, in the woods, or on the mountains; whence they acquire prodigious muscular activity and strength. We have no *game* laws, such as exist in Europe, to prohibit the possession and use of fire-arms to the great body of the people. Our boys carry a gun almost as soon as they can walk ; and the habitual practice of shooting at a target, with the rifle, renders the Americans the most unerring marksmen, and the most deadly musketry in the world ; as was singularly evidenced at *Bunkers Hill,* in the commencement of the revolutionary conflict, and at New-Orleans, at the close of the last war. Every male, from the age of eighteen to forty-five, is liable to be enrolled in the militia ; of which the President's Message of the second of December, 1817, informs us the United States have now eight hundred thousand. These men make the best materials for a regular army, as they learn the use of arms in platoons, and the elements of military discipline, in their militia exercises and drills. The Americans are excellent engineers and artillerists, and serve their guns

F f

well, both in the field and on the flood, as their enemies can testify;—whereas, the people in Europe are
not suffered to be familiar with the use of arms ; whence
neither their seamen nor their soldiers fire with any
thing like the precision and execution of the American
army and navy.

Thus the people of the United States possess, in an
eminent degree, the *physical* elements of national greatness and strength. Add to these, the general prevalence of elementary instruction, which enables the great
mass of the people to develope their natural faculties
and powers, and capacitates them for undertaking any
employment, success in which depends upon shrewdness, intelligence, and skill ; whence their singular ingenuity in mechanical and manual operations, and their
sound understanding, enterprise, and perseverance in
the practical concerns of life. And to crown all, the
political sovereignty of the nation residing in the people,
gives them a personal confidence, self-possession, and
elevation of character, unknown and unattainable in any
other country, and under any other form of governmeut;
and which renders them quick to perceive, and prompt
to resent and punish any insult offered to individual or
national honour. Whence in the occupations of peace,
and the achievements of war, the Americans average a
greater aggregate of effective force, physical, intellectual, and moral, than ever has been exhibited by a given
number of any other people, ancient or modern. Individuals, in other countries, may, and do exhibit as much
bodily activity and strength, as much intellectual acuteness and vigour, as much moral force and elevation, as
can be shown forth by any American individuals ; but
no country *can* display such a population, *in mass,* as
are now quickening the United States with their prolific energy, and ripening fast into a substance of power,
every movement of which will soon be felt in its vibra-
tions to the remotest corners of the earth.

Sagacity and shrewdness are the peculiar characteristics of American intellect, and were in nothing more
pre-eminent, than in the advice of President Washing-

ton's secretary of the navy, that the United States should build their ships *nominally* of the same rate with those of Europe, but really of greater strength, of more speed, tonnage, and guns, than the corresponding classes of European vessels, that they might ensure victory over an enemy of equal, or nearly equal force, and escape, by superior sailing, any very unequal conflict. This was good policy; as it served materially to raise the naval character of the country, to lessen that of England, and to put out of use and service the European navies, and compel other nations to construct their ships anew, after the American model. This policy is still persisted in, and our seventy-fours are equal in tonnage, bulk, strength, guns, and crew, to any hundred gun ships in the British navy. The American crews also are far superior to those of Europe: every seaman is a good gunner, and the ships are manned with picked men, and a full complement of real, able-bodied, skilful sailors; whereas the European ships seldom have more than one-third of their crews able seamen, the other two-thirds generally consisting of landsmen and boys. When we shall have a navy, as large as we ought to have, in proportion to our long line of sea-coast, our immense lake and river navigation, and our immense and rapidly-augmenting resources, it will not be easy to man our fleets and squadrons as we now do our few single ships; nay, it is doubtful, if they can be manned at all, without the aid of *impressment*, which, indeed, was strongly recommended to Congress by our secretary of the navy, towards the close of the last war, as the *only* possible mode of filling up the complement wanted for the two and twenty vessels, of all sizes, frigates, sloops, and brigs, which we then had in commission.

There are, however, drawbacks upon the high elements of national greatness above enumerated, to be found in some of our political and social institutions. For example, *slavery* demoralizes the southern, and those of the western states, which have adopted this execrable system. *Lotteries* pervade the middle, southern, and western states, and spread a horribly increasing mass of idleness, fraud, theft, falsehood, and profligacy throughout all the classes of our labouring population. The crying iniquity and evil of this system are compelling the British parliament to abolish it altogether in that country. Our state-legislatures never assemble without augmenting the number of lotteries. Our favourite scheme of substituting a *state prison* for the gallows is a most prolific mother of crime. During the severity of the winter season, its lodgings and accommodations are better than those of many of our paupers, who are thereby incited to crime in order to mend their condition. And the pernicious custom of *pardoning* the most atrocious criminals, after a short residence in the state-prison, is continually augmenting our flying squadrons of murderers, house-breakers, foot-pads, forgers, highway robbers, and swindlers of all sorts. The effect of Mr. Bentham's plan of a penitentiary, with its panorama and whispering gallery, is not known, because it has never been tried in this country; but, beyond all peradventure, our state-prisons, as at present constituted, are grand demoralizers of our people.

Our state insolvent laws, likewise (for we are too patriotic to permit Congress to pass an uniform bankrupt law, that might compel our merchants to pay their *foreign* creditors), acts as a perpetual bounty for dishonesty and fraud. A few favoured creditors, by whose false representations the debtor has obtained large credits, are secured, and the rest of the creditors, more especially if they happen to be British, are sure to get nothing. The insolvent is discharged, as a matter of course, from all responsibility, and left at liberty to renew his depredations upon the property of others according to his own inclination, experience, and dexterity.

The *poor-law* system, as an awful encouragement to pauperism and profligacy, requires no further comment. With the exception of *forgery*, in the ingenuity and audacity of which our *native* Americans far surpass all other people, and for which our state-prisons do not afford even a palliative, much less a remedy, the *foreigners* and free blacks are the most numerous and atrocious of our criminals. The "*low Irish*," as they are called, who come out to us in shoals from their own country, and are by far the most noxious donation which the United States receive from Britain, fill up our lowest departments of labour in the manufactories, or the manual operations of our large cities, as hod-men, porters, and so forth, are in general, rude, intemperate, and abandoned. They tenant our bridewells and state-prisons in great numbers. The next in the scale of profligacy, as criminals, are the freed negroes; then come foreigners, other than Irish; and lastly, our own native citizens, of which few find their way into confinement for crime, excepting, as before stated, for forgery; of adepts in which the United States produce a greater number, in proportion to their population, than any country in Europe; their numbers, however, might be materially diminished, if our legislators could be persuaded to try the experiment of the gallows upon them.

The prevailing vice throughout the Union, excepting New-England, is *immoderate drinking;* encouraged doubtless by the relaxing heats of the climate, in the southern, middle, and western states, by the high wages of labour, and by the absence of all restriction, in the shape of excise, or internal duty. Not only our labourers generally, but too many of our farmers, merchants, and other classes of the community, are prone to a pernicious indulgence in spirituous liquors.

The alarming increase of pauperism, drunkenness, and general profligacy, in the city of New-York, has induced our most respectable citizens of all classes to appoint a committee to examine into the causes, and devise the means of checking this great national evil, which menaces the very existence of our social fabric. This committee is now in session; and every succeeding day presents them with an accumulating mass of facts, all conspiring to show forth the loathsome deformity of our city, with respect to its rapidly augmenting poverty and vice. In the year 1817, our corporation expended *one hundred and twenty thousand* dollars in the poor law system ; which sum is in addition to other public charities, as the hospital, asylum for orphans, widow's society, charity schools, &c. and in addition to the private charities, which in this city are numerous and expensive. Indeed, the Americans, generally, are a charitable benevolent people, both in private and in public. The city of New-York has very recently, raised five thousand dollars for the sufferers by the late fire at St. John's in Newfoundland. And Boston, with only one-third of the New-York population, subscribed ten thousand dollars for the same object. But Boston has always been peculiarly munificent; witness a few years since, when some of our principal citizens subscribed twelve thousand dollars for the support of the widow and children of the British Consul for that district, who had died in indigent circumstances.

In consequence of the extreme suffering of the poor in the city of New-York, during the winter of 1816-17, in January, 1817, a large meeting of the citizens was convened for the purpose of devising some means of immediate relief for their brethren in affliction. Committees were appointed, in each ward of the city, to raise money by subscription, and administer to the more pressing wants of the dependent classes of the community. Six thousand dollars were instantly raised, and entirely consumed in the course of a few days ; so prodigious was the number of distressed applicants for food, fuel, and clothing. Indeed, the number of indigent poor, destitute of all the first 'necessaries of life, as covering, provisions, fuel, lodging, upon careful examination, was found to far exceed that of any former period of distress. The several committees faithfully discharged their important but painful duties ; they visited the habitation of *every* family that applied for relief. It was *not* possible for any city in Europe—for London, for Paris, for Dublin itself—even at *that* awful hour of universal distress and visitation, to exhibit a greater *proportional* number of wretched objects, sunk to the lowest pitch of barren sorrow and destitution, than were exposed to the astonished view of the various committees, in their rounds of inquiry through the city of New-York.

Full *fifteen thousand* men, women and children, during that season, received aid from the hand of public and private charity; that is to say, about *one-seventh* of the whole population of our city. It raised a cry of alarm and horror throughout all the corners of their extended empire, when, in the year 1816, it was discovered that *one-ninth* of the population of the British isles was reduced to a state of pauperage and dependence on the bounty of others. Ought *such* to be the condition of the mass of the people in *any part* of the United States; where a comparatively small population is spread over an immense territory, blessed with a fertile soil and genial clime; where the burden of government expenditure is scarcely felt; where the national debt is trifling, and the taxes nothing; where there are no *tithes;* and where the demand for agricultural labour is constantly outrunning its supply?

It is a lamentable and alarming fact, that the number of destitute poor in the city of New-York has averaged an annual augmentation far exceeding *the rate* of its actual increase of population for several years past; more especially since the winter when the battery, at the confluence of the North and East rivers, was broken up, and distributed for firewood amongst the indigent; and the corporation proclaimed that it would give food and fuel, at the Almshouse, to *all* distressed applicants. This is the very essence of the impracticable folly, and positive evil of the *poor-law* system, which promises work and support to all that want; as if it were possible for any human scheme to create either food or employment where neither is to be found in existence.

It is not, however, to be dissembled, that a large proportion of our New-York paupers are *foreigners,* chiefly from Europe, and some from the neighbouring states and towns. Nor can it be concealed, that the leprosy of wickedness and crime has tainted the lower class of our citizens in a most awful degree; as was to be expected, in consequence of their progressively increasing pauperism.　It will scarcely be credited in Europe, that a large proportion of these profligate paupers are *free and independent* voters at our elections, for charter-officers, for State Representatives, and for Congress-men !

The several committees laboured to investigate the *causes* which have produced the present wretched and degraded condition of the poor in our city.　Some of the distress, undoubtedly, is to be attributed to the vast influx of indigent, and not immaculate, foreigners; to the present depressed condition of commerce and manufactures ; to the prodigious number of benevolent societies, which have, with the best and most charitable intentions, undesignedly offered a standing bounty for the continual increase of needy applicants ; and to some *other* causes not proper, perhaps, now to be enumerated, but which our legislators and city magistrates can easily remove if they will ; and, perhaps, to the natural tendency of human society to deteriorate, if not constantly watched and guarded by religious and moral culture.　A greater portion of the distress, probably, is occasioned by our system of *poor-laws*, which we have borrowed from England.　The *British Review* for November, 1817, contains an elaborate, masterly, and temperate exposition of the evils which that system has burned, in characters of the nether fire, into the heart and vitals, the body, soul, and spirit of the English population.

But beyond all controversy, the most fertile source of the present unparalleled distress among the poor of the city of New-York, is the general, not to say universal, use of *spirituous liquors* by the lower orders of the community, of each sex and every age.　There are nearly *three thousand* houses *licensed* to sell poison to the poor, in the shape of alcohol ; in addition to which there are great numbers of cellars and vaults, where ardent spirits are vended *without license.*　And do we wonder at the rapid augmentation of mendicity and crime in this city, when there are so many charnel houses of industry, health, religion, and morals, open day and night, and every hour, for the consignment of their victims to an untimely grave ?

By information from the mayor of Philadelphia, communicated to a committee of our *Humane Society*, in December, 1809, it appears that there were then in the city of Philadelphia only *one hundred and ninety* licensed houses ; and in the whole county of Philadelphia, including the suburbs of the city, several considerable towns and villages, and a large tract of country, containing altogether a population of more than one hundred and fifty thousand souls, only *two hundred and forty* houses licensed to sell spirits.   Since that period up to the present hour, the magistracy of Philadelphia have been most laudably employed in diminishing even that comparatively moderate number, which comprehends all the taverns, beer-houses, groceries, and other places, licensed to sell spirituous liquors by retail.   So that our sister city of Philadelphia permits less than *one-tenth* of inflammable poison, in proportion to her population, to be distributed among her citizens, in comparison of the heedless prodigality with which the official guardians of New-York waste the health and integrity of the poor committed to their charge.

Nay, even in London, that mart of all the world, it appears from a recent report on the mendicity of the British empire to the House of Commons, that there are no more than *four thousand two hundred and twenty* houses licensed to sell spirits ; and that number is complained of as being too great for a city and its neighbourhood, containing about one million, three hundred thousand inhabitants, and continually receiving into its capacious bosom a prodigious influx of profligacy and crime, from every tongue, and every nation, and every quarter of the globe.   The population of New-York is not much more than one hundred thousand ; and therefore it is necessary for her, young as she is in her national career, and simple as she is in all her forms and habits of social institution, to reduce the licensed houses to at least three hundred, in order to reach the level, *in incentives to iniquity,* of an overgrown metropolis, hoary with age, and presenting the most artificial and complicated state of society ever yet exhibited in the history of the human race.

On a very moderate computation, the licensed houses in New-York sell a yearly aggregate of spirits, amounting to three millions of dollars. One-tenth of the population of the whole state resides in this city, and, allowing that *they,* owing to the greater tendencies of a crowded city to idleness and profligacy, consume as much as all the other nine-tenths, the annual expenditure of our state in spirituous liquors will amount to *six* millions of dollars. Now it is an enormous evil, that so large a portion of our annual income should be diverted from the service of productive industry; from administering to the agriculture, commerce, manufactures, conveniencies, comforts, and embellishment of the state. The sum so expended is about equal to a *capitation* tax of *six* dollars upon every man, woman, and child, throughout the state. But the mere detraction of so much money annually from the public service, from private comfort, from social ornament, is, by no means, the greatest evil resulting from *such* an application of the funds of labour. The *habitual* use of ardent spirits enervates the bodily frame, renders it irritable, and liable to disease, lays the sure foundation of constitutional decay, and premature death; it dissipates all the powers of the mind in shapeless idleness, quenches the fires of genius, and puts out the lights of learning; it corrupts and debases the whole moral nature of man; sears up his conscience against every obligation of duty, stifles the voice of affection, extinguishes in his bosom all the charities of parent, child, and brother; eradicates every principle and every sentiment of religion, and renders him an incarnate fiend, ripe for the perpetration of every enormity that can carry anguish and ruin into the recesses of private life, and convert society itself into a scene of rapine, and violence, of fraud, injustice, anarchy, and blood.

This evil is too great, too deeply rooted in the habits

and passions of our people, for individual charity, however active and persevering, to remove, or even sensibly to diminish. It is to the *legislature* of the state that we must look for a remedy to an evil, which is eating, like a cankerworm into the heart of the community, and rendering that structure of human society, which is so fair and glistening in its exterior form, full of dead mens' bones and all uncleanness within. What should forbid our legislature?—nay, but is it not their imperious duty, instantly, without the delay of a moment, as they regard the welfare, temporal and eternal, of the people committed to their trust, by the *Governor among the nations*, to put a stop to this great and growing evil, by the wise and wholesome restraint of efficient laws? Can it be deemed a sufficient objection to the diminution of these receptacles of vice and misery, that such a measure will lessen the *state revenue?* Are the guardians of the commonwealth, who are appointed to their high office for the express purpose of promoting the *well-being* of the people, to put into one scale a little paltry tax, and into the other the health, the industry, the morals, the prosperity, the happiness, of the great mass of the community, and make their miserable peppercorn of revenue weigh the heaviest? But for a moment, putting aside all reference to morality and religion, which however *ought* always to be the most powerful and conclusive arguments to the magistrates of a Christian country, the state revenue itself may be infinitely augmented by the increase of industry, social order, public and private wealth, which would instantly spring up from amidst the ruins of the present demoralizing system. Since writing the above, the *New-York Committee* have published a report, in which, with great wisdom and judgment, they state the evils, and point to the remedies of pauperism.

With regard to the manners of the United States, M. Volney, in the preface to his view of this country, says, " that he would dissuade his countrymen from settling here, because, although many facilities and benefits attend the establishment of English, Scots, Ger-

mans, and Hollanders, from the *resemblance* that prevails between their manners and habits, and those of
America, yet there are disadvantages and obstacles, from
a *contrariety* in these respects, attending natives of
France. There is nothing in the social forms and habits
of the two nations that can make them coalesce. They
tax us with levity, loquacity, and folly, while we reproach
them with coldness, reserve, and haughty taciturnity ;
with despising those sedulous and engaging civilities,
which we so highly value, and the want of which is
construed by us into proofs of unpoliteness in the individual, or of barbarism in the whole society. This
national incivility appears to flow from the mutual independence of each other, and the general equality, as
to fortune and condition, in which individuals in America are, for the most part, placed."

The truth however, is, that the United States exhibit
a *medium* of manners, between the rude vulgarity of the
lower orders, and the artificial refinement of the higher
classes in Europe. The great body of our people exhibit an erect manliness of behaviour, equally remote from
the brutal ferocity of a revolutionary ruffian, and the
elaborate politeness of a *petit maitre*. The only exces-
sively polite people we have are the *negroes*, who " *Sir
and Madam*" each other everlastingly ; and know no
other order amongst themselves than that of " *gentlemen and ladies*." Some of our young men who visit
Europe, on their return exhibit what they call fashionable European manners, that is to say, a studied *indifference* to all persons and things, as if politeness could
consist in the apparent absence of all sense and feeling.
These travellers, however, are soon compelled, either
to resume their native habits and manners, or to revisit
Europe, or to lounge away their lives in solitary idleness. For our people are almost universally employed
in some calling : the southern planters are lawyers and
politicians ; the northern, middle, and western states,
are employed in every variety of pursuit. And it generally happens that the sons of our opulent citizens become idle, good for nothing, and eventually paupers ;

while needy adventurers, from the country, urged by the twofold stimulus of necessity and ambition, gradually win the heights of political, legal, and commercial eminence.

Our wealthier classes, particularly in the large cities, exhibit as great an average of real politeness and good breeding, as the corresponding orders in Europe: for example, the *middle* class of Britain, whose intelligence, good manners, and virtue, have always been reckoned the bulwark and ornament of the empire, and which includes within its range the learned professions, the army and navy, the merchants, agriculturists, and men of letters. The incomes of our " decent livers," as they are called, reach from five hundred to ten thousand sterling a year; although very few individuals in the Union possess revenues so large as the latter sum indicates. Our American ladies are, in their persons lovely, in their manners easy and graceful, in conversation lively and sensible, in their various relations of wives, daughters, and mothers, exemplary and excellent. The aspect of society in the United States is somewhat clouded by the marvellous facility with which *foreigners*, of every sort, species, and complexion, gain access to our most respectable circles. A pattern-card, a pair of saddle-bags, and a letter of credit, appear to be all the qualifications necessary to enable the agents of European traders to mingle intimately with company in America, far superior to any that they could ever command in their own country.

Although the origin of the American people is not homogenous, yet the primary causes of their migration hither were similar; and the liberal freedom of their social institutions, their general intelligence, and common interests, have approximated their habits and manners so much, that, notwithstanding a comparatively small population is spread over an extensive territory, there are fewer provincial diversities of character and behaviour in the United States than in any other country. Nine-tenths of our people speak the same language, without any variety of dialect; which is, in itself, a bond of national unity, not to be found in any part of Europe; every different section of which, even in the same nation, speaks its own peculiar provincial *patois*. The laws, government, policy, interests, religion, and opinions of the inhabitants of all the different states essentially correspond and coincide. They are all bound together by the same mighty bands of political and commercial liberty. Our civil institutions, and religious toleration, tend to produce habits of intelligence and independence; we have no division into the higher, middle, and lower orders; we have no grandees, and we have no populace; we are all *people*.

Natural equality we cannot have, because some men will be taller, or stronger, or richer, or wiser than others, in spite of every effort of human legislation. But *political* equality we possess in a degree far superior to what has been known in any other country, ancient or modern. All our civil and religious institutions are framed in the spirit of social equality. By the high wages of labour, the abundance and facility of subsistence, the general diffusion of elementary education, and the right of universal suffrage, every man, not black, is a citizen, sensible of his own personal importance. Not more than *one* million of our people reside in the large cities and towns; the other nine millions live on farms or in villages: most of them are lords of the soil they cultivate, and some are wealthy. This subdivision of property, operating as a kind of Agrarian law, and aided by the abolition of the rights of primogeniture, the repeal of the statutes of entails, and the equal distribution of land and money among all the children, gives an individual independence and an equality of manner to our population, unknown in Europe; every country of which is yet deeply scared by the stabs and gashes of baronial dominion and feudal vassalage.

The personal independence which every one in the United States *may* enjoy, in *any* calling, by ordinary industry, and common prudence, is in itself one of the greatest of political blessings. So long as a man obeys that injunction of Scripture, to " owe no one any thing," (and in this country debt must arise from idleness, or vice, or misfortune, or folly,) he is as free as the air he breathes; he knows no superior, not even the President, whom his vote has either helped or hindered in the career of exaltation. But this personal independence can only be supported by a man's cleaving exclusively to his own calling, and diligently discharging its duties and demands; for the moment he wants the aid of his fellow-citizens, in *any* capacity or character, and has competitors for that aid, he is subjected to a scene of intrigue, electioneering, influence, and cabal, that would not have disgraced a conclave of cardinals, when the popedom was worth having.

Generally speaking, those are most attached to a country who own a part of its soil, and have therefore a stake in its welfare. But a great majority of the American people have this stake. In other countries low wages and unremitted labour stupefy the understanding, break the spirit, and vitiate the virtue of the great body of the population. In the United States the price of labour is high, and constant toil merely optional; but the ocean and the land offer continual incitements to industry, by opening inexhaustible regions of enterprise and wealth. In consequence, all is motion; every one follows some vocation, and the whole country is in perpetual progress; each industrious individual feels himself rising in the scale of opulence and importance; and the universal nation, growing with the growth of its aspiring children, hastens onward, with continually augmenting velocity, towards the maturity of resistless strength and unrivalled power.

A people so lately sprung from, and so closely connected with, Europe, must greatly resemble it in manners. But the universality of employment, and general equality of fortune, enable, and cause the Americans to steer equally clear af the luxurious refinement and the rude vulgarity of Europe. Hospitality and politeness are the common virtues of the United States. Mr. Birkbeck was peculiarly struck with the urbanity and civilization that prevail throughout this country, even in situations the most remote from our large cities. In his journey from Norfolk, on the Virginia coast, to the heart of the western country, he did not for a moment lose sight of the manners of civilized life. He found neither the excess of artificial refinement, nor the extreme of vulgarity, which exist in his own country. In every department of common life, he here saw employed persons far superior in education, habits, and manners, to the corresponding classes in England. He complains, however, that the taverns in the great towns east of the Alleghany mountains, which lay in their route westward, afforded nothing corresponding with their habits and notions of convenient accommodation, except the expense.

He says, that every thing in these places is gregarious; every thing is public by day and by night; for even the night affords no privacy in an American inn. Whatever be the number of guests, they must eat *in mass*, and sleep *in mass*. Three times a day, the great bell rings, and a hundred people rush from all quarters to eat a hurried meal, composed of fifty different dishes. The breakfast consists of fish, flesh, and fowl, bread, butter, eggs, coffee, and tea; the dinner resembles breakfast, with the omission of tea and coffee, and the addition of fermented liquors; the supper is a repetition of the breakfast. After which, the guests are crammed into rooms crowded with beds, like the wards of an hospital; where they undress in public, and generally receive a human partner in their bed, in addition to the myriads of *gentlemen in brown livery*, who occupy every house on a perpetual lease. Into the horrors of the kitchen of an American inn, with its darkness and negroes, and dirt, I have no appetite to follow Mr. Birkbeck, who, however, accounts properly for the independent air of the landlord, so entirely in contrast with the obsequious civility of an English tavern-keeper, by stating, that he is generally a man of property, cultivating his own farm, and a general, or colonel, or, at least, a captain of militia, and, consequently, feels himself fully as great as the guests whom he entertains, and behaves rather as if he confers than receives a favour, by accommodating them and their attendants, and receiving their money.

The political equality which pervades the United States opens all official ranks to all persons; and, accordingly, we have innkeepers, and tailors, and shoemakers, and retail shop-keepers, as well as merchants, and lawyers, and farmers, among our generals and colonels; whence arises that equal air of demeanor and manner that so much surprises Europeans who have been accustomed to the insolence of wealth and power on one hand, and to the servility of pauperism and dependence on the other. Besides, the Europeans generally do *not* receive so much civility from our taverners, because they are very apt to insult us by exaggerated comparisons of the marvellous superiority of European wisdom, convenience, comfort, elegance, and refinement, to those of the United States; and an American citizen, who is taught from his cradle to despise the nations of Europe, as paupers and slaves, is not very nice in showing his contempt at these sublimated parallels.

In another part of his notes, Mr. Birkbeck proceeds to offer the result of his own observations on the manners of that section of the Union which he saw; namely, part of the southern, and nearly the whole of the western division. He thinks, that as the Americans have no central focus of fashion, or local standard of politeness, no remote situation affords any apology for sordid apparel or coarse behaviour; and he found no examples of that rural simplicity, that embarrassed, awkward, sheepish air, so frequent among the peasantry, and even the farmers, of England. This self-possession he attributes very justly to the political equality of our people; the consciousness of which accompanies all their intercourse, and operates most powerfully on the manners of the lowest class. He complains, however, that *cleanliness*, in house and person, is neglected to a degree quite disgusting to an Englishman; and tells of court-houses in the western country, used as places of worship, in which

G g

all kinds of filth have been accumulating ever since they were built.

The truth is, the people of the southern and western states, generally speaking, are *not* cleanly either in their persons, or houses, or habits. The inhabitants of the New-England and middle states are, in general, given to cleanliness, particularly the Dutch settlers and their descendants. There is, however, one *very filthy* custom, which pervades the whole union; I mean the habit of eating and smoking tobacco. Our judges and lawyers, politicians and parsons, doctors and merchants, army and navy, farmers and mechanics, in a word, our whole people, from the president of the United States down to the pauper in the alms-house, smoke and chew tobacco, and abundantly eject its concocted juice in all places, at all times, and under all circumstances, without any remorse of conscience, or regard for the white draperies and finer sensibilities of our most delicate ladies; or for its execrable annoyance to all those who did not happen to be cradled in America. The late Mr. Gouverneur Morris, during his residence abroad, saw that the use of tobacco, save in the shape of snuff, was confined, in Europe, to the lowest orders of soldiers and sailors, boors and mechanics. On his return home, two of his male cousins began to question him on European habits and manners, keeping him all the while under the cross-fire of their segars. At length one of them said, " Mr. Morris, do the gentlemen in Europe smoke much?" " Sir," replied Mr. Morris, striking his *jambe de bois* sharply on the ground, " *Gentlemen* smoke in no country."

The *amusements* of the Americans do not exhibit so ferocious an aspect as those of the English; they being more addicted to dancing and music, than to bull-baiting, cock-fighting, and boxing. Not that the English are, really, more ferocious than the American people; but the United States either never adopted, or have laid aside, certain savage customs still preserved in England. Theatrical exhibitions, balls, routs, the sports of the field and turf, and the pleasures of the table, are the chief amusements of our people, and conducted much in the same way as in Europe; from which quarter we generally import our players, dancing-masters, singers, and musicians; such commodities, as yet, making no part of the staple of the United States. When Pericles was asked if he could play on any instrument, he answered, " No, I cannot fiddle, but I can make a little empire a great one." Our *routs* resemble those of London: we cram a hundred people into a room not large enough to contain fifty; making it, as an Irish member said of the House of Commons, after the union, " as full as it can hold, and *fuller*." They create human intercourse without human sympathy, and cut down all distinctions of talent and information to the dead level of frivolous vacuity. They seem entirely to have superseded, in our large cities, the good old family way of visiting friends and acquaintance, without ceremony, and without a tremendous invitation of six weeks ahead.

Marriages in the United States are earlier than in Europe; there being no constraint by statute, and no fear of not being able to maintain a family in so young a country, whose extensive territory offers an abundant provision to every species of industry, when regulated by discretion. Any clergyman of any sect, or any justice of the peace, may marry any couple without asking any questions. And, notwithstanding Dr. Johnson's sarcasm, " That marriages are made in haste, and repented of at leisure," celibacy is an unnatural, as well as an unsocial state:

> " For earthlier happy is the rose distill'd,
> Than that wh'ch withering on the virgin thorn,
> Lives, grows, and dies in single blessedness."

And, however the yearnings of ambition, or the pursuits of learning, or the occupations of business may, for a time, absorb a vigorous spirit, yet every man, in whose heart the charities of life are not extinguished, nor the milk of human kindness dried up, wishes, before he falls into the sere and yellow leaf of autumn, that his blood may run in the veins of some living thing; and that his age may be surrounded by those whose affection and reverence may double unto him the delight of well-earned reputation and honour. For all the purposes of connubial happiness, *early* marriages are best fitted, because the youthful pair have time, and opportunity, and power, gradually, to mould themselves to each other's temper, and disposition, and habits, and manners; whereas, later marriages require much good temper, good sense, and, above all, confirmed domestic habits on both sides, to render the union happy; because the character of both parties is already fixed, and not capable of that flexile adaptation to the circumstances of life, so characteristic of ardent and ingenuous youth. Perhaps, within the whole compass of human learning, there is not a more pathetic appeal to the heart, than when Eliza says to Dido, "Nec dulces natos, Veneris nec præmia noras."

Marriages, in the United States, are not only contracted at an early age, but, in general, from disinterested motives. Indeed, owing to our social institutions and habits, individual fortunes are seldom sufficiently large, compared with the overgrown family opulence of Europe, to induce mere money matches, where the estates, not the parties, are united. There is no fear with us of the proverb, so commonly levelled in England against sentimental affection, that love in a cottage generally ends in the cottage without love; because any man, in any calling, if he be industrious, honest, and careful, may make ample provision for his wife and children. With us, the sanctity of the marriage bed is seldom profaned; nor is seduction frequent. The familiar, but innocent, intercourse of the sexes renders American society peculiarly interesting and delightful. It is not confined, either before or after marriage, as in some parts of Europe, to a narrow circle of exclusive aristocracy, where the portion, and not the person, is the object of affection. In the United States it is unrestrained, chaste, and honourable. Our well-educated and virtuous women are kindly and affectionately treated by their husbands, loved and reverenced by their children, and respected by society—of which they compose the brightest ornament and honour. Hence it is, that without pretending to so high a polish of elaborate and artificial refinement as some of the selecter societies in Europe exhibit, the United States display a more general urbanity and civilization than are to be found in any other country.

An extensive territory, a fertile soil, a good climate, are all well calculated to afford abundant means of subsistence, to quicken the growth of population, to ensure the health, activity, and strength of the human species. The occupations of agriculture, the ranging in the woods for game, the locomotive and migratory habits of the Americans, have all a direct tendency to impart agility and strength to the sinews and muscles of the body. An *increasing* and *efficient* population does not depend, however, merely upon the multitude of early marriages, and frequency of births, but chiefly upon the great proportion of children that are born being reared to maturity. In the United States the marriages average *six* births, of which *four* are reared. Mr. Storch, in his " *Historico Statistical Picture of the Russian Empire*," says the boors in Russia have generally *twelve* children to one marriage, of which seldom more than *one-fourth* are reared. This great mortality among the children, occasioned, no doubt, by hardship and want on the part of the peasantry, caused Catharine the Second to complain, in her celebrated " *Instructions*," to her different ministers, and ask of them the causes, why " this hope of the government is defeated?" Now, the political doctors of Russia ought to have informed their mistress, that the only wise institutions by which the evil could be remedied, would be the establishment of such a frame of civil society, as to secure permanent liberty, public and private, by equitable laws, a regular administration of justice, the general diffusion of sentiments of personal respectability, moral restraint, reli-

gious feeling, industry, sobriety, and cleanliness, among
the people.

Wherever these social blessings occur, there never
will be, necessarily and of course, that is to say, without
the intervention of epidemics and fatal diseases, any
very great mortality among the children born in *any*
country; because in old and long-established nations,
where the population presses hard upon the means of
subsistence, the marriages will be late, the births proportionally few, and the children generally reared to
man's estate; and in a young country, as in these United States, where these social blessings do actually exist,
where the means of subsistence are abundant, and there
is plenty of land to give elbow-room for a rapid increase
of population, the marriages will be early, the births
frequent, and most of the children reared.

M. Volney, in his "*View*" of the United States, emphatically notices the idle, babbling, uneffectual life of a
colony of French farmers in the western country, when
contrasted with the patient, plodding industry of the
Scottish, English, and German agriculturists in the same
neighbourhood; and more especially when contrasted
with the far superior activity and enterprise of the native American settlers in reclaiming the waste and wilderness from the dominion of the beasts of the forest,
making the valleys wave thick with the teeming grain,
and causing the solitary places to blossom as the rose.
Indeed, these United States possess unrivalled advantages for promoting a rapid increase of their inhabitants;
and also for rearing *a most efficient* population; so that,
if America shall spring forward during the next, with
the same velocity and force with which she has moved
progressively during the last fifty years, she will then
whiten every sea with her commercial canvass; bear her
naval thunders in triumph to earth's extremest verge;
peer above the sovereignty of other nations, and cause
the elder world to bow its venerable head, white with
the hoar of ages, beneath the paramount power and influence of this younger daughter of the civilized globe.

The habits and manners of the United States are considerably influenced by the eager appetite for the acquisition of wealth, which is necessarily the great absorbing passion of all new and thinly settled countries; and also by the perpetual proneness to mingle in the party-politics of the day, which is the natural consequence of our popular and democratic institutions. Of course, these pursuits prevail most in the large cities on our seaboard, because they afford the greatest facilities of commercial enterprise, and the busiest scene of political exertion. Yet the *trading spirit* is diffused over all the country: our farmers, mechanics, soldiers, seamen, lawyers, legislators, physicians, nay, sometimes, even our clergy, indulge in mercantile speculations. Even politics themselves give way to the universal desire of speedily amassing money. The peculiar circumstances of the Union have conspired to foster the growth of this trading spirit. During five and twenty years, while war impoverished and wasted Europe, commerce enriched the United States with a rapidity, and to an extent unexampled in the history of nations. Since the peace of 1815, indeed, the diminution of our foreign trade, and the incredible number of insolvencies, *ought* to teach us both to moderate our eager craving after wealth, and that extravagance of expenditure far surpassing the rate of living among the corresponding classes in Europe, which has been almost the necessary effect of our sudden and unexampled opulence.

America has profited in more ways than one by British capital; that is to say, she has grown rich, not merely by the amount and length of credit which the merchants of Britain have given her, but also by her own numberless insolvents, having made it a point of conscience never to pay a single stiver to a British creditor. From the peace of 1783 to 1789, the British manufacturers did not receive more than *one-third* of the value of all the goods which they sold to their American customers; and since the peace of 1815, up to the present hour, they have not received *one-fourth*. This horrible piracy upon British property is supported, if not created, by our system of *state insolvent* laws. No honest man can devise a valid reason why Congress should not exert its constitutional power of passing a uniform bankrupt act, and thus give our foreign creditors some chance of an occasional dividend. At present, every state has its own insolvent law, that is to say, there are twenty different legal modes of evading the payment of debts in the Union. According to the present system, the creditor has no security for the recovery of his money but the personal honesty of his debtor, which, sometimes, is *not* the best of all possible bonds. If the debtor thinks the money better in his own pocket than in that of his creditor, he has twenty different governments out of which to select the theatre best fitted for the purposes of fraud and knavery. And, to speak tenderly of our insolvents, they seem to understand their business very well.

As a natural consequence of the sudden influx of wealth into the United States, too many of the Americans have departed from the salutary habits of *economy* which characterized their English and Dutch ancestors, and have become the most extravagant people on earth. In proportion to its wealth and population, our city of New-York far surpasses all the rest of the civilized world in its rate of expenditure and amount of insolvencies, of which last, upwards of *six thousand* occurred in 1811. It costs, at least, one-third more to live here than in London ; which, on the whole, is perhaps the dearest place in Europe. To be sure, there is no occasion in this country to feel that perpetual anxiety about pecuniary matters, which is entailed upon all the people in England, excepting a few overgrown capitalists, by the enormous expenditure of the government, and the pressure of universal taxation. But our people, generally, and particularly in the large cities, have fallen into habits of personal and family expense, not only far surpassing those of the corresponding classes in Europe, but also far exceeding the fair earnings of our merchants and professional men; many of whom become their own executors, and leave their children paupers, and the more helpless for having been brought up in idleness and extravagance. It is the more surprising that the Americans should hasten to impoverish themselves with such heedless prodigality ; because, as there is neither birth nor rank in the United States, wealth is our only mark of distinction : it is, in fact, our great social virtue, as poverty is the unpardonable crime; and in no part of the world is the learned pate required to duck to the golden fool with more obsequious servility than in our free and independent republic.

But well-regulated *economy*, equally removed from parsimony on one hand, and from extravagance on the other, is alike the basis of all domestic independence and comfort, and of all national wealth and prosperity. Women can seldom *earn*, but they may often *save* a fortune by judicious management. The American ladies, however, are not generally taught the importance and use of economy. And it requires more moral nerve than most men possesses to practise frugality amidst the surrounding extravagance of the whole neighbourhood. Whence, a man's own personal and domestic vanity, seconded by the eternal exhortations of his wife and daughters, leads too many of our respectable families into that poverty, which, in itself, is one of the greatest of all social evils, which neither prevents nor softens any other evil, but exasperates and darkens all other calamities. Of course, no one in his senses supposes that the rich and the poor are to live according to the same rate of penurious expenditure, since the magnificence of the opulent puts in motion a considerable amount of productive industry and ingenuity, and is a better mode of distributing money, by employing the labouring classes, than by giving it as alms. Nor is it any part of sound philosophy for men of talents to live like ascetics, or self-denying monks, under pretence of being abstracted from the allurements of time and sense. When Descartes was dining with the Stadtholder of Holland, the worthy Dutch magistrate observed the metaphysician demolish the dessert with indefatigable perseverance, and bawled out : " What ! does a *philo-*

sopher eat ice, and creams, and sweetmeat ?"   " Why,"
answered Descartes, " should your highness think that
all the good things of this world were made only for
blockheads ?"

In addition to the general extravagance, there are
other causes which prevent the accumulation of *family*
wealth in the United States.   The abolition of the statute of entails, and of the common law of descent, prevents the formation of new, and ensures the extinction
of old families.   There are scarcely a dozen of the ancient Dutch and British stocks now remaining in the
city of New-York.   Say, an industrious frugal man
amasses wealth, by a long life of successful trade or
laborious law, or lucky land-jobbing ; he dies, and all
his property is divided among his children ; of which
a large squadron is generally left, and the share of each
is about enough to make them all idle, and not sufficient
to afford a decent independence.   In numerous instances they sink eventually into paupers, and new men
from the country gradually rise into eminence and
wealth, and leave their offspring to run a course of idleness, folly, extravagance, and ruin.   Whence, a perpetual fluctuation of property and of family takes place
throughout the Union.   Some great men in Europe,
among whom Mr. Burke is one of the most conspicuous,
have undertaken to demonstrate that the power of *perpetuating* property is essentially necessary to give
strength and ballast to a nation, and link the present
with the past and future generations of men.   But this
right of primogeniture was known only to the artificial,
unnatural state of society called the feudal system.   And
it seems contrary to the first principles of natural justice,
that the eldest son should take all the real estate, and
the other children be left destitute, for no other crime
than being younger than he.   This scheme also bears
peculiarly hard upon the daughters, who are doubly
helpless, on account of their luxurious habits as well as
their poverty.

Strictly speaking, there is no such thing as *social subordination* in the United States.   Parents have no com-

mand over their children, nor teachers over their scholars, nor lawyers, nor physicians, over their pupils, nor farmers over their labourers, nor merchants over their clerks, carmen, and porters, nor masters over their servants. All are equal, all do as they list, and all are free *not* to work, except the master, who must be himself a slave if he means his business to prosper, for he has no control over any other head, eyes, or hands, than his own. Owing, perhaps, to the very popular nature of our institutions, the American children are seldom taught that profound reverence for, and strict obedience to, their parents, which are at once the basis of domestic comfort, and of the welfare of the children themselves. Of course, where there is no parental authority, there can be no discipline in schools and colleges. If a preceptor presume to strike, or effectually punish a boy, he most probably loses at least one scholar, perhaps more. And as no inconvenience attaches to a boy's being expelled from school or college, the teachers have no authority, nor learning any honour, in the United States.

Nay, the independence of children on their parents is carried so far, as to raise doubts if a father or mother has *any right* to interfere in the marriage of a son or daughter. A few weeks since, this question was publicly discussed at one of our New-York debating clubs, for the edification of a numerous audience, both male and female, and it was determined by a stout majority that in a free and enlightened republic, children are at liberty to marry whom they please, without any interference on the part of the parents, either in the shape of advice or command, or otherwise; and for this most sagacious reason, that the child, and not the parent, is about to commit matrimony; it being quite an exploded prejudice, that parents can have any possible concern in the welfare and happiness of their offspring. This doctrine, doubtless, is palatable to every needy and unprincipled adventurer, who wishes to persuade some silly daughter of an opulent father to accompany him to the next trading justice, who, for a few shillings, will perform the marriage ceremony, and consign her to a husband, and disgrace, and misery, for life.

There is no such relation as *master and servant* in the United States: indeed, the name is not permitted :— " *help*" is the designation of one who condescends to receive wages for service. This help is generally afforded by free blacks, and Irish ; our natives seldom lowering the dignity of free-born republicans so much, as to enter a house in the capacity of servants. Even Mr. Birkbeck, who is so much enamoured of our democracy, is somewhat troubled at what he calls the bigotted aversion of the Americans to domestic service ; and that they, confounding the term servant with that of slave, should prefer keeping their children at home, in idleness, and often in rags, when they might be profitably and pleasantly employed in attending upon their more affluent fellow citizens. He concludes with the discovery, that if a gentleman wishes to be waited on and served in the United States, he must wait upon and serve himself; which is true enough. I remember, at Boston, a few years since, the mistress of the house where I lodged desired her negro man to go on some errand for her : the answer was, " I cannot, for I am engaged to meet some gentlemen and ladies (all negroes), at an assembly this evening, in —— street." And the lady was obliged to have her service unperformed, while a stout fellow, to whom she gave twelve dollars a month wages, was regaling himself at a black ball in the neighbourhood.

The *national vanity* of the United States surpasses that of any other country, not even excepting France. It blazes out every where, and on all occasions, in their conversation, newspapers, pamphlets, speeches, and books. They assume it as a self-evident fact, that the Americans surpass all other nations in virtue, wisdom, valour, liberty, government, and every other excellence. All Europeans they profess to despise, as ignorant paupers and dastardly slaves. Even during President Washington's administration, Congress debated three days upon the important position, that "America was the *most enlightened* nation on earth;" and finally decided the affirmative by a small majority. At the breaking out of the late war with England, General Moreau, who then resided in this city, was asked if our officers did not seek to avail themselves of his military skill and experience, by propounding questions to him? He replied, "there is not an ensign in the American army who does not consider himself a much greater tactician than General Moreau." And our present President, in his recent tour through the Union, told the people of Kennebunk, in the district of Maine, "that the United States were certainly the most enlightened nation in the world."

The causes of this national vanity are obvious; our popular institutions, vesting the national sovereignty in the people, have a direct tendency to make that people self-important and vain. Add to which, the incessant flattery they receive in newspapers, and public talks, about their collective majesty, wisdom, power, dignity, and so forth; their unexampled prosperity in the occupations of peace; and lastly, their actual achievements in war. Twice have they grappled, in deadly encounter, with the most powerful, the bravest, and the most intelligent nation in Europe; and twice have they triumphed over the most skilful commanders, and best appointed troops of that nation, in the battlefield, and on the ocean.

The result of all is, that the American people possess physical, intellectual, and moral *materials* of national greatness, *superior* to those of any other country; and in order to render the United States the *greatest nation* in the world, they have only gradually to augment the power of their general government; to tighten the cords, and strengthen the stakes of their federal union; to organize a judicious system of *internal* finance; to provide for the more general diffusion of religious worship; to enlarge and elevate their system of liberal education; to increase the dimensions, and exalt the standard of their literature, art, and science.

CONCLUSION.

In order to show the necessity of radically strengthening and vigorously administering the general government of the United States, the remaining pages will be devoted to exhibiting an eye-glance of the present condition of Europe, and its probable consequences to the world at large, and to this country in particular.

What portion of Europe, insular or continental, promises a continuance of repose? Does *France*, with a feeble throne, recently reinstated, amidst a discontented, mortified, vain, unprincipled people, torn to pieces by contending factions, and bent to the earth by the increasing difficulties of her finance? Can England alone, reeling as she is beneath the weight of her own burden, stem the tide of that revolutionary fury which pervades Europe from the Tagus to the Neva, and threatens, once more, to dissolve the elements of social order, and roll into ruin those principalities and powers which have been so recently restored or elevated to their present eminence? In Italy, in Germany, in Poland, and in the United Netherlands, all seems to be disjointed; every thing is afloat; the ancient boundaries and landmarks of kingdoms are removed; the people are transferred, like herds of cattle, from one master to another, and all their feelings, passions, and prejudices kept in a state of continual ferment and exasperation.

The shock occasioned by twenty-five years of revolutionary conflict has been too violent, to permit the mere re-establishment of the old dynasties to produce a secure and permanent repose. Two of the main props of European society have been grievously impaired; namely, the influence of the intermediate bodies, or orders, and the balance of power. The importance of the clergy and nobility, as component parts of the state or commonwealth, has been too much diminished, ever to recover its former weight and strength. For want of the influence of these intermediate bodies, which, prior to the French revolution, served at once to secure to the sovereign the respect and obedience of his people, and to the people mildness and moderation on the part of the sovereign, it is to be feared that Europe now will perpetually oscillate between the struggles and triumphs of sedition and despotism. The only ground of hope for European peace would be the extension of the *representative* system, which might enlighten the executive councils, strengthen the authority of the sovereign, establish and preserve the liberties of the people.

For political revolutions are always occasioned, or preceded by disaffection in the great mass of the community ; and ambitious and profligate men, consulting only their own interests, would in vain labour to produce a national convulsion, if the people were contented, and at ease. By what possible means could any unprincipled demagogues incite the American people to a revolution, in their present happy and prosperous state ? Moderation, justice, and an easy yoke can, alone, give stability and permanence to governments. But the danger is, that, after so terrible an explosion, a spirit of distrust or resentment, and the predilection for arbitrary power, which is too common with *all* rulers, whether imperial, or monarchal, or republican, may lead the governments of Europe to adopt maxims of severity and restraint—the necessary consequence of which, in the present feverish state of the world, must be a perilous popular reaction, that nothing but magnanimity and mildness in the ruling powers can either avert or disarm, when once excited. This revolutionary reaction, an incident of human nature, in all ages and countries, but peculiarly characteristic of the present period of insurgency and turbulence, the wisdom and forecast of every good government will labour not to provoke. In the present generation, certainly, and perhaps in the next following, there will be great danger of this reaction. Its symptoms, in various gradations of violence and force, have already broken out, under the popular monarchy of England, the, as yet, undefined sovereignty of France, the senseless, imbecile despotism of Spain, the limited and guarded government of the United Netherlands, and some of the smaller Italian and German principalities.   The military sway of Russia, Austria, and Prussia, have, hitherto, kept down this natural insurgency against all arbitrary rule in their subjects, whose reaction, however, will be the more terrible, in proportion to the protracted resistance of their respective governments, to the introduction of a representative system and popular institutions.

Notwithstanding the re-establishment of the old dynasties, the *balance of power*, in Europe, cannot be restored, as it existed prior to the French revolution, when Austria, and England, and Russia, were generally ranged on the same sides, in order to counterpoise the ascendency of France, and the growing greatness of Prussia.   The system of equilibrium is, at all times, and now more than ever, merely a system of provident jealousy for the great powers ;   than for those of a secondary order, it arises out of the necessity of a mutual support against the encroachments of over-bearing neighbours.   A slight eye-glance at the present condition of Europe, will show at once that it is not easy to regulate the balance of power in that quarter of the world ; nor probable that peace and harmony can be long maintained among its different sovereigns.

The course of the smaller states will, as heretofore, be determined by that of the primary powers.   *Prussia* has only a population of *ten* or *eleven* millions, scattered over a disjointed territory, that has neither frontier nor centre ; a population too, multiform and dissonant, not bound together in themselves, or towards their government, by long habits of kindred feeling, and loyal attachment.   Its government is purely military, and, consequently, ill adapted to the present tendencies towards popular representation and sovereignty, that prevail all over Christendom.   The Emperor Joseph the Second used to say, in reference to Prussia, " if she be ever pressed vigorously by a powerful neighbour, she will find that an army and an exchequer are *not* a nation."

Austria numbers a population of nearly *thirty* millions, but her dominions are scattered over Germany, Poland, and Italy; her Italian and Polish subjects are not well affected; her fine provinces of Hungary, Bohemia, Styria, Carinthia, and Gallicia, in themselves capable of developing vast resources, and maintaining an immense number of inhabitants, are so strangely mismanaged as to be comparatively in a state of nature, and unproductive;—whereas, if well regulated, they, together with the hereditary dominions of Austria, might supply the Austrian government with a sufficient force in men and money, to enable it to stride the balance, and preserve the equipoise of Europe. But the government of Austria is inert and feeble, her finances are shattered, and her people have not enough of the redeeming spirit of liberty in them to enable her to stay the progress of the Giant of the North, when he rises to direct his steps towards the supremacy of Europe.

The physical advantages of Spain are at least equal to those of any country in Europe. Her localities are admirably calculated to make her a great and predominating nation. Placed as she is between the ocean and the Mediterranean, and bulwarked in by the Pyrenean mountains on the only side where she touches the European continent; with a territory covering a hundred and fifty thousand square miles, and blessed with an abundant soil and luxuriant climate; rich in all navigable capacities; containing a population of *twelve* millions of inhabitants, and able to maintain, under a due culture of the land, and a well administered government, at least *thirty* millions of souls; with a numerous peasantry, patient, hardy, and bold; with mountaineers, vigilant, active, and intrepid; with borderers on the ocean, expert, adventurous, invincible seamen. Previous to the battle of Rocroi, the Spanish infantry was the best in Europe ; and, even now, after her long night of darkness, ignorance, and superstition, Spain has only to develope the *mind* of her children, by the free and general diffusion of art, science, and literature, in order to enable her to rank in power, influence, and renown, with the most civilized and illustrious nations of the earth.

But Spain is an awful instance, *e contrario*, of the truth of the position, that the strength, prosperity, and greatness of a country are intimately connected with the liberty and intelligence of its people. *Human reason* is *not* the ability or the effort of any one human being; but it is the great result of the learning and reflection of numbers, arising from the intellectual lights, mutually communicated, and examined, either verbally, or in writing, and, consequently, human reason itself, is just in its conceptions, clear, profound, and comprehensive in its views, precisely in proportion to the number of generally educated and well informed minds that are actively employed, at any given period of the world, in exploring and disseminating the lights of science and literature, throughout those sections of the earth which the rays of knowledge are permitted to penetrate. Hence, the enormous difference between the actual power and information of the human mind, in different ages and countries. At one time and place, the intellect of man blazes forth in excessive strength and splendour over all the horizon—at another place and period, it is only dimly discerned in the distance, darkling in ignorance and superstition, upon the borders of chaos and old night.

Hence the necessity of affording to the great mass of the people of every community the means of elementary instruction; if the nation desires to be permanently prosperous and powerful in the general activity of its intelligence; employed and guided by the superintendence of the few *master spirits* that are created the natural guardians of the age in which they live; the beacons and bulwarks of the country they adorn. This is most necessary, because as native talent is scattered by the Almighty with an impartial hand, among the children of men, the greater portion of natural genius must always be produced amidst the lower and poorer orders of society; precisely for this reason, that they *are* the most numerous class of the community; and an *illiterate* nation is almost entirely deprived of the means of unfolding its native capacities into strength and precision, by its inability to approach the fountains of information.

In the year 1808, it was required of the universal Spanish nation to rise in resistance to the most atrocious, and most formidable invasion of their rights and claims as a people: they were called upon to strain every bodily nerve, to direct every ray of intellect, to devote every pulsation of the heart, in physical and moral fearlessness, against their terrible and remorseless enemy. Nor were the people of Spain wanting in patriotic ardour and courage; they listened to their country's call, and pressed forward with one heart, and one accord, to dedicate themselves, body, soul, and spirit, to rescue the soil of their nativity, the bones of their fathers, their wives, and their little ones, from the grasp of the invader. But Spanish courage was *not* seconded by Spanish intellect. The *mind* of Spain had been stifled in the sink of ignorance, through the lapse of centuries; and more especially during all the reigns of the Bourbon dynasty. So that in the year 1808, at the bursting forth of the revolution, the want of previous general education exceedingly narrowed and crippled all the national efforts. The Spanish nobles, generally, were immersed in ignorance, sloth, and profligacy; the great body of the people were unacquainted with even the simplest rudiments of instruction ; they could neither write nor read; the little miserable information that was afloat was confined to the *clergy*, and consisted chiefly of the scholastic theology, and inquisitorial sophistry and cruelty of the dark and barbarous ages.

So great indeed was the dearth of native *disciplined* talent in Spain, that for more than a century preceding the revolution her government had been principally directed by *foreigners* as ministers of state; obscure adventurers, Irish, Scottish, Italian, and French, who were hangers-on about the court, and supplied the want of Spanish intelligence, by their own superior address and skill. Spain, perhaps, is the only instance on the record of nations, of a country of any extent, power, and influence, being so extremely deficient in all general education, as to be obliged to have recourse to obscure foreigners to administer her finances, and guide her political movements. Owing to this ignorance of the community, retarding and confining the growth and operations of native talent, the whole seven years of peninsular warfare passed away without Spain's being able to produce a single first-rate warrior, one superior

statesman, a solitary efficient engineer, a profound financier, an able negociator; any one individual, of great
and comprehensive genius, to redeem his country from
civil and military death. All her *own* fighting was hill
and glen, and partisan warfare. No military tactics
were displayed on a large scale by the Spanish commanders. Her colonial governments, also, were still
suffered to labour under all the vices of the old mal-
administration. Such were the political and military
defects of Spain, in consequence of her extreme and
general ignorance, that in all probability she must have
sunk for ever under the superior mind and means of
France, had not Britain interposed between her and
ruin; had not the British armies, by their skill and prowess, vanquished the most accomplished generals, and the
best appointed, and most highly disciplined veterans of
Napoleon.

Nor were they wiser in their *civil* than in their military capacity; for they passed in what they called their
new government, from the extreme of single despotism,
under which they were afflicted by their Bourbon kings,
into the other extreme of many-headed democracy.
The Spanish *Constitution*, fabricated in the year 1812,
gives to the King much less positive power than the
federal constitution bestows upon the President of the
United States: only *one* legislative assembly is allowed;
the order of nobility, or hereditary aristocracy, is not
even recognized; no senate is established; and the press
is placed under the guardianship of a committee. A
worse government could not be devised, than one in
which the executive power is weak and unsupported;
where there exists no senate, no permanent representative body to interpose its check, its weight of property,
character, and talent, between the pressure of the single executive, and the fluctuations of the immediate and
temporary representatives of the people; where nearly
all the power of the country, executive, legislative, and
judicial, is engrossed by the House of Representatives,
the single branched Cortes, which is filled up *by rotation*,
alike from the inhabitants of Old Spain and Spanish
America; and all the members chosen for so short a

period of service, that the peninsular representatives could not possibly become acquainted with the national wants, and the means of remedying them ; and the Hispano-American members would perform the whole of their legislative functions, in the act of sailing backward and forward upon the Atlantic Ocean. This single-handed representative assembly was the chief wreck-rock of the French revolution. The observations of Mr. Burke upon this subject ought to be treasured up in the remembrance of every political student.

The return of Ferdinand the Seventh, in the year 1814, put an end to this strange constitutional medley, and restored to the Spaniards the blessings of the Inquisition, and of a despotism at once cruel and weak, alike terrible and despicable ; from the effects of which nothing short of a popular revolution can rescue Spain. Such a revolution, *well conducted,* (of which, indeed, the hope is very faint,) might eventually render that country a first-rate power ; by establishing a *free* government, with full religious toleration, giving to each Christian sect and denomination equal political rights and privileges, with a free press, permitting every man to publish what he pleases, with *no other* control than the subsequent animadversions of a jury of his countrymen; with a strong well-guarded executive ; a permanent senate, comprising the aristocracy of property, talent, and character ; a powerful democratic branch of the legislature, immediately representing the great mass of the people ; each of these three branches, the executive, senate, and house of representatives, having a legislative check upon each other's proceedings ; with an independent, enlightened judiciary, appointed by the executive, and not removable, except from malconduct ; with a numerous, well-appointed regular army; an extensive and formidable navy ; a skilfully organized system of taxation; a wide and enterprising foreign commerce; and above all, free scope and full protection for every individual citizen to better his condition by the unrestrained exertions of his own industry, skill, and genius, in whatever occupation he may choose, without the intervention of *poor*-laws, or the bondage of *apprenticeships.*

France has, for several centuries, been a great and formidable power; she has always maintained a military predominance in Europe, both by her arms and by her language, giving names and terms to every species of military tactics. Shorn of her beams as she now is, and somewhat narrowed in her territory, she still retains the means of reappearing as a primary power, when a few years of peace shall have enabled her to repair her shattered finances, and recruit her exhausted population. In addition to her valuable colonial possessions she has a compact home territory, covering a surface of more than 250,000 square miles, and containing a population of nearly *thirty* millions of souls, and situated in the very heart and centre of Europe. The climate is excellent, and the soil fertile; the political strength of the country is greatly augmented by the annihilation of the monasteries and convents, and the resumption of their endowments; by the sale and consequent cultivation of the national and ecclesiastical domains; the great royal and signorial forests, parks, pleasure-grounds, and chases; by the subdivision of the large estates into small farms, and their transfer to persons possessing more capacity and inclination for improvement than had distinguished the former feudal proprietors.

Add to this the consolidation of her municipal laws into one national code; whereas, before the revolution, every different province had its distinct system of laws; a circumstance that materially thwarted the equal administration of justice, impeded the circulation of property, clogged the growth of productive industry, and obstructed the progress towards national improvement, opulence, and strength. The country, likewise, is more thickly crowded with military institutions, that at once diffuse a greater eagerness for a soldier's life, and render the means of carrying on offensive warfare more abundant and more effectual. And above all, France is rendered more formidable to every civilized community, by the increased activity, restlessness, spirit of injustice, rapine, insolence, and oppression, which the revolution has engendered and established.

The contra-indications to the exhibition of vast national power by France, are the exhaustion of her *effective* population ; that is to say, her men able to bear arms, by the waste of twenty-five years of sanguinary warfare; the entire derangement of her national system of finance ; the annihilation of her foreign commerce; the destruction of her military marine ; the disabling of her internal manufactures; the general impoverishment of the country, by the military contributions, and armies of occupation of the allied sovereigns. Nevertheless, a few years of prudent domestic government, aided by the prodigious natural advantages of the country, would be sufficient to repair all these national breaches. But the *moral* evils of France cannot so easily be healed. The extreme prevalence of infidelity, profligacy, fraud, and cruelty, for so many years, has nearly stifled all public spirit. During the several revolutionary usurpations, all noble sentiments were opposed; every generous and manly opinion was ridiculed and proscribed. These governments, both republican and imperial, were not contented with condemning to inaction the virtues which they dreaded; but they excited and fomented all the bad passions, whose exercise they wanted for the furtherance of their own nefarious designs.

In order to obliterate the traces of public spirit, these revolutionary governments tampered with the personal interests of individuals; they silenced the still small voice of conscience, amidst the uproar of tumultuous ambition; they made every condition of life intolerable, except that of devotedness to themselves; they suffered no hopes to live, save those alone which they chose to gratify ; they industriously taught that no ambition, however boundless, on the part of the *great nation*, could be improper ; that no pretensions, however arrogant, could be exaggerated. Hence, revolutionary France presented a scene, in which was exhibited an incessant agitation of interests, wishes, hopes, and desires, among all classes of people: nothing was permanent; nothing was quiet; all was commotion, all was change; the instability of every situation left to no man the performance of the duties, or the practice of the virtues of his condition, because he thought of emerging from it as speedily as possible. In a word, a universal battery was incessantly kept up against religion, morals, common honesty, all that can cheer private life, or adorn public conduct, by such seductions of power, fraud, pleasure, and corruption, as the virtue of revolutionary Frenchmen was not sturdy enough to withstand.

France, therefore, is yet an unextinguished volcano, from whose burning crater probably will be again thrown out the smoke, and flame, and northern lava of desolation upon all the surrounding nations.

At the bursting out of the French revolution, in the year 1789, the *mind* of France was in a state of high cultivation, at least, so far as regards mere intellectual acquisition, without respect to religious and moral culture; that is to say, in the physical sciences, in arts, and letters. At that period, too, the *people* of France, generally, felt an eager enthusiasm for liberty; and, although this popular disposition was afterward most flagitiously abused, by unprincipled demagogues and military despots, yet it did then exist in a very high state of sublimation; and perhaps a portion of this republican feeling still survives all the horrors of the revolution. Prior to this awful epoch the French press had been busily employed, for more than half a century, in disseminating throughout all France the *dead-lights* of infidelity and jacobinism. The whole public mind was in agitation. The very princes of the blood royal professed the *new* philosophy, while the king himself was poring over the pages of ancient history; the nobles encouraged the progress of atheism; the clergy had pretty generally discovered popery to be a grave farce, and many of them took refuge from the mummery of superstition in profligate unbelief of all religion; the *sçavans*, the literati, had persuaded themselves that none but men of talents ought to govern France, and that they themselves were the only men of talents in the community; the negotiators of France were intriguing with, disturbing, and influencing every court in Chris-

tendom ; the great body of the people were made drunk
with dilirious notions of vague, unattainable, impracticable liberty.

All the talent of this fine populous country was in
tumultous movement.   In this critical state of things,
this precise juncture of affairs, the revolution exploded;
and levelled every barrier of the French government ;
beat down every bulwark of habit, rank, order, and
establishment ; and let loose all the mighty mass of native and diciplined talent of twenty-seven millions of
the most active, ingenious, restless, turbulent, and unprincipled people in Europe, to prey upon their neighbours first, and then to disturb and set fire to the four
corners of the world.   Situated in the centre of continental Europe, girt round about on all sides with a
triple frontier of unassailable fortresses ; full, to the
overflowing, of a people, abounding in military genius
and science, and yearning after an increase of their
already great patrimony of military renown, France,
almost immediately after the first eruption of her revolution, poured forth her armed myriads from all quarters, north, east, west, and south, and soon overran,
with her victorious legions, Holland, Spain, Italy, the
German principalities on the Rhine, Switzerland, Prussia, Austria, Poland, and the borders of Russia.   She
out-fought all her opponents, by the ascendency of her
military talents and tactics ; she out-negotiated all other
nations, by the depth and subtlety of her dexterous diplomacy ; she domineered over all the earth by the
weight and reach of her political interlect.   France,
springing upward, as a tiger from its thicket, and shak-
ing from off her shoulders the shackles of a feeble,
worn-out government, poured out her impetuous and
unrestrained *mind* in political and military movements,
that shook all Europe to its foundations, and struck a
blow of destruction at the pillars of human society, from
the horrible effects of which the whole fabric of the
universe is, even now, reeling.

By what magical charm or incantation is the Congress of Vienna to find a remedy for the healing of all
the complicated, radical evils imposed upon Europe,

by five and twenty years of revolutionary cruelty and conflict? How is it to re-adjust the balance of power in that quarter of the globe; how to restore harmony; how to ensure the continuance of repose and peace, amidst the jarring elements of disorder and contention?

Is *Russia* to be the grand pacificator? Is Alexander " the Deliverer" to perpetuate the blessings of peace over all the circumference of Christendom? Russia has a home territory of nearly *four* millions of square miles; is unassailable in flank and rear, and presents a most formidable frontier to the rest of Europe. More than five-sixths of her population inhabit her European dominions, which number nearly *fifty* millions of souls. She is also susceptible of indefinite augmentation, by the growth of wealth, people, and power, on account of her natural means, existing in the prodigious extent of her dominion, and the variety of its soil, climate, and productions. Its government uses every effort to improve the essential strength of the country, and to direct its force towards ulterior aggrandizement, by the diffusion of arts and sciences, by the liberal rewards given to talents and learning, whether found among its own people or contributed by foreigners. Her soil is capable of containing, and supporting with all ease, at least *four times* the present number of its inhabitants. The people are brave, patient, hardy, and obedient, capable of enduring great fatigue, and of performing rapid and long continued marches. Her commanders are able,a nd her military tactics excellent; her government is absolute, and can (as it uniformly has done, for the last hundred years,) pursue, steadily and perseveringly, the most long-sighted schemes of ambition and policy, alike by the force of arms, and the still more efficient instrument of dexterous diplomacy.

The improvement of her agriculture, and consequent increase of her population, are great and progressive. Her rivers and canals, in summer, and the sledge-roads on the snows, in winter, facilitate her internal communication and commerce. Her present Emperor appears intent on improving the condition, both physical and moral, of his people, by emancipating the serfs, encouraging agriculture and commerce, diffusing literature, art, and science, and, above all, by promoting Bible and Missionary Societies throughout the whole extent of his immense dominions. The recent exploits of Russia, in stemming the tide of revolutionary France, have wonderfully augmented her power and influence; and facilitated the means of her further extension and aggrandizement; by developing the amount, and displaying the official management of her national resources, by disciplining her enormous strength, by inspiring her own people with self-confidence, by dispiriting and overawing her enemies.

It is not in the nature of great power to set limits to its own progress. Peter the first said, " he had land enough, and only wanted water;" yet Catharine and Alexander have added a very large portion of land to the Russian empire since their imperial predecessor utterred this speech. Alexander himself has enlarged his dominion by the annexation of Finland, Moldavia, Wallachia, Bessarabia, a part of old Gallicia, lower Georgia, Circassia, and the kingdom of Poland. With one part of her territory she threatens Asia, and with the other alarms Europe. What is to prevent her extension into Germany, her entire control of the northern powers, Sweden, Denmark, Prussia, and her possession of Constantinople? Once mistress of the Bosphorus and the Dardanelles, in addition to her present empire, and what is to become of Austria, what of the whole European continent?—Nay, what of England's maritime superiority? It has always been the aim of the Russian cabinet, from the reign of the first Peter to that of Alexander, to render their country a great naval, as well as a great military power. The dominion of the Black Sea, of the Morea, of the Grecian Archipelago, of Constantinople, of some ports in the Mediterranean, might render Russia a far more formidable rival on the ocean to England than she has ever yet found in Europe. Lord Nelson used to say, " that in encountering with *French* ships the best way was to run along side and board them; but with *Russian* ships to keep at a distance, and manœuvre." And Russia has often evinced her jealousy of the maritime pre-eminence of Britain, particularly when she led the armed neutrality in 1781, under Catharine, and in 1801, under Paul, and at the treaty of Tilsit, in 1807, under Alexander, when he and Napoleon stipulated, that Russia might take possession of Turkey in Europe, and pursue her conquests in Asia, at her own discretion ;—that she should assist France with her marine for the conquest of Gibraltar ; that the towns in Africa, as Tunis, Algiers, Tripoli, &c. should be taken possession of by France ; that no peace should be made with England, unless the island of Malta be ceded to France ; that Egypt be occupied by the French ; that *no other* than French, Russian, Spanish, and Italian vessels be purmitted to navigate the Mediterranean ; that *no* power be allowed to send merchant-ships to sea, unless they have a certain number of ships of war.

The British empire in India, also, has been long an object of desire to Russia ; and Catharine, at one time, projected to march an army over land, to drive the English from the Indian Peninsula ; and, at a more recent period, Alexander and Napoleon agreed to accomplish this scheme. It is supposed that Britain could *not* prevent the occupation of Constantinople by the Russian arms ; and that any one of her able generals, with a sufficient body of troops, might march strait to the Turkish capital, and win, and hold it, in spite of the world. No one imagines that the Turks, themselves, could defend their European empire against the undivided assaults of Russia, who might well alarm all the other powers of Europe for their independence, if she could lay her schemes for their subjugation in her two capitals of Constantinople and Petersburgh. It is doubtful, if she be allowed a few years of peace to organize her resources, to consolidate her strength, to develope her schemes, whether or not a coalition of the other European States could stop her progress towards universal dominion in that quarter of the world. At all events, the prodigious preponderance of Russia is not likely to restore the balance of power, nor to ensure the perpetuity of peace in Europe. See Sir Robert Wilson's " Sketches of the power of Russia," for facts

proving the extent of her alarming strength; although I
by no means subscribe to his *ultra whiggish* inferences
against England, who certainly means to survive his
predictions.

In glancing the eye over the present condition of the
European powers, in connexion with a view of the resources of America, it is necessary to bear in mind the
strongly marked difference between all the governments
of the United States, and those of other countries. In
the United States they have consisted, from their commencement, of *written* constitutions, of certain fixed
codes; whereas, in other countries, they have grown
up incidentally, from existing circumstances. In Holland and France, indeed, written constitutions have been
lately adopted; which appears to be not the least momentous of the consequences imposed upon Europe by
the French revolution; namely, a tendency to infuse a
greater spirit of *democracy* into the European governments. It is asserted, likewise, that Prussia and Wir-
temberg, and some other of the continental powers,
propose to form written constitutions, and admit the representative system into their municipal institutions.
Prior to the French revolution, all the governments of
Europe were composed amidst the chapter of accidents,.
and time and chance were there nursing-mothers. When
the government of imperial Rome, in the west, was sub-
verted by the barbarous tribes of Northern Asia, and
Northern Europe, the victorious nations every where
established an *elective* aristocracy, consisting of an elective chief, and elective nobles. After a time the *feudal*
system grew up into an hereditary monarchy and aristocracy; nevertheless, some traces of popular liberty
still survived, although they were rendered faint and
feeble in Spain, by the abolition of the *cortes ;* in France,
by the depression of the *tiers etat ;* in Denmark and
Sweden, by the usurpations of the sovereign over the
privileges of the nobles ; in Italy and Germany, by the
combined encroachments of both nobles and sovereign
upon the mass of the people ; while, in England, the
gradual advance of the House of Commons, or democratic branch of the government, eventually rendered it,

at least, equal to, if not an over match for, the two other branches, consisting of an hereditary aristocracy, and an hereditary monarchy.   Mr. Burke developes this subject in his *Regicide Peace*, and labours to show that England is the *weakest*, and revolutionary France the *strongest*, of all the European governments.

Indeed, it may be taken as a general proposition, that the more *free* a government is, whatever be its *form*, whether a republic or a monarchy, the more it consults and provides for the individual, domestic, and national happiness of its own people, the less able it is to watch over, and influence the actions of other sovereignties; and *so far* it is deficient in its system of *foreign* policy. And this defect applies, not only to its diplomatic department, but also to the mode of conducting its foreign wars; in the management of which it never exhibits the secrecy, despatch, and effective energy that characterize the military operations of more absolute governments.

But peace and war are the great hinges upon which the safety and existence of nations turn.   Diplomatic negotiations are the means of making peace or preventing war; and are, therefore, in themselves, and in their consequences, of more serious importance than any single events of war or peace.   It is not too much to affirm that England has suffered and lost more by her unskilful diplomacy, during the ninety years which elapsed from the peace of Utrecht, in 1713, to the peace of Amiens, in 1801, *including both those deplorable treaties*, than by all the battles she has fought for the last five centuries.   Yet such is the construction of her internal government; so well adapted is it to secure the personal liberty, promote the productive industry, and protect the individual enjoyment of her people; and, at the same time, build up the intrinsic, permanent strength of the nation, that, notwithstanding the frequent blunders of her foreign policy, she has, in spite of her confined home territory, and small population, raised herself to the rank of a first-rate power; and, in more than one period of her national history, has been the saviour and the arbitress of Europe.

The French revolution, however, has materially shattered and deranged the political fabric of England, by compelling her to maintain a large and disproportionate military force; by grievously augmenting the public expenditure and taxation, and by adding seven hundred millions of pounds (more than three thousand millions of dollars,) to the national debt. That revolution has likewise torn up from their foundations all the governments on the European continent. Into what forms of civil polity, whether into a preponderance of democracy or aristocracy, or monarchy, the states of Europe will eventually subside, when the more immediate consequences of the French revolution shall have produced their full effect, is not given to human wisdom to foresee. At present, the *representative* system, which is the *only* certain and permanent basis of national liberty, prevails to a small extent, and in different degrees, in Europe: for example, in England, Holland, France, and Sweden, the executive and nobles are hereditary, and the popular representatives elected; while in Switzerland, the executive and both branches of the legislature are elective. The system of representation hitherto has gained no effectual entrance into Spain, or Portugal, or Italy, or Germany, or Russia, containing, altogether, a population of one hundred and forty-five millions of souls.

There seems, however, among some of the nations of continental Europe, a desire to imitate the constitution of England, in their own municipal institutions. Indeed, it is no new thing for continental Europeans to admire and praise the fabric of British polity; for instance, M. Montesquieu has devoted the whole of the sixth chapter of the eleventh book of his *Esprit des Loix*, to an investigation of, and eulogium on, the English constitution; and Voltaire, in his letters on the English nation, chap. 21, 22, follows the same track; and M. Gourville also expresses similar sentiments, as may be seen in Sir William Temple's Memoirs. To these may be added the decisive testimony of the Duke de la Rochefaucault, in the Supplement to his Reflections; and the incidental praises of many of the best French historians, from the

Sieur de Comines to Father Daniel. Frederic the Second of Prussia, likewise, has shown his acquaintance with, and his approbation of, the English constitution, in his Memoir of the House of Brandenburgh. But the fullest and ablest account of the British polity is given by De Lolme, who says expressly, that it combines the three essentials of good government, namely, " the most certain protection, the exaction of the least sacrifices, and the capacity of progressive improvement." Since De Lolme wrote, perhaps the weight of taxation, and amount of the national debt in England, may incline sober persons to modify the second member of his laudatory sentence. M. Fouche, in his celebrated letter to the Duke of Wellington, after the battle of Waterloo, says, " that the establishment in France of a constitution similar to that of England would be a sufficient recompense to her for all the horrors of the revolution; and that Frenchmen do not desire *more*, nor will they be contented with *less*, freedom than the British nation enjoys."

It may be remarked, that some of the wisest men of all antiquity have declared their conviction, that a due blending together of monarchy, aristocracy, and democracy, in one political system, would be the best form of government, if it could ever be realized. *Plato*, in his Πολιτικος, says, " Μοναρχια τυχθεισα εν γραμμασιν, ους νομους λεγομεν, αριστη πασων," A monarchy, which is kept within the limits prescribed by the *laws*, is the best form of all. In his fragments of a Treatise upon a republic, *Cicero* says, "Statuo esse optimam constitutam rempublicam, quæ ex tribus generibus illis, regali, optimo, et populari, confusa modice." I determine that to be the best constructed commonwealth which is temperately compounded of the three different forms of government, the royal, the aristocratic, and democratic. *Tacitus*, in the fourth book of his Annals, says, " Cunctas nationes, et urbes, populus, aut primores, aut singuli regunt; delecta ex his, et constituta reipublicæ forma, laudari facilius quam evenire ; vel, si evenit, haud diuturna esse potest ;" all nations and cities are governed, either by the people at large, or the leading men of the community, or a single soverei n; the frame of a commonwealth, constructed out of all these forms of government, it is more easy to praise than to establish; and if ever established, it cannot possibly be lasting. *Polybius*, in the sixth book of his History, says, " Δηλον γαρ, ως αριστην μεν ηγητεον Πολιτειαν, την εκ παντων των ειρεμενων ιδιωματων συνεστωσαν τουτου γαρ του μερους ου λογω μονον αλλ' εργω πειραν ειληφαμεν. Λυκουργου συστησαντος πρωτου κατα τον τροπον το Λακεδαιμονιων Πολιτευμα," for it is evident that is to be considered the best form of government which is constituted from all these three simple forms, of democracy, aristocracy, and monarchy, already enumerated; and of this position we have had proof, not in theory only, but in fact; Lycurgus having established the first model of this threefold constitution of government in the system of polity which he framed for the Lacedemonians.

It is to be remembered, however, that these sentiments of the great writers of antiquity, and the praises bestowed upon the English constitution by continental Europeans, were all pronounced *before* the United States had given to the world an example, (yet unfollowed,) of a whole people meeting, by delegates, in a national convention, and deliberately framing for themselves a system of government, *purely representative*, altogether elective, as well in the executive as in both the branches of the legislature. And, above all, it is to be remembered, that the form of government, and the legal code of *every* country, are then most natural and most likely to last, when they are accommodated to the *habits* and disposition of the people among whom they are established. The individual materials of national strength can never be fully united, unless the will and inclination of the people be combined in favour of the government. The union of this inclination and will, makes emphatically the state, or body politic. *Laws* themselves, in general, are nothing more than the application of human reason and experience to the practical concerns of social life; and the laws, civil and political, of any particular country, are only the practical application of reason and experience to the existing interests of that particular country. Indeed, they are, generally, so exactly fitted to the people, among whom they grow up, that it scarcely ever happens that the laws of one nation *can* be made to suit the habits and dispositions of another community; whence the extreme folly of attempting to introduce, *suddenly*, new laws and a new government into any country.

The *Americans*, who framed a form of representative government towards the close of the eighteenth century, thitherto unparalleled in the history of the world, and, as yet, unimitated by other nations, were the descendants of men, who had, in preceding ages, fled from religious persecution and civil oppression in England, and sought a refuge from the intolerance of the old world in the waste and wilderness of the regions of the west. These men cherished an hereditary horror of single sovereignty, of feudal aristocracy, of ecclesiastical dominion; and, therefore, in their constitutions, whether of the separate or of the United States, abolished all the vestiges of royalty, swept away every ensign of nobility, placed every religious denomination upon the same footing, made every branch of their government elective and popular, provided for the personal, domestic, and social liberty of all their citizens, and laid the foundations of their whole civil polity broad and deep in the soil of national freedom.

The French revolution having, in its consequences, abolished the *feudal* system on the European continent, the governments in Europe, henceforth, will be either military or commercial, or both. France, Prussia, Austria, and Russia, lean to the military, while Britain and the United Netherlands support the commercial system. And, in proportion as the one or the other predominates, will the nations be free and prosperous, or enslaved and miserable. In their extremes, they are incompatible: trade cannot flourish, it cannot live under the withering blasts of a military government; nor can a military tyranny exist under the quickening influence of the commercial system. The prevalence of mercantile enterprise implies great individual liberty, extensive national credit, abundant wealth, and progressive improvement. The military system makes the government all, and the people nothing; gives to the single despot the property, person, industry, mind, will, and life of all his slaves, to do with them as he lists, for the forwarding his own views of external conquest, internal aggrandizement, sensual sloth, and arbitrary caprice.

If the military power preponderates, the people are crushed beneath the weight of their fetters, and ignorance, idleness, and poverty, convert the finest climate and most fertile soil into a desert waste. If the commercial spirit predominates, the people are free, and industry, skill, and wealth, create a garden of Eden out of the most churlish soil, and beneath the most ungenial sky. But, in order to ensure at once the individual liberty of the people, and the personal strength of the government, it is necessary to combine, in due proportions, the military and mercantile systems. Holland was merely commercial; her citizens were individually free, enterprising, and opulent; but, *as a nation*, she soon fell into decay, and, eventually, into extinction, owing to the weakness of her government, which was unable to resist the pressure of foreign war from without, combined with the turbulence of faction within the bowels of the state. Revolutionary France was merely military: her people were ground down to the dust beneath the burden of their unmitigated bondage; but her government, absolute in its dominion over its own subjects, was portentous and terrible in power to other nations; against whom it could, at will, direct *all* the physical and intellectual resources of its own territory, for the purpose of extending the ravages of tyranny over a larger portion of the earth. Britain unites military power with commercial influence in her system of government; whence her people are individually free, industrious, enterprising, intelligent, and wealthy; and her government has sufficient permanency of strength to protect its own subjects from injury, to punish the aggressions of other nations, to guard the weaker powers from wrong, to awe the mightier sovereignties into justice and moderation, to diffuse the blessings of civil and religious liberty over the most distant regions of the habitable globe. It was, under Providence, owing to *her* fortitude, perseverance, and public spirit, during twenty-five years of unexampled warfare, that continental Europe was at length rescued from the thraldom of revolutionary France.

There is one objection to the administration of the British government, which requires a more minute notice.   It is urged, as a common topic of reproach, both in England and in these United States, that the English government does *not* employ a sufficient portion of talent in its service.   This complaint is natural in the mouths of the *opposition* in Britain, and means nothing more, than that if *their* party were in power, the government would be very wisely administered; a circumstance, which must be left to the votes of the people of England, when they elect their knights and burgesses to represent them in the House of Commons.   This charge, also, is quite natural in the English *reformers,* who clamour, incessantly, about the dulness and ignorance, as well as the corruption and profligacy, of the administration; all which is a mere effusion of disappointed malignity and rage, because the talent, skill, and strength of the government, render all *their* efforts to destroy the country vain and ineffectual.   Such language is still more natural in the United States, because the Americans do *not* often witness any very bright specimens of English intellect, either in the private citizens, who come out here, or in the public officers, who represent their government.   And this country has witnessed the egregious mismanagement of Britain in her mode of conducting both the revolutionary and the late war; and still continues to see the marvellous mal-administration of her North American colonies, which appear to be governed by the mother country, for the express purpose of rendering them an easy prey to the United States, whenever our government shall enter into a *national,* instead of a party, war against England.

It is *not,* indeed, easy to defend the British government against the charge of general incapacity in its foreign policy, and in its colonial administration, particularly in the Canadas, where they never, by any accident, employ a *statesman* in any one of their public

offices, civil, legal, or military. This apparently strange
conduct may be, however, susceptible of some explanation.   It is admitted, I believe, on all hands, that there
exists a sufficient quantity of talent of every various
gradation in Britain; but the objection is, that it is not
employed in the service of government, which, therefore, labours under an habitual, permanent imbecility.
This inference is incorrect in itself, and founded on erroneous premises; for it rests on the assumption, that
all the great talent of a country ought to be employed
in the guidance of its government.   But, if this were
ever to take place in *any* nation, it would, of itself, ensure a perpetuity of resistless despotism; because, as
power has always a natural and necessary tendency to
increase in the hands of its holders, all the existing
great talent combined together would, of course, bear
down into hopeless subjection the general mass of folly,
ignorance, and weakness, that is always floating in every
community.

In every free country great talent is necessary to administer the government with wisdom, energy, and effect: and great talent is also necessary to constitute a
formidable *opposition* to the existing administration of
government, in order to prevent it from degenerating
into an arbitrary and illegal use of its power, and to
produce a most salutary exercise of the understanding
in the reciprocal collision of mighty intellects: great
talent is likewise necessary to carry on the learned professions of divinity, physic, and law, and the more active
occupations of the army and navy, to enlarge the
boundaries of literature and science, to improve the
arts, to beautify, adorn, and strengthen the interior of
the country, so that it might present a vast aggregate
amount of intelligence, industry, wealth, population,
physical and moral strength, for the government to
wield, as an offensive and defensive weapon, with which
to control other nations, to secure its own independence, to maintain its *progression* in power, to augment
its resources, to consolidate its aggrandizement.

It is not disputed, that a high bounty is perpetually
offered for the exercise of the greatest talents in general

science, letters, and arts, both speculative and practical, by the vast patronage, public and private, of wealth and honour, in Britain; and that this demand, in consequence, has produced the most splendid and successful effusions of genius and knowledge, in all these various departments of intellectual pursuit. To those who are acquainted with the past and present situation of the British empire, no proof is necessary to show, that there never was a period of its history in which so much talent was employed in *all* the departments of service and pursuit, whether private or public, as is now put into constant requisition. And, as to the *government* itself, in the guidance of which so great a deficiency of wisdom is supposed always to exist, it is simply impossible to prevent *a very large proportion* of the talent and information of the country from being constantly employed in carrying on the administration of so extensive and complicated a system of policy as that of England, which unites great energy of action in itself, with an ample extent of personal liberty to its people. A vast amount of intelligence, skill, experience, discretion, and wisdom, is required, to give direction to her immense naval and military departments; to marshal and guide her parliamentary troops; to watch over, and guard the political well-being of her established national church; to manage and conciliate the great landed, moneyed, manufacturing, and commercial interests of the empire; to contend, both in and out of the senate, with an incessant and formidable *opposition*, of wealth, rank, influence, talent, and learning, employed in declaiming, writing, and acting against *all* its measures, whether right or wrong, from the most important down to the least significant of its transactions.

In examining the position, that Britain never employs a sufficient quantity of talent in the administration of her government, it may be remarked, that it is easier to guide the movements of a machine already made, and the uses of which are known, than to make the machine and set it in motion. A well-established government, like that of England, does *not* require all the highest talents of the country to be crowded into the administration. Having grown up in the habits, affections, and feelings of the people, its business can be regulated, and energetically carried on, by the superintending genius of a few great men, to guide its primary movements; and by men of decent, respectable talents, to execute its subordinate functions. The residue of its greatest and most commanding talents would be employed to the best advantage in diffusing the lights of science, art, and literature, over the whole community. A wide field for the production and display of great talent is opened in England, by always calling a respectable portion of high intellect into the service of the government; by occasionally raising up powerful minds, from the middle and lower orders of the people, to the great offices of state, and thus perpetually fanning the flame of honourable competition; and by encouraging the exertions of genius in every various department of scientific and literary pursuit, by rewards and honours. Perseverance in large and liberal study, and a regular adherence, through successive ages, to the great fixed principles of moral and political science, have raised and maintained the national spirit, and rendered its government, laws, intelligence, agriculture, manufactures, commerce, and marine, at once the envy and admiration of the surrounding world. The exhibitions of great talents always follow the demand for their display; and no effectual bounty *can* be offered for their *general* appearance, except in a *free* country, whose civil and military institutions are on a large and magnificent scale, holding out the only adequate incitements of wealth, influence, honour, and power, for their full developement.

It is a question of great importance for the statesman to decide, how far the *letting loose* all the talents of a community would unsettle every thing, and fix nothing. Certain land-marks, and boundaries of authority and habit, are necessary to govern men. If the *judiciary*, for example, were not by the veneration attached to their high office to restrain the license of the bar, no business could be transacted in a court of justice; but all the time necessary for the trial and determination of legal suits would be consumed in the clashing of judicial with forensic intellect; and the same disorder would prevail, under similar circumstances, throughout all the departments of a government. Whence, it appears both wise and necessary to establish habits of implicit obedience to authority, to call a due portion of high talent into the administration, and to reward, by public applause and patronage, the exertions of genius, and the display of knowledge, in all the various branches of intellectual inquiry. The two only aristocracies of human nature, *talent* and *property*, must govern every country, or it will infallibly be destroyed, either by foreign conquest or domestic tyranny. But talent is merely personal and fleeting, while property is fixed and permanent, accumulating through successive generations, and consequently gives a poise and stability to the community.

If talent alone have sway, it produces a perpetual vibration of society from scheme to scheme, by its clashing interests and discordant collisions. But property, whether it belongs to a wise or a weak possessor, is in its nature stable; is a balance-wheel, which keeps the main-spring of talent from dashing the machinery of society to pieces; and in *old* well-established governments, the weight of property, by opposing the *too rapid* rise of talent, renders the talent which ultimately rises more mature, more powerful to combine the joint forces of experience, discretion, wisdom, and foresight, for the public service; and thus ensures a continual succession of able, and well-traine d men, in all the great departments of state. In France, the revolutionary politicians did actually destroy the influence of property, and give to talent an undivided sway. What was the consequence?—an incessant hurrying of the whole community from one scheme of theoretic insanity to another; from one set of tyrants to another; until a military despotism fixed all the nation in the frost of universal bondage.

It requires a whole life of labour and wisdom, directed to the prosecution of mental and moral improvement, to build up the exalted character of a single individual; what, then, is necessary, in order to construct the permanent greatness, and magnificent exaltation of a whole community ? Mr. Burke, after long and profound reflection upon the different forms of government, both ancient and modern, concluded, that nothing short of the *hereditary* transmission of property, and civil polity, through a long series of ages, is adequate to rear a nation into extensive and durable power. And yet Rome, during the space of eight hundred years, made herself absolute mistress of the greater part of the then known world, *without* the aid either of an hereditary civil polity, or an hereditary transmission of property. Undoubtedly, the number of great discoveries, or improvements, which have been *suddenly* made, in any branch of knowledge, is extremely small. For example, the greatest discovery in the science of political economy, the *balancing system*, has been gradually unfolded by the observation and experience of several centuries. That vast theory of political expediency regulates the mutual actions of contiguous nations ; subjects each to the influence of others, however remote ; connects all together by one common principle ; regulates the movements of the whole ; and maintains the order of the stupendous, complicated system of modern Christendom.

In the sixteenth century, the balancing system preserved Europe from subjugation to the Emperor Charles the Fifth ; in the seventeenth century it rescued Europe from the grasp of French dominion, under Louis the Fourteenth ; in the nineteenth century it broke the chains of slavery, which Napoleon Bonaparte was casting over the whole civilized world ; and ere the close of this same century, probably, all its efforts will be wanted to stop the progress of Russia towards universal supremacy.

In a community where the legislature is composed of the effective aristocracy of the country; that is to say, of the best birth, talent, wealth, and character of the country ; where the officers of the government sit in the representative assembly ; and where large and liberal salaries are allowed to the public servants—there *must* always be a great portion of intelligence in the administration ; and the affairs and destinies of the country, whether domestic or foreign, are but little liable to be influenced or deranged by the occurrence of accidental, unforeseen, or sudden events. For instance, the death of a civil or military chief, who had supported the greatness of the state by the vigour and wisdom of his councils, or by the glory of his arms, is seldom, if ever, the cause of great change, either in the positive strength or the relative importance of such a country. Four of the greatest men, in their respective departments, whom England ever produced, all died within the space of two years; these illustrious men were Lord Nelson, Mr. Pitt, Mr. Fox, and Lord Thurlow; nevertheless, the British empire, although deprived of the stupendous talents, the vast experience, the political wisdom, the daring and felicitous heroism of these exalted characters, bore herself steadily onward, and grappling, single-handed, with a whole world in arms against her, finally redeemed all Europe from bondage, and placed herself upon the pinnacle of national glory.

Such important and salutary results can only occur in *representative* governments; they can never be produced either in a single despotism or in an unbalanced democracy; both of which systems depend upon the temporary exaltation of single individuals for their own momentary ascendency. Neither of these forms of government provides for the training up of great men for the public service, in any regular succession. The truth of this position is exemplified in the whole history of the Asiatic despotisms; the different kingdoms of which alternately rise into influence over, or sink into dependence upon their neighbours, as they happen to be governed by an able, active, and warlike, or a weak, indolent, and dastardly monarch. Nay, almost within our own remembrance, Frederic the Second of Prussia, by the exertions of his single political and military talents, raised his kingdom from a very inferior rank, to that of a first-rate European power. But, after his death, his successors, not possessing his genius or activity, were first conquered and stripped of half their dominions, by revolutionary France, and then leaned upon Russia for the preservation of the miserable remnant of their na-

tional existence. In ancient story the democracy of
Thebes was great and flourishing, and domineered over
all Greece, as long as Pelopidas and Epaminondas led
her armies, and guided her councils; but as soon as
these two great men died, Thebes fell rapidly into the
degradation of national insignificance and contempt.
Athens, whenever an able statesman was in office, was
an overmatch for all the other Grecian republics; this
was particularly shown, during the administration of
Pisistratus, and Pericles; but whenever her more ignorant and noisy demagogues took the lead, she invariably
bowed her head beneath the military ascendency of her
aristocratic rival, Lacedæmon. As long as Rome remained a military aristocracy, she produced a regular
succession of great statesmen and warriors, and went
on steadily for several centuries, conquering the whole
world. But as soon as she became an unbalanced democracy, she fell into internal anarchy and weakness,
sunk into single military despotism; and was finally
burned up, both in her eastern and western thrones,
by the victorious watchfires of the Asiatic Saracens and
Turks, and of the European barbarians of the north.
Nay, revolutionary France, herself, fell in the fall of
her military tyrant.

But in extensive and well balanced communities,
which unite strength in the government with liberty
in the people, great men are continually rising up
amidst the existing exigencies; they are disciplined to
excellence in particular schools, whether civil or military; they regularly train up able and adequate successors for themselves, when they shall retire from
public conflict, into the arms of death, or of quiescent
age; they are incessantly called forth by the pressing
emergencies of national affairs.

Lord Castlereagh had from his earliest youth exhibited the marks of great talent, the efforts of which he
always seconded by habitual industry and application;
but he actually astonished all his friends, and quite confounded all his enemies, by the transcendent mind which
he displayed in those political negotiations that led to
the deliverance of Europe from the extreme degradation

of universal bondage. In the year 1812, he concluded a convention with Sweden, at a time when it was generally supposed that the Crown Prince Bernadotte was in close league with Bonaparte, for the destruction of Russia. He was repeatedly warned of his danger in the House of Commons; his answer was, that he was well aware of the difficulty and delicacy of such a negotiation; but that, in the existing crisis of Europe, and of the world, he was willing to run all the hazard, and take upon himself all the responsibility of that perilous transaction. In the year 1814, he went over to Chatillon, in France, where he found the allied powers of Russia, Austria, and Prussia, dispirited by five successive defeats, which their armies had experienced, and inclined to conclude a peace with Bonaparte. But Lord Castlereagh again took upon himself the enormous responsibility of refusing to negotiate, on the part of England, until the French revolutionary system was destroyed, by the dethronement of Napoleon, and the restoration of the Bourbons.

What a responsibility was this! If Bonaparte had succeeded in rousing the spirit of the French people, and in levying armies sufficiently numerous to enable him to overwhelm the allied squadrons, Castlereagh's name would have been handed down to everlasting execration, as the destroyer of Europe, by his own obstinacy and short-sightedness. If the allies had rejected his advice, and concluded a separate peace with Napoleon, Castlereagh would have been stigmatized as the destroyer of England, by again arming all the millions of the European continent in a fresh coalition, and with increased rancour, against her alone. But as his great mind peered above the intellects of the allied statesmen, he distinctly saw that perseverance and daring alone were wanting to crown the exertions of humanity with success, and redeem the world from the pressure of military despotism; and as the allies followed his counsel to victory, to the capture of Paris, the overthrow of Napoleon, and the reinstating of the Bourbons on the throne of their ancestors, Lord Castlereagh deserves the most honourable appellation of the pacificator of Europe, the deliverer of England.

The main object of *every* country should be to remove all political impediments and checks to the rising of *such* men into the high public stations for which their natural faculties, and acquired information, so peculiarly fit them. Under a free representative government, whose national institutions and departments of public service, both civil and military, are extensive and magnificent, the restrictions upon the rise of real merit are much fewer and less pernicious than under a single despotism, or an unbalanced democracy; and the road to legitimate preferment is extended to a much wider circle. Whence, in those countries, much less consequence may be attached to the existence or loss of any particular great man; because the appearance of those illustrious characters, in whose hands the national destinies are placed, is not regulated by accident, but it is provided for *in regular succession*, from age to age, by the internal organization, and ordinary administration of government. Thus, Chatham was reproduced in Pitt, and Pitt reappears in Castlereagh and Canning. Mr. Brougham, in his " Colonial Policy," discusses this subject at length, and with vast ability.

These observations respecting the best means of training up, and preparing a regular succession of great men for the public service of the nation, might be illustrated by an analysis of the internal or *home* government of England, whose system of *foreign* policy, however, as it consists in the prosecution of external warfare, in the ordinary transactions of diplomacy with other nations, and in the extraordinary negotiations for peace with her enemies, is, in general, very defective, and ought to be improved. Her mode of conducting the war in Spain, France, and Flanders, from the year 1808 to 1815, and her negotiations for the peace of Europe in 1814 and 1815, are magnificent exceptions to the usual imbecility and errors of her foreign policy. But notwithstanding all her imperfections and difficulties, there is yet sufficient ground to expect that Britain will be able to weather the storm, and again lift her head on high, above the waves of revolutionary violence and foreign assault, that beat with unceasing tide against all her most venerable establishments.

This expectation is founded on the prevalence of pure religion and sound morals, throughout her dominions ; her well-balanced government, her free and equal laws, her pure and unstained administration of justice, her lofty and unyielding spirit, her talents, learning, and intelligence, and the industry, enterprise, and perseverance of her people. All these, we trust, under the blessing of Providence, will enable her to stand erect and unmoved, in spite of the pressure of her finances, the deficiency of her revenue, the vast amount of her public expenditure, the diminution of her commerce, the rage of her reformers, the defects of her foreign policy, as well in diplomacy as in war, the hatred and intrigues of France, the fear and jealousy of the United Netherlands, the preponderance of Russia, and the growing power and deadly enmity of the United States. While Britain remains pre-eminent, the liberties of Europe are safe ; when she falls, the light, moral and intellectual, of that portion of the earth, will be extinguished in Egyptian darkness. As Britain, however, cannot enlarge her own home territory, nor contend with Russia on land, it is her imperative duty to increase her maritime resources, by adding the Grecian Isles, Cuba, the Isthmus of Darien, and the junction of the Atlantic and Pacific, to her empire, in order to place herself in so commanding a situation, as to be able to save Europe once more, in the event of Russia's hereafter menacing that quarter with subjugation, as revolutionary France has so recently done.

The recent extinetion of *lineal* royalty in Britain is, indeed, an awful dispensation to an hereditary monarchy. But there never went by an hour in the tide of time, when the national destinies of twenty millions of a free and enlightened people hung suspended upon the life or death of any individual, however exalted in rank, talent, or virtue. This calamitous event—the untimely death of a lovely woman, an empire's pride and hope, has called forth the clamorous joy of many of our more ardent politicians, as portending the speedy dissolution of the British government; which, however, will, most probably, survive its present, as it has outlived many generations of its past enemies.

The result of all this is, that it is the duty of every prudent government, while it acknowledges the supremacy of the Governor among the nations, in whose hands are the issues of life and death, to avail itself of all the means in its power to confirm and strengthen the prosperity of the people committed to its charge. Wherefore, considering the precarious condition of Europe, its germinant and springing seeds of disorder, the little probability of readjusting its balance of power, or of preserving its peace for any considerable length of time, the difficulty of preventing the *United States* from being embroiled in the general conflict, the rapid growth of the wealth, population, and power, the continual enlargement of their territories, and the constant multiplication of new states, our general government ought, immediately, to lay the foundation, broad and deep, of a solid system of *internal* finance; that it might have the command of an ample and a growing revenue, arising out of the territorial resources of the country, for the purposes of administering the home department liberally and effectively; of conducting its foreign policy vigorously and magnificently; of promoting the progress of letters and science, and every species of internal improvement; of training up, in regular succession, able men for the public service, and rewarding their labours splendidly; of establishing the national credit on an imperishable basis, so as to be able to raise any amount of money by voluntary loans, in the event of any sudden emergency, as the breaking out of war, or of a long-continued demand, in case of a protracted conflict for sovereignty, or aggrandizement, or existence.

The President seems to be aware of the necessity of giving to the United States all possible means of offensive and defensive strength, when, in his Message to Congress, on the 2d of December, 1817, he states the public credit to be at an extraordinary elevation; the preparations for defence, in future wars, to be advancing under a well-digested system; the general government to be daily gaining strength; local jealousies to be rapidly yielding to more generous, enlarged, and enlightened views of national policy; the militia of the several states to amount to eight hundred thousand men, infantry, artillery, and cavalry, great part of which is already armed, and measures are taken to arm the whole, and Congress is recommended to improve its organization and discipline. The message also states, that the regular army amounts nearly to the number required by law, and is stationed along the Atlantic and inland frontiers; that of the naval force, strong squadrons are maintained in the Mediterranean, and in the Gulf of Mexico; that by lands recently purchased from the Indians, bordering on Lake Erie, and from the Cherokees, the United States will be enabled to extend their settlements from the inhabited parts of the state of Ohio, along Lake Erie, into the Michigan Territory, and to connect their settlements, by degrees, through the state of Indiana and the Illinois territory, to that of Missouri; and a similar advantageous effect will soon be produced to the south, through the whole extent of the states and territory which border on the waters that empty themselves into the Mississippi, and the Mobile; thus affording security 'to our inland frontiers; and a strong barrier, consisting of our own people, planted on the lakes, the Mississippi, and the Mobile, with the protection of a few regular troops, effectually to curb all Indian hostility. A few great fortifications along the coasts, and at some points in the interior connected with it, will ensure the safety of our towns, and the commerce of our great rivers, from the Bay of Fundy to the Mississippi. From all this will spring a rapid augmentation in the value of all *public* lands, and emigrations be facilitated to the remotest parts of the Union. Several new states have been created to the west and south, and territorial governments organized over every place where there is vacant land for sale; whence an immense increase of our population is to be expected, at once augmenting the wealth and strength of the whole country.

But all these bright prospects are clouded by Mr. Monroe's saying, at the close of his Message, that the revenue arising from imports and tonnage, and from the sale of public lands, will be adequate to support the civil government, the present military and naval establishments, including the annual augmentation of the navy, and provide for the payment of the interest on the national debt, and its gradual extinction, without the aid of *internal* taxes; wherefore he recommends Congress to *repeal* them.   Now, it is sinning against all past experience, and all the most approved principles of political philosophy, to endeavour to carry on a government without any system of internal taxation in time of peace, and when war breaks out, *then* to begin to tax, when the diminution of revenue, and the increasing necessities of the people, peculiarly indispose and disable them from bearing the imposition of new burdens; whereas internal taxes, laid during peace, and so adjusted as to increase in productiveness with the national growth in population and wealth, will easily admit of such a gradual augmentation in time of war, as not to press too heavily on the community, and at the same time most materially to strengthen and establish the public credit; which *alone* can enable a government to call out and effectually wield the resources of the country, so as to secure its permanent prosperity, power, and reputation.

As soon as Congress met in December, 1817, they passed a bill through both houses, for the *repeal* of the *internal duties,* which the President immediately signed; and the law now is, that the United States government have *no internal revenue.* And yet, probably, the recent occupation of Amelia Island by our American troops, under the provisions of the *secret* act of Congress, passed in 1811, but not published till December, 1817, will, ere long, call for a large appropriation of the public money.   Is Cuba to follow the fate of Amelia; and are our land limits to be stretched beyond the horizon of Mexico?

P. S. Since the foregoing sheets were printed, the Treasury documents for 1817 have been received; from them the following summary is extracted:

TREASURY DEPARTMENT.

16th January, 1818.

Sir,

I have the honour to transmit a statement of the exports of the United States, during the year ending the 30th of September, 1817, amounting, in value, on articles

Of domestic produce or manufacture, to $68,313,500
Of foreign produce or manufacture, to   19,358,069

$87,671,569

Which articles appear to have been exported to the following countries, viz. :

	Domestic.	Foreign.
To the northern countries of Europe.	$3,828,563	2,790,408
To the dominions of the Netherlands.	3,397,775	2,387,543
Do. of Great Britain,	41,431,168	2,037,074
Do. of France,	9,717,423	2,717,395
Do. of Spain,	4,530,156	3,893,780
Do. of Portugal,	1,501,237	333,586
All other.	3,907,178	5,198,283
	$68,313,500	19,358,069

I have the honour to be,
Very respectfully, Sir,
Your most obt. servant,
WILLIAM H. CRAWFORD.

The Hon. the Speaker of the House of Representatives.

By this Report it appears that there were exported from the United States, from the 1st day of October, 1816, to the 30th day of September, 1817, of the growth and manufacture of the United States, 17,751,376 dollars worth of flour, and 23,127,614 dollars worth of cotton, making in these two items alone, 40,278,990 dollars. The whole value of exports for the same year, including foreign articles, amounts to 87,671,569 dollars. Of this sum 18,707,433 was exported from the port of New-York.

Summary of the value of exports from each State.

States.	Domestic.	Foreign.	Total.
New-Hampshire,	170,559	26,825	197,424
Vermont,	913,201	——	913,201
Massachusetts,	5,908,416	6,019,571	11,987,997
Rhode-Island,	577,911	372,556	950,467
Connecticut,	574,290	28,949	604,139
New-York,	13,660,583	5,046,700	18,707,433
New-Jersey,	5,849	——	5,849
Pennsylvania,	5,538,003	3,197,589	8,735,592
Delaware,	38,771	6,083	48,454
Maryland,	5,887,884	3,046,046	8,933,930
Dist. of Columbia,	1,689,102	79,556	1,768,658
Virginia,	5,561,238	60,204	5,611,442
North Carolina,	955,211	1,369	956,580
South-Carolina,	9,944,343	428,270	10,372,613
Georgia,	8,530,831	259,883	8,790,714
Ohio,	7,749	——	7,749
Louisiana,	8,241,254	783,558	9,402,812
Territory of U. S.	108,115	——	108,115
Total	68,343,500	19,358,069	87,671,569

APPENDIX,

Containing some few Miscellaneous Matters, omitted in the preceding pages.

———

SINCE the chapter on the government of the United States has been printed off, it has been suggested as a desideratum, that a table of the rates of pay, or wages allowed to our public servants, whether at home or abroad, should be given, in order to show what pecuniary incitements to ambition are applied to the governors, ambassadors, judges, and other public functionaries of the American commonwealth. The consequences of this republican frugality, in *underpaying* our government officers, are, that the governors and judges of some of the states are actually employed in prosecuting some other calling, in addition to that of discharging the functions of the executive and judicial; for instance, in keeping taverns, selling tenpenny nails, dealing in flour, and many similar employments, equally well adapted to the sciences of political philosophy and jurisprudence.

The President of the United States receives a
salary of. . . . . *$*25,000
The Vice-President of the United States. . . . 5,000
The Secretary of State. 5,000
The Secretary of the Treasury, War, and
Navy, each. . . . . . . , ... 4,000
The Chief Justice of the United States. . . . 5,000
The puisne Judges, each. 4,000

The United States Ambassadors to the *first-rate*
   European Courts $9,000
The Judges of the Supreme Court of New-York,
   one of the most liberally paid States in the
   Union, each 3,500
The Governor of the State of New-York . . 7,500
The Mayor of New-York 7,000
The Governor of Rhode-Island 800
The Governor of Vermont 600
The Governor of Connecticut 1,000
The Judges of Connecticut, each 1,000

It is needless to multiply instances: in many of the
states the governors and judges are even more scantily
paid than in Connecticut, Vermont, and Rhode Island ;
and, of course, this state parsimony produces all the
evils pointed out in the Chapter on Government, as resulting from the mistaken policy of *underpaying* the
public servants.

The pay of the legislators, whether of the United or
separate States in the Senates, or Houses of Representatives, ranges from two to six dollars a-day, during their
legislative session. If it be really wise to give the legislators any wages at all, their present stipend seems
to be fully as disproportionate as that of other public
servants; although, doubtless, in some instances, among
our twenty separate independent republican sovereignties, it amounts to a *quantum meruit*.

Mr. Wirt makes some very sensible and judicious observations, in his Life of Patrick Henry, on the evils
resulting from the mistaken policy of *underpaying* all
our public servants. Indeed, this beggarly system literally *starved* Henry and Hamilton out of the service of
their country, and drove them back into their professional practice for a morsel of bread.

The following memoranda, taken from the government
paper of March 14, 1818, will show in what a continual flux of mutation men and things are rolled under
our popular institutions ; and it should be remembered
that this eternal rotation is so favourite a feature in our

republican polity, that the most stupendous consequences are augured from its operation; so much so,
that one of our profoundest philosophers very gravely
informed me yesterday, that, " in the course of a few
years, there would be only *two* empires in the world,
the United States and Russia."

In the House of Representatives of the United States
there are now, out of 184 members, only *six* who were
members of the Tenth Congress, (1807-8-9,) and have
continued in the house without intermission.   Of those
who were members of that Congress, and are members
of the present house, but who have had intermissions of
service, there are but six or seven.   Yet the principle
of rotation is even more strongly illustrated in the
senate of the United States, though intended by the
constitution to be the more permanent service.   In that
body there is but one individual who was a senator in
the Tenth Congress.   In the senate, at present, eight
members out of forty were members of the House of
Representatives in the Tenth Congress; and of the
present House of Representatives two members were
in that Congress senators, both from the State of Maryland.

These facts afford materials for much reflection on the
practical operation of our system of government.

It may be added, that there is no member of the executive department of the government who was then concerned in the administration of the government.   Mr.
Monroe was then a minister abroad, and Mr. Adams a
member of the senate.   Of the present governors of the
several states there is not one who at that day filled the
same office.   Of the twenty, two were then representatives in Congress.

We are, also, to the full, as fond of variety as of rotation; for the rate of interest on money, and the current value of the dollar, differ in the several states;
for instance, by act of Congress, government receives
six per cent. on the bonds due to the United States;
New-York regulates the rate of interest at *seven*; Massachusetts at *six and a half* per cent.   In New-York

the dollar is valued at *eight*, in Pennsylvania at *seven*, in Massachusetts at *six* shillings.   Travellers and foreigners reap the richest harvest of inconvenience from the want of a uniform standard of weights, measures, and values; and if *any* rate of interest must be imposed on money, the trouble would certainly be much less, if our neighbouring states would establish it equally throughout their respective dominions.   Indeed, it is expressly given to Congress, by the federal constitution, to coin money, regulate its value, and fix the standard of weights and measures.

By the late arrivals from Europe, we learn some facts, which, had they transpired sooner, would have found a place in their appropriate chapters; as it is, they must be thrown, with other miscellanies, into an Appendix.

The papers laid before the two Houses of Parliament, by order of the Prince Regent, on the 27th of January, 1818, manifest a great improvement during the year 1817, in almost every branch of domestic industry, throughout the United Kingdom of Great Britain and Ireland.   The estimates for the year 1818, give the annual government expenditure at *fifty-eight* millions sterling, the revenue at *fifty-two* millions, making a *deficit* of *six* millions.   Out of the expenditures, however, nearly *sixteen* millions, will be paid to the commissioners of the sinking fund for the reduction of the national debt; and the supposition is, that the Chancellor of the Exchequer, instead of issuing Exchequer bills, or raising a loan, will take six millions from the existing income of the sinking fund, in order to supply the gap between the expenditure and revenue, and leave the remaining ten millions to be applied to the liquidation of the public debt.   The expenditure is to be lessened from sixty-five to fifty-eight millions, by a reduction of the army to its peace establishment, and by the saving of interest, on paying off the five and four per cent. stocks.

Treaties have also been concluded between Britain, Spain, and Portugal, respecting the abolition of the slave-trade; the Treaty with Spain is laid before Parliament; that with Portugal yet remained incomplete, because its ratification on either side had not been exchanged. By a proclamation, dated Madrid, December, 1817, the King of Spain prohibits, from the day of the date of the proclamation, all his subjects, both in the Peninsula and America, from going to buy negroes on the coast of Africa, *north* of the line; and from the 30th of May, 1820, a similar prohibition is extended to those parts of the coast of Africa, *south* of the line.

The rumour of the day, (25th March, 1818) is, that our government have determined to declare war against Spain. Before they plunge the nation into hostilities, it well becomes the wisdom of the senate to pause and ponder, whether or not the powers of Europe will be inclined to sit tamely by, and see the United States strip the nerveless and impotent Spaniard of the Floridas, Cuba, and Mexico, and thus endanger, or render useless, all the West-India possessions of every European sovereignty; and whether or not America, with only ten millions of people, scattered over two millions of square miles, is *at this moment* prepared to encounter the *coalition of crowns* in Europe, with their embattled veterans at leisure for any new enterprise, weary of peace, procinct for war, and looking with a jealous and fearful eye upon the rapidly growing strength of our giant republic? Is the impending rupture with Spain one of the firstfruits of *western* predominance; and are the Atlantic states to purchase a President from *Kentucky* at the price of all the blood and treasure that may be expended in a conflict with universal Europe?

THE END.

B. Clarke, Printer, Well Street, London.